Introduction to
THERAPEUTIC COUNSELING

Second Edition

ABOUT THE AUTHORS

Jeffrey A. Kottler is an associate professor of counseling and educational psychology at the University of Nevada, Las Vegas. He received his Ph.D. in counseling from the University of Virginia and has worked as a counselor, psychologist, educator, and consultant in a variety of settings, including schools, mental health centers, universities, industry, and private practice. He has lectured extensively throughout North and South America and served as a Fulbright Scholar in Peru, where he helped establish counseling programs in underdeveloped regions.

Jeffrey is the author or coauthor of the books *Pragmatic Group Leadership* (1983), *Ethical and Legal Issues in Counseling and Psychotherapy* (1985), *On Being a Therapist* (1986), *The Imperfect Therapist: Learning from Failure in Therapeutic Practice* (1989), *Private Moments, Secret Selves: Enriching Our Time Alone* (1990), *The Compleat Therapist* (1991), and *Compassionate Therapy: Working with Difficult Clients* (1992).

Robert W. Brown is an associate professor and chair of the Department of Counseling at Oakland University in Rochester, Michigan. He received his Ph.D. in counselor education from Wayne State University and has worked as a teacher and counselor in schools, colleges, and universities. Bob is a licensed psychologist, and his clinical experience includes work in hospitals and community agencies. His specialty areas include group counseling, educational and psychological testing, and developmental counseling; his current research is in the area of adult transition. He publishes and lectures on these and other topics.

Introduction to
THERAPEUTIC COUNSELING
Second Edition

Jeffrey A. Kottler
University of Nevada, Las Vegas

Robert W. Brown
Oakland University

BROOKS/COLE PUBLISHING COMPANY
PACIFIC GROVE, CALIFORNIA

 A CLAIREMONT BOOK

Brooks/Cole Publishing Company
A Division of Wadsworth, Inc.

Printed in the United States of America
10   9   8   7   6   5   4   3   2   1

Library of Congress Cataloging in Publication Data

Kottler, Jeffrey A.
   Introduction to therapeutic counseling / Jeffrey A. Kottler,
Robert W. Brown. -- 2nd ed.
      p.   cm.
   Includes bibliographical references and index.
   ISBN 0-534-17286-5
   1. Counseling.   I. Brown, Robert W., [date]– .   II. Title.
   [DNLM: 1. Counseling. 2. Psychotherapy. WM 55 K87i]
BF637.C6K678   1991
616.89' 14--dc20
DNLM/DLC   91-36607
for Library of Congress   CIP

Sponsoring Editor: *CLAIRE VERDUIN*
Editorial Associate: *GAY C. BOND*
Production Coordinators: *MARLENE THOM* and *KAY MIKEL*
Manuscript Editor: *ALYNE M. LAWLER*
Permissions Editor: *CARLINE HAGA*
Interior and Cover Design: *LISA BERMAN*
Art Coordinator: *CLOYCE J. WALL*
Photo Researcher: *RUTH MINERVA*
Desktop Typesetter: *GRAFIKZ™*
Printing and Binding: *ARCATA GRAPHICS/FAIRFIELD*
Credits continue on page 394.

Dedicated to: *elli* and *mlo*

PREFACE

We wrote this book out of a very personal need to create a student-centered introduction to our field. We've felt frustrated because at times the personalized warmth and sensitivity that are the basis of our profession have not been reflected in academic experiences. Too often education emphasizes theoretical knowledge and scholarly inquiry to the exclusion of student involvement. We hope that this book not only meets the stringent demands of traditional scholarship but also provides a lively and dynamic overview of therapeutic counseling.

Throughout the text we speak directly to students, challenging them to explore their personal motives for choosing the counseling profession, as well as helping them to personally integrate much of the research and theoretical concepts. We use case examples, personal experiences, practical applications, and humor to make the material informative and exciting. A student-centered workbook designed to accompany this text, *Self-Guided Exploration for Beginning Counseling Students* (Kottler, 1992), contains a series of experiential and reflective exercises that will further help the reader personalize material.

Introduction to Therapeutic Counseling is designed for initial courses in human service programs with titles such as "Principles of Counseling," Professional Orientation," Counseling Theory and Practice," Introduction to Helping," and "Human Resource Development." The book emphasizes the development of a professional identity, ethical standards, basic process skills, the therapeutic relationship, personal theory building, and understanding of meaningful research, as well as a contemporary focus on the practical realities of counseling. Particular attention is devoted to the major specialties and diverse settings in which counseling takes place, such as schools, clinics, and medical, industrial, mental health, and community agency settings. We quite deliberately made the size of the book realistic for a semester's work and planned the number and length of chapters to be manageable for the student struggling to digest a new world of terminology and technology. The book is organized into four broad focus areas: professional identity factors, theoretical and research foundations, counseling applications, and issues in therapeutic practice.

Whereas the first two sections (Chapters 1 through 8) help the student learn the foundations of therapeutic counseling, the latter two sections (Chapters 9 through 16) apply these concepts to the various specialties within the field. The student is thus encouraged to master the basic theory and research of the field and become familiar with the generic therapeutic skills, as well as to begin thinking about the realities of developing a flexible specialty, making oneself marketable, finding suitable employment, and staying passionately committed to the profession.

In the years since we completed the first edition of *Introduction to Therapeutic Counseling*, there have been many changes in the field. These advances cover innovations not only in theory and research but also in such areas as licensure and professional regulation. We have thus made a number of significant changes for this second edition that you will see reflected in the content and scope.

Consistent with the Zeitgeist of our times, we continue to emphasize a philosophy of counselor education and training that we first proposed a number of years ago—one that is integrative and pragmatic and that seeks to combine the best of existing approaches. The text has also been expanded considerably to include more detailed discussion on today's major issues—multicultural sensitivity, historical roots of our profession, licensure and credentialing, family violence, sexism and age discrimination, legal and ethical conflicts, and women's issues, to name a few. We have added and expanded sections on counseling specialties that have blossomed in recent years—pastoral counseling, marriage and family counseling, rehabilitation counseling, and counseling in private practice, higher education, and industry.

Finally, we have followed the advice offered by many of the students and faculty who valued the first edition of this text: we have continued our effort to distill the common factors that operate in all effective helping efforts, seeking to integrate and simplify the essence of our profession. We are especially grateful to a number of professionals who helped us refine our ideas and offered us much constructive input during the exacting revision process: Robert Bowman, Northwestern State University; Tim Clinton, Liberty University; Ray Hillis, California State University at Los Angeles; Robert Nielsen, North Dakota State University; and Kathleen Ritter, California State University at Bakersfield.

Jeffrey A. Kottler
Robert W. Brown

CONTENTS

PART ONE

THE PROFESSIONAL COUNSELOR   1

CHAPTER ONE

THERAPEUTIC COUNSELING: WHAT IT IS AND HOW IT WORKS 3

Why Be a Counselor? 4

To Be a Counselor 6

Making a Commitment 7

Striving for Excellence 8

Adopting a Neutral Posture 8

Subjugating Personal Needs 9

Being a Generalist 10

Coping with Discomfort 10

Teaching Through Self-Discovery 11

Dealing with Ambiguity 11

Definitions of Counseling 12

Why Does Therapeutic Counseling Work? 15

Significance of the Self 16

Perceptual Base of Effective Counselors 17

Summary 18

Suggested Readings 19

ix

CHAPTER TWO

HISTORICAL AND CONCEPTUAL FOUNDATIONS OF COUNSELING 20

The Identity of Therapeutic Counseling 21

Counseling and Psychotherapy 21

The History of Therapeutic Counseling 24

   The Ancient Philosophers 25

   The First Psychiatrists 26

   Influences from Psychology 28

   The Guidance Era 28

   The Counseling Era 29

   The Era of Therapeutic Counseling 32

Licensing and Regulation in Counseling 33

Summary 34

Suggested Readings 35

CHAPTER THREE

SETTINGS FOR THERAPEUTIC COUNSELING 36

What Counselors Have in Common 39

   A Unique Identity 39

   Many Different Roles 39

   A Set of Generic Skills 40

   A Set of Common Goals 41

   Both Developmental and Remedial Orientation 42

   Teamwork 44

A Day in the Life 44

   Private Practice 44

   Mental Health Center 46

   Crisis Center 47

   High School 48

   Preschool 50

   Street Ministry 51

   University Counseling Center 53

   Rehabilitation Center 54

   Counseling in Industry 55

The Value of a Flexible Specialty 57
    Specialty Areas in Counseling 58
    Guidelines for Selecting a Counseling Specialty 59
Summary 61
Suggested Readings 62

CHAPTER FOUR

THE THERAPEUTIC RELATIONSHIP 63

Qualities of Counseling Relationships 64
Historical Perspectives 66
Counselors as Relationship Specialists 67
Characteristics of the Helping Relationship 71
    Congruence, Positive Regard, and Empathy 71
    Attending Skills and Responding Skills 73
Practical Dimensions of the Therapeutic Relationship 74
    Commitment 74
    Trust 75
    Empathy 75
    Confidentiality 76
    Benevolent Power 76
Creating a Relationship in the Initial Interview 76
    Establishing Rules 77
    Planting Hope 77
    Assuring Confidentiality 78
    Assessing Expectations 78
    Collecting Information 79
    Identifying Problems 80
    Beginning Intervention 80
    First-Session Agenda Review 80
Summary 82
Suggested Readings 82

PART TWO

COUNSELING ANTECEDENTS AND APPROACHES 85

CHAPTER FIVE

INSIGHT-ORIENTED COUNSELING APPROACHES 87

Introduction to Theory Construction 88
Client-Centered Counseling 91
Originator and Revisionists 91
Basic Assumptions 92
Personality Development 92
Favorite Techniques 93
Criticisms of Client-Centered Counseling 95
Personal Applications   95
Existential Counseling 96
Originators 96
Premises of Existential Counseling 97
Criticisms of Existential Counseling 98
Personal Applications 99
Psychoanalytic Counseling 100
Originators 100
Basic Psychoanalytic Concepts 100
Criticisms of Psychoanalytic Counseling 105
Personal Applications 105
Gestalt Counseling 106
Originators and Basic Concepts 106
Techniques of Gestalt Therapy 108
Criticisms of Gestalt Counseling 109
Honorable Mentions 109
Transactional Analysis 110
Adlerian Counseling 111
Character Analysis 113
Summary 114
Suggested Readings 114

CHAPTER SIX

ACTION-ORIENTED COUNSELING APPROACHES 115

Behavioral Counseling 116
    Conceptual Perspective 116
    Behavioral Technology 118
    Criticisms of the Behavioral Approach 122
Rational-Emotive Counseling 122
    Originators 122
    Basic Points of RET 123
    Therapeutic Techniques 126
    Criticisms of RET 126
    Personal Applications 126
Strategic Counseling 128
    Origins 128
    Strategic Interventions 128
    Criticisms of Strategic Counseling 128
    Personal Applications 131
Multimodal Counseling 132
    Originators 132
    Basic Concepts 132
    Premises of the Multimodal Approach 132
    Some Multimodal Techniques 134
    Criticisms of the Multimodal and Other Eclectic Approaches 134
Honorable Mentions 135
    Reality Therapy 135
    Expressive Therapies 135
Summary 137
Suggested Readings 137

CHAPTER SEVEN

DEVELOPING A PERSONAL STYLE 139

A Personal Journey 140
Grabbing Truth by the Tail 142
A Personal Theory 143

Criteria of Effectiveness 143

Guidelines for Usefulness 144

Stages in Developing a Personal Theory 145

Entry 145

Mentorhood 147

Eclecticism 148

Experimentation 148

Pragmatism 149

Summary 150

Suggested Readings 150

CHAPTER EIGHT

THE ASSESSMENT PROCESS 152

What is Assessment? 153

The Role of Testing in the Assessment Process 154

The Value of Testing 155

Standardized Measures 156

Tests of Ability 158

Tests of Aptitude 159

Tests of Achievement 159

Tests of Typical Performance 159

Selecting Tests 161

Nonstandardized Measures 162

Observational Assessment 162

Rating Scales 162

Self-Assessment 163

Using Assessment in Counseling 163

Test Interpretation 163

Summary of Assessment Principles 164

Formal and Functional Diagnosis 164

Psychiatric Diagnosis 168

Ethical Concerns 171

Behavioral Diagnosis 172

Summary 174

Suggested Readings 174

PART THREE
APPLICATIONS OF COUNSELING   177

CHAPTER NINE
GROUP COUNSELING 179
Survey of Groups 180
  Encounter Groups 182
  Guidance Groups 182
  Counseling Groups 183
  Therapy Groups 184
Some Considerations in the Use of Group Modalities 184
Counteracting Potential Limitations 187
Advantages of Group Work 188
  Cost Efficiency 188
  Spectator Effects 188
  Stimulation Value 188
  Opportunities for Feedback 190
  Support 191
  Structured Practice 191
Basic Assumptions about Groups 192
Cues for Intervention 197
  Abusive Behavior 197
  Rambling and Digressions 197
  Withdrawal and Passivity 198
  Lethargy and Boredom 198
  Semantic Errors 199
Specialized Skills of Group Work 199
Summary 201
Suggested Readings 201

CHAPTER TEN
MARITAL, FAMILY, AND SEX COUNSELING 203
Family Counseling Theories 205
Power in Relationships 208

Symptoms as Solutions 211
Case Example of Family Counseling in Action 212
Interpreting Symptoms as Metaphors 214
Diagnostic Questions 215
Reframing 215
Directives 218
  Forcing the Spontaneous 219
  Opposition Through Compliance 219
  Pretending 220
  Slowing Down 220
Ethical Issues in Family Counseling 221
Sex Counseling 221
  Clinical Assessment Interview 222
  Physical Exam and Medical History 222
  Exploration of Relationship 223
  Sensate Focus Exercises 223
  Specialized Techniques 223
  Evaluation 224
Summary 224
Suggested Readings 224

CHAPTER ELEVEN

CAREER COUNSELING 226

The Functions of Work 227
Roles of Counseling 228
  Facilitating Self-Awareness 229
  Becoming Familiar with the World of Work 230
  Teaching Decision-Making Skills 230
  Teaching Employability Skills 231
Theories of Career Development 231
  Theodore Caplow's Theory 233
  Donald Super's Theory 233
  John Holland's Theory 235
  Robert Hoppock's Theory 236
  Anne Roe's Theory 238
  John Krumboltz's Theory 239
  Other Theories 240

Career Education 240
    Abilities 243
    Interests 243
    Values 243
Career Decision Making 243
Trends and Issues in Career Counseling 245
    Changes in the Workplace 245
    Work and Leisure 246
    Use of Technology 246
Summary 247
Suggested Readings 247

CHAPTER TWELVE

DRUG AND ALCOHOL COUNSELING 249

Drug Use and Drug Abuse 250
The United States as a Drug Culture 252
What Counselors Should Know about Drugs 253
    Marijuana 253
    Depressants 254
    Stimulants 255
    Narcotics 256
    Hallucinogens 256
Effects of Drug Abuse 256
Adolescent Drug Use 257
Abuse in Special Populations 259
    The Elderly 260
    The Disabled 260
Principles for Counseling the Chemically Dependent 262
    Medical Model 262
    AA/NA Model 262
    Therapeutic Model 263
Summary 264
Suggested Readings 265

CHAPTER THIRTEEN
COUNSELING SPECIAL POPULATIONS 266
Influence of Biases 267
Beliefs and Attitudes 269
Preferred Client Types 270
Counseling Women 271
Counseling Ethnic Minorities 273
Counseling the Aged 276
Counseling Lesbian Women and Gay Men 279
   Gay Identity Development 280
   Other Issues for Gay/Lesbian Clients 281
   The Counselor and AIDS 282
Counseling Clients with Disabilities 284
Summary 285
Suggested Readings 285

PART FOUR
PROFESSIONAL PRACTICE   287

CHAPTER FOURTEEN
RESEARCH AND PRACTICE 289
The Marriage Between Research and Practice 290
Research for the Counselor 292
Research on Therapeutic Attributes 297
   Reliability and Validity in Counseling 298
   Outcome Effects in Counseling 300
The Generic Skills of Counseling 302
   Significance of Attending Skills 302
   Skills that Facilitate Client Change 303
Summary 305
Suggested Readings 306

CHAPTER FIFTEEN
ETHICAL AND LEGAL ISSUES 307
Professional Codes 309

Our Divided Loyalties 310

Areas of Ethical Difficulty 311
    Seduction 311
    Misjudgment 313
    Deception 313
    Confidentiality 313
    Recent Trends 316

Making Ethical Decisions 317

Legal Issues in Counseling 321

Summary 323

Suggested Readings 324

CHAPTER SIXTEEN
TOWARD CLOSURE 325
Advice for the Passionately Committed Counseling Student 326
    Be Self-Directed 326

    Read 326

    Find a Mentor 326

    Volunteer to Do Research 327

    Ask Questions 327

    Challenge Your Teachers 328

    Challenge Yourself 328

    Experience Counseling as a Client 328

    Personalize Everything 329

    Become Active in Professional Organizations 329

    Develop a Flexible Specialty 329

    Resist Burnout 330

    Confront Your Fears of Failure 330

Variations on a Theme 331

Suggested Readings 332

References   333

Appendix A Ethical Standards, AACD   355

Appendix B Ethical Principles of Psychologists, APA   366

Appendix C Code of Ethics for the AAMFT   376

Index   383

PART ONE
THE PROFESSIONAL COUNSELOR

1

THERAPEUTIC COUNSELING: WHAT IT IS AND HOW IT WORKS

WHY BE A COUNSELOR?

TO BE A COUNSELOR
  Making a Commitment
  Striving for Excellence
  Adopting a Neutral Posture
  Subjugating Personal Needs
  Being a Generalist
  Coping with Discomfort
  Teaching Through Self-Discovery
  Dealing with Ambiguity

DEFINITIONS OF COUNSELING

WHY DOES THERAPEUTIC
    COUNSELING WORK?
  Significance of the Self
  Perceptual Base of Effective
    Counselors

SUMMARY

SUGGESTED READINGS

WHY BE A COUNSELOR?

It is both interesting and useful to begin the systematic study of the counseling profession by initially exploring the motives and expectations of students. The decision to become a counselor is as complex and multifaceted as any concern with which our clients might wish help. We expect—even demand—that our clients be completely honest with themselves, that they confront their self-deceptions, ambivalence, and motives behind actions. It is only fair that we attempt to be honest with ourselves as well.

Students enter the counseling field, as they do any other profession, for a variety of reasons. Some people genuinely wish to save the world; others, more modestly, wish to save themselves. Many persons, including the authors, quite deliberately chose this field because there are so many opportunities to apply classroom and book studies to our own lives. Other persons have quite unabashedly admitted that it was a toss-up for them between going to see a counselor for their own problems and becoming a counselor.

The personal motives behind our own career decisions are indeed important to examine as this introduction to therapeutic counseling begins. Such an understanding will permit a more thoughtful and clear-headed approach to the material presented. Within a typical class there are often students who see themselves as missionaries. They choose the counseling profession because they have a strong desire to help others: to make a difference in the lives of those who are suffering. They frequently have a kind of empathy that comes from personal experience. They suffered and were saved; now the roles can be reversed. They wish to make the world a bit more civilized. Perhaps this reason belongs, even if only slightly, to everyone who selects this path; after all, it can't be for the liberal financial rewards, lack of stress, and open job market.

Apart from altruism and idealism, there are many other reasons why people choose counseling as a profession. The selection could be pragmatic: grades or GRE scores may prevent a move into highly competitive programs. Or the time commitments required by some disciplines may seem excessive or overwhelming. Counseling seems a reasonable compromise; the program can be completed in a few years and then the credentials will permit practice in many attractive settings. Some writers feel that there is a narcissistic motivation for entering the helping professions, since the counselor is able to satisfy unfulfilled nurturing needs by rescuing people with problems as well as to participate in intimate relationships while always maintaining control (Robertiello, 1978; Herron & Rouslin, 1984). Some people are attracted to counseling because they enjoy the power they can wield in influencing other people's lives. Counselors and other therapeutic practitioners are, in fact, the real power brokers in our society. They have become the oracles, the witch doctors, the gurus, the wizards, the mentors. They listen with compassion and speak with authority. They have the answers and, although they won't reveal them directly, if clients behave and do what they are supposed to, they will be gently prodded to discover truth for themselves.

Students also select counseling for many of the same practical reasons that lead to any other career. They need the degree for a pay raise or promotion. The courses are offered at convenient times. Tests are infrequent, or the program doesn't appear too demanding. And, indeed, counseling does not, at first glance, seem as rigorous as training in engineering, nuclear physics, or neurosurgery.

But don't be fooled. A counseling program is about the most challenging emotional experience a student can undertake. Although some counseling programs do not create intense academic pressure, all emphasize skill mastery and performance competencies. Counseling programs are usually less interested in your ability to succeed at academic tasks and more interested in your ability to translate book and classroom learning into action. The bottom line for success in a counseling program is what you can do and what you can deliver.

The pressure and inward journeys necessary for growth and counseling skill development are well worth the effort. This profession offers the student more advantages on both a personal and a professional level than almost any other field. Where else can all life experiences, books, films, travels, relationships, fantasies, jobs, losses, disasters, and triumphs help the professional to be more effective? Everything and everyone teaches a counselor to understand the human world better, to have more compassion, to be a better communicator, to comprehend more completely the intricate complexities of behavior. Every experience allows us to teach from what we know.

What other profession teaches skills and competencies applicable to work that can be so easily applied to one's personal world? Counseling trains people to be more vibrant lovers and livers. Intensive training in observing nonverbal behavior, analyzing motives, handling confrontations, and reflecting feelings helps counselors to be more attractive human beings, experts at efficiently developing trusting, productive relationships. If counselors can do that in their offices, they can certainly do it with their friends, children, partners, and parents.

Counseling inspires the student to be a knowledgeable generalist, a Renaissance scholar, a devourer of truth in any palatable form. We are not restricted to our texts for learning. We read literature, history, anthropology, sociology, biology, biochemistry, education, psychology, and philosophy, and they are all beneficial, even necessary, if we are truly to understand this abstract thing called the human mind.

Counseling permits practitioners to make a difference in people's lives and to see the results in their own lifetimes. One of the ways in which we attempt to confront our own mortality is by preserving our spirit long after physical death. Certainly the principal reward for a dedicated teacher, counselor, or therapist is the knowledge that a generation of clients will remember and use the help that was offered. Our profession allows us to productively face our own fears of death by leaving behind those who, because of our efforts, fill less pain. One counseling student confronted his own anxiety, fear, and despair with this realization: "I know only two things—one, that I will be dead someday, two, that I am not dead now. The only question is what shall I do between those two points" (May, 1983, p. 169).

Counselors become more wise and self-aware with every client they see. Each presented concern forces us to consider introspectively our own degree of stability.

In all cultures, therapeutic counselors are empowered to act as models of wisdom, serenity, and guidance.

Every discussed problem reminds us of those problems we still have unresolved. A client complains of periodic urges to break out of the mold and run away, while the counselor silently considers his or her own rebellious impulses. A boring relationship, fear of failure, career stagnation, sexual frustrations, loneliness, parental dependence—all subjects that are commonly presented—force the counselor to resolve them, once and for all, in his or her own life. The profession thus continually encourages its practitioners to upgrade their personal effectiveness.

At this very moment in may be profitable for *you* to examine your personal motives for studying counseling. Although you may never fully understand all the factors, needs, interests, values, and unconscious processes that are influencing your decision, the quest is, nevertheless, valuable. It is likely that only years after graduation, and perhaps after your own experiences as a client, will you ever have a focused picture of your honest motives. This process of self-inquiry, once begun, is self-perpetuating because of the growth it fosters. And the beginning is *now*.

TO BE A COUNSELOR

The action of choosing counseling as a career sets into motion a chain of events and leads to a series of direct and indirect consequences, the impact of which is often initially unclear. The choice to be a counselor, for example, not only will dramatically affect the education, training, and molding of the student who made the decision but also will affect that individual's family and friends. Imagine, for example, that you just studied the impact of birth order on personality development. How can you *not* look at your life and your relationships with family members differently after that? Or consider the very real possibility that, in any given week in your professional life, you will listen to clients struggle with fears of dying, infidelity, loneliness, dependency, boredom, suicidal thoughts, and a hundred other issues that have haunted you throughout your life.

Choosing to be a counselor means opening yourself up to intense self-scrutiny and personal growth. It means examining your strengths and limitations as a human being, exploring your vulnerabilities, and identifying those aspects of your functioning that you need to improve. All these changes emerge as the consequence of simply selecting studies in counseling. A number of other implications flow from choosing to be a counselor.

Making a Commitment

To be a counselor means making a commitment to a profession and a lifestyle.

For every spectacular success there are also failures. Counselors must learn not only to temper their exhilaration after witnessing phenomenal change but to cope with the frustrations of resistant clients, rigid institutional policies, overworked administrators, irate parents, and confusing laws. Although there are few greater victories than the feeling of knowing that a person has been helped as a direct result of our efforts, oftentimes clients do not accommodate our wishes or cooperate with our interventions. They may stubbornly insist on staying miserable in spite of our best attempts at helping them to find another way.

There are times when a counselor will do everything perfectly: patiently build a trusting relationship with a client and gently lead her through the successive counseling stages—exploring, reflecting, analyzing, interpreting, and confronting—and then, finally, the time comes for action. Let's say the client agrees that a divorce is imminent. The marriage has become destructive, her husband abusive. She realizes she cannot grow further while handcuffed. She has worked through her guilt over deserting him, her fear of disapproval by mutual friends, and her fear of making it on her own without a man to lean on. She is ready—or so she says. But time is up for this week's session. She will do her homework and be prepared by next week to make the commitment to beginning her new life as a single woman.

Eagerly, the counselor awaits the report next week. He tries hard not to pat himself on the back because he *does* feel proud. He has done good work. The next week arrives. The counselor waits in his office. And waits. The client doesn't show. She doesn't show! He calls her, only to receive the cold announcement, without any explanation, that she will no longer be returning for sessions. That's it. Before the counselor can sort out the mess there is a knock on the door. His next client is waiting impatiently for the session.

Striving for Excellence

To be a counselor means taking responsibility for one's own growth, striving for excellence in one's personal behavior.

Every client presents a novel challenge. Five persons who are depressed will act differently as a result of the symptoms they may call depression. Even though there are maybe a dozen major problems that frequently present themselves to a counselor, there are endless variations on those themes. In order to be maximally helpful to each client, the counselor should understand the problem thoroughly and have had some experience in handling it.

Whereas a male counselor cannot directly relate to the struggle of a female client considering an abortion, and can never have worked it through himself, it is likely that this counselor has accumulated rich personal experiences in resolving similar value conflicts. And although a female counselor can never know the shame of her male client who is impotent, she does know the awful dread of being unable to perform adequately.

There is a consensus among many counselors that each client provides them an opportunity, after the session, to look inward, personalize the material, and ask the question "To what extent is this a problem for me?" When a client complains of stagnation in his life, of too many predictable routines and boring people, how can the counselor not examine this pattern in his or her own life? Fears of growing old, of failure, of rejection, of loving, of hating—all hit a familiar chord. And the degree to which the counselor has successfully struggled with any of these themes presented in the sessions will determine, to some extent, his or her capacity for understanding the client's fears and resolving them.

A client complains of a bad temper and uncontrolled explosive outbursts. But the counselor *knows*, not just theoretically but personally, the value of a bad temper—how it provides an instant excuse for abusing others: "Sorry. I couldn't help it. I have a bad temper." Beyond such insight, the counselor also knows personally just how to stop himself cold whenever he catches himself acting angry.

Counselors, then, are constantly striving for more mastery in their lives, applying the technology of psychological helping to themselves. At any moment in time the counselor ought to be able to articulate three or four specific personal areas in need of upgrading—and be actively involved in the process.

Adopting a Neutral Posture

To be a counselor implies a dedication to helping other people without having a vested interest in the particular directions that they may choose.

Based upon his or her particular religious beliefs, lifestyle preferences, and value system, every counselor has a notion about what is generally good for people, whether it be brown rice, plenty of fresh air, a God-fearing home, or an orgasm. Clients, therefore, present the counselor with the dilemma of which way to influence them: in a way that is consistent with the counselor's own beliefs or in quite another direction, one that the client may genuinely prefer.

In the social world people are quite liberal in dispensing their opinions on a variety of issues; in the counseling session such casually stated advice can be harmful. Counselors are interested in creating neither disciples nor dependents. They will understand that, by answering the client's persistent question "What should I do?" they fall into one of two traps. Either they offer poor advice, which then teaches the client to resent the profession forever and not to take responsibility for the negative outcome, or, worse, they offer sound advice, giving the client the clear message that the thing to do with a difficult question is just to run back to the counselor for help.

Yet a counselor always has strong personal opinions on whether clients should join the Army or go back to school, get a divorce or have an affair, tell off nosy parents or buy them a present, turn themselves in to the authorities or learn to be more discreet, punt or go for a touchdown. It is first necessary for the counselor to be aware of his or her own values and then, as far as is humanly possible, to block their effects on a client's decisions. Neutrality is the catchword of a therapeutic relationship. Although the counselor may feel strongly about choices that clients make, it is also important to accept the consequences of communicating those preferences. This caution does *not* mean that the counselor attempts to hide his or her true feelings from the client, using the mask of professional distance and neutrality. Rather, the counselor works toward conquering the need for an investment in client decisions beyond a professional counseling responsibility to the client.

It is also a necessary survival mechanism for counselors to do everything within their power to be helpful during the session but to refrain from needless worry afterward. The counselor may plan strategy and honestly be concerned with what clients are doing between sessions; however, there is no productive payoff in permitting one's work to interfere with one's personal life. All experienced counselors who have lasted in the field have devised ways to avoid thinking about client problems when they are not in a position to do anything about them.

Subjugating Personal Needs

To be a counselor involves subjugating one's own needs, desires, and preferences in favor of the best interests of the client.

The principal reason why counseling is such difficult work is that the professional makes a deliberate decision to suspend all distractions—both internal and external—while in session. Whether the phone rings in another room or a siren blares through the streets, the counselor blocks out all stimuli that are extraneous to the task at hand. Even more difficult to banish are internal distractions. To be maximally helpful to the client, to focus all of one's energy therapeutically, it is necessary to immerse oneself totally in the helping role. Attention to a grumbling stomach or an ingrown toenail will reduce one's concentration. To daydream or indulge in fantasy while pretending to listen is obviously counterproductive. And to permit oneself the luxury of liking or disliking clients during a session will only further reduce effectiveness. The counselor, therefore, becomes quite adept in the meditation-type skills of gently pushing aside distracting thoughts, indulgent feelings, and any other internal behavior that reduces concentration, without sacrificing the genuineness of being human.

A rationale for the necessity to receive some compensation in exchange for delivering a therapeutic service is that it does require such extraordinary effort to stifle one's natural urges. It is for this reason that counseling is an activity that is far from "natural." It is highly *un*natural to push aside one's urges of attraction, indulgence, and selfishness.

Being a Generalist

To be a counselor means learning to use all of one's capabilities, knowledge, and training to help others with their concerns.

Unlike the engineer who needs only assimilate the theory and mechanics of physics or the surgeon who intensively studies practical medicine, the counselor must study everything related to human behavior. It is not enough merely to master the set of generic skills that compose a professional's repertoire without personalizing the knowledge; the counselor must understand why people do the things they do.

The counselor studies mathematics and logic as a foundation for understanding relationships among ideas. Biochemistry, physiology, and psychopharmacology have value for grasping an overall view of body/mind interactions. Sociology and anthropology aid the counselor in understanding interpersonal behavior.

Literature, films, and television illuminate the psychology of characters faced with conflict. They provide the counselor with metaphors for understanding human processes as well as for conveying ideas to clients. In addition, philosophy, science, and every other discipline help the counselor more fully to appreciate people and their self-inflicted suffering.

In a typical session, the counselor may be expected initially to use a variety of traditional skills, such as rephrasing, summarizing, and questioning. As the process develops, the counselor may employ more sophisticated strategies— role playing or dramatic confrontation. Next, personal devices may be helpful— modeling and self-disclosure about life experiences. The counselor might create intricate metaphors as well as powerful verbal images reflecting experience. In the end, the counselor is willing to try almost anything that could motivate the client to change.

Coping with Discomfort

To be a counselor requires that a person learn to become comfortable in the presence of others' discomfort.

One goal of counseling is to make people squirm. Until clients become dissatisfied with themselves, disgusted by their self-sabotaging behaviors, they will rarely change. Counselors often help to intensify this discomfort as a means of encouraging continued flight toward mental health. Confrontation is intended to force the client to face discrepancies, incongruence, and inconsistency. And the counselor must get used to despair. The one place in the world where people feel safe to cry and honestly express their pain is in the counselor's office. Often the feelings of desperation are even exaggerated because the therapeutic environment is so nurturing and accepting. Clients will complain and show rage and hurt. They will cry and scream and stamp their feet. And counselors take the full force of this emotional energy.

It is advantageous to become proficient at facing outbursts calmly. Often it is necessary to reinterpret psychological discomfort as a sign that things are going according to plan rather than as a signal to retreat. Only when clients are uncomfortable may we be certain they are seriously working on themselves. They do not come for a good time.

Teaching Through Self-Discovery

To be a counselor involves learning to teach others without their knowing that they have been taught.

> I developed the Great Teacher Theory late in my freshman year. It was a cornerstone of the theory that great teachers had great personalities and that the greatest teachers had outrageous personalities. I did not like decorum or rectitude in a classroom; I preferred a highly oxygenated atmosphere, a climate of intemperance, rhetoric, and feverish melodrama. And I wanted my teachers to make me smart. A great teacher is my adversary, my conqueror, commissioned to chastise me. He leaves me tame and grateful for the new language he has purloined from other Kings whose granaries are famous. He tells me that teaching is the art of theft: of knowing what to steal and from whom [Conroy, 1982, p. 271].

Counselors teach through the force of their personalities and the richness of their experiences, focusing the reality of the client so that insights may be gleaned and learnings generated. They do so in subtle ways, recognizing that their job is to stimulate and structure, helping the client to learn through self-discovery. This point is part of the art of counseling, because the counselor wants no credit or acknowledgment for his or her contributions, preferring to allow the client to experience fully the sense of accomplishment that accompanies self-learning. Clients need to feel ownership of their learning so they can take the responsibility for both successes and failures.

Dealing with Ambiguity

To be a counselor requires that a person learn to function well with abstract ideas and ambiguous circumstances.

Counselors inhabit a professional world characterized by uncertainty and ambiguity. Clients are often not fully aware of what their real problems are. They report discomfort, vague and abstract, but circle relentlessly when the counselor attempts to help them focus. Very often clients want counseling because they are experiencing a true dilemma wherein no answer or response is truly satisfactory. Consider, for example, the man who has met a woman he deeply loves and wishes to spend his life with. However, she has a child, and he, after some traumatic past experiences, has realized that he is not comfortable in the parenting role. He wants to be with her yet is unable to share her role as a parent. The dilemma is real, and no alternative is completely satisfying. He comes for counseling, and your job is to help him resolve this thorny issue.

Counselors must develop empathy for clients who seem unfocused, who vacillate daily, and who seem unhappy but don't know why. In a sense, as Tramel (1981) has observed, counselors (and other social scientists) must abandon their search for cause and effect and come to terms with ambiguity and uncertainty, which reflect the reality of the individual. Counselors must relinquish the quest for answers and instead relish the challenge of helping clients with their abstractions and the uncertainty inherent in reality. *To be a counselor means dedicating oneself to the resolution of conflicts that are often irreconcilable, solving problems that have no right answers, and mediating disputes among parties who enjoy fighting.*

DEFINITIONS OF COUNSELING

Counseling is indeed an ambiguous enterprise. It is done by persons who can't agree on what to call themselves, what credentials are necessary to practice, or even what the best way is to practice—whether to deal with feelings, thoughts, or behaviors; whether to be primarily supportive or confrontive; whether to focus on the past or the present. Further, the consumers of counseling services can't exactly articulate what their concerns are, what counseling can and can't do for them, or what they want when it's over.

The authors went all the way through master's-level programs and most of the way through doctoral programs in counseling without ever really understanding what the profession was all about. Naturally we could recite textbook definitions that sound as if they describe what counselors do. And most of our professors and fellow students would eagerly nod their heads in agreement, particularly when our explanations included key phrases such as "actualizing your potential" (whatever *that* is) or "helping people to understand who they are" (as if they might be someone else).

For a definition to be useful, practical, or of any value whatsoever except as a professional prayer to memorize, it should have certain elements. At several points in his or her professional life—if not on comprehensive examinations, then certainly with every astute client—the practitioner will be asked to define what it is she or he does. This definition ought to be as specific as possible, describing in detail what counselors do, why they do it, and how it works.

We believe that a definition, like counseling itself, should be a process—a process designed to stimulate thinking so that ideas can ferment, evolve, and grow into a *personal* conception. Textbook definitions, although elegant, incisive, and comprehensive, almost always lack one essential ingredient: personalized meaning. As a beginner to this complex field who is already somewhat confused regarding what counseling is, the *last* thing in the world you need is another academic-sounding description of something that you don't really understand but that nevertheless sounds good to others (who don't understand it either). We therefore offer, for your perusal, a process definition of therapeutic counseling that we believe most people in the field could live with—regardless of differences in their treatment approaches. Further, we have tried to present our definition in such a way that, after you have studied it a bit, you can actually describe to someone else what counseling is and give a fairly intelligible explanation of why and how it works. (We would even suggest you try that to boost your confidence.)

Counseling is a profession with a history and set of standards, distinct from other related disciplines such as social work, psychology, and psychiatry.

Counseling is an activity that is geared for working with relatively normal-functioning individuals who are experiencing developmental or adjustment problems.

Counseling involves a relationship, either in a group, family, or individual format, that is caring, honest, accepting, and open.

Counseling is multidimensional, dealing with human feelings, thoughts, and behaviors as well as with the past, present, and future.

Counseling is a process that has the following components:

- Helping people to articulate why they are seeking help
- Formulating goals and expectations for treatment
- Teaching clients how to get the most from the counseling experience
- Developing a high degree of trust and favorable expectations for change
- Diagnosing those concerns and dysfunctional areas in need of upgrading
- Exploring the client's world, including past and present functioning
- Facilitating the release of pent-up frustrations and conflicts
- Supporting and accepting the client as a person while selectively reinforcing those behaviors that are most fully functioning
- Confronting inconsistencies in the client's thoughts, language, and behavior
- Challenging assumptions that are inappropriate, self-destructive, or irrational
- Uncovering hidden and unconscious motives behind actions
- Encouraging people to accept more responsibility for their choices and actions
- Helping clients to develop more options for their lives and to narrow alternatives to those that are most suitable
- Providing constructive feedback
- Structuring opportunities for practicing new ways of acting and being
- Facilitating greater independence in the client so that counseling ends in the most efficient period of time

The best definitions of counseling are those that are clearly understood and relevant to the needs of clients. Pictured here is a counselor who has been successful communicating to a group of teenagers what counseling can do to help them with a variety of concerns.

Yes, this definition *is* long, and certainly too cumbersome to memorize and spit back exactly as you read it. But remember that the objective is for you to be able to describe this wonderful and complex process *in your own unique way.* The following example illustrates how a counselor would actually use this definition in his or her work.

CLIENT:
    My mom thinks I should come to see you, but I don't really see what you can do. *(This confusion is not unusual in a first interview.)*

COUNSELOR:
    What is it that your mother thinks I can do? *(Rule number one in counseling is: when you don't know what else to do, put the ball back in the client's court to buy time until you can think of something else to say.)*

CLIENT:
    I don't know. She mentioned that maybe you could hear my problem and then fix it for me. *(Again, this is pretty typical that clients believe that we have magic wands.)*

COUNSELOR:
    Without knowing exactly what problem you are referring to, maybe it

would be helpful for you if I could explain a bit about what I do. If you were to interview people on their way out of my office, and ask them what their problems were, most of them would be unable to tell you anything specific. The clients that I see want to learn about themselves, about why they do the things they do; they want to understand better why they keep repeating the same mistakes over and over. *(The client looks perplexed. I better bring this more down to earth.)*

People come to see me because they feel safe here. They can talk about anything they want and know that I will listen carefully and I won't ever criticize them. I will keep whatever we talk about private, unless you seem inclined to hurt yourself, or someone else. Most people also appreciate the fact that I am completely honest with them, that I do everything in my power to help them. Sometimes I am very gentle; at other times I can be pretty tough if that's what the situation calls for. But basically people come to see me because they enjoy having a place where they can talk about whatever they want and work on whatever part of themselves they want to improve. So where would *you* like to start?

Although it is hardly as specific and clear an explanation of counseling as a client (or you) might like, this definition-in-action illustrates the value of being able to describe the process in a personal way. It also raises other questions, notably how and why counseling works in the first place.

WHY DOES THERAPEUTIC COUNSELING WORK?

Although at this juncture the jury has not yet returned to deliver its verdict, we do know that therapeutic counseling probably works as a combination of factors that many theorists find significant. You will learn in later chapters about how *client-centered* theorists believe that the nurturing relationship between counselor and client plays the biggest role in facilitating change; the *behaviorists* have evidence to indicate that reinforcement, modeling, and structured practice make the greatest difference; the *psychoanalytic* practitioners prefer to emphasize unconscious desires; and the *cognitive* clinicians claim that counseling works by teaching people to think more rationally. And so on ... and so on. By now it must have occurred to you that in this first chapter (and in a beginning course) it is not likely that you are going to get a very acceptable answer to the question "Why does counseling work?" Have patience.

On a more optimistic note, the field of counseling is currently driven by a movement toward synthesis and integration of existing knowledge. This is true of research, which is applying new methodologies such as "meta-analysis" as well as synthesizing what is known in the field into a single research volume (Marmor & Woods, 1980; Rice & Greenberg, 1984; Garfield & Bergin, 1986; Norcross, 1986). This is also true with counselor education in the standardization of curricula across the nation and the development of generic training models. And this is certainly the case in theory development, in which efforts are directed toward finding common factors that operate in all helping systems as well as toward combining the advantages of several therapeutic approaches into a unified model (Truax & Carkhuff, 1967; Wachtel, 1977; Palmer, 1980; Lazarus, 1981; Goldfried, 1982; Beutler, 1983; Prochaska, 1984; Driscoll, 1984; Zeig, 1986; Mahrer, 1989; Kottler, 1991).

Eclecticism, pragmatism, and integrationism have become the watchwords of the profession. Many years ago, several writers such as French (1933), Kubie (1934), Rosenzweig (1936), Dollard and Miller (1950), Thorne (1950), Strupp (1973), and Frank (1973) began to look at the common elements of various helping approaches in an effort to find the essence of what makes counseling and therapy most helpful. You must understand that, prior to these years, and even up to the present, there have been furious debates—even outright wars—among various theoretical camps, each convinced that they have cornered the market on what is "truth." You may even sense conflicts within your own department in which each instructor may present a different version of what constitutes "good counseling."

Perhaps of all the attempts to sort out this confusion, Brammer and Shostrum's (1982) classic book *Therapeutic Psychology* (now in its 4th edition) became most influential in its effort to bring together diverse elements into a unified model of helping. It is in this very tradition and spirit that we attempt to integrate many of the factors that various schools of thought find significant. Although there are individual differences in every practitioner's style of practice, depending on such factors as personality, theoretical preferences, and setting in which one works, empirical research does support that certain elements such as an effective counseling relationship, collaboratively structured roles, and instilling positive expectations in the client, consistently lead to constructive changes (Sexton & Whiston, 1991).

Counseling is less likely to be effective when the counselor is inexperienced, self-indulgent, and rigid and forces compliance to a personal agenda. Similarly, counseling is more likely to be helpful when the clinician's role is flexible, genuine, and accepting. Counseling effectiveness is often the result of the practitioner's use of self as an instrument of communication and treatment.

Significance of the Self

What counseling is and how it works are important concepts that can be defined and illustrated. But any explanation of counseling, however precise, exists only in a static sense. Life can be given to a definition, vitality breathed into a process, only in the context of a person—the self of the counselor. It is to this self that we now turn our attention.

The self is the crucial, the undefinable, and the most variable component of counseling. Yet it is the most therapeutic dimension of the counseling process. The need to integrate the richness of the person within the boundaries of the process is a major challenge for both prospective counselors—*you*—and counselor educators—*us*. It is not a challenge that either of us can take lightly. We must respect and prize one another's uniqueness, personal preferences, and individual values, remembering that our task is to preserve the salient richness of the self as we direct the learning of a profession. For your part, it is necessary that you be open, flexible, honest, and nondefensive as you work to implant the professional skills within your essential self. The goal is simple: growing toward increased effectiveness both as a counselor and as an evolving being. Necessary as it may be, the task of sharing our self, using it to perceive our clients, make sense of their actions, and communicate our reactions, is also quite difficult.

Thomas (1979) explains that the functional purpose of self is to maintain the individuality of every creature, to mark off distinguishing features so that each organism can defend itself against the rest. It is therefore our uniqueness rather than our sameness that gives our self an identity. And the threat to our self increases proportionately to risks we take in joining with another—an experience that is both exhilarating and terrifying.

Perceptual Base of Effective Counselors

It is helpful to think of the self as the primary tool in therapeutic counseling. The idea of self-as-instrument (Combs, Avila, & Purkey, 1971) emphasizes the importance of humanness and the counselor's perceptions as essential to the counseling process. In a sense, the self programs how the counseling skills, once learned, are put to work. The perceptual base of the self also defines the texture of the counseling process. Personal attitudes and self-characteristics that are facilitative include perceptions about self, others, and purposes.

According to Combs et al. (1971), the most effective counselors are able to perceive primarily from an internal rather than an external frame of reference. They tend to perceive others as being capable, as internally motivated, and in positive but realistic terms. They identify themselves strongly with others and feel an affinity for the human race. Additionally, they perceive their mission as altruistic rather than self-indulgent, as freeing rather than controlling, and as self-revealing rather than self-concealing.

Each of these characteristics aids in organizing personal reality and serves as a foundation from which the counselor's self mediates the counseling process. In a classic study, Fiedler (1950) illustrated the importance of the self in the counseling process by comparing the quality of the therapeutic relationships in psychoanalytic, nondirective, and Adlerian therapies. He found that experts in each of the three approaches were more similar than different in terms of style and personal relationship. He also found that the nonexperts were more different from one another in relationship style than were the experts and, further, that the nonexperts tended to be less similar than the experts in their own orientation. He therefore concluded that theoretical orientation was not the distinguishing variable separating expert from nonexpert therapists; rather, the difference was more related to personal style independent of conceptual affiliation. It appeared that a common thread unified the expert therapists, particularly with regard to relationship variables. In those instances in which there is a difficulty creating an alliance in counseling, it is due more often to the counselor's personality than to the client's motivation (Fromm-Reichmann, 1952).

Those counselors who are expert at using the self as an instrument, and who are powerful models with the capacity for influencing others, tend to cross theoretical boundaries. In spite of how they label themselves—as behaviorists, humanists, Adlerians, Gestaltists, or rational-emotivists—the most dynamic practitioners are intensely aware of the potential influence their selves can wield: as modelers of personal expertness, as reinforcers of appropriate behavior, and as nurturers of warmth and support.

Thus the self is the most significant dimension in therapeutic counseling; what counseling is and how it works depend to a large extent on the personal characteristics of the counselor. The existentialist Rollo May believes that, because counselors work through their personalities and selves as the primary instruments of treatment, it is crucial that certain qualities be evident. According to May (1967), good counselors are at ease in others' company, are free of personal prejudices, have the courage of imperfection, enjoy the process of living, have developed self-understanding, and are spiritually attractive.

Many other authors, such as Maslow (1954), Carkhuff and Berenson (1977), Patterson and Eisenberg (1983), Corey and Corey (1989), Trotzer (1989), and Kottler (1991), have compiled lists of those qualities they feel are necessary for the counselor's self to be in proper operating condition. A composite of these personality characteristics includes self-confidence, high energy level, sense of humor, neutrality, flexibility, emotional stability, experience in risk taking, analytic thinking, creativity, enthusiasm, honesty, and compassion.

In reading these lists of qualities, you cannot help but evaluate the extent to which you possess them and reflect upon how much personal growth lies ahead. Yet in counselor training the development of self as a more masterful person parallels the evolution of therapeutic skills. The self becomes refined and nurtured as a sensitive and operative component of the counseling process. As the self evolves, the counselor becomes more aware of personal assets and limitations, biases, and areas in need of upgrading. Actually, this opportunity to examine your own personal functioning is the greatest benefit to joining the counseling profession. On a daily basis, you not only have the opportunity to make a difference in other people's lives but can also continue to work on improving the quality of your own existence.

SUMMARY

In this chapter we have explored the decision to enter the field of counseling from a personal perspective. Honesty and self-awareness are themes that you will encounter again in this book and on a daily basis in the field; they need to be applied at the onset of your studies. Your personal awareness and understanding of the motives and payoffs for choosing counseling as a career objective will affect the energy, vitality, and commitment you bring to this introductory course and, ultimately, to the field.

In this relatively young profession there are many opportunities for creative individuals to make an impact. However, this flexibility of roles also results in confusion among people as to exactly what counseling is, how and why it works, and how it differs from other mental health disciplines. It will therefore become necessary for the beginning counselor to define the counseling process and profession assertively, both to carve out a useful identity and to provide a realistic and explicit portrait for clients who wish to know what services can and will be delivered.

SUGGESTED READINGS

Brammer, L. M., & Shostrom, E. L. (1982). *Therapeutic psychology: Fundamentals of counseling and psychotherapy* (4th ed.). Englewood Cliffs, NJ: Prentice-Hall.

Collison, B. B., & Garfield, N. J. (Eds.) (1990). *Careers in counseling and human development*. Alexandria, VA: American Association for Counseling and Development.

Corey, M. S., & Corey, G. (1989). *Becoming a helper*. Pacific Grove, CA: Brooks/Cole.

Kottler, J. A. (1986). *On being a therapist*. San Francisco: Jossey-Bass.

Meier, S. T. (1989). *The elements of counseling*. Pacific Grove, CA: Brooks/Cole.

Ram Dass, & Gorman, P. (1985). *How can I help? Stories and reflection on service*. New York: Knopf.

CHAPTER TWO

HISTORICAL AND CONCEPTUAL FOUNDATIONS OF COUNSELING

THE IDENTITY OF THERAPEUTIC
COUNSELING

COUNSELING AND
PSYCHOTHERAPY

THE HISTORY OF THERAPEUTIC
COUNSELING
The Ancient Philosophers
The First Psychiatrists
Influences from Psychology
The Guidance Era
The Counseling Era
The Era of Therapeutic
Counseling

LICENSING AND REGULATION IN
COUNSELING

SUMMARY

SUGGESTED READINGS

T his is the chapter that students dread reading almost as much as we resisted writing it. In most disciplines history is usually relegated to one of those requirements that everyone thinks is necessary but very few people relish studying. Who cares, after all, about what some obscure philosopher or educator said a hundred years ago? I just want to help people.

Yet the past is the basis for the present and future. One of the first tasks that occurs in every counseling endeavor, regardless of the practitioner's theoretical preferences, is the taking of a thorough client history. We explore childhood experiences, medical history, family lineage. We track every aspect of the client's social, emotional, physical, religious, educational, and vocational background in order to develop a complete portrait of functioning. And if personal history is important to understand and help the client, then a knowledge of the profession's history is necessary for you to function as a literate professional—even to understand how counseling fits within the context of other helping professions.

THE IDENTITY OF THERAPEUTIC COUNSELING

As you may already be aware, there are tremendous disagreements regarding professional identity and who is the rightful heir to the title "helper." There are psychiatrists, social workers, psychiatric nurses, psychologists, marriage and family therapists, and counselors all claiming that their training and abilities are superior to those of their colleagues. There are various titles that describe the work of helping others (Table 2-1), depending on the school they graduated from and the state in which they practice. Yet amongst these divergences there is a central core, an essence of effective practice, regardless of how it is labeled.

Whether it takes place in schools, community agencies, or private practice, the act of helping clients work through *personal* issues is best called *therapeutic counseling*, a hybrid term that distinguishes "counseling" as the professional identity and "therapeutic" as the modality. This practitioner is thus distinguished from some of the predecessors in the evolution of our field, such as "guidance counselor" or "career education consultant." This is not to say that therapeutic counselors (especially those in schools) don't regularly provide the services of career guidance among their other functions. However, the *therapeutic* aspect has to do with far more than merely providing information or facilitating decision making; it involves helping clients to personalize their decisions in such a way that they become part of them—that their underlying feelings and thoughts are dealt with as well.

COUNSELING AND PSYCHOTHERAPY

There has been much debate concerning the relationship between counseling and psychotherapy. Many contend that there is no essential difference between them and that any distinctions drawn tend to be artificial, to focus on superfi-

TABLE 2-1. Allied Mental Health Professional Groups

Group	Specialization	Clientele	Training	Degrees	License
Counselors	Developmentally based interaction with nonpathological clientele having problems in daily living, including career, education, family, marriage, and personal/esteem issues.	Normally functioning individuals with adjustment problems that typically do not retard daily functioning.	Minimum 2-year program with practicum and internship.	M.A. M.Ed. Ph.D. Ed.D.	Professional Counselor (most states)
Psychologists	Psychodiagnosis, psychotherapy, intervention with persons evidencing psychopathology, clinical management of cases.	Persons with psychopathological symptomology who are often dysfunctional in normal, everyday living.	Minimum 2-year program with practicum and internship.	M.A. Ph.D. Psy.D.	Psychologist (most states)
Psychiatrists	Medical and psychiatric management of clients with clinically significant psychological problems. Provide psychotherapy, pharmacological therapy, hospitalization services to patients.	Persons with psychological symptoms that either are psychopathological or require medical management, including drug therapy. Persons are often dysfunctional in everyday life.	Minimum 3-year residency following medical school and medical internship.	M.D.	Physician
Social Workers	Social casework, family relations, social impact of client problems. Organize and structure social resources for clients. Mediate clients' relationship with social structures, including schools, government, and health care facilities.	Persons who are experiencing problems and need to gain access to social services system. Persons who experience problems managing or responding to demands of society or social systems.	Minimum 2 years postgraduate training with internship.	M.S.W.	Social Worker (most states)
Marriage and Family Therapists	Systemic approach to diagnosing and treating problems in a family context. Extensive use of more active, directive interventions that realign hierarchies, coalitions, and boundaries within family.	Persons presenting developmental issues or psychopathological symptoms that are affected by, and influence, other family members.	Minimum 2-year program with practicum and internship.	M.A. M.Ed. Ph.D.	Marriage and Family Therapist (most states)

cial rather than substantial aspects, and to present a barrier rather than a help to practitioners (Pietrofesa, Hoffman, & Splete, 1984; Patterson, 1986). The differences, then, may be only a matter of degree along a continuum of depth, emphasis, and usage (see Table 2-2).

TABLE 2-2.   Counseling and Psychotherapy: Some Distinctions

	Counseling	*Psychotherapy*
Clients	Persons from a variety of walks of life who are functioning and are able to maintain psychological autonomy in spite of concerns or problem situations. Are not classified as mentally ill.	Persons from a variety of walks of life who are often dysfunctional in their natural environment, tending to be overwhelmed by the problems and situations they experience. May be classified as mentally ill.
Coping Abilities	Tend to cope with issues, although they may expend much energy on coping at the expense of growth. Will normally resolve problems or problem issues without counseling, although at much greater personal cost and by sacrificing growth potential.	Clients tend to cope very poorly, feel overwhelmed, at times are unable to respond. Are unlikely to resolve problems without outside help.
Length of Treatment	Generally short term.	Generally long term.
Approaches	Developmental, adaptive, growth oriented. Help to increase personal mastery and sense of self-worth. Build upon strength. Teach new skills.	Psychopathological, remedial, diagnostic. Attempt to develop coping skills, sense of worth. Restructure personality; define skills; provide support.
Goals	To facilitate personal growth; to increase adaptive behavior; to master negative emotions and situations; to improve decision-making and problem-solving skills. To increase autonomy and improve relationship skills.	To develop basic coping skills; to establish some psychological autonomy. To resolve past issues. To manage emotions and initiate some constructive relationships. To cure mental illness.
Setting	Variety of settings with which people come into daily contact, such as schools, churches, adult education facilities, recreational facilities, government agencies; also mental health clinics.	Settings requiring referral or intentional contact. Mental health clinics, psychiatric hospitals, private practice.

The other side of the debate argues that counseling is a profession unto itself and that the services delivered, approaches used, and underlying assumptions are distinct from those used in psychotherapy (Belkin, 1981; Ivey & Simek-Downing, 1987). Psychotherapy, for example, tends to rest upon a psychopathological base in which the medical model—emphasizing diagnosis and treatment—is commonly used. Counseling, in contrast, often rests upon a developmental model emphasizing learning and adaptation in response to problem situations. Thus many practitioners see clear differences between counseling and psychotherapy and believe that, although overlap may at times occur, the typical client interaction reflects those basic differences.

It is our position to deemphasize these issues in our daily practice. Although it is useful to have a clear professional identity, it is more useful for the practi- tioner to conduct an effective session with a client, regardless of what it is called. An unfortunate correlate of this debate is the implicit assumption that counseling is relatively "easy" whereas psychotherapy is relatively "difficult" and that therefore less skill is needed by "counselors," especially as compared to "psy- chotherapists." We could not disagree more with this position. Working with clients, regardless of the labels applied, requires enormous skill. Period.

One final point: it is important to remember that counselors are *not* in com- petition with allied professional groups; each discipline reflects specialized skills and various professional competencies, which overlap yet have distinctive com- ponents. For example, although clinical psychologists do counseling, their area of training and expertise is more centered on psychodiagnosis, psychotherapy with patients demonstrating psychopathological behavior, and the management of clinically significant mental illness. Counselors do not generally develop expertise in these areas as much as they specialize in briefer treatment modali- ties with less disturbed individuals. These distinctions, however, become even more muddled when we consider that in recent years the specialties of "clinical counseling" and "mental health counseling" have been geared toward work with client populations that previously had been restricted to social workers, psychologists, and psychiatrists. There are settings, in fact, such as community mental health centers and hospitals, where master's-level practitioners do essen- tially the same things regardless of their professional identity.

It is useful to think of the allied professional groups as forming a mental health treatment team that responds to various clients who experience problems within their areas of specialization. The team concept recognizes the responsibil- ity of professionals to provide relevant services within their respective areas of competence and, further, demands effective communication and cooperation among professionals. Working toward increased professional recognition and cooperation of various mental health specialties reduces the negative effects of implied competition and presents a coherent public profile.

THE HISTORY OF THERAPEUTIC COUNSELING

A unique aspect of counseling as a profession is that its foundation is grounded in so many other disciplines; it is a hybrid of knowledge from philosophy, edu- cation, psychology, psychiatry, sociology, and family studies. Even today, pro- grams that train counselors are found in academic units as diverse as colleges of education, departments of psychology or family studies, schools of human ser- vices, and religious institutions.

The field of therapeutic counseling and its related disciplines of psychiatry, psychology, social work, and guidance have undergone an uneven progression of development. In the days of our palaeolithic ancestors, the first mental health professionals were fond of drilling holes in a client's head to permit demons to escape. Through the days of ancient Mesopotamia and Persia, the Classical Greek and Roman eras, and into modern times, early therapeutic counselors were primarily philosophers, physicians, or priests.

The primitive days of the 19th century spawned the first real counselors, the experts who attempted to heal by talking (even if they did so in ways we now find a bit bizarre). It is incredible to think that 100 years ago therapeutic counseling, as we know it, did not exist. And it has only been in the past 50 years that counseling has emerged as a distinct field apart from its related mental health disciplines.

The "talking cure" is a concept that we take for granted today, yet a century ago it was a revolutionary idea that was not only unaccepted but held in disrepute, smacking of witchcraft and the occult. The cathartic method of talking out problems was pioneered by Freud at the turn of the 20th century as a method for treating persons with psychological problems. Although the concept had existed for many years, it took Freud to build credibility for the technique. Today, most people agree that talking over problems is helpful, sharing feelings and concerns is useful, and professional helpers are reasonable alternatives for those faced with problems or difficult situations. Interpersonal communication and verbal interaction form the heart of therapeutic counseling, albeit in a substantially different format from what Freud envisioned. Counselors, clients, and the "person in the street" all accept the interactive therapeutic process and believe that constructive change can occur when a counselor and a client participate in a verbally mediated therapeutic relationship.

The Ancient Philosophers

The first counselors were leaders of the community who attempted to provide inspiration for others through their teachings. They were religious leaders like Moses (1200 B.C.), Buddha (500 B.C.), and Mohammed (600). They were also philosophers like Lao-tzu (600 B.C.), Confucius (500 B.C.), Socrates (450 B.C.), Plato (400 B.C.), and Aristotle (350 B.C.).

Many of these philosophers and religious leaders functioned as "counselors" in that they worked with a group of disciples, trying to impart wisdom to stimulate emotional, spiritual, and intellectual growth. Although their approaches to helping are considerably different from those of most contemporary counselors, we have inherited a few of their basic tenets:

- There is no single right answer to any question worth asking.
- There are many possible interpretations of the same experience.
- Any philosophy is worthless if it is not personalized and made relevant to everyday life.

These same principles, spoken in the forums of Rome, Athens, and Mesopotamia, are very much a part of what today's counselors work with on a daily basis—helping clients to find their own path to inner peace.

The First Psychiatrists

Besides those who sought to "heal" others' suffering through educational and spiritual paths, there were also those pragmatic practitioners who tried to combine philosophy with what they observed about human behavior. Foremost among these medical philosophers was Hippocrates (400 B.C.), who introduced many ideas that we now take for granted, including the concepts of "homeostasis," the natural balance of the body, and "prognosis," the prediction of outcomes.

Hippocrates emphasized the importance of a complete life history before undertaking any treatment (which unfortunately was usually bloodletting) and devised the first comprehensive classification of mental disorders. He is also credited with developing, over 2000 years ago, the first counseling interventions, relying on many techniques that are still in use today: systematic diagnostic interviews, detailed history taking, trust building in a therapeutic relationship, and even dream interpretation and acknowledgment of repressed feelings!

In September 1909, Sigmund Freud was invited to the United States to give a series of lectures on his theories. He is pictured here (bottom left) sitting next to the American psychologist G. Stanley Hall, and colleague Carl Jung (before they parted ways). In the top row (from left to right) are three of Freud's disciples: A. A. Brill, Ernest Jones, and Sandor Ferenczi.

There really were not that many improvements on Hippocrates's theories until the last century or two. (Remember, the favored "treatment" in the Middle Ages for those suffering from emotional problems was being burned at the stake.) But when Sigmund Freud and his collaborator Joseph Breuer evolved their "talking cure" of healing through catharsis, the professions of counseling and psychotherapy were truly born. Not only was Freud a talented physician, writer, teacher, thinker, and astute observer of the human condition, but he was also remarkably persuasive as an influencer of others. He recruited into his camp a flock of followers from all over the world to spread the word about his newfound cure for emotional suffering; many of their names may be familiar to you: Carl Jung, Alfred Adler, Wilhelm Reich, and even his own daughter, Anna Freud.

The 19th century had produced a number of great philosophers who were to have a significant impact on the development of Freud and his students. Such thinkers as Søren Kierkegaard, G. W. F. Hegel, and Friedrich Nietzsche were to be just as influential on this new profession as were his own colleagues in medicine. In addition, a number of brilliant mentors had instructed Freud in the intricacies of the brain as well as introduced him to the technique of hypnosis as a means of accessing the mind's inner secrets. Add to that training Freud's own penchant for philosophy, literature, and archeology, and he was ideally suited to pull all this knowledge together into the first comprehensive model for understanding and changing human behavior.

Throughout his prolific life, churning out volume after volume of meticulously documented theories on the human condition, Freud accomplished several remarkable feats, including:

- plotting the anatomy of the human nervous system
- developing the first form of local anesthesia for eye surgery
- adapting the technique of hypnosis for studying the inner world
- formulating models of personality development and psychopathology
- emphasizing unconscious motives behind human behavior
- suggesting that dreams have meanings that can be uncovered and interpreted
- studying the underlying structure of society
- developing the first formal methodology of therapeutic counseling

Although it is popular nowadays to ridicule many of Freud's ideas, to call him obsolete, sexist, controlling, sexually obsessed, neurotic, and a host of other names, it must be remembered that he was the primary mentor of the first generation of therapeutic counselors. Many of the most famous names in the field, representing quite diverse approaches—Albert Ellis, Fritz Perls, Carl Rogers, Eric Berne—were all at one time practicing Freudian analysts. It would be difficult, therefore, to underestimate Freud's importance in the development of counseling, even if contemporary practitioners no longer employ his methods the way they were originally intended. (But, then, how many techniques in *any* profession remain intact after a hundred years?)

Influences from Psychology

About the same time that Freud was laying the foundation for psychiatric counseling, another discipline was making its own contribution to the field: the burgeoning field of psychology. As was the case with the first psychiatrists and counselors, all the first psychologists were philosophers. Beginning with René Descartes (1596–1656), who was among the first to study the mind as distinct from the body and soul, and continuing through the British empirical philosophers like John Locke (1632–1704), George Berkeley (1685–1753), David Hume (1711–1776), and John Stuart Mill (1806–1873), who analyzed human experience in terms of its basic elements, the discipline of philosophy gave rise to the new science of psychology.

Every undergraduate psychology major memorizes that psychology was born when Wilhelm Wundt (1732–1920) founded the first experimental laboratory in 1875. However, it was really the American philosopher William James (1842–1910) who was the first to be awarded the title "Professor of Psychology." For our purposes, James's ideas are more relevant to the development of therapeutic counseling as a separate discipline. He was intensely interested in the concepts of "free will," "consciousness," and "adaptive functioning" and believed humans to be creatures of emotion and action as well as thought and reason.

There are, of course, many other names associated with the development of psychology, such as G. Stanley Hall, who received the first doctorate in psychology and became the bridge between this new science and the field of education. Certainly the behaviorists, led by John Watson and B. F. Skinner, also made significant contributions to the understanding and management of human behavior through their experimental studies of reinforcement. A number of other experimental psychologists, such as Max Wertheimer and Wolfgang Köhler, approached things from quite a different perspective. From their studies of how apes solve problems, they concluded that learning does not necessarily follow an orderly progression; sometimes sudden insights play a part, whereby a person conceptualizes the whole as greater than the sum of its elemental parts.

The Guidance Era

In the years from about 1895 to 1915, a completely different movement was taking place. It was a time of significant social reform, and there was an emerging recognition that social forces and individual development could be assisted, directed, and, more important, guided. This awareness was especially evident in the field of education and the specialty of career guidance.

The industrial age was then flourishing; technical training and skilled workers were becoming necessary, and new programs in vocational guidance attempted to respond to these needs. Although there were a number of pioneers who took the initiative in this field, Frank Parsons is often credited as the founder of the vocational guidance movement. In his book *Choosing a Vocation* (Parsons, 1909), he described a three-part model for career counseling: (1) an analysis of one's own personal interests, abilities, and aptitudes; (2) an exploration of available occupations; and (3) the application of a systematic reasoning process to find a good match between the two. This procedure, Parsons believed, would place individuals in work settings most appropriate to their skills and education.

Parsons and several colleagues applied their new technology of testing and interviewing to help Boston's unemployed youth identify interests and abilities and find suitable work. Thus the vocational guidance field became respectable, enabling counselors to specialize in a particular aspect of human conflict. It carved a niche for guidance personnel in educational settings; however, it also prevented the integration of the structured teaching model of vocational guidance into the mainstream of therapeutic counseling. For the next 60 years counselors were seen primarily as school specialists who helped children make educational and occupational decisions.

The Counseling Era

Not all of the contributors to the mental health movement were philosophers, psychiatrists, psychologists, or educators; one of the most influential figures in the early part of the 20th century was an abused mental patient! In *A Mind That Found Itself*, Clifford Beers described his harrowing experiences at the hands of an insensitive system that treated him as a lunatic rather than as a human being. In this classic work (which eventually led to the establishment of the National Association for Mental Health), Beers proposed that what the emotionally disturbed person needs most of all is a compassionate friend. It was the field of therapeutic counseling that finally responded to his plea.

The prevailing "medical model" espoused by psychiatrists and some psychologists had reigned supreme. This framework emphasized the diagnosis of psychopathology; patients who sought therapeutic services were viewed as afflicted with a form of mental illness that could be treated by a number of medical options—electroconvulsive shock treatment, psychosurgery (frontal lobotomies), psychopharmacology, and, as a last resort, medical psychotherapy—which usually took the form of long-term psychoanalysis with sessions three to four times a week for a half-dozen years or more.

At the midpoint of this century a lone voice was heard above the throng of psychiatrists and psychologists. Carl Rogers began to argue persuasively that the traditional doctor/patient pattern of interaction proposed by the medical model was not appropriate for working with the vast majority of human beings. According to Rogers, people with emotional problems are not "sick" or "mentally ill"; most people simply need a safe environment in which to work out their difficulties. He maintained that the most effective vehicle to accomplish this task was within the context of a counselor/client relationship.

In spite of the initially cool reception to the ideas in client-centered theory, Carl Rogers emerged as a significant force in the field of counseling, changing previous thinking about the nature of the therapeutic relationship. In retrospect, it seems difficult to imagine counseling today without the impact of Rogers and his ideas about the importance of relationship variables.

Client-centered counseling became the theoretical focus of many counselor education programs during the 1950s and early 1960s. On the whole, Rogers was enthusiastically embraced and legions of counselors were trained in nondirective, client-centered techniques. However, in spite of the general acceptance of client-centered counseling, some concerns were emerging that questioned the nature of this approach and criticized its relevance for many client populations. Additionally, the operational difficulties involved in defining the tasks of the counselor and the difficulties in gathering empirical evidence to support the client-centered approach caused further questioning and exploring.

The 1960s and early 1970s saw much change and refocusing in the counseling field. The wide acceptance of the Rogerian approach came under increased scrutiny. Carkhuff and Berenson (1967) and Krumboltz (1966) wrote books that were very influential in challenging the field to move toward a more behavioristic slant, while Ellis (1962) and other cognitive therapists emphasized the role of thinking in the counseling process. Other theorists joined the defection: Gestalt therapy, transactional analysis (TA), values-clarification strategies, reality therapy, and others all clamored for attention and vied for influence.

From this rich inquiry and challenge there seemed to emerge a focus that gained wide credibility in counselor education. Carkhuff (1969) imposed a systematic and generalist approach to the task of helping. He suggested that counselors must be skilled, reliable, and capable of delivering effective levels of core counseling skills. He defined the skills and developed methods of assessing effectiveness. By and large the work of Carkhuff is widely accepted, with much counselor training emphasizing the development of generic skills that provide a base for effective helping relationships. It should be noted that Carkhuff's "core conditions" were built directly on the work of Rogers, but with more attention given to defining relevant skills operationally and developing a quantitative base for those skills. Today, therapeutic counseling is built upon the work of Carkhuff, who has developed a base for the skill-development process; Rogers, who emphasized the importance of the relationship dimension in counseling; and Freud, who gave credibility to the idea of treatment through talking.

Table 2-3 summarizes the contributions of many individuals to the field of therapeutic counseling. In a sense, it represents the generic foundation for training in therapeutic counseling. To achieve maturity as a therapeutic counselor, it is necessary to integrate the various approaches to counseling within the generic model used in most training. It is a mistake to assume that minimal generic skills will prepare a person to function as a therapeutic counselor. Therefore, in your training you will first learn the basic skills of reflecting, confronting, summarizing, attending, and goal setting and will then expand upon this base from the diverse sources of theory and technique available to therapeutic counselors.

TABLE 2-3.   Summary of Historical Figures in Therapeutic Counseling, with
Contributions from Philosophy, Education, Medicine, Literature, and Social Science

400 B.C. Hippocrates	Classified types of mental illness and personality disorders
400 B.C. Socrates	Encouraged self-awareness as purest form of knowledge
350 B.C. Plato	Postulated human behavior in terms of internal states
350 B.C. Aristotle	Designed first rational psychology to manage emotions
A.D. 100 Aretaeus	Studied personalities associated with depression
A.D. 400 St. Augustine	Prescribed introspection to master emotions
1250 Sprenger and Kraemer	Wrote text of psychopathology and symptoms of witches
1500 Leonardo da Vinci	Combined science with art to recreate human reality
1500 Niccolò Machiavelli	Brought attention to group dynamics and social interaction
1550 Johann Weyer	Documented case histories of depression
1600 Shakespeare	Created a literature of psychologically complex characters
1625 René Descartes	Attempted to resolve dualism of mind and body
1675 John Locke	Theorized that all knowledge originates from experience
1675 Baruch Spinoza	Developed an integrative personality theory with the unconscious
1800 Johannes Müller	Plotted the physiology of the nervous system
1800 Philippe Pinel	Described various forms of neurosis and psychosis
1800 Anton Mesmer	Used hypnotic suggestion to cure psychological symptoms
1850 Fyodor Dostoyevsky	Wrote complex character studies of anxiety and dread in novels
1850 Charles Darwin	Set forth an evolutionary theory of individual differences
1850 Jean Charcot	Scientifically studied hypnosis to give it respectability
1850 Søren Kierkegaard	Developed an existential concept of giving meaning to being
1880 G. Stanley Hall	Began first child guidance clinic
1880 Wilhelm Wundt	Founded first psychological laboratory
1890 James Cattell	Coined the term "mental tests"
1890 Jesse Davis	Became first school counselor
1900 Emil Kraepelin	Systematized the classification of mental disorders
1900 William James	Postulated comprehensive theory of emotions
1900 Ivan Pavlov	Described behavioral theory of conditioned reflexes
1900 Sigmund Freud	Invented first systematic form of therapeutic counseling
1905 Alfred Binet	Invented first intelligence test
1910 Frank Parsons	Established field of vocational guidance
1920 Carl Jung	Proposed theory of collective unconscious
1920 Alfred Adler	Authored theory of individual psychology
1920 J. L. Moreno	Invented psychodrama
1920 John Watson	Propounded behavioristic notions of prediction and control of behavior
1930 Robert Hoppock	Studied levels of job satisfaction
1940 B. F. Skinner	Formulated theory of operant conditioning
1940 E. G. Williamson	Published standard text on school counseling
1945 Gregory Bateson	Emphasized family influences in psychological disturbances
1945 Kurt Lewin	Used training-group format for personal development
1950 Erik Erikson	Proposed theory of personality development

(continued)

TABLE 2-3.   *(continued)*

1950	Jean Piaget	Proposed theory of cognitive development
1950	Viktor Frankl	Introduced system of existential therapy
1950	Milton Erickson	Focused on linguistic aspects of therapeutic encounter
1950	Carl Rogers	Proposed theory of client-centered counseling
1955	Abraham Maslow	Studied self-actualized people
1955	Donald Super	Introduced theory of vocational decision making
1960	Joseph Wolpe	Devised systematic theory of behavior therapy
1960	Jay Haley	Began strategic family therapy
1960	Eric Berne	Introduced transactional analysis (TA)
1960	Albert Ellis	Began rational-emotive therapy (RET)
1960	Albert Bandura	Researched modeling processes in change
1960	Frederick Thorne	Made systematic attempt to create an eclectic system
1965	Fritz Perls	Popularized Gestalt therapy
1965	George Gazda	Popularized methods of group counseling
1965	Robert Carkhuff	Organized the skills of helping
1965	Lawrence Kohlberg	Proposed theory of moral development
1965	Jane Loevinger	Proposed theory of ego development
1965	John Krumboltz	Published theory of behavioral counseling
1965	Salvador Minuchin	Developed structural family therapy
1965	Murray Bowen	Brought attention to family-of-origin issues
1965	Virginia Satir	Described communication theory in family therapy
1970	Heinz Kohut	Developed theory of self psychology
1970	Aaron Beck	Refined methods of cognitive therapy
1970	Jerome Frank	Authored seminal work on persuasion in healing
1970	Allen Ivey	Developed microcounseling as an innovation for training counselors
1975	Allan Bergin	Edited first comprehensive research handbook on psychotherapy
1975	Arnold Lazarus	Proposed integrative multimodal treatment approach
1975	Helen Kaplan	Published classic work on sex counseling
1975	Irving Yalom	Refined practice of group treatment
1980	Paul Pederson	Championed cause of multicultural awareness in counseling
1980	John Norcross	Represented new movement toward integration of theories

The Era of Therapeutic Counseling

There was a time when 80% of all students enrolled in counseling programs were following a school-based employment track. Now that trend has shifted, and the majority of new counselors are targeting themselves for employment in community agencies. Clearly, the focus of counseling is now less educational and more therapeutic. This fact is reflected in the name change of the American Association for Counseling and Development (AACD) several years ago (it used to be called the American Personnel and Guidance Association). It is evident in the divisions of AACD that are growing the fastest (the American Mental

Health Counselors Association is now the largest). And it is certainly obvious from the emergence of licensing and credentialing for professional counselors.

This cadre of new counselors is still using the core skills of practice that have been identified for some time but is also drawing heavily from other fields while researching, developing, and expanding the intervention base. The emphasis is on approaches that are developmentally oriented and that use relatively short-term, dynamic strategies designed to reduce symptoms, eliminate self-defeating behaviors, and increase self-esteem, self-efficacy, and self-management skills. Therapeutic counselors focus on developing a therapeutic relationship, identifying core issues, understanding them from a developmental perspective, and employing interventions best suited to the particular client and clinical situation.

The latest movement within the helping professions has been a drive toward greater integration of existing research and theory into a coherent model that most practitioners can follow. As a result, counselor training programs are becoming more standardized across the continent as current theorists attempt to reconcile the conflicts and differences among competing schools of thought. (See Norcross, 1986; Mahrer, 1987; Corey, 1990; and Kottler, 1991, as examples.)

Of particular note is the work by Zeig (1986), who organized a series of conferences in which the most prominent theoreticians in the field were invited together to try to reach some consensus regarding what works in counseling. These "Evolution of Psychotherapy" conferences best symbolize the direction we are headed in the future. We are coming to terms with our history as a multidisciplinary and multidimensional profession—one that can find common ground among its practitioners regarding what constitutes the best ways to help people.

LICENSING AND REGULATION IN COUNSELING

The best evidence for how far we have developed in our history is found in the progress made in the credentialing of counselors across the country (Vroman & Bloom, 1991). There was a time, just a few decades ago, when there were no standards for the preparation of counselors, no licensure laws, no certifications for specialties in any area. As a result, therapeutic counselors did not enjoy the professional autonomy and respect granted to our colleagues in social work, psychology, and psychiatry.

Efforts to standardize counselor training and to regulate the practice of clinicians began in 1973, when the Association for Counselor Education and Supervision developed a knowledge base to provide the foundation for future licensing efforts (Brooks & Gerstein, 1990). Before we could decide who should be allowed to practice counseling, it first became necessary to establish minimum standards of training and education. Soon after this report was created, a number of states in succession, beginning with Virginia, passed licensing laws.

The licensure initiative must be understood in the context of two other attempts to legitimize counseling as a profession that evolved simultaneously. In 1981 the American Association for Counseling and Development (AACD) established an independent agency to accredit training programs in the field. This Council for the Accreditation of Counseling and Related Educational Programs (CACREP) developed minimum requirements for graduate programs at the master's and doctoral levels, including specialties in mental health, school counseling, student personnel, community/agency counseling, and marriage and family counseling. The National Board for Certified Counselors (NBCC) has also been influential in gaining increased recognition for our profession. The NBCC developed generic standards for rehabilitation counseling, mental health counseling, and career counseling. In order to become board certified in any of these areas, or to become licensed in most states, it is necessary to pass a written exam and to document your training and supervision experiences.

These organizations, as well as others, such as the American Association for Marriage and Family Therapy, have been instrumental in upgrading the quality of training and practice in therapeutic counseling. It is no longer necessary for our profession to rely on psychology, social work, education, philosophy, psychiatry, or any other discipline for our models (Van Hesteren & Ivey, 1990). Graduates from our programs are as qualified and skilled as those from allied helping professions.

Now, finally, we are earning greater respect and recognition from colleagues in other fields and from clients who prefer to work with practitioners employing a developmental rather than a medical model. Our legitimacy is even attested to by our eligibility for third-party reimbursement from clients' insurance companies.

It is probably a very good idea, even this early in your program, to begin researching the licensing requirements in your own state as well as the certification options that will be available for you upon graduation. Almost every region of North America has a unique professional climate, and each specialty you may be interested in—whether in schools, agencies, rehabilitation settings, religious organizations, private practice, universities, or industry—will have different requirements in course content, internships, and supervision.

We turn now, in the next chapter, to a more detailed look at just what counselors do in the various settings in which they practice.

SUMMARY

Counseling is an interdisciplinary profession that has evolved from fields such as education, philosophy, medicine, and social sciences. Although there are many similarities among what all helping professionals do, such as their emphasis on the therapeutic relationship, their interest in fostering client growth, and their use of interpersonal skills, there are also several important distinctions. The counseling profession is unique in that: (1) we work more toward prevention rather than the remediation of problems, (2) we follow a developmental rather than a psychopathological model of assessment and treatment, (3) we attempt to intervene in relatively short time periods rather than establish lengthier treatments, and (4) we specialize in helping people through normal life transitions and adjustments rather than only during times of major dysfunction.

Whereas the power and rights that we have earned through legislative acts are still not where most of us would like them to be, therapeutic counselors now enjoy an unprecedented degree of professional autonomy and respect.

SUGGESTED READINGS

Brooks, D. K., Jr., & Gerstein, L. H. (1990). Counselor credentialing and interpersonal collaboration. *Journal of Counseling and Development, 68,* 477–484.

Council for the Accreditation of Counselors and Related Educational Programs (1985). *Standards for the preparation of counselors and other personnel-services specialists.* Alexandria, VA: Author.

Dingman, R. L. (Ed.). (1988). *Licensure for mental health counselors.* Huntington, WV: Marshall University.

Heppner, P. P. (Ed.). (1991). *Pioneers in counseling and development: Personal and professional perspectives.* Alexandria, VA: American Association for Counseling and Development.

Herr, E. L. (1989). *Counseling in a dynamic society: Opportunities and challenges.* Alexandria, VA: American Association for Counseling and Development.

Rossberg, R. H., & Band, L. (1978). Historical antecedents of counseling: A revisionist point of view. In J. Hansen (Ed.), *Counseling process and procedures.* New York: Macmillan.

Van Hoose, W. H., & Pietrofessa, J. J. (1970). *Counseling and guidance in the twentieth century.* Boston: Houghton Mifflin.

Whiteley, J. M. (1982). A historical perspective on the development of counseling psychology as a profession. In S. D. Brown & R. W. Lent (Eds.), *Handbook of counseling psychology.* New York: McGraw-Hill.

CHAPTER THREE
SETTINGS FOR THERAPEUTIC COUNSELING

WHAT COUNSELORS HAVE
   IN COMMON
   A Unique Identity
   Many Different Roles
   A Set of Generic Skills
   A Set of Common Goals
   Both Developmental and
      Remedial Orientation
   Teamwork
A DAY IN THE LIFE
   Private Practice
   Mental Health Center
   Crisis Center
   High School
   Preschool
   Street Ministry
   University Counseling Center
   Rehabilitation Center
   Counseling in Industry

THE VALUE OF A FLEXIBLE
   SPECIALTY
   Specialty Areas in Counseling
   Guidelines for Selecting a
      Counseling Specialty
SUMMARY
SUGGESTED READINGS

STUDENT:

Where can I work after I get my counseling degree?

PROFESSOR:

Nowhere and everywhere.

STUDENT:

Huh?

PROFESSOR:

You're feeling confused and frustrated because the question is more complex than you thought.

STUDENT:

Actually, I'm angry because you're evading my question with that active listening stuff.

PROFESSOR:

What would you like to do with your degree?

STUDENT:

See what I mean? There you go again.

PROFESSOR:

OK. The reason I answered your question the way I did is that I wanted to be honest with you.

STUDENT:

Yes. I appreciate that. But I'm putting all this time and work into my studies. I have a right to know what my degree will qualify me to do.

PROFESSOR:

Yes, you have a right to know. In one sense your counseling degree qualifies you to do nothing at all. You will see very few job openings in the paper under the heading "Counselor." Very few people—employers, friends, family—will know what a counselor is qualified to do. There aren't many precedents from the courts, the legislature, or the media that will prescribe what you are entitled to do and where you are entitled to do it.

STUDENT:

This I already know. I looked in the Yellow Pages under "Counselor" and found astrologers, dietitians, palm readers, finance companies, employment agencies—not to mention the usual assortment of mystics, and guidance people....

PROFESSOR:

That's true. However, there are also a number of fairly specific slots for counselors to fit in and a virtually unlimited market for creative professionals to develop needed services. That's what I meant when I said that counselors work nowhere and everywhere. Although your degree does not qualify you to do one particular job, there are a hundred different ways that you could put your training to work.

STUDENT:

But outside of school counselors and ministers, and perhaps a crisis center, college dormitory, or probation department, I've never heard of any other places where counselors can work. I mean, we're not exactly like psychiatrists—everyone knows what they do and where they are supposed to work.

PROFESSOR:

That's just it. Counselors aren't as limited to working in specific settings, such as hospitals or clinics, or with specific populations like neurotics and psychotics. Counselors work with relatively normal people in almost any place where they hang out—in senior citizen's homes or playgrounds.

STUDENT:

I know I'm supposed to get better at dealing with ambiguity and abstractions, but couldn't you be a little more specific?

PROFESSOR:

Sure. But the possibilities that I name are limited by my own meager imagination. Counselors create jobs for themselves in industry, for example. It's relatively easy to convince corporate executives that profit can be increased if morale is improved among workers. We've had graduates hired to reduce absenteeism, drug abuse, and interpersonal conflicts in companies. Sometimes they also get jobs in public relations or personnel offices. In fact, what training could possibly be better for people management at any level? Counseling teaches you to be sensitive to others' feelings, to respect their rights, to selectively reinforce productive behavior. You learn to confront people nondefensively, to stimulate creativity, to encourage growth at all levels. You tell me where counselors could work.

STUDENT:

I just thought about all the creative roles counselors could play in a hospital, for instance. Patients don't exactly feel good about being there. Maybe a counselor-at-large could help prepare people psychologically for their operations.

PROFESSOR:

Exactly. Graduates have been hired to do just that, for one thing. Counselors also work as part of teams in other settings. They work with medical personnel in mental health clinics, with teachers, with attorneys, and with administrators. They work everywhere and anywhere that they can persuade people their services are helpful.

STUDENT:

Now I'm really confused. How can I possibly decide which direction I should go in?

Several years ago it would have been unheard of to include a chapter such as this one in an introductory text. Historically, counselors were prepared for only one setting—schools. But times have changed. And the demand for counselors in almost all settings is on the rise.

WHAT COUNSELORS HAVE IN COMMON

The needs and requirements of a particular environment determine, in part, the adaptations and behavior of organisms in that setting. The Manhattan pigeon, for instance, a mutant bird form that has accommodated to city life, has survived—even flourished—because of its ability to evade taxis, shoppers' feet, and dogs. As Charles Darwin discovered in his travels, there is a staggering variety of species that have successfully adapted to their environments—20,000 different butterflies, 40 kinds of parrots, and 300 species of hummingbird. There is also potentially an endless variety of counselors, each species having successfully adapted to the demands of the work environment. Every client population, geographical area, cultural heritage, institutional policy, physical facility, and psychological climate subtly shapes a new species of counselor. It is even difficult, on the basis of the everyday practice of professionals, to recognize that they are nevertheless members of the same evolutionary family. Even so, there are probably more similarities than differences among therapeutic counselors in various settings. Before we profile the roles of counselors in the places where they work, it will be helpful for you to understand what they all share in common.

A Unique Identity

All counselors, irrespective of their work settings, identify themselves as part of a shared profession that is distinguished from other helping disciplines. Counseling is *not* the same as social work, psychology, guidance, psychiatry, or education, even though those other professionals often practice counseling in some form. Each field, however similar in its methods and goals, arises out of quite different settings. Psychiatry is a specialty of medicine. Social work came from the streets, psychology from the university, and counseling from the schools. In spite of their recent trends toward convergence, each helping profession is indelibly marked by its birthplace.

Many Different Roles

Counselors have many varied roles, regardless of the setting in which they practice. These may be grouped into several categories.

1. *Individual counseling* consists of those one-to-one interactions with clients in which the therapeutic process is applied to resolving personal concerns, career and educational decisions, and problems of human adjustment.

2. *Individual assessment* comprises observation, information seeking, and interpretation of a person's behavior in areas that might include performance, achievement, aptitude, personality, and interests. The results of assessment are valuable for screening, placement, diagnosis, evaluation, and planning of treatment approaches.

3. *Family counseling* focuses on the interaction patterns that lead to dysfunc-

tional behavior. By thinking in terms of the family system to which a client belongs, the counselor is able to intervene by understanding and changing communication patterns and coalitions of power.

4. *Group work* structures may be used to accomplish more efficiently the goals of individual counseling. Participants have the added advantages of interaction. Counselors also work in guidance groups in which they serve a more active role, designing educational exploration experiences, providing information, and stimulating personal awareness and growth.

5. *Consultation* activities involve initiating changes on an organizational level, often by working on program development. Counselors consult with the human and organizational components of systems to help the individual parts make a more unified whole. Counselors, as human relations specialists, will intervene to fix or prevent the problems that arise from interpersonal conflict.

6. *Administration* plays a part in many counselors' work; it involves directing the activities of a school, agency, or organization. Public relations, quality control, fund raising, the conducting of meetings, paperwork processing, and decision making are major components of this kind of work.

7. *Supervision* is a significant role of all experienced practitioners in helping those who are less capable. The counselor may conduct in-service workshops and provide individual or group supervision sessions that may be either emotionally or behaviorally focused. Responsibility for staff training and development may also include attention to improving morale.

8. *Research* is an important part of determining professional effectiveness. Counselors are frequently required to justify their existence and to demonstrate to funding agencies, regulatory commissions, citizens' advisory groups, and boards of trustees that they are earning their salaries. Research is also crucial in communicating the results of experimentation to other professionals so the field can continue to grow.

A Set of Generic Skills

Regardless of their work settings, theoretical orientation, training program, and client population, counselors all use the same intervention skills:

- self-disclosure—sharing aspects of the self to deepen the relationship and facilitate movement
- confrontation—inviting a person to examine discrepancies between personal behaviors and their consequences
- active listening—attending to all the messages, both verbal and nonverbal, communicated by the client
- goal setting—assisting the client to set behaviorally measurable courses of action
- interpretation—attempting to impart meaning to the client by introducing new concepts and/or frames of reference
- questioning—designing queries to elicit further information and/or stimulate further exploration

- reassurance—using psychological or emotional supports during periods of high client anxiety
- modeling—helping a client to learn new behaviors through vicarious experience and imitation
- reinforcing—rewarding adaptive behavior through the use of praise or other techniques in an attempt to help a client repeat desired behaviors
- empathy—communicating both the feelings and the meanings implied in a client's statements
- immediacy—helping the client to focus on the here-and-now aspects of counseling, including the counselor/client relationship
- respect—communicating the counselor's prizing and valuing of the client;
- genuineness—communicating a sense of sincerity, honesty, spontaneity, and openness to the client

The use of these generic skills is by no means limited to counselors; however, counselors tend to depend on them as a basis for initiating the counseling process and developing an effective counseling relationship. In addition, counselors also use a wide variety of other specialized intervention skills, which depend on theoretical preferences.

A Set of Common Goals

Goals that are common to all counselors and that serve to clarify professional identity include the following:

1. helping clients to work constructively toward life/career planning
2. helping clients to anticipate, plan, and react constructively to developmental issues and transitions
3. helping clients to integrate thinking, feeling, and behavior into a congruent expression of self
4. helping clients to respond productively to stress and reduce its negative impact on their lives
5. helping clients to develop effective interpersonal skills so that relationships with peers, family, and colleagues can have constructive potential
6. helping clients to assess strengths and identify weaknesses so that they may develop more personal awareness
7. helping clients to become aware of the holistic nature of life and to integrate effective principles of living into psychological, physical, and social aspects of their lives
8. helping clients develop more choices in their lives, with accompanying skills to make constructive decisions
9. helping clients to become independent of the counseling in the shortest time possible.

Both Developmental and Remedial Orientation

Counselors are interested in and trained for helping individuals to anticipate issues and concerns, develop adaptive life skills, respond constructively to issues and problems, and work toward psychological growth and increased personal mastery. Counselors choose and prize their role because of its orientation toward life-skill development, with an emphasis on improved problem-solving abilities and decision-making skills, as opposed to an orientation that focuses exclusively on diagnosis, evaluation, and remediation.

Although counselors can and do use their knowledge of personality theory, psychopathology, and emotional dysfunctions to work therapeutically, they often focus on prevention of problems before they become severe. Counselors tend to distinguish themselves as well-trained experts working with those who don't necessarily have neurotic or psychotic symptoms. There are, however, many counselors operating within the mental health system who also do remedial work. The principal advantage of counseling practitioners, in contrast to social workers, psychologists, and psychiatrists, is that they can help people who aren't stigmatized as dysfunctional. One need not be "sick" or "mentally ill" to seek the services of a professional counselor, whereas insurance regulations specifically mandate to the other professions that there must be evidence of a medically defensible diagnosis of mental illness or a significant disturbance of conduct before treatment can be administered.

The role of the counselor is not to instruct but to stimulate the natural growth and potential inherent in human beings (Ivey, 1991). As persons develop, they have the capability to initiate, expand, and maintain psychological growth. In fact, many (Neugarten, 1968; Troll, 1975; Schlossberg, 1984; Newman & Newman, 1991) consider this capacity to be an essential feature of adult development. The crystallization of a client's irreconcilable conflict and the client's resulting discomfort are tools often used by counselors. The client can resolve that anxiety by moving to a more mature developmental stage, which will allow for an integration of the conflict and subsequent reduction in personal discomfort.

Counselors rely heavily on the work of developmental theorists as they attempt to stimulate clients to initiate developmentally relevant growth. Developmental work focuses on client issues and may include psychosexual development (Freud, 1924), cognitive development (Piaget, 1926), psychosocial development (Erikson, 1950), career development (Super, 1957), moral development (Kohlberg, 1969), or ego development (Loevinger, 1976), among many possibilities (see Table 3-1). This core of knowledge may be described as follows:

1. Human development proceeds in a series of stages leading to increasingly complex behaviors.
2. These stages are invariant and sequential.
3. They are genetically determined and adaptive to the culture and environment.
4. The stages alternate between periods of well-adjusted equilibrium and periods of unstable disequilibrium.

TABLE 3-1. Developmental Stage Theories

Theorist	Aspect of Development	Age Period			
		Infancy	Childhood	Adulthood	Old Age
Sigmund Freud	psychosexual	oral stage	anal stage phallic stage latent stage	genital stage	
Jean Piaget	cognitive	sensorimotor	preoperational concrete operations	formal thought	
Erik Erikson	psychosocial	trust versus mistrust	autonomy versus shame and doubt initiative versus guilt industry versus inferiority	identity versus role confusion intimacy versus isolation generativity versus stagnation	integrity versus despair
Donald Super	career	growth of self-concept	exploration of occupational roles	establishment of career maintenance of position	decline in power
Lawrence Kohlberg	moral	punishment orientation	individual self-interest approval seeking	authority maintaining social contract universal ethics	
Jane Loevinger	ego	presocial symbiotic	impulsive self-protective	conformist conscientious autonomous	integrated

5. Growth may be encouraged by stimulating a person to restore equilibrium at a higher stage of development.

It is the work of the counselor to help the client translate immediate issues of concern into a relevant developmental framework so the necessary growth can be identified and initiated. Pragmatically applying developmental theory, the counselor seeks to stimulate client growth toward successive stages of human maturity. During counseling sessions, therefore, conflicts are examined that cannot be resolved at current primitive levels of moral or emotional development. For example, a person operating at Kohlberg's Stage-3 level of moral maturity, wherein the reason for conforming to ethical standards is to avoid others' disapproval, would have great difficulty resolving personal struggles. The counselor would work toward helping the person to develop standards of a more personal nature in order to deal with such questions as these: "Can I lie in order to avoid hurting my brother's feelings?" "Ought I to have an affair?" "Is smoking pot OK even though it's illegal?" "Am I allowed to pursue my own goals selfishly, even at the expense of others' progress?"

Teamwork

It is rare to find a counselor who works alone; most counselors work in institutional or clinical settings as part of a team that is responsible for a range of activities or services, only one aspect of which is counseling. For example, many counselors work in business and industry settings, helping employees with personal, marriage, career, or substance-abuse problems that can affect their work attitudes and productivity. There the counselors frequently consult their manager, as well as supervisors, union representatives, personnel department representatives, and others in the work environment. The counselor is a vital member of a team and strives to work in concert with colleagues to advance institutional goals and provide help to individual employees. Counselors also maintain an active professional liaison with community agencies, mental health clinics, and so on. The same pattern holds true in most other settings, for counselors are specialists in resource identification, consultation, and individual counseling.

A DAY IN THE LIFE

The diversity of counselors' work in various settings can best be illustrated by a typical day at the office. What follows is a realistic glimpse of counselors in each of several traditional and nontraditional roles, including a sampling of the frustrations and problems as well as the excitement and satisfaction.

Private Practice

Through the groggy dream mist the counselor struggled toward alertness, finally achieving enough to figure out whom she was talking to and what the situation was. She calmed the man down and firmly instructed him to take a hot bath, try to relax, and write his feelings down on paper. She scheduled an appointment for him the next day and then tried to go back to sleep.

The counselor has now arrived at her office, which she shares with other professionals in private practice—a few social workers, a psychologist, and a part-time psychiatrist. Her 9:00 client already sits in the waiting room, but first she returns her telephone messages. One call is from a client who wants to cancel her appointment in the middle of the day. The counselor doesn't know whether to feel disappointed because it is too late to fill that spot or relieved because now she has an unanticipated but needed break to catch up on her paperwork. Next she calls a physician whom she has been trying to reach for months, hoping to arrange a lunch meeting and discuss possible referrals. He is out of his office.

The first of six clients for the day then enters her office. The client is relatively easy to work with, is highly motivated, pays her bills on time, and will make rapid progress. The counselor struggles with herself during the session because they have just successfully completed working on the originally stated problem. The client feels great. Her marriage has stabilized. But she wants to continue the sessions. The counselor reinforces the idea that one can never have enough counseling but silently wonders if she is saying that because she means it or because she needs the money. It is such a pain for her to get new referrals.

Yet she feels so proud of her work, her competence, her ability to make a difference in people's lives. In private practice there is the constant pressure to become more skilled at helping; if not, the clients won't return or send their friends. And all over the community she can see the results of her efforts. Her reputation is slowly beginning to build.

Two more clients in the morning. Then lunch. She loves the freedom of answering only to herself and decides to do some shopping and visit with a friend. Back to the office and an hour of paperwork—progress notes, correspondence, forms. A new referral calls, but the counselor can't persuade her to come in for an appointment because there are financial difficulties. Maybe she'll call back. A few colleagues are free, so they sip tea together and chat about their day. One colleague in particular is feeling much stress because he has just had a draining session with a client skilled at playing games. Back to work.

The counselor makes a few more calls, including one seeking referrals from a school system and one offering an in-service program for staff on stress management. The company agrees to let her make a presentation. She feels ecstatic: at last, a breakthrough! Then she makes a follow-up call to an ex-client who is still doing quite well and appreciates the counselor's continuing concern.

The clients file through until early evening. She feels exhausted after so many consecutive sessions. "Is the money worth all the energy it takes?" she wonders as she puts the finishing touches on her case notes. "But it *is* lucrative, and the freedom is wonderful. I like being an important part of so many people's lives, and I especially appreciate not having to answer to a boss."

Mental Health Center

The community mental health center is an oasis of support in an isolated rural area. The counselor is still apprehensive about fitting into a culture that is so foreign to his experiences as a city dweller. Yet in a tight economy he felt it a necessary adjustment to go where the work is—in this case, to a large organization of social workers, psychologists, psychiatrists, health educators, and counselors who service a three-county area populated mostly by farmers and factory workers.

The day begins with a planning session for his team. Predictably, the administrator once again reminds everyone to keep up with the paperwork. The counselor groans inwardly as he remembers the stack of progress notes and treatment plans that require his attention. He is then happily distracted by a proposal to do more outreach with the aged. He quickly volunteers to head up a study group to do a needs assessment in the community and prepare materials for several grant proposals. What a coup it would be to direct his own project— especially in such a novel area as counseling older adults. His mind drifts away from the more boring parts of the meeting as he thinks about his own relationship with his grandfather. He resolves to interview the 81-year-old man to see how he thinks counselors could be more helpful to his generation.

Various other staff members present their reports, all jockeying for power and more money to run their individual projects. Although the counselor deplores the politics, the personality conflicts, and the interpersonal struggles, he nevertheless jumps in with both feet so he isn't left behind. The clinical director schedules supervision conferences. The medical director reviews the medications of several clients. Finally, one hour late, the administrator closes the meeting with tips on appropriate conduct during the upcoming accreditation audit.

Finally the real fun starts. The counselor completes two counseling sessions before lunch, the first with a family of six, two of them teenagers whose strivings for independence are hard on all of them. The second session seems calm by comparison: a depressed man discloses the emptiness in his life and his frustration in trying to find a mate.

As the counselor joins several colleagues for lunch, he rethinks how to regain more control with the family. The food is lousy, but the conversation is always lively, usually centered on bits of gossip and different perspectives on particular cases. Before he can finish dessert, he is sidetracked by the assistant director, who wants to know if she can count on his support for proposed changes in promotion policy. The counselor gives an ambiguous response until he can figure out the political consequences of taking one side or the other during the fight. He decides to be neutral—the safest plan considering his own vulnerable position.

He rushes to a group session he has scheduled with seven teenagers to help them become more vocationally marketable; they are most cooperative, possibly because they get to leave school early for the experience. The counselor absolutely loves his groups—the energy is incredible! This week the kids spend time complaining about their parents' expectations. The counselor structures a successful role-playing activity in which they act like their parents, eventually realizing that complaining can sometimes be an expression of love.

The counselor has a bit of free time before his other appointments. He meets with his supervisor about the uncooperative family, then catches up on his paperwork. All is going well until he gets the day's phone messages. One of his clients decides to discontinue treatment. No explanation. Just a phone call. Now he will have to do a bunch of paperwork and follow-up to close the file. One afternoon appointment talks of depressing matters so intensely that the counselor notes that even he is starting to feel depressed: "This poor woman is going to be depressed her whole life, and there's probably nothing I can do but hold her hand. That is depressing. I've got to put this stuff behind me. My last client is waiting. I'm so glad I thought to schedule her at the end of the day. She'll be her usual entertaining, cheerful self. It feels so fine to know that I'm partially responsible for helping her to feel so good."

Crisis Center

The day begins with a crisis: the coffee is all gone. The crises continue—staff will be short today, so the counselor must handle more calls. The first call is from a "regular customer," a gentleman who enjoys waking himself by masturbating over the phone. The counselor giggles, then remembers her training and quickly hangs up.

Next call: a routine referral to Legal Aid for divorce information. Next: a kid who wants information about the Valium his mother is taking. Then—crisis. A boy calls and says he thinks he just killed himself. He sounds distraught, confused. He took a bunch of pills, but he doesn't know what kind. He doesn't care anyway. He just wants to die. He just wanted to say goodbye to someone, anyone; he has no one else. The counselor tries to get his address but to no avail; he hangs up. The counselor starts trembling, but, before she can talk her feelings through the boy calls again. This time he's laughing, screams "sucker," and hangs up once again. With all the lambs crying "wolf," how will she ever know for sure when the games and manipulation stop? She feels abused and disgusted.

Someone is asking for her in the lobby. It's an ex-client who just dropped in to say hello and give her a progress report: he is doing fantastically, thanks to her caring work. No time for reveling in the glory or bemoaning the fake calls— she is late for a program at the junior high school, where she is scheduled to give a talk on drugs.

The counselor spends an hour with the kids, giving accurate information, answering questions, discussing her observations about how children are introduced to the drug scene. Afterward one teacher solicits her advice about what he can do to help prevent further problems in the school. A few appointments are then set up to meet with any kids who wish more information. She has several valuable encounters—helping one child to work on resisting the pressure of his peers to get high, helping another to realize how dangerous it was for him to be taking pills that he couldn't identify. The counselor next meets with the school counselors to lend assistance and lead an informal workshop on strategies for fighting drug abuse.

She returns to the crisis center, spends two more hours fielding mostly routine calls, then a half-hour with her colleagues discussing the frustrating morning. They mutually decide, for their own protection, that it's better to stay more detached and neutral with their clients. The counselor also vows: "I must talk to myself harder so that I don't permit the few bad experiences to overshadow the productive work that I've been doing." The thought is interrupted by the jangling phone. It is a 74-year-old woman, frightened, alone; she just wants to make human contact. The counselor spends a half-hour offering reassurance and then decides to leave work a little early so she can meet the woman for coffee.

High School

At 7:25 A.M., when the counselor walks into her office, there are already seven students waiting. Right away she knows why. There was a glitch in the computer yesterday, and third-hour English was double loaded. The teacher about blew her fuse, but at least she has now settled down. As the counselor finishes rescheduling the last student 30 minutes later, she wonders what this activity has to do with counseling.

Not only is scheduling classes boring administrative work, but it really eats up time, keeping her from getting to what she wants to be doing—working with kids and their problems. She makes a mental note to mention this concern in the afternoon meeting with the principal, knowing she won't even have the full support of the staff. Some of them actually prefer scheduling to counseling; they consider the work less demanding. The thought is depressing.

On the way to the attendance office to check on a student, she suddenly hears shouts and a commotion around the corner. Cringing, she moves toward the disturbance and finds two senior boys wrestling against a locker, each twice her size. Using what she hopes is her most authoritative voice, she pushes between them and manages with the help of another teacher to separate them. Her heart sinks when she recognizes one of the offenders as a client for whom she went out on a limb two weeks ago—he was in danger of being suspended for fighting. Now this!

An hour later she feels better. The fighting business has been cleared up, and she has just finished a successful interview with a student whose parents have been pushing him toward a military career. It felt good to help him explore what he wants and to become more aware of his tendency to please his parents at all costs. The session seemed to be productive, and she felt confident that the student would make some changes.

Her meeting with the principal is grim. Teachers, says he, are complaining because the counseling staff is overloading classes and allowing friends to alter their schedules so they can be together in their mischief. The counselor points out (once again) that class scheduling is administrative work and not the primary responsibility of the counseling department; further, if teachers are having

A school counselor reviews a behavioral checklist with a problem student before she can return to class.

discipline problems in their classes, they should consult with a counselor instead of complaining to the principal.

Lunch provides a needed break. A teacher stops by and suggests that they get together to talk about his frustrations with his job and hassles with the department chair. The talk with him seems to help. Sometimes the informal sessions over lunch seem to make more difference than all the appointments during the week.

The counselor tries to keep the afternoons open for working with kids. She has two appointments and will finish the day with a group. However, she is worried about the first appointment: a 17-year-old senior who is depressed and very worried about smoking too much pot. The session is taxing, and she reflects on how difficult it is to work with kids having drug problems. The last individual appointment is a bonus. She has been working with this girl for four months now and can really see the difference. The girl has overcome her shyness, is involved in extracurricular activities, and reports a much improved relationship with her parents. She even has a boyfriend. At the finish of the session, the counselor feels great. As she is leaving for the group, the secretary motions urgently. An irate parent is on the phone demanding an explanation for her son's suspension. She's really hot. The counselor calms her down and makes an appointment to see her after school.

Now for the group. Today's topic is love again. As always, she is amazed at how sensitive the kids are and how they really do confront each other as they interact. They know what honesty means.

Hurrying to meet with the irate parent, the counselor reflects on her day, thinking: "The good parts do make up for the bad, but, boy, is it draining and frustrating at times! And there's one more challenge yet to go."

Preschool

The counselor arrives at work to find a 3-year-old hiding under a picnic table, surrounded by two teachers and his parents, all urging him to come out. Instead he screams "Never!" and continues to cry. The counselor reassures the parents, sends them off to work, and disperses the crowd of children and teachers. She then crawls under the table and sits silently for ten minutes, until the child halts his tears long enough to ask why the counselor is acting silly by sitting under a table. Without hesitation the counselor replies simply that she is a little scared today, and angry at her parents for dumping her off, and this seems like as good a place as any to hide. The 3-year-old understands immediately, nods his head, and tells the counselor that he'll pay extra attention to her today so she won't feel so lonely. He then crawls out and joins the other kids in the sandbox as if this entrance were a natural beginning to a day of school. The counselor, too,

A counselor communicates with a 3-year-old child about her concerns through the use of play therapy techniques.

crawls out but makes her way to the morning staff meeting, which she will direct in planning the day's psychological education.

After the play activities for the day have been discussed, the counselor reviews the past week's discipline problems—how they were managed, and how they could have been handled differently. She reports on the outcomes of various conferences she conducted with children and their parents, then makes specific recommendations to the teachers about strategies that might be helpful in the future: "When Alice throws a temper tantrum, it is best to isolate her calmly in the 'time-out' room." "Pay special attention to Brian—give him lots of hugs today because his father beat him last night." "Don't let Jennifer test you."

As the art classes begin, the counselor works on test evaluations of the children's aptitude strengths and weaknesses, detailing treatment plans for each child. She then spends some time with the director going over administrative chores before an appointment with parents.

The mother and father of a particularly disturbed child show up 20 minutes late and then proceed to pick at each other about whose fault it was. When the counselor tries to intervene, they turn on her and then launch into an abusive tirade against the school, the teachers, and especially the counselor for being responsible for their child's problems. They decide to pull the child out of the school, and they march up to him while he is occupied on the swings, grab him by the neck, and yell at him all the way to the car. As the child cries for his friends, the parents start arguing again about who is responsible for their having such a screwed-up kid. They spank the child for good measure, throw him into the back seat, and drive off.

Another child sees the counselor fuming, with tears in her eyes, and invites her to play on the slide. They talk about what just happened, and other children ask questions about why parents sometimes get so mad. When the kids resume their play, the counselor excuses herself to break up a fight.

The counselor is exhausted; the children are still literally running circles around her. She mobilizes her energy for the afternoon parent-education class she teaches. Eleven participants attend, almost all of them single parents who have concerns about their effectiveness. She rates the class only "fair" because she feels tired and a few parents are unusually rigid in their beliefs and therefore reluctant to try anything new ("Spankings were good enough for me. Why the hell shouldn't they be good enough for our kids?"). While the counselor patiently explains the negative side effects of punishment, she sees the last of the kids departing. As their cute little legs scurry off, she wonders if she is really preventing any of them from having emotional problems in the future. "I sure would like to see them about 20 years from now," she thinks. "That's an idea! I think I'll talk to the director about organizing some follow-up research."

Street Ministry

Sam is an ordained minister, but he does not have a church. Several years ago he decided to give up his pulpit so he could more intimately and effectively help disadvantaged people in their natural habitats. Based in a soup kitchen in a ghetto area, Sam works with the most impoverished and neglected population in his city. Since these people would never have come to him in his church, he has decided to reach out to them.

Sam finds that most of his counseling training and religious instruction is more for *his* benefit than for his clients. Very little that worked in his nice, quiet office is helpful in the streets, where chaos, violence, and noise reign supreme. Yet the single most important thing of all that he remembers from his training— that, without trust, compassion, and understanding, you have nothing—serves him well in his street ministry.

Since without food and shelter anything else he might do for his clients is irrelevant, Sam's first priority every morning is to help prepare and serve food to the throngs of people who are waiting for the doors of the soup kitchen to open. As he passes out bread, wipes off tables, and cleans dishes, he makes an effort to make contact with each and every person he encounters—a smile, a nod, a pat on the shoulder, a few words, or even a quick jibe. It is obvious that he is comfortable among his "congregation" and that they, in turn, have accepted him.

It is during this meal that he scans the room searching for his first client— someone in need to whom he can offer assistance. Sometimes people approach him, wanting advice, a referral, or funds to feed or clothe their children, but usually he must initiate the contact. He sees a man huddled in the corner, his lip cut and cheek bruised, so Sam escorts him to get medical attention.

On his walk back to the soup kitchen, he stops and talks to most everyone who will meet his eyes, joking, jostling, yet watching his back—the streets are a dangerous place, and he has already had more than his share of injuries while attempting to settle arguments or rescue a child from abuse. Finally he settles down on a stoop where people have learned to expect him. These are his "office hours," when he performs his most important service—referring people to places where they can get financial aid, medical attention, protective services, legal aid, or even college scholarships. Sam has developed a vast network of contacts he can draw upon.

In the afternoon, with his own energy depleted by all the action, he tries to settle down with one person he can talk to—sometimes a runaway child or a pregnant teenager or a drug addict or a lonely elderly person. He has nobody standing over him telling him where he has to be; in his work he wanders the streets doing whatever he can.

Sometimes at night, just before he falls into an exhausted slumber, he smiles to himself, feeling so good about what he is doing: counseling and helping the people nobody else cares about—the homeless and the poor who have given up hope of ever escaping their miserable existence. And yet there are other, sleepless, nights, when he feels that he is just wasting his time—that he and a thousand others just like him couldn't put a dent in all that needs to be done.

The injured man he helped to get medical attention died two weeks later in another fight. The runaway girl he coaxed back home is now on the loose again—probably beginning her career as a prostitute. Yet Sam keeps offering soup and bread, a smile, and all the love he can give. He has nothing else to offer. And this is his calling.

University Counseling Center

If there is one thing she enjoys most about her job in this medium sized university, it is the diversity of activities that she is part of. Of course, there is also the excitement in being part of such a highly charged environment—young people in search of wisdom, identity, independence. And satisfying their raging hor-

The greatest need in our profession is for dedicated counselors to reach out to those disadvantaged people who would not ordinarily seek out their services.

mones. But most of all she likes being part of a team in Student Services whose primary function is to facilitate the adjustment of students. And because most of the staff is somewhat flexible (except for the Vice President of Student Affairs, who can be a major pain), she has the opportunity to do so many things.

The bread and butter of her job description consists of the fairly routine task of helping confused students select a major (which they will probably change a few months later). Fortunately, with self-guided computer programs available, she can concentrate mostly on helping the students interpret and personalize what they have learned from the data they generated. She much prefers the group work that she does—conducting study-skills seminars, leading assertive-ness-training workshops, and offering seminars on AIDS, drug abuse, and eth-nic and cultural diversity.

Whereas her mornings are sometimes "political" (attending staff meetings, writing Student Services literature, talking to on-campus organizations), her afternoons are free to do what she enjoys. She sees several clients in fairly long-term counseling, and she especially appreciates these cases as a contrast to the relatively short-term problem solving she is often called upon to participate in (with someone who is having trouble with a roommate, a parent, or a professor).

She carries a half-dozen intense counseling cases, for which she receives excellent supervision from a doctoral student who is doing an internship in the Counseling Center. This supervision (three hours per week) may be the best part of all (besides the free tuition to take any class she wants). These benefits are especially important to her, given the frustrations that are part of university life—the low salary, the power games among administrators fighting for their turf, the repetitive nature of some of her duties.

For the seventh time this month she is on her way to conduct a human relations workshop for the resident assistants in the dormitory. Then she can hurry back for a session with one of her favorite clients. Her day will end with supervision, process-ing her active cases, and letting off steam about some of her frustrations.

Rehabilitation Center

"One of the most interesting parts of my day is the first staff meeting. In rehabil-itation counseling it is imperative to work as part of a team. I come in first thing, grab a cup of coffee, and then walk into the conference room where our staff is congregating. Sitting around the table are a neuropsychologist, a speech thera-pist, an occupational therapist, a physical therapist, a physiatrist (a doctor who specializes in rehabilitation), a few miscellaneous social workers, and me, a rehabilitation counselor.

"My job is to help people with closed head injuries—mostly accident and stroke victims—to learn to adjust psychologically to their disabilities and to work on morale to aid recovery. During our planning session in the morning, we discuss cases in an interdisciplinary way so that we are clear on what role each of us will be playing in the patient's recovery process. I must say it's really fun to hear how other professionals apply their specialties—assessing areas of dysfunction, mapping out treatment programs, thinking through strategies. While each of them concentrates on a different area of rehabilitation (physical, career, family, relationships), my job is to try to bring things together—to be the liaison between the experts and the patient.

"It is after this meeting ends that the hard work starts. By and large, the patients I work with are disabled in a major way. They have cognitive deficits, speech difficulties, physical limitations, emotional problems. And practically all of them are depressed. Furthermore, the majority of these people are going to struggle with lingering disabilities their whole lives. No matter how compassionate and skilled I am, there are limits to what I can do to help. Sometimes that tears me up inside.

"For example, my first client of the day is a man in his fifties—a handsome man with a crooked smile. The stroke he has suffered wiped out the left side of his brain. He has short-term memory problems as well as visual impairments; he can't think straight, and his right side is paralyzed. I look at this guy and I want to cry. What can I really do to help him? He tells me he's going to play tennis again, but I know he'll be lucky if he can walk. He repeats himself constantly and doesn't remember many things we talk about. But I'm doing my best to help him adjust. I get his family in together and try to help them understand what he can and can't do. I let them vent their anger and rage; unfortunately, sometimes it is directed toward me—as if I should be able to make things the way they were.

"After a half-dozen of these sessions a day, I'm beat. Yet sometimes people do make excellent recoveries. They are able to resume the productive and enjoyable activities of their lives. Even this man with the stroke is happy much of the time, although he often resides in a fantasy world. And I would like to think that, in my own small way, I really help these people do the best they can with what they have. Isn't that what counseling is all about?"

Counseling in Industry

Squeezed between a dozen other glass and steel structures is a building that resembles all the others. It is the corporate headquarters for a medium-sized manufacturing company that employs tens of thousands of people in the area—factory workers, skilled craftspeople, engineers, marketing and sales personnel, and administrative, financial, and support specialists.

In one suite of offices, tucked away in the back of the building and flanked by departments with signs reading "Personnel" and "Affirmative Action," is an enigmatic label reading "Human Services." The services performed in this department are quite innovative for corporate environments.

Once it was discovered that employee morale and productivity could be increased, while absenteeism could be reduced, through certain support services, a number of progressive companies began hiring counselors to help their

employees address personal problems that may interfere with their professional functioning. These problems may include drug and alcohol abuse, compulsive gambling, marriage and family problems, divorce adjustment, racial or
sexual discrimination, developmental issues, career decision making, or conflicts in the workplace.

The Department of Human Services is staffed by three counselors, two
administrative assistants, and a secretary. Their mandate is to serve employees
of the company, improving their life satisfaction and helping them to resolve
personal problems that may be impacting their productivity and efficiency in
the workplace. Services provided include (1) individual, group, and family
counseling, (2) crisis intervention and conflict management, (3) career guidance
and job placement, (4) substance-abuse prevention and treatment, (5) retirement
planning and counseling, (6) quality-of-work-life seminars, and (7) referral to
specialized agencies in the community. The staff also coordinates its activities
with those of Personnel and Affirmative Action.

What the counselors like best about their jobs is that they have the relative
freedom to implement a number of new programs that are on the "cutting
edge" of human services. They also enjoy excellent fringe benefits and salary
packages, which are the hallmark of corporate settings. And they appreciate
working as part of a team of professionals who are overseeing the quality of life
for thousands of employees.

On the negative side of the ledger, working for any large organization is
frustrating. The work hours are fairly rigid. Most employees tend to be somewhat suspicious of what the counselors do. (Are they really there to help people,
or are they spies of management who will report everything they see and hear?)
Also, because what they are doing is so new, there is a certain amount of resentment and resistance associated with introducing their programs, especially
among the senior employees.

On the whole, though, the counselors feel that they have a great thing
going—that is, as long as upper management provides support for their programs. They also realize that, in such a small department, things work smoothly
because everyone gets along quite well. As would be the case with any small
group, if one member of the staff were obstructive or incompetent, things could
be very unpleasant. This group does work well together, however, and they are
able to be supportive and yet confront one another when the need arises. (A
number of counselors, working in many different settings, report that this last
characteristic is one of the most important in any job—being part of a team in
which colleagues are helpful to one another and there is a spirit of cooperation
and mutual caring. Counseling *is,* after all, a stressful job, requiring that we have
built-in components to help us function well without feeling burned out. It is for
this very reason that beginning counselors look for first jobs that have very supportive environments with friendly coworkers and a benevolent supervisor who
makes it feel safe to learn and grow as a professional.)

THE VALUE OF A FLEXIBLE SPECIALTY

The days of the counseling generalist are numbered. No longer can the counselor indulge in the luxury of acting like a country doctor who knows a little bit about everything and yet nothing in depth about anything. The technology and knowledge in the field are growing so rapidly that it is impossible to stay current on subjects as diverse as general systems analysis in organizational development, genetic predeterminants of emotionally disturbed children, nutritional imbalances in geriatric senility, indirect hypnotic trance inductions, and unionism among school personnel specialists.

Most counselors, by design or by circumstances, find themselves a flexible specialty. Because of a need in a particular community for family mediation experts, a counselor may choose to affiliate with a court system to fill the gap. A counselor newly hired by an agency may need to adapt to handling drug-abuse cases, sex counseling, or another area in which the counselor has specialized expertise. Sometimes clientele, by sociometric homogeneity or geography, will present similar problems of economic hardship, bored marriages, or free-floating anxiety. Again the counselor ends up reading and studying more about those particular concerns and thereby becomes an expert in dealing with future cases.

Although it is probably intelligent to market oneself as a specialist in a few related areas, to increase both one's employability and one's professional mastery, it is not necessary to become so narrow in focus that one typifies Toffler's (1970) victim of "future shock." Whether one is a financier, physician, or counselor, the consequences of overspecialization can be equally undesirable, resulting in rigidity, obsolescence, and a narrow field of vision.

It may therefore be advantageous to select a particular field in which to concentrate one's study while continuing efforts to survey the wide educational spectrum. Certain specialties even fit well together, depending on one's interests and skills. A student's career-developmental scenario might run as follows: "As soon as I completed the introductory course, I knew immediately the things I *didn't* like, even though I had no idea what I did like. The idea of sitting in an office seemed intolerable to me. I had to find something where I could move around a lot, have variety in my job, try different things all the time. In the class on career information, I took a lot of those tests we're supposed to give to clients, but they only told me what I already knew. So I visited five different agencies, interviewed counselors in the field as part of a school project, and did two different internships. I tentatively settled on working with small kids for a number of reasons: (1) you can help them before they get into too much trouble; (2) you get to run around a lot while chasing them, so you don't stay cooped up in an office; (3) you get to see their changes in a matter of weeks instead of years; (4) it's a relatively new field, so I should be able to get a job; and (5) if I don't like it, I will already be prepared to work with children in any setting I choose." The decision-making process exemplified by this student's reasoning is typical of what ought to go on in every prospective counselor's mind. The marketability of a counseling degree, as illustrated in the dialogue that began this chapter, is dependent almost totally on what the graduate is able to represent effectively to a potential employer.

Specialty Areas in Counseling

A survey of broad specialty areas that permit career flexibility and the opportunity to develop expertise in the field is illustrated in the following list.

Child Development
> elementary school counseling
> preschool counseling
> early childhood education
> parent education
> work with abused or neglected children

Adolescent Development
> high school counseling
> youth probation officer
> career development specialist
> college placement
> youth work in a residential facility

Adult Development
> adult education
> midlife transitions
> counseling for the aged
> spiritual/pastoral counseling

Interpersonal Relationships
> marriage counseling
> family counseling
> sex counseling
> divorce mediation
> sex education

Health
> nutritional counseling
> exercise and health education
> stress management
> patient education in hospitals
> lifestyle consultation
> weight loss or smoking reduction

Careers
> employment counseling
> occupational therapy
> vocational rehabilitation
> career development

The Disabled
>   rehabilitation counseling
>   special education
>   counseling for the physically handicapped

University
>   student development
>   college administration
>   student counseling
>   student activities

Drugs
>   substance-abuse counseling
>   drug education
>   crisis intervention
>   primary prevention

Clinical Mental Health Counseling
>   private practice
>   community mental health centers
>   hospitals
>   public and nonprofit agencies

Industry
>   organizational development
>   corporate consulting
>   personnel specialist
>   public relations
>   Affirmative Action officer
>   employee assistance programs
>   staff training and development
>   quality of work life

Guidelines for Selecting a Counseling Specialty

You should at least consider concentrating in one or more of the categories in the list. The task of considering them is no less overwhelming than any other career decision and needs to be based on a systematic process of solid self-evaluation and the collection of pertinent information about each subspecialty. Beginning this process early in a graduate program allows maximum opportunity for exploration and can guide a student's class and field work so that the eventual decision on a subspecialty can emerge rather than be forced at the last minute. The choice of some specialties will involve further training beyond the M.A. level, a factor that may be important for some students.

The following guidelines may be helpful in thinking about specialty areas and creating an innovative personal approach to this important task.

1. *Assess personal strengths and weaknesses.* In thinking about your personal strengths and weaknesses, strive to be brutally honest with yourself and assertively seek feedback from trusted friends, peers, colleagues, and professors. Often a disappointing specialty selection can be traced back to an inaccurate self-assessment. It is important to be scrupulous in all aspects, avoiding any tendency to be overcritical, underplay strengths, or be defensive about weaknesses. Accuracy and honesty are twin hallmarks of an effective self-assessment.

2. *Clarify values related to work.* Personal values exert a substantial impact on work satisfaction and can influence burnout, career development, and professional effectiveness. It is useful to spend some time early in graduate study confronting personal values and testing them within possible specialty areas. The counseling field is so large and diverse that it provides ample opportunity for individuals to seek or create work settings and specialties that are consistent with personal values. Nothing is more frustrating than choosing a career or specialty that requires considerable investment, only to discover that it doesn't feel right— for instance, that the job requires evening hours and you hate working after dark. You can avoid, or at least minimize, such disappointments and frustrations by paying careful attention to values early in the specialty-selection process.

3. *Visit as many different specialty settings as possible.* There is no replacement for reality testing in career selection. Although a specialty might sound interesting and comfortable to you, a visit to a site could provide a completely different perspective on what the job is really like. Many counseling students, for example, believe that they would like to work in a hospital setting. However, upon visiting a site, they may discover that much of their work would be routine and depressing and that counselors are at the bottom of the pecking order. This awareness may cool initial enthusiasm, or it may reinforce a tentative commitment. Regardless of the outcome, decision making will be based more on reality considerations than on fantasy.

4. *Interview as many counselors in the field as possible.* Selecting a specialty depends on awareness of opportunities as well as personal preferences and goals. Interacting with professional counselors allows the student to collect a wealth of valuable information, rooted in day-to-day reality, on work situations and opportunities. A limitation of graduate education is that it is often removed from the experiences of clinicians. You can work to reduce this separation and in the process enrich the base for choosing your specialty.

5. *Maximize internship and practica experiences.* The heart of a professional training program in therapeutic counseling is internship and practica. These dual experiences provide an indispensable source of knowledge and experience for specialty selection. Students should *maximize* internship and practica experiences, seeking as wide a range as possible. This is a time to experiment and to broaden professional experiences. The field portion of your training is, in a sense, the last "free" opportunity to explore professionally. Once you have graduated, it will be much more difficult to avoid making firm commitments.

6. *Develop a "future" orientation.* Essayists have repeatedly observed that change is the only stable characteristic of the future. In order to prepare for a

vital and pertinent specialty area, you will need to develop a professional orientation that looks to the future rather than the past for definition and career opportunity. For example, school systems—historically the largest employer of counselors—are not currently a promising career setting. To ensure professional relevance, you will have to anticipate settings and opportunities wherein counseling skills and attitudes will be useful and in demand. Creatively forecasting the future will allow you, as a counselor-in-training, to select specialties carefully and to target emerging employment opportunities.

SUMMARY

The selection of a specialty is, in a sense, a subgoal of counselor training. It is useful to begin the process of specialty selection early in your education but to avoid making rigid or premature commitments. Counselors need to be flexible and open to change as they develop as persons and professionals. Specialty selection is really the first step in professional development, which is an ongoing aspect of your work as a therapeutic counselor.

This chapter has provided an overview of the work of professional counselors in a variety of jobs. Each setting for therapeutic counseling is vital, dynamic, and filled with both substantial rewards and grinding frustrations. Such is the nature of the profession. Helping people, particularly within an institutional context, is not an easy task but does offer a unique and creative opportunity to make a difference in the world.

Professional counselors work in many settings and perform a variety of tasks. Opportunities for employment in the field are extensive and require a proactive orientation. A major task for students in counselor training programs is to begin to think about their careers and to initiate careful research and planning to ensure maximum opportunity. One aspect of this planning is the tentative selection of a specialty area.

PROFESSOR:
So much for our overview of the places where counselors work. Are you any more clear on what you can do with your degree?

STUDENT:
You're feeling unsure of yourself and your ability to help me deal with a problem so complex.

PROFESSOR:
Yes, it is frustrating. All the time I must—ah, yes, I see you *have* learned something. And I know how it feels to be evaded with active listening.

STUDENT:
To answer your question: I learned that it is up to me to market myself for the job I really want. The counseling program provides me with a core of basic skills to apply in any setting I choose.

PROFESSOR:

Yes, and it is up to me to help you in your choices by providing honest feedback about your assets and limitations concerning possible specialty areas. In addition, I need to stimulate and challenge your thinking about possibilities.

STUDENT:

So I guess it's up to me to use the skills and techniques I'm learning in the program and somehow to combine them with my personal strengths and figure out what I'm going to be when I grow up.

PROFESSOR:

You bet—and the process doesn't stop. In fact, right now in my own life I've been doing some thinking and evaluating....

SUGGESTED READINGS

Blocher, D. H. (1987). *The professional counselor*. New York: Macmillan.

Clinebell, H. (1984). *Basic types of pastoral care and counseling: Resources for the ministry of healing and growth*. Nashville: Abingdon Press.

Palmo, A. J., & Weikel, W. J. (Eds.) (1986). *Foundations of mental health counseling*. Springfield, IL: Charles C Thomas.

Rubin, S. E., & Rubin, N. M. (Eds.) (1988). *Contemporary challenges to the rehabilitation counseling profession*. Baltimore: Brookes.

Seiler, G. (1990). *The mental health counselor's sourcebook*. New York: Human Sciences Press.

Worzbyt, J. C., & O'Rourke, K. A. (1989). *Elementary school counseling: A blueprint for today and tomorrow*. Muncie, IN: Accelerated Development.

CHAPTER FOUR

THE THERAPEUTIC RELATIONSHIP

QUALITIES OF COUNSELING
    RELATIONSHIPS
HISTORICAL PERSPECTIVES
COUNSELORS AS RELATIONSHIP
    SPECIALISTS
CHARACTERISTICS OF THE
    HELPING RELATIONSHIP
    Congruence, Positive Regard,
        and Empathy
    Attending Skills and
        Responding Skills
PRACTICAL DIMENSIONS OF THE
    THERAPEUTIC RELATIONSHIP
    Commitment
    Trust
    Empathy
    Confidentiality
    Benevolent Power

CREATING A RELATIONSHIP IN
    THE INITIAL INTERVIEW
    Establishing Rules
    Planting Hope
    Assuring Confidentiality
    Assessing Expectations
    Collecting Information
    Identifying Problems
    Beginning Intervention
    First-Session Agenda Review
SUMMARY
SUGGESTED READINGS

R egardless of the setting in which you practice counseling—whether in a school, agency, hospital, or private practice—the relationships you develop with your clients are crucial to any progress you might make together. For, without a high degree of intimacy and trust between two people, very little can be accomplished.

Make a mental list of the important relationships in your life. Include friendships. Add your parents, siblings, and other relatives. Perhaps a few teachers, coworkers, or classmates might also be considered influential in your world. Now, what do your best relationships—all those you have ever known— have in common? What are the characteristics you consider to be most crucial in your past, present, and future interactions with other people?

Important relationships in almost *any* context, except adversarial, have certain desirable elements—trust, for one. Mutual respect, openness, acceptance, and honesty are others. Whether we are examining personal relationships or the unique contact between counselor and client, there will be similarities. For in all kinds of relationships, helping or otherwise, we desire intimacy and intensity. And we might say that the quality we are able to create in these dimensions is directly related to the personal enrichment of our lives. We *might* say the same for helping relationships. We might . . . but we won't.

QUALITIES OF COUNSELING RELATIONSHIPS

Counseling takes place chiefly within the context of a very special kind of relationship—one that is similar to other successful relationships but is also distinctly different. In this chapter we will explore the fundamental aspects of the therapeutic relationship, describe how these qualities are developed, and show how several primary relationship-enhancing skills and interventions may be applied to an initial counseling interview.

In a comparison between personal and helping relationships, the most outstanding distinction would be the inherent *inequality* of the latter. It is clear, from the outset of the first encounter, that the client is in need of some assistance and that the counselor is identified as an expert with specialized talent and skills to provide the desired help. The relationship, therefore, involves a contract in which both parties agree to abide by certain rules: the client to show up on time, to pay bills promptly, and to make an effort to be as open as possible; the counselor to be trustworthy, to protect the welfare of the client, and to do everything possible to help the client reach identified goals in the most efficient period of time. The power between the client and the counselor is thus embodied in a unique structure wherein the client is primarily responsible for the content of the relationship while the counselor has most of the responsibilities for directing its style and structure. Although counselors do make an effort to demonstrate complete sincerity and respect to the client, there nonetheless remains an uneven distribution of status and power. After all, the relationship takes place on the counselor's home turf. There are diplomas and books on the wall. A warm professional atmosphere pervades. Yet the counselor gets the more comfortable chair, and, when both speak simultaneously, the counselor usually prevails.

There are many practitioners, such as Rogers (1957), Boy and Pine (1990), and Egan (1990), who try to minimize the power dimensions of the relationship, believing that equality is crucial to change. There are also others (Haley, 1984, 1989; Erikson, 1950; Minuchin, 1974) who make a strong case for the counselor's deliberately and strategically cultivating a powerful position in order to be more influential. In other words, some counselors find downplaying their status to be effective in facilitating change, whereas others wish to emphasize their capability as powerful models.

The therapeutic relationship is also different from other interactions in that there are relatively specific objectives and stringent time limitations: the relationship exists to seek solutions, and the discussion ends once the minute hand of the clock reaches a previously agreed-upon point. Thus, in addition to many of the characteristics found in other successful human relationships, the counselor/client relationship has several identifying features:

1. There is an explicit goal and purpose to the relationship—to *end* it as soon as therapeutically possible.
2. There is an understanding that one person (the counselor) has more control, responsibility, and expertise in making things go smoothly and helpfully, while the other person (the client) is more important.
3. The relationship is essentially one of interpersonal influence in which the counselor seeks to promote changes in the client through skills, powers, and the force of interacting personalities.
4. The interactions are structured to make the most efficient use of time. Small talk and other meaningless prattle common to personal encounters are not in evidence during counseling, where time is viewed as a valuable commodity.
5. The helping relationship can deal with a variety of human behavior— thoughts, attitudes, and actions—but is often focused on expression and exploration of feelings that are rarely disclosed outside the encounter.
6. To best facilitate learning in any form, Rogers (1969) suggested that the qualities of realness, genuineness, freedom, acceptance, trust, prizing, and empathic understanding must be in evidence within the relationship. He felt it imperative to value the worth of each individual: "And I am very grateful that I have moved in the direction of being able to take in, without rejecting it, the warmth and the caring of others, because this has so increased my own capacity for giving love, without fear of being trapped and without holding back" (p. 237).

The therapeutic relationship, as the core of all helping encounters, follows a pattern of successive stages. Greenspan and Wieder (1984) use a developmental approach to describe this predictable evolutionary process. *Stability* is initially established through the willingness of the client to cooperate with the structure of counseling. *Attachment* follows as the dimensions of trust, acceptance, and

emotional interest are fostered. The final *process* stage includes the more traditional therapeutic work that leads to insight and change.

In their provocative thesis on the evolutionary basis for therapy and counseling, Glantz and Pearce (1989) noted that human beings originally functioned
as part of a tribe—a close-knit unit of hunter/gatherers who depended on one
another for survival. However, after about 100,000 years of intense social existence in which people lived as part of an extended family numbering in the hundreds, contemporary life has literally disbanded our intimate connections.
Siblings now live in different cities from one another, and from their parents.
Careers require periodic relocations of family. Our cultural, ethnic, and family
histories have become diluted, and our friends and family are scattered around
the globe. Human beings now walk the earth alone.

It is the absence of bandlike social structures that Glantz and Pearce believe
has created such feelings of alienation, estrangement, loneliness, anxiety, and
depression in contemporary life. Counseling in general, and the therapeutic
relationship in particular, supplies the nurturance, support, and caring that are
now missing from daily life. It is this relationship with others, whether in individual or group treatments, that rekindles the feelings of belongingness and
acceptance that were once part of tribal life.

HISTORICAL PERSPECTIVES

From whence has come the conception of the therapeutic relationship as we
now know it? Carl Rogers was quite open about his feelings on the subject.
Many other practitioners also have strong opinions about helping relationships,
the ideal form they should take, and how they may best be created. Knowing
the evolution of these ideas is helpful in understanding the contemporary status
of the counseling relationship.

In modern times, helping relationships began within a religious context:
clergy members and other spiritual experts acted as go-betweens in issues
between a client and God. The relationship was rigidly defined according to the
values of the Middle Ages. At the onset of the Renaissance came Johann Weyer,
considered by many to be the world's first psychiatrist. He condemned the
archaic witch-purging practices of religious healers and instead extolled the
value of a benevolent, kind, and understanding relationship between doctor and
patient. A few centuries later, Sigmund Freud also gave considerable attention
to the structure of patient/doctor interactions but stressed a more benign, formalized, and unobtrusive relationship. He was, of course, concerned about such
things as "transference" and so warned practitioners of its value and danger.

Historically, the roles within the counseling relationship have not been static.
Every theoretical approach has distinct notions about how best to work with
clients. Some counselors deliberately encourage dependence in their client relationships, thereby facilitating the transference struggle that Freud found to be so
crucial in overcoming unresolved problems with authority. In this type of thera-

peutic relationship, the counselor remains aloof, dispassionate, and neutral, so as not to fall victim to an erotic involvement that could so naturally proceed from the role of omnipotent love object.

In the therapeutic relationship, according to Carl Rogers and his client-centered school, the counselor becomes the prototype of nurturance, warmth, genuineness, and effective honesty. The relationship is a mutual involvement, a sharing of feelings in an open, accepting atmosphere; the counselor accepts responsibility not only for creating these fertile conditions but also for communicating his or her own attitudes and feelings within the session. In his personal equation for creating an ideal relationship in counseling, Rogers (1961) explains: "I would like my feelings in this relationship with him to be as clear and transparent as possible, so that they are a discernible reality for him to which he can return again and again" (p. 67).

A third and quite distinct position is the no-nonsense instructional model of the relationship in cognitive/behavioral counseling. The practitioner creates a businesslike contract with the client to meet certain specific goals, with an action plan for reaching them. In these circumstances the relationship becomes an encounter between teacher and student.

Recently researchers have been exploring the counseling relationship from another perspective, that of interpersonal influence. Strong and Claiborn (1982), for example, have argued that the interpersonal influence variables of perceived expertness, attractiveness, and trustworthiness all affect the counselor's ability to facilitate change in clients. The relationship is viewed as the vehicle for establishing power and influence.

Regardless of orientation, it is clear that the counseling relationship is a special and necessary aspect of the therapeutic counseling encounter. Indeed, counseling effectiveness has been found to be a function of the quality of the alliance (Parloff, 1956; Truax & Carkhuff, 1967). But, although the importance of the relationship is well documented, it is necessary to recognize that a helping relationship in and of itself is not a sufficient condition for behavior change. As Egan (1990) has pointed out, putting too much attention on the importance of the therapeutic relationship can be as detrimental as ignoring it altogether. The purpose of all helping is to assist clients to manage their lives better. "The goal won't be achieved if the relationship is poor, but if too much focus is placed on the relationship itself, both client and helper are distracted from the real work to be done" (Egan, 1990, p. 59).

COUNSELORS AS RELATIONSHIP SPECIALISTS

The helping relationship can be defined as a systematic and intentional attempt, using a specified cluster of interpersonal skills, to assist another person to make self-determined improvements in behavior, feelings, and/or thoughts. Whereas daily helping encounters such as those between parent and child, teacher and student, or supervisor and employee could also be included, it is primarily counselors who are specialists in developing nurturing and productive encounters. May (1983) prefers the use of the term *presence* to describe the counselor's real alliance with a client, who is less an object to be analyzed than a being to be understood. Yalom (1980) states that the single most important lesson for a beginning counselor to learn is that "it is the relationship that heals" (p. 401). The therapeutic involvement with the counselor symbolically illuminates other relationships in the client's life, besides providing the opportunity for a real, caring, respectful encounter with someone who is safe. The client feels minimal danger of seduction, manipulation, or betrayal, for the stated bounds of the interaction provide for protection of privacy, confidentiality, trust, and benevolence. It is at once both refreshing and frightening to be involved with a professional who is expert at listening and nonpossessively loving.

The therapeutic relationship helps the client work through feelings of isolation, a condition that the existentialists such as Kaiser (1965) and Yalom (1980) consider the "universal symptom" of humanity. The only cure is communication with someone who is sensitive, receptive, neutral, interested, and psychologically healthy. Imagine the deep pleasure, satisfaction, freedom—the complete and total freedom—to be genuinely open with another person who is doing *everything* within his or her power to subjugate personal needs and focus only on *you*. For one uninterrupted hour you have the absolute attention, full concentration, and vast resources of a specialist in building relationships. This person is caring yet honest, fully capable of perceiving things beyond your awareness and explaining things beyond your understanding. This is a relationship you can truly depend on and use as a model for the kinds of experiences you deserve.

Yalom (1980) further explains that, although the therapeutic relationship is only temporary, the experience of intimacy is permanent. The key to developing such a meaningful encounter, irrespective of technique, is through the full engagement with the client in the present moment:

> I listen to a woman patient. She rambles on and on. She seems unattractive in every sense of the word—physically, intellectually, emotionally. She is irritating. She has many off-putting gestures. She is not talking to me; she is talking in front of me. Yet how can she talk to me if I am not here? My thoughts wander. My head groans. What time is it? How much longer to go? I suddenly rebuke myself. I give my mind a shake. Whenever I think of how much time remains in the hour, I know I am failing my patient. I try then to touch her with my thoughts. I try to understand why I avoid her. What is her world like at this moment? How is she experiencing the hour? How is she experiencing me? I ask her these very questions. I tell her that I have felt distant from her for the last several minutes. Has she felt the same way? We talk about that together and try to figure out why we lost contact with one another. Suddenly we are very close. She is no longer unattractive. I have much compassion for her person, for what she is, for what she might yet be. The clock races; the hour ends too soon [p. 415].

In addition to sharing the attitude implicit in Yalom's moving statement, counselors are quite skilled in their ability to foster helping relationships with a wide diversity of people. From research and experience summarized by Wolberg (1967), Goldstein (1980), and Derlega, Hendrick, Winstead, and Berg (1991), we know there is a specific set of behaviors likely to facilitate a therapeutic relationship, as well as behaviors that will inhibit the alliance.

Facilitative Behaviors	Inhibiting Behaviors
Acceptance	Exclamations of overconcern
Open-mindedness	Expressions of overconcern
Reflection of feelings	Moralistic judgments
Open-ended questioning	Punitive responses
Physical closeness	Probing of traumatic material
Self-disclosures	Criticism
Sympathetic remarks	False promises
Demonstrations of warmth	Threats
Supportive statements	Self-indulgent disclosures
Expertness	Rejection
Consistency	Displays of impatience
Diplomatic honesty	Political/religious discussions
Structuring	Ridicule/sarcasm
Respect	Belittling of client
Patience	Blaming of failures
Genuineness	Intolerance
Paraphrasing of content	Dogmatic statements
Positive reinforcement	Premature deep interpretations

Counselors must, of course, be consistent in their ability to create constructive relationships with *anyone* who walks in the door. This skill and attitude take practice as well as an openness to new people. The place to start, naturally, is in one's own personal life. To what extent are you, the reader, able to relate to people from all walks of life?

In his study of human relationships, Nelson-Jones (1990) found that a series of specific skills will allow you to initiate, maintain, and nurture your connections to others. Since this repertoire of behaviors is so crucial to being able to conduct counseling successfully, he recommends that beginning students assess their degree of competence in each of several areas. For each of these categories we have listed a few of the skills that are considered most significant in creating solid counseling relationships. Read through this list, and consider the degree to which you can improve your effectiveness in each of the broad categories.

As you read through your self-ratings on these items, especially those marked with a 1 or 2, you will see where you most need to improve. It is hardly our expectation that you would already be a master of these relationship skills—that's why we have counselor training programs to help you learn and develop them. But it should be exciting to you to consider that, by the time you have completed your education as a professional helper, you will be reasonably competent in each of these dimensions. This will, of course, not only make you a successful counselor but also help you to become more loving and intimate in all your personal relationships. A prerequisite to beginning this work is a clear understanding of the characteristics of the helping encounter.

Relationship Skills Rating Scale

(5) All of the time   (4) Most of the time   (3) Sometimes   (2) Rarely   (l) Never

Self-Awareness

___ I am in touch with my inner feelings.
___ I am comfortable with myself.
___ I am aware of my fears, anxieties, and unresolved conflicts.

Self-Disclosure

___ I express my feelings honestly and clearly.
___ I am concise and expressive in my communications.
___ I am open in sharing what I think and feel.

Active Listening

___ I can focus intently on what others are saying and recall the essence of their communications.
___ I show attention and interest when I listen.
___ I am able to resist internal and external distractions that may impede my concentration.

Responding

___ I am perceived by others as safe to talk to.
___ I can demonstrate my understanding of what I hear.
___ I reflect accurately other people's underlying thoughts and feelings.

Initiating

___ I have the ability to put people at ease.
___ I am able to get people to open up.
___ I am smooth and natural in facilitating the flow of conversation.

Attitudes

___ I am nonjudgmental and accepting of other people, even when they have different values and opinions than I do.
___ I am trustworthy and respectful of other people.
___ I am caring and compassionate.

Managing Conflict

___ I can confront people without them feeling defensive.
___ I accept responsibility for my role in creating difficulties.
___ I am able to defuse explosive situations.

CHARACTERISTICS OF THE HELPING RELATIONSHIP
Congruence, Positive Regard, and Empathy

Rogers (1951) followed his early theorizing about the importance of the counseling relationship with a series of research studies during the 1950s and 1960s in which he attempted to develop some empirical evidence for his ideas. The results of these research efforts led him to conclude that there were several major characteristics of the helping relationship (Rogers, 1957).

The first characteristic so identified was congruence: a correspondence between feelings experienced internally and feelings displayed externally. This referred to the ability of the counselor to exhibit a sincere concern for the client. Rogers felt that counselors must not merely use certain techniques and processes but also *feel* a genuine concern for the client. To pretend to care when the inner feelings are uncaring is to be phony, insincere, and incongruent, thereby negatively affecting the development of a therapeutic alliance. Rogers learned that clients need to perceive the counselor as openly and honestly communicating real feelings so that trust can evolve. He believed that congruence is the most important ingredient in the helping relationship and encouraged counselors to work toward developing more congruence between what they are feeling on the inside and what they are communicating on the outside.

Positive regard, the unqualified acceptance of the client by the counselor, was the second characteristic that Rogers identified. This quality is closely related to warmth and exists independent of the client's behavior, whether positive or negative. It means that the counselor does not evaluate and judge clients' actions or statements; behavior is viewed neutrally, and all people are worthy of respect.

Rogers's research identified empathy as the third characteristic. This denotes the process of attempting to understand, from the client's frame of reference, the thoughts and feelings underlying behavior—that is, the ability to walk around in the client's shoes and know how he or she feels. Empathy communicates to clients that the counselor understands their experience and through this understanding is able to facilitate an increased self-awareness of the client's emotional and cognitive processes. Empathy provides the context in which the counselor can help the client to work toward reintegrating aspects of the personality that have been stressful and problematic.

Numerous other writers besides Rogers have also postulated that certain qualities implicit in the therapeutic relationship have remarkable healing properties. Moustakas (1986) believes that the ideal counseling model consists of three principal elements: *being in, being for,* and *being with.*

The act of *being in* refers to "empathic resonance," or the willingness to enter into a client's world—to feel, sense, perceive, and experience what it is like to be in the client's body and mind. This is, naturally, quite difficult to do— to suspend temporarily your own sense of self while you enter into the client's existence—and especially to do without losing yourself in the process. Further, this empathy toward the client must not only be felt but also be communicated in a way that he or she feels heard and understood.

An intimate conversation between friends demonstrates the healing powers of supportive relationships in which a person in pain feels understood, accepted, and nourished.

Being for symbolizes the strong advocacy position that we take on the client's behalf. The counselor unconditionally accepts the client as a person (even while selectively disapproving of certain self-destructive *behaviors*). The client feels as if there is truly someone in his or her corner, an enthusiastic source of comfort and support.

Being with is that part of the relationship between two people that recognizes their distinct separateness. Yes, counselors are in synch with their clients. Yes, they support, encourage, and are active advocates for their welfare. However, when a therapeutic relationship is truly working—really humming along—counselors are able to *be with* their clients and simultaneously offer their own perspectives on what is going on. Even when these perceptions differ from the client's point of view, the sanctity of the relationship does not become jeopardized or compromised.

Therein lies the true value of a caring and constructive therapeutic alliance: the counselor has developed sufficient trust, and solicited enough cooperation and patience from the client, that he or she can sometimes make mistakes or misjudgments and not risk losing everything that has already been built. This awareness should be especially reassuring for the beginner who may erroneously believe that, if you make an error or say the wrong thing, clients always fire you or jump out the first open window. Within the context of a good counseling alliance in which empathy, congruence, and positive regard have developed, *both* participants enjoy a great deal of freedom.

Attending Skills and Responding Skills

Rogers's original research on the counseling relationship was expanded by Charles Truax and Robert Carkhuff (1967) during the late 1960s. Their work attempted to identify more precisely and behaviorally those central characteristics of the counseling relationship that produce therapeutic change. The most important contribution they made was to conceptualize the characteristics of the counseling relationship as skills rather than as attributes that were a function of personality. Their reconceptualization allowed for further research based on skill-learning models and further identification of relevant subskills important to the counseling relationship. It also makes it possible for most counselor educators to believe genuinely that all students can learn to be more empathic.

Carkhuff (1969) reorganized the basic relationship skills into broad categories of skills and subskills that provided a generic model for the counseling relationship and process. The first two stages of the model—attending skills and responding skills—have direct relevance to our discussion of constructive relationships.

Carkhuff identified two important aspects of attending: physical attending and psychological attending. Physical attending refers to the arrangement of the physical surroundings so that they reduce distraction and maximize the potential for interaction. Physical attending also includes variables such as the counselor's body position and posture and other nonverbal aspects of behavior. It means that we communicate to the client, with all our body and mind, our respect and our readiness to be helpful. Psychological attending, the second component, usually involves the use of reflection of feeling and content to demonstrate to the client full and complete concentration. The skills of empathy, respect, and acceptance are important in psychological attending.

The second general area identified by Carkhuff was responding skills, which involve reflecting back to clients both their feelings and the meaning of their communications in such a way that exploration and awareness are facilitated. Skill at responding shows the client that the counselor understands, from the client's perspective, the issues presented in the interview, and it adds to the base of respect and regard in the relationship.

Gordon (1974) mentions several other benefits of the active listening/reflecting mode for relationship building, which we have illustrated with supporting examples:

1. It communicates our intense interest in what the client is saying:

   "You seem to be saying that you care deeply about what others think, that you feel overwhelmed by their expectations. And that we, you and I, should work together on this concern."

2. It proves not only that we have been listening, but that we truly understand what the client means:

   "If I am hearing you clearly, you would like to break out of your shell, but feel so scared that *then* you would be vulnerable."

3. It checks out the accuracy of our interpretations:

"You are saying that it's not so much a matter of being able to do the work; it's just that you feel so listless and helpless."

4. It invites the client to ventilate feelings that are held inside:

"So you're spinning your wheels, going round and round, feeling more overwhelmed, more frustrated, more out of control."

5. It moves communication from a superficial to a deeper level:

"You want men to acknowledge the total you . . . yet you're concerned that, if you demand that, you may end up with nothing—and that really scares you."

6. It promotes insight:

"Even though you say you want close relationships, it sounds like you choose people who won't or can't give this to you. I wonder if you're the one who's afraid of intimacy."

7. It helps the client to take responsibility for solving his or her own problems:

"Even though you feel stuck, you're not willing to share this with your husband. I wonder what kind of relationship you really want to create with him."

The skills of reflecting feeling and active listening thus promote a relationship of warmth and intimacy. A base of trust is created from which all future interventions can be implemented.

PRACTICAL DIMENSIONS OF THE THERAPEUTIC RELATIONSHIP

The client usually comes to counseling with a history of impoverished relationships. With family members, friends, or colleagues there have been some misunderstandings—even conflicts—that lead the client to seek help. The initial suspicions of a client toward new, intense relationships, even a client who feels lonely and isolated, will only be compounded within the strange, artificial boundaries of the counseling encounter.

As we have said, there is an inequality inherent in most professional relationships: the presumed expert controls most of the power. Thus the client begins the relationship at a disadvantage—unbalanced, overwhelmed, anxious, and confused. Before she or he even has the chance to adjust to the surroundings, check out the environment, and study the counselor, the session usually begins with the question "How can I help you?" Given the difficulties present in the initial encounter, most practitioners agree, on the basis of research, theory, and experience, that the therapeutic relationship must possess certain dimensions to create a favorable climate for change.

Commitment

As in all other meaningful contacts between people, there is an implied, if not explicit, contract in the counseling relationship to act in certain ways and follow certain agreed-upon rules. The commitment to each other is both mutually and flexibly determined but nevertheless specifies the form and texture of the relationship that will develop. The counselor feels bound to this agreement with respect to promises made about what constitutes professional behavior: avoidance of self-indulgence, manipulativeness, and deceit; delivery of specified services; total commitment, in fact, to doing everything possible to aid the client's growth.

The client is also strongly urged to feel a commitment to the relationship, although this personal contract is often difficult to enforce. By modeling honesty, the counselor encourages the client to live under agreed-upon rules: to come on time, give sufficient notice when canceling appointments, and pay fees as negotiated. Of equal importance is the client's commitment to work with the counselor, to work on himself or herself, and to invest energy and personal risk taking in the relationship. All successful relationships a client has, whether with an attorney, a mechanic, a spouse, a friend, or a counselor, involve a commitment to be fair and just with each other.

Trust

The development of trust in counseling relationships is crucial to productive work. It is the primary responsibility of the counselor to offer interpersonal conditions to the client that are likely to result in trust. But trust is a catch-all word meaning various things and consisting of a number of factors. Several aspects of a trusting relationship are worth repeating: respect for the client's intrinsic right to be his or her own person, warm regard for the client as a unique being, and genuineness, which means being honest and real.

Although it may seem obvious to you that a counselor must be trustworthy to be helpful to a client, this trust is not as easy to maintain as it might seem. There has been serious, and unfortunately all too common, occurrences of ethical transgression in which a practitioner violates the client's trust to meet his or her own needs (Sell, Gottlieb, & Schoenfeld, 1986). Chapter 15 will explore this issue in greater depth, but for now we'll just stress that maintaining trust in the relationship requires constant vigilance and a high level of professional commitment.

Empathy

Empathy refers to the ability of the counselor to truly understand the client, from a unique perspective. It often involves communicating accurately the feelings and meanings of clients' statements, thereby demonstrating an active understanding of clients' concerns. Egan (1990) distinguishes between two levels of empathy: primary-level and advanced-level accurate empathy. Primary-level empathy refers to the interchangeability between the client's statements and the counselor's responses. At this level of empathic responding, the counselor communicates a basic understanding of the thoughts, feelings, and behavior of the client. Advanced empathy is built upon the primary-level base and emphasizes the counselor's responding in a way that facilitates the deeper exploration of relevant issues. Effective therapeutic counseling relationships are based on the sensitive and timely use of both levels of empathy.

Confidentiality

An essential and unique feature of the counseling relationship (as compared to a personal or informal relationship) is the maintenance of confidentiality to assure safety and privacy. Just as an attorney, clergy members, or physician must be able to guarantee that whatever is revealed will be considered privileged communication, trust and openness in counseling hinge on a similar promise. It is precisely the knowledge that a counselor's professional and ethical standards protect individual rights that makes it easier for the client to confide personal secrets.

Benevolent Power

Interpersonal influence is that dimension of counseling that involves the application of expertise, power, and attractiveness in such a way as to foster self-awareness and constructive change. Lazarus (1981) believes that the most important function of the initial interview in counseling is to inspire hope, to help the client believe in the process and in the expertise of the counselor as an influencer. One theorist has even created a whole therapeutic system that capitalizes principally on the placebo effects in counseling, structuring the expectations of the client to maximize favorable results. In this "placebo therapy," Fish (1973) recommends using power, expertise, and the aura of omnipotence, in addition to nurturance and acceptance, to increase one's influencing capabilities in the therapeutic relationship.

Examples include evidence of expertise (for instance, diplomas on the wall), attractiveness (dress, surroundings), and power (control of the interview). Each of these social-influence parameters can be used and communicated in a manner likely to develop a constructive relationship and lead to productive change (Bandura, 1977). The use of social influence is a sensitive area because of the danger of manipulation and deceit, which do not enhance therapeutic relationships; thus, interpersonal-influence factors must be communicated openly and within a trusting, warm, and empathic context in order to minimize the potential negative effects of these elements.

We have mentioned several dimensions of the counseling relationship that seem to us to be important. There are many others. However, focusing on developing skill in the sensitive use and targeted application of the characteristics we have described will build a strong base for developing a productive counseling relationship.

CREATING A RELATIONSHIP IN THE INITIAL INTERVIEW

Some of the theory and research underlying the counseling relationship has been reviewed. The characteristics, components, and skills essential to these relationships can be identified. However, each of these individual aspects must be integrated into the person of the counselor during the interview with the client. The integration process is crucial, because the relationship variables will define the context and texture of the interaction that follows. The initial interview provides the opportunity to operationalize relationship skills and provides the first test of the effectiveness of counseling.

Establishing Rules

The relationship between client and counselor is established in their first encounter. Even before the first words are spoken, the two size each other up, assessing the other's personal competence. The client, usually confused and nervous, will wait for the professional to begin and define the parameters and tone for the sessions. The counselor also bides his or her time, knowing how crucial the first interchange will be to the entire therapeutic process. If ineffective or unsuccessful, the result will be unforgiving: the client will not return for more counseling. Worse yet, the client may return, but with grossly distorted perceptions of what will be involved in the future.

Perhaps the client will view the relationship as unequal, seeing the counselor, an expert, as the authority, the parent, the controller. The client may then adopt behavior appropriate to that situation, showing deference and asking questions. Transference, power, and dependence variables will exert themselves optimally as in other unequal relationships, such as those between parent and child, boss and employee, and, often, doctor and patient.

The client could also perceive the relationship as mostly equal, especially if the counselor introduces himself or herself by first name and does not respond with formal detachment. In this case the client will adapt to the situation and internally define the relationship according to his or her perceptions: "The counselor recognizes that we are equal, that what I have to say is intelligent and important, but we both really understand that I need help and I'm here because *he* can offer it."

The initial interview, therefore, serves the function of creating and communicating rules for future interaction that are likely to be beneficial to a productive relationship. It establishes the norms for appropriate conduct and capitalizes on the trust, respect, acceptance, and warmth that are so much a part of the therapeutic encounter.

Planting Hope

The client is motivated to make an appointment out of a sense of helplessness. People rarely pay money, risk embarrassment, or inconvenience themselves to hire a professional if there is another way to resolve their concerns. Counseling is usually the last resort, the final step before self-destructive acts are likely to occur.

Clients show up at the first session ambivalent about their behavior and unable to trust their feelings. They want help; they want to change. Yet they have also invested themselves in preserving the status quo and will therefore almost always resist, on some level, the interventions of the counselor. They want reassurance, easy solutions to their problems, and simple answers to their complicated questions. But most of all they want to believe that they can learn to trust themselves. Clients want to hope that working for the future is worthwhile. They want to believe in their capacity to make needed changes in their lives. They want hope that, eventually, their pain will diminish and will someday be replaced by something better. Clients have hope that we, as professionals, know what we're doing, that we actually can make a difference. Therefore, favorable expectations for treatment, consistent with what can be delivered, must be quickly established in the initial interview.

Assuring Confidentiality

Confidentiality is the verbal contract between two people in which the counselor promises to keep private the communications heard in counseling and the client agrees to believe the promise. Unless such an understanding and basic level of trust can be reached, it is unlikely that the relationship can proceed any further.

For this reason the issue of confidentiality is always discussed early in the initial interview, both to allay fears about how private the sessions will be and to convince the client that the relationship will be safe and sacred, impervious to the questions of a curious parent, spouse, employer, or judge. The therapeutic relationship thus begins with a mutual commitment—that of the counselor to work ethically and competently in the best interest of the client while safeguarding privacy, and that of the client to be as open, truthful, and self-revealing as possible. These commitments will form the temporary bond of the relationship until real respect and intimacy evolve as a function of working together.

Assessing Expectations

Often in conjunction with delivering a statement about confidentiality, the counselor further defines the therapeutic relationship to assure that both parties enter into the verbal contract in ways that will be compatible and satisfying. Clients can come to the first session with fairly outlandish notions about what is possible, probable, or likely to occur. These unrealistic expectations may include any of the following:

- "I talk. You listen. Then you talk. I listen. We take turns until one of us gets too bored."
- "I tell you my problems. Then you tell me yours. Afterward, I can figure out what I should do by what you have done."
- "I tell you my dreams and then you tell me what they mean."
- "You're like a lie detector. Whenever I don't tell the truth, or exaggerate a little bit, or go through my standard lines, you interrupt me and tell me I'm full of crap."

- "You give me a tissue and hold my hand and tell me everything will be OK. That's what a helpful person should do."
- "I tell you my problems. You tell me what to do so I can change situations that keep me from getting what I want."

Images of a friend, father-confessor, lover, teacher, and coach all emerge in the client's mind as models for what the therapeutic relationship will be like. Many of the misconceptions and distorted expectations can be cleared up after they are discussed in the interview. As the counselor explains what counseling is and how and why it works, the client's images can be modified to reflect a more accurate portrayal. In this process, client and counselor discuss who will do what, in which order, and what is likely to happen as a result of the fulfillment of these expectations.

Collecting Information

Before the counselor can really go to work, some form of data collection usually needs to take place in the first interview. The extent and depth of this activity will depend on the theory to which the practitioner subscribes; a psychoanalytic counselor might spend several entire sessions creating a history, whereas a behavioral counselor would devote much less time, limiting the focus to specific information about the presenting problem.

Other models for collecting relevant background information about a client's environment are available, most including some preliminary explorations into the client's development, the evolution of the problem, and a description of self-defeating behaviors. In addition, it would be important to know which solutions have already been tried and why the client is seeking help at this particular time.

Most clinicians have a list of favorite questions to elicit useful information about how the client characteristically functions. Insightful queries can also create greater intimacy, openness, self-disclosure, and trust in the relationship. The following questions often facilitate the self-examination process and produce valuable data for the counselor. Simultaneously, the client begins to experience the excitement and discomfort of looking inward. Answer these questions for yourself as you review them:

Who are the most important people in your world, and how do you spend time winning their approval?

Who else knows that you are having this difficulty, and what will you tell them?

What is your favorite part of each day?

When you feel a lot of pressure, what kinds of things do you usually do to calm yourself?

When are the specific times in your daily life in which you feel most uncomfortable and out of control?

Regardless of which questions or data-collecting model is selected, the intention in the initial interview is to complete a preliminary inventory of the client's complaints, symptoms, and concerns.

Identifying Problems

The identification of a client's complaints eventually leads to a working diagnosis. Since counselors aren't restricted to a medical model that limits labels to categories of psychopathology, they are able to concentrate on functional diagnoses that describe specific behavior patterns for each client. It is not necessary for the counselor to think in terms of "neurotic," "schizophrenic," or "dependent personality." Instead, efforts are made for the counselor and client to label self-defeating behaviors in specific, operational, and useful ways during the initial interview.

Beginning Intervention

In addition to the traditional uses of the initial interview to begin the therapeutic relationship and collect useful information, Kovacs (1982) feels that other goals take even greater precedence. The counselor must intervene in the very first session on some level "to make at least a small dent in the stasis into which the patient has been locked for some time now" (p. 148). Counseling starts immediately in the first session. It is not enough merely to initiate the relationship, fill out forms, set goals, or create structure. These steps are but the means of bringing a sense of commitment to the counseling relationship.

First-Session Agenda Review

We were both so apprehensive when starting out as counselors that we drew comfort from a degree of structure regarding how a first session should be conducted. One of us even carried a "cheat sheet" into practicum sessions with reminders of what essential tasks should be completed during an initial interview (Vriend & Kottler, 1980).

Fortunately, a number of authors have spent the time to construct lists of those components that constitute a first-session agenda (Dyer & Vriend, 1974; Gottman & Leiblum, 1974; Haley, 1989). The following list summarizes the steps that many practitioners consider to be important in a first session. Each of these components is part of a flexible agenda in which the counselor simultaneously collects needed information and establishes a therapeutic relationship that is equitable, productive, and caring.

> *Opening.* Begin the interview dynamically and enthusiastically, sensitizing the client to the excitement of change.
> *Route.* Find out through which avenue the client decided to seek help, how the decision was made, and why this particular choice was made.

Reason. For what reason is the client deciding to get help? Why now?

Experience in counseling. What is the client's previous experience with counseling? Who has she/he seen before, and what was it like?

Expectations. What are the client's expectations for treatment? Do they relate to previous counseling experience? What does the client believe will happen?

Definition. Misconceptions and predictably unrealistic expectations can be corrected when the counselor provides a definition of counseling, detailing how the process works and who has responsibility for each part.

Confidentiality. Discussing confidentiality is very important in establishing trust.

Search for content. Identify areas appropriate for counseling content, including presenting problems, self-destructive behavior, and unresolved conflicts.

Important people. Explore the people most important in the client's world, especially those who have a vested interest in the treatment outcome.

Functional level. Assess the functional level of the client across a broad spectrum of behaviors—intelligence, resilience, confidence, exercise, sleeping and eating routines, dexterity, perceptual and cognitive capacities, life skills, and values.

Structure. Determine a structure for the particular client and counseling situation that will make significant progress likely to occur.

Commitment. Secure a commitment from the client to change and to work toward counseling goals.

Goals. Specifically work with the client to define realistic goals for the counseling that can be reduced to subgoals for and between future sessions.

Summary. Review or—better yet—have the client evaluate what his/her perceptions and feelings are about the first session, the counselor, and their relationship.

Homework. Translate the issues highlighted in the summary into a self-determining homework assignment so that action may continue between sessions.

Closing. Ending the first session, solidifying the relationship, and setting future appointments are relevant details in this final step.

Although this list may seem comprehensive, it is also a bit daunting to think about working all the way through the items in a first interview without alienating the client along the way. By way of summary, your principal job as a counselor is to create an alliance with your clients in which you establish a degree of trust and intimacy. This must be done efficiently and effectively or your clients will develop unrealistic expectations (or, worse, they won't return; and if they don't come back, you can't help them).

The steps of an initial interview translate into several core therapeutic tasks: (1) establishing a bond between you and your client, (2) providing preliminary information regarding what counseling is and how it works, (3) assessing client issues and expectations, (4) instilling a sense of hope, and (5) obtaining a commitment to be patient and to work hard in the sessions. From these humble beginnings, the success of all future counseling efforts is firmly established.

SUMMARY

Considering the energy, motivation, courage, and desperation required for a client to initiate the first appointment, anxiety during the first encounter is usually quite high. This initial interaction in the counseling relationship is marked by fear— fear of what might or might not happen; fear that there is no cure; fear that there *is* a cure but that it will involve a lot of work; fear the counselor might tell someone else about the session; fear about what friends, family, even the receptionist might think about the fact that the client needs help; fear of revealing deeply guarded secrets; and perhaps most of all, fear of entering into an intense human relationship.

That the counselor is able, often within the first few minutes, to relieve a client's apprehensions is a testimony to the consummate skill of the professional who is experienced at relationship building. Everything in the easy manner, the calm self-confidence of the counselor indicates that this is a person who is comfortable with intimacy. The soft smile, soothing voice, relaxed posture, and interested eyes all communicate an authenticity that helps the client trust, open up, and feel prized. Rapport is developed not by accident, nor by magic, but by the deliberate efforts of the well-trained counselor who understands the core conditions of nurturance in human relationships and can create them at will.

SUGGESTED READINGS

Avila, D. L., & Combs, A. W. (Eds.) (1985). *Perspectives on helping relationships and the helping professions.* Boston: Allyn & Bacon.

Bugental, J. F. T. (1990). *Intimate journeys.* San Francisco: Jossey-Bass.

Derlega, V. J., Hendrick, S. S., Winstead, B. A., & Berg, J. H. (1991). *Psychotherapy as a personal relationship.* New York: Guilford Press.

Egan, G. (1990). *The skilled helper: A systematic approach to effective helping* (4th ed.). Pacific Grove, CA: Brooks/Cole.

Lambert, M. J. (1983). *Psychotherapy and patient relationships.* Homewood, IL: Dow Jones-Irwin.

Nelson-Jones, R. (1990). *Human relationships: A skills approach.* Pacific Grove, CA: Brooks/Cole.

Patterson, C. H. (1985). *The therapeutic relationship: Foundations for an eclectic psychotherapy.* Pacific Grove, CA: Brooks/Cole.

Rogers, C. R. (1980). *A way of being.* Boston: Houghton Mifflin.

PART TWO

COUNSELING ANTECEDENTS AND APPROACHES

CHAPTER FIVE

INSIGHT-ORIENTED COUNSELING APPROACHES

INTRODUCTION TO THEORY
    CONSTRUCTION
CLIENT-CENTERED COUNSELING
    Originator and Revisionists
    Basic Assumptions
    Personality Development
    Favorite Techniques
    Criticisms of Client-Centered
      Counseling
    Personal Applications
EXISTENTIAL COUNSELING
    Originators
    Premises of Existential
      Counseling
    Criticisms of Existential
      Counseling
    Personal Applications

PSYCHOANALYTIC COUNSELING
    Originators
    Basic Psychoanalytic Concepts
    Criticisms of Psychoanalytic
      Counseling
    Personal Applications
GESTALT COUNSELING
    Originators and Basic Concepts
    Techniques of Gestalt Therapy
    Criticisms of Gestalt Counseling
HONORABLE MENTIONS
    Transactional Analysis
    Adlerian Counseling
    Character Analysis
SUMMARY
SUGGESTED READINGS

SOCRATES:

Come, lie down here.

STREPSIADES:

What for?

SOCRATES:

Ponder awhile over matters that interest you.

STREPSIADES:

Oh, I pray not there.

SOCRATES:

Come, on the couch!

STREPSIADES:

What a cruel fate.

SOCRATES:

Ponder and examine closely, gather your thoughts together, let your mind turn to every side of things. If you meet with difficulty, spring quickly to some other idea; keep away from sleep [Alexander & Selesnick, 1966].

INTRODUCTION TO THEORY CONSTRUCTION

Theory has been both a plague and a challenge for students since presocratic times, when philosophers would aggressively query their disciples about the meaning of life. Certainly the contemporary student finds little solace in historical precedent for his or her own struggles to understand the differences among the various theoretical systems that are part of the counseling profession. "What good is theory?" students often ask. "I want to be a counselor, not a philosopher."

Yet confusion abounds within the realm of counseling itself, as the differences of opinion on the structure of the therapeutic relationship have shown. Whereas the more insight-oriented counseling approaches focus on creating an authentic human encounter for its intrinsic healing properties, the action-oriented approaches use the relationship as a means to another end. And even within a particular orientation there is much disagreement as to style, form, and content. Carl Rogers, for example, proposed that it is the realness of the encounter that is important, and so he described an insight theory that encourages naturalness, genuineness, and humanness in the relationship. On the other hand, Sigmund Freud's insight theory postulated that the relationship should be as anonymous and formalized as possible so that the client can work through resistance and transference issues.

A theory, therefore, is a blueprint for action. The counselor's choices of interventions, reactions, analysis, and understanding all flow logically from a theoretical model of what people are like, what is good for them, and what conditions are likely to influence them in a self-determined, desirable direction (Geis, 1973). Some students may be surprised to learn that counselors actually have quite complex and well-developed theories of metaphysics (how the world works), ethics (how people should act), logic (cause/effect relationships), ontology (meaning of human existence), and epistemology (how people know) (Kottler, 1983). It is precisely these theories that guide what a counselor does with a particular client at a particular moment.

Theories are valuable because they organize knowledge and information in an easily retrievable fashion. They are no more nor less than models for consistency in action; they permit all practitioners, whether of architecture, medicine, or counseling, to repeat those strategies that have worked previously in similar circumstances (Argyris, 1974). Theories, of course, have other useful functions, such as attempting to simplify the world and developing rules to explain, predict, or guide behavior.

Although they are valuable constructs for aiding action, theories are not indelibly inscribed in stone as truth. When you study the various counseling approaches, remember that each is a single attempt to explain the therapeutic process, albeit with emphasis, values, and strengths in some areas and limitations in others. In deciding which ideas have the most personal relevance for you, bear in mind the attributes of good theories set forth by Burks and Stefflre (1979): good theories are clearly and precisely described, as simply expressed as possible, comprehensive in scope, useful in the real world, and valuable in generating new knowledge and research.

In theory construction we are indirectly trying to establish a basis for predicting (1) a client's prognosis, (2) likely consequences of certain interventions, (3) connections among experiences (and nonexperiences) in a client's life, and (4) the impact of our therapeutic efforts. But since no prediction can ever be 100% certain, we also use theory to approximate some degree of consistency. Theories are working hypotheses, subject to change and revision as new information about the world, our clients, and ourselves becomes available. We cannot accurately and precisely describe what we see; instead, we filter our experiences through slightly focused images, and inadequate language approximates what we think we perceive. Theory is, in a sense, our beliefs about how we explain reality (Burks & Stefflre, 1979).

Gregory Bateson (1979) describes the problem of theory construction in science by listing many of the inherent logical weaknesses in the ways we organize our knowledge:

1. Science can never prove anything, not only because prediction is imperfect and our methods of collecting data are flawed but also because *proof* occurs only in the realm of abstraction.

2. In human perception, all experience is subjective and hence colored by individual perceptions, as well as by unconscious motives. We can be certain that the reports of our senses will be slightly distorted, viewed through individual prisms that have been shaped by unique genetic structures and experiences.

3. Explanations are the results of descriptions, and these descriptions can

be organized in more than one way. Convenience determines how things are classified, and, no matter which model is used, some information will be lost or downplayed.

4. For a theory (and hence its predictive power) to be perfect, it would have to deal with factors that are 100% controllable. Far from the whimsical, impulsive nature of the human world, even physical laws are minutely capricious.

5. Theories are constructed from information. Information is subject not only to inadequate description and arbitrary classification but also to flawed methods of measurement. Researchers in counseling, for instance, have been debating for decades about whether it can even be reliably demonstrated that therapeutic interventions cure people, since we can't agree on definitions of "cure," much less figure out a way to measure the degree to which it occurs.

For the purposes of counseling students, each of the theoretical systems represented in these chapters should be viewed within the aforementioned human context. Each theory is an approximation of truth, one person's or a group's attempt at explaining phenomena that are difficult to understand and virtually impossible to describe fully. These theories, as with all other human structures,

Carl Rogers (1902–1987), creator of client-centered counseling and advocate for the value of the therapeutic relationship.

are imperfect working hypotheses subject both to random error of the samples of behavior investigated and to the distinctions, limitations, and expectations of the inventors. We advise you to read the following sections openly and critically. Assume that each theory has some merit and value, some practical use and interesting ideas that can help you better understand the process of counseling.

The distinction between insight theories (this chapter) and action theories (Chapter 6), although a convenient demarcation of counseling approaches, is hardly a clear-cut one. No longer can we say that any theory is now applied in the "pure" form in which it was invented. Insight practitioners who identify strongly with psychoanalytic or existential frameworks nevertheless make use of behavioral structures to help their clients translate insights into action in their lives. And even the most staunch cognitive and behavioral practitioners will sometimes help their clients understand the source of their suffering. Even in a more natural way, some degree of self-knowledge accompanies every form of action—no matter how concretely it is formulated (Westerman, 1989).

The theories grouped together in this chapter have one principle in common: it is through the process of self-awareness, self-understanding, self-revelation that true growth occurs. Whether in a gradual clarification of feelings or in a brief spurt of insight, whether facilitated through open sharing or in-depth interpretations, whether focused on the present, past, or future, the theories treated in this chapter work through the process of self-discovery. Their unifying dimension is the belief that insight into one's problems, along with a grasp of implications, connections, consequences, and perspectives, is a necessary prerequisite before any real and lasting change can occur.

CLIENT-CENTERED COUNSELING

Aliases: Nondirective, Person-Centered, Humanistic, Rogerian, Self Theory

Originator and Revisionists

Before Carl Rogers entered the scene, therapeutic counseling was largely a directive, prescriptive enterprise consisting of advice, diagnoses, interpretations, and authority. With the publication of his books (Rogers, 1942, 1951), the field was irreversibly pushed in the direction of giving clients more autonomy and responsibility for their treatment. Client-centered counseling caught on quickly because of its optimistic philosophy, which emphasized the wonderful potential of humans to learn, grow, and heal themselves when given the opportunity within a nurturing therapeutic relationship. Further, nondirective counseling became attractive to North Americans as their first native-born approach, one that stressed positive concepts and relatively simple interventions.

Rogers also strongly influenced two other theorists who were later to refine and adapt his ideas, thus reaching a larger audience. Robert Carkhuff and his colleagues (Truax, Berenson, and Gendlin) ingeniously combined techniques of behavioral analysis into a helping model that presented simplified counselor skills as the essence of constructive intervention. Carkhuff has become the most frequently quoted professional of our time through his systematic research on the dimensions of human nourishment originally identified by Rogers: empathy, respect, genuineness, and concreteness. Carkhuff also helped to convert Rogerian philosophy into a system of action. Thomas Gordon is another adapter of client-centered counseling; he created a popular educational system for training parents (Gordon, 1970) and teachers (Gordon, 1974) by applying the skills of "active listening" to clarify a person's feelings.

In more recent times the client-centered approach has been championed by such writers as Boy and Pine (1990), who have sought to bring Rogers's concepts of humanism into the mainstream of all counseling practice.

Basic Assumptions

Most client-centered counselors are in basic agreement that:

1. Human beings are growth oriented and tend toward self-actualization. This natural process of development toward higher stages of moral, emotional, and behavioral evolution can be facilitated by professional helpers who are able to stimulate the inherent capacity for progress in clients who are temporarily stymied or faltering.

2. The necessary and sufficient condition for change to occur is the therapeutic relationship, which exudes qualities of trust, openness, acceptance, permissiveness, and warmth. The degree to which the counselor is able to create this nurturing atmosphere will influence the client's possibilities for growth.

3. The legitimate focus of counseling content is on affect and thorough exploration of feelings. Both interpersonal relationships and the self-concept may be improved by becoming aware of feelings about oneself and others and by learning to express these emotions in sensitive and self-enhancing ways.

4. The client/student has primary responsibility for the course of treatment/study—what constitutes appropriate content and whether, ultimately, it succeeds. There is thus a goal shared by client and counselor and a mutual understanding of the client's world.

5. Human beings are intrinsically good and trustworthy. They will instinctively move, in a deliberate way, toward goals that are satisfying and socially responsible. Irresponsible or socially undesirable behavior emerges from a defensiveness that alienates human beings from their own nature. As defensiveness declines and persons become more open to their own experiences, they will strive for meaningful and constructive relationships.

Personality Development

Client-centered counseling has not developed an elaborate, well-integrated theory of personality functioning but, rather, has defined a series of formal propositions

(Rogers, 1951, 1959). These statements reflect a perspective about human beings that is philosophically phenomenological and has drawn much from self theory:

1. "Every individual exists in a continually changing world of experience of which he is the center" (Rogers, 1951, p. 483). This proposition emphasizes the central importance of the individual and the subjective nature of personal experience. One can never really "know" the full experiences and perceptions of another person.

2. "The organism reacts to the field as it is experienced and perceived. The perceptual field is, for the individual, 'reality' " (Rogers, 1951, p. 484). Reality, for the individual, exists only in subjective terms. Therefore, to work effectively with another, one must enter that person's perceptual field and begin to experience his or her reality.

3. "Behavior is basically the goal-directed attempt of the organism to satisfy its needs as experienced, in the field as perceived" (Rogers, 1951, p. 491). Persons are intentional in their behavior, which is defined by their perceptual field and experienced needs. A lack of awareness of needs or options tends to limit and restrict behavior. Psychological reality for an individual is based on experienced needs and perceptions, regardless of the objective truth.

4. "The best vantage point for understanding behavior is from the internal frame of reference of the individual himself" (Rogers, 1951, p. 494). To understand another requires concentrating on the reality that exists subjectively for that person. Therapeutically, it is necessary to experience people from an empathic, subjective frame of reference while helping them to expand their awareness to include a greater proportion of the external, objective reality.

5. "Most of the ways of behaving adopted by the organism are consistent with the concept of self " (Rogers, 1951, p. 507). Rogers believes that the *self-concept* is essential to an understanding of the individual. The self-concept is the organized and integrated image that is a compromise between the self perceived by others and that perceived by oneself. It tends to be a relatively stable guide for behavior and changes only when internal dissonance is experienced.

Favorite Techniques

Client-centered counseling is hardly technique oriented, preferring instead to explore curative variables and refine philosophical assumptions; nevertheless, there are a few standard intervention strategies. The bread-and-butter technique of the client-centered counselor (as well as of many others) is reflection of feelings, also referred to as active listening. Communicating from a posture of empathic understanding, the counselor intently attends to a client's verbal and nonverbal messages, interprets the surface and underlying meanings, and then formulates a response that demonstrates a deep-level understanding of the client's feelings. This technique has its advantages:

1. Although it is the most difficult counseling skill to master, it is relatively simple to learn and fosters an open and honest helping relationship.

2. Even if the reflection of feeling is inaccurate and ignores the client's actual messages, it still encourages further self-exploration.

COUNSELOR:
    You sound so angry at your brother for not writing you to join him.
CLIENT:
    No. Not really. I'm not so much angry at him as I am frustrated at myself
    for not telling him it was important that I go.

3. It helps the client to feel reassured that he or she is deeply understood
and accepted for his or her feelings.

STUDENT:
    I really think it's stupid to give us an exam in a class like this that empha-
    sizes skills instead of stuff to memorize.
PROFESSOR:
    You feel like I don't treat you with enough respect, and you also have
    some real concerns about how well you are doing in this class.

4. It clarifies a client's feelings so that the situation may be viewed more
objectively.

CLIENT:
    My father always butts into my life when he can't take care of his own.
COUNSELOR:
    You are really afraid that, although you love your father very much, you
    may follow in his footsteps as a disaster in love relationships.

5. It provides an opportunity for emotional catharsis, bringing relief of
pent-up tensions and pressure.

CLIENT:
    I don't know how I feel about it.
COUNSELOR:
    You're afraid to let yourself feel.
CLIENT:
    You're damn right I am! I gave that bastard the best years of my life. I
    don't know whether to cry, scream, fight, or give up. I'm so confused.

6. It encourages the client to move from superficial concerns to deeper,
more significant problems.

CLIENT:
    I don't know. I've just never had good study habits. You have any tricks
    for doing better on "true/false" exams?

COUNSELOR:
> You have some real reservations about your ability to discipline yourself. You sometimes feel like you aren't smart enough to hack college and are afraid that, even if you do study, you'll flunk out anyway.

Encounter groups are another favorite application of the client-centered approach, since they provide additional opportunities for developing a climate of trust, freedom, honest feedback, interpersonal interaction, and improved communications, as well as a reduction of defensiveness, inhibitions, rigidity, and game playing (Rogers, 1970). In the client-centered group format, ground rules are established that encourage participants to be as honest as possible with themselves and others. They are urged to stay in the present, to become aware of their feelings, to express them straightforwardly, and to take risks within the safety of a trusting, cohesive, and intimate group experience.

It is important to mention that client-centered counselors subordinate the use of techniques to the attitudes of the counselor and the relationship created with the client. Those interventions that are emphasized include active listening, reflection of feelings, and clarifications, whereas directive techniques such as interpretation, questioning, probing, and diagnosis are minimized.

Criticisms of Client-Centered Counseling

Although a valuable and, at the time of its inception, a radical departure from psychoanalysis, client-centered counseling can be criticized on several grounds:

1. It may give too much responsibility to the client and reduce the role of the counselor as the trained expert. Counselors may merely reflect back what the client has said.
2. It may be somewhat naive in its view of clients as naturally evolving and lofty in goals that may not be possible. Counselors, for example, may be unable to create "unconditional positive regard," since everything is ultimately conditional.
3. It does not respond to the difficulties encountered in translating feelings into action.
4. It is narrow in its focus on affect and tends to ignore thoughts and behavior.
5. It may overemphasize the importance of relationship factors, which may be a necessary but not sufficient condition for therapeutic change.
6. It is not useful for clients who are in crisis and require directive intervention.
7. It tends to be more useful for highly verbal clients and less appropriate for those who have difficulty expressing themselves.

Personal Applications

Principles of client-centered counseling can help you to:

1. Create greater self-awareness, especially with regard to your feelings, and

thereby expand growth and congruence. It helps one to create a growth orientation and encourages an active attitude toward life and personal growth.

2. Gain appreciation for the importance of genuineness, unconditional acceptance, and empathy in dealing with other persons.

3. Take more responsibility for your own education and life experiences.

4. Recognize the importance of exploring your feelings, risking, and sharing
them with others.

5. Acknowledge the need to suspend your own values and judgments as you
encounter other persons so that you may experience their inner reality.

EXISTENTIAL COUNSELING

Aliases: Humanistic, Phenomenological, Experiential

Originators

Existentialism is a particularly rich and difficult theory because it intersects so
many different fields. It had a long and distinguished career as a philosophy
long before it was recruited to the more practical dimensions of reality in therapeutic counseling. Beginning with Socrates and continuing onward into the 20th
century, such well-known philosophers as Kierkegaard, Nietzsche, Heidegger,
Husserl, Tillich, and Marcel have led an international search for the ultimate
meaning of human existence. These complex philosophies were later absorbed
into the world of art (Cezanne, Picasso, Van Gogh, Chagall) and literature
(Kafka, Camus, Sartre, Dostoyevsky). Existentialism has now been translated
into a style of living, a way of being that encourages a person to use and accept
anxiety constructively (May, 1983). Fortunately, it is not necessary to comprehend fully existentialist philosophy in order to make use of its concepts in therapeutic counseling. For our purposes, we will concentrate our discussion on its
practical applications. Frankl (1962) adapted existential thinking to survival
strategies in Nazi concentration camps during World War II. The main determi-
nant, according to Frankl, of an inmate's likelihood of living or giving up and
dying was the ability to create a personal meaning to the experience: "If there is
a meaning in life at all, then there must be a meaning in suffering. Suffering is
an ineradicable part of life, even as fate and death. Without suffering and death
human life cannot be complete" (Frankl, 1962, p. 106).

Whether a rationalization or justification of the unjustifiable, Frankl
observed the importance of the basic existential hallmarks in the everyday life of
anyone who suffers humiliation and pain—in a hospital, death camp, or counselor's office. Freedom, choice, being, responsibility, and meaning are the ideas
that helped him to survive and those that help clients to flourish:

> We who lived in concentration camps can remember the men who walked through
> the huts comforting others, giving away their last piece of bread. They may have
> been few in number, but they offer sufficient proof that everything can be taken

from a man but one thing: the last of the human freedoms—to choose one's attitude in any given set of circumstances, to choose one's own way [Frankl, 1962, p. 104].

May (1958) introduced this previously European philosophy to North American psychotherapists and counselors. The focus of therapeutic intervention is to help clients become responsible for their choices, to manage their freedom and thereby transcend the meaninglessness of their lives, moving into a more authentic existence. May has contributed a series of books on love, power, creativity, anxiety, freedom, and various other issues of existential relevance. His goal has been to assist the client to develop insight regarding the life forces that can be mobilized to overcome the existential crises of powerlessness and freedom:

> After many a therapeutic hour which I would call successful, the client leaves with more anxiety than he had when he came in; only now the anxiety is conscious rather than unconscious, constructive rather than destructive. The definition of mental health needs to be changed to living without *paralyzing* anxiety, but living with normal anxiety is a stimulant to a vital existence, as a source of energy, and as life enhancing [May, 1981, p. 19].

If anxiety has its usefulness, so too does the concept of death to the existentialist. Yalom (1980), in his definitive text *Existential Psychotherapy*, writes about the idea of death as the primary savior of humankind because it motivates an intense appreciation of life's value. By confronting our own vulnerability, the ultimate threat to our existence, we are made aware of people and things that are truly important. Death and the companion existential issues of isolation, meaninglessness, and freedom are seen as the legitimate focus of counseling. Yalom (1985) was able to translate much of the confusion, complex language, and abstract ideas of existentialism into a system of helping and an attitude for the helper, complete with methodologies for analyzing and solving human problems.

Existential counseling is richly endowed in its affiliations with Rogers's person-oriented approach, Maslow and Shostrom's self-actualization psychology, and Freud's theory of psychoanalysis. Far from postulating a rigid set of therapeutic procedures, the existentialist offers a way of thinking about clients and their concerns, about humans and their dilemmas, and about life and its puzzles.

Premises of Existential Counseling

The existential approach has been minimally concerned with the techniques and specific interventions of counseling, concentrating instead on philosophical principles that aid the understanding of the client. As an insight-oriented theory, its main goal is to help people to find personal meaning in their actions, their lives, and their suffering. A counselor working from an existential posture would assist people primarily to develop the range of their choices, and hence their freedom to be. The four basic concepts of existential theory are (1) existence, (2) encounter, (3) authenticity, and (4) experiencing.

Clients who present the symptoms of existential anxiety (lack of meaning, fear of death, isolation, avoidance of responsibility) can be helped to become more capable of determining the outcome of their daily life. They become aware of their fears. They understand the significance and personal meaning of their refusal to enjoy freedom. They confront the naked fact that each person, from the moment of birth, stands alone. Yet, far from necessarily condemning the self to loneliness, we may choose to take responsibility for our aloneness, our freedom, our choices, and the consequences of what we choose. "The one who realizes in anguish his condition as being thrown into a responsibility which extends to his very abandonment has no longer either remorse or regret or excuse, he is no longer anything but a freedom which perfectly reveals itself and whose being resides in this very revelation" (Sartre, 1957, p. 59).

The existential counselor seeks to enter into the client's world and, remaining in the present, to use the therapeutic alliance—the relationship—as a fulcrum by which to lever more involvement and commitment to living, to being. This process of counseling and change is more than a little ambiguous. The existential approach is a philosophy, an attitude, a way of thinking, analyzing, and experiencing; it is, therefore, difficult to describe specifically how the counselor acts, even though a few techniques reluctantly emerge from the theory.

The basic distinguishing features of an existential approach include the following:

- a focus on issues of freedom
- a confrontation with fears of death, alienation, and aloneness
- an emphasis on taking responsibility for one's life
- a compatibility with other, more action-oriented, theories
- a challenge to discover the meanings behind one's choices and actions
- a search for a personal philosophy to guide daily life

Existentialism is basically an attitude toward living and, as such, emphasizes the role of understanding and insight into the human condition. The counselor works toward knowing the client rather than knowing *about* him or her. The process of knowing includes the three separate modes of human existence: the client's natural, biological world; the interpersonal world; and the uncharted territory of the solitary individual in relationship to itself. It is the counselor's presence with the client rather than any specific technique that encourages growth to greater autonomy (May, 1983). The emphasis is on helping people to become more aware of how they limit themselves (Bugental, 1991).

Criticisms of Existential Counseling

Existentialism is often misunderstood by philosophers and can be obtuse to those of us who are untrained in this discipline. It has been described as a particularly abstract, ambiguous, mystical theory that is difficult to apply to the circumstances of everyday living. Also, because the philosophy is so intellectually complex, it is not often appropriate for clients who are of low to average intelligence or for people with severe emotional and cognitive disturbances. Needless to say, other individuals who are in the midst of a crisis or who are barely surviving in their basic economic needs are going to be relatively unconcerned with their "existential Angst" or "phenomenological nonbeing" as compared to other, more pressing problems.

The existential approach is also hard to study because it is nonempirical and doesn't lend itself to scientific scrutiny. Further, although practitioners of this theory are extremely versatile and flexible in their willingness to use a variety of techniques, there are relatively few specific interventions available.

Personal Applications

One exception to the criticism of ambiguity in the applications of existential techniques is the work of Viktor Frankl (1978) in the development of one strategy that is remarkably behavioral. Paradoxical intention is a means of reducing anticipatory anxiety for those with inhibiting obsessions/compulsions by breaking the vicious cycle of fearing fear itself. Paradoxically, "the patient is encouraged to do, or to wish to happen the very things he fears" (Frankl, 1978, p. 117).

Frankl describes the case of a 54-year-old woman addicted to sleeping pills. She was ordered to continue her symptoms; if the sleeplessness persisted, she would only be following her doctor's orders (and thus her anxiety would be reduced), and, if she disobeyed (as was more likely), she would thereby cure herself of the symptom. The technique works equally well with problems such as anxiety, obsessional neuroses, and vicious-cycle syndromes.

Yalom, an expert on group techniques as well as an active proponent of the existential approach, describes several practical strategies that force clients to consider introspectively their phenomenological positions with respect to issues of responsibility, isolation, death, and freedom. One dramatic exercise works well in group sessions and is also constructive for individual reflection. In fact, even in this moment you are reading *about* existential ideas instead of *experiencing* them. The purpose of this exercise is to help participants to experience rather than to understand cognitively. It might be helpful for you to try this experience in your "here and now."

On eight separate slips of paper, write answers to the question "Who am I?" (Do that now.)

Next, arrange your answers in order of importance to you. (Go on—do it!)

Taking the cards in order of their personal significance, spend a few minutes with each one, thinking about how your life would be different without that attribute. This journey to the "center of pure self-consciousness" can be possible only after the layers of intellect, emotion, and desire are stripped away.

Here is a second existential exercise that is even simpler (or deceptively so at first glance): on a sheet of paper draw a straight line (or feel free to use the line provided). One end of that line represents your birth; the other end, your death.

Sigmund Freud (1856–1939), founder of psychoanalysis and all therapeutic counseling.

Draw an intersected line to represent where you are now (Yalom, 1980, p. 174).

Birth ———————————————————————————————— *Death*

Meditate on your feelings, thoughts, and reactions for a few minutes.

Anyone can become more existentially grounded by attempting to live more in the present, to appreciate every waking moment, to use the idea of eventual death as a strong motivation to become more intensely involved in life. We can give meaning to our lives only by directly confronting our motives and values and by choosing our life and world.

PSYCHOANALYTIC COUNSELING

Aliases: Psychoanalysis, Analysis, Freudian Psychotherapy, Psychodynamic Therapy

Originators

The profession of therapeutic counseling can be traced to Sigmund Freud and his early experimentations with hypnosis and the "talking cure," in which he allowed hysterical patients to reveal their innermost unconscious desires. From the late 19th century until his death in exile from his native Austria at the out-break of World War II, Freud not only revolutionized our conceptions of human psychology but singlehandedly recruited an army of psychoanalytic thinkers to continue his work. Carl Jung, Otto Rank, Alfred Adler, Wilhelm Reich, Karen Horney, Theodore Reik, Franz Alexander, Harry Stack Sullivan, Erik Erikson, Erich Fromm, Heinz Kohut, and Anna Freud form an impressive list of theorists, brilliant in their own right, who were able to expand, revise, and adapt the psychoanalytic approach to their respective settings, situations, and personalities. As a footnote, it is important to realize that even the creators of completely new schools of counseling, such as Fritz Perls, Albert Ellis, Eric Berne, and Rollo May, were once practicing psychoanalysts who grew beyond the confines of traditional psychoanalysis.

An additional point of clarification: there is a difference between "psycho-analysis," the orthodox application of Freudian theory, and "psychoanalytically oriented approaches," which make use of some Freudian concepts but are more flexible in their application, according to the preferences of the practitioner. Some theorists have successfully abbreviated psychoanalytic methods into a short-term psychodynamic approach that can be more efficient, economical, and appropriate for counseling settings (Malan, 1963; Sifneos, 1967; Davanloo, 1978; Bauer & Kobos, 1984; Strupp & Binder, 1984). Our discussion will focus on some of the more universal and practical ideas of psychoanalytic theory, those that are most relevant to the practice of counseling.

Basic Psychoanalytic Concepts

Traditional psychoanalysis is very complex. Its practice requires five years of intensive postdoctoral training, which includes undergoing personal treatment as well as seminars in order to have a working knowledge of the theory. Many terms and words of psychoanalysis have crept into our everyday language—for example, "ego," "catharsis," "unconscious," "oral stage," and "rationaliza-tion"—making a basic understanding of some important ideas necessary for any practicing counselor. Even for those who have no intention of ever using this particular style of helping, the conceptual vocabulary of psychoanalysis has become crucial as a mode of communication with other professionals, as an ori-entation toward analyzing the etiology and development of human problems, and as a foundational base for constructing new therapeutic strategies. The fol-lowing sections discuss some of the most basic psychoanalytical concepts.

Layers of Awareness. Freud introduced the concept of different levels of awareness that motivate behavior. He postulated that there are several regions of the mind: the *conscious mind,* which contains those thoughts and feelings that are always accessible; the *preconscious mind,* which holds elements on the edge of awareness that, with minimal effort, can be made immediately accessible; and the *unconscious mind,* which harbors the secrets of the soul.

Each layer of awareness can be peeled away, providing deeper access into the human psyche, only by permitting unconscious thoughts to surface. This task may be accomplished through *analysis of dreams, free association* of thoughts, *catharsis* of feelings, and *interpretations* that provide a level of insight sufficient to release unconscious, inhibiting desires and facilitate their continued awareness.

Stages of Personality Development. As a medically trained physician, Freud had a particular interest in neurology and the instinctual basis of behavior. He thus viewed the development of human personality as following a series of biologically determined stages, each an expression of the *pleasure principle*—the child's insatiable urge to reduce tension and maintain psychic equilibrium by self-indulgence in oral, anal, or genital preoccupations. Freud's original conception of psychosexual development is often paired with a more recent adaptation by Erikson (1950), which has more contemporary relevance for counselors seeking to understand the orderly progression of human development. Freud was concerned mostly with early childhood development and its impact on later life; Erikson's stages more accurately reflect growth throughout the life cycle, with a particular emphasis on social influences. The two sequences of stages are compared in Table 5-1.

Structure of the Psyche. The healthy personality, according to Freud, consists of three separate systems, which function harmoniously and cooperatively to satisfy a person's basic needs and desires. Each of these aspects of personality is less discrete than the structure suggests and should more accurately be considered as an approximate description of processes that influence who one is and how one reacts to the world around one.

The *id* is the source of all energy and instinctual drives. Its sole psychological function is to reduce tension, discomfort, and pain at all costs. The id is impulsive, demanding, and infantile in its wishes, acting without thought or consideration of consequences.

The *ego* is the contact between the id's uncontrolled energy and the world of reality. The ego rationally, intelligently, and logically attempts to harness and moderate blind action. The ego is an integrator, pacifier, negotiator, and compromiser that seeks in socially acceptable and appropriate ways to fulfill a person's needs.

The *superego* is concerned primarily with moral issues. It is the ideal part of oneself, as contrasted with reality or pleasure. Operating as one's conscience, it strives for perfection and virtuousness. In its battle waged against the hedonistic id, the superego often takes home the spoils of "pride" or "guilt," depending on the ego's chosen resolution of the conflict.

Defense Mechanisms. The *defense mechanisms* are a major contribution of psychoanalysis to practicing counselors. According to their descriptions, the defenses used by the ego to guard against perceived attack are analogous to the workings of our body's immunological system to maintain a constant equilibrium of fluid temperature, pressure, and content. Change is the enemy. Just as

TABLE 5-1. Developmental Stages of Personality

Age	0–1	2–3	4–5	6–11	12–18	Early Adulthood	Middle Age	Late Maturity
Freud's stages of psychosexual development	Oral	Anal	Phallic	Latent	Genital			
	Mouth as source of pleasure. Oral deprivation leads to oral fixation. Origins of aggressive impulses. Character of greediness, trust, rejection, insecurity, jealousy, hostility is established.	Parental demands require bowel control. Origins of frustration, independence, anger, fastidiousness, stubbornness, control of self and others.	Growth of incestuous desire for parent and birth of repression. Origins of fear, fantasy, unconscious, identification, sexual attitudes, and guilt.	Resting reprieve from tension; origins of narcissism in self-perception, socialization process.	Need for satisfaction in sex and work. Development of altruism and love relationships. Healthy personality stabilized.			
Erikson's stages of personality development	*Trust versus mistrust*	*Autonomy versus shame and doubt*	*Initiative versus guilt*	*Industry versus inferiority*	*Identity versus role confusion*	*Intimacy versus isolation*	*Generativity versus stagnation*	*Integrity versus despair*
	Quality of maternal relationship leads to security, affection, hope, or fear and suspicion. Consistent, dependable care will foster a trusting nature.	Freedom and support of free will and struggle for independence. Origins of fear of failure and doubt; shame over rebellious nature.	Child can initiate rather than respond—inquisitive and adventurous spirit evolves. Excessive restrictions will foster more guilt over natural urge to explore.	Realization of basic competencies, striving to compete and excel; criticism leads to sense of inferiority.	Search for sex, age, and career identity—for individuality as a person. Inability to establish stability creates confusion.	Overcoming safety of social distances to love and the fear of losing self in the process.	Issues of productivity and guiding next generation take precedence unless self-absorption and stagnation dominate.	Realization of wisdom and period of reflection about life or regret over lost opportunity.

we are unaware of the antibodies in our bloodstream when they are activated to fight foreign protein molecules, our psychological defense mechanisms operate without our conscious awareness in an attempt to reduce anxiety and lower tension. They are ingenious strategies, impressive in their variety and flexibility; but these unconscious mind-directed defenses make the job of counseling and facilitating changes much more difficult. Better we should recognize the opponents that will be resisting our best treatment efforts:

repression—the selective exclusion of painful experiences of the past from conscious awareness; a form of censorship used to block traumatic episodes.

projection—the art of putting onto another person those characteristics that are unacceptable to ourselves, such as accusing someone of being angry when we are actually feeling the anger.

denial—distortion of reality by pretending that undesirable or unacceptable events are not really happening. In contrast to repression, denial occurs on a preconscious rather than unconscious level.

sublimation—the disguised conversion of forbidden impulses into socially acceptable behaviors. For instance, athletes may unconsciously choose their profession as a way to release aggression. Creative enterprises such as da Vinci's paintings or Shakespeare's sonnets were seen by Freud as sublimated unacceptable sexual desires.

reaction formation—used to counter perceived threats, the substitution of an opposite reaction for the one that is disturbing. Guilt can be replaced by indignation, hatred by devotion, or resentment by overprotection.

rationalization—intellectual misuse of logic to overexplain or justify conflicting messages. For example, "It doesn't matter if I type the paper or not; I'll probably flunk the class anyway."

displacement—rechanneling of energy from one object to another, as when an infant sucks a finger or another object in place of the desired breast.

identification—incorporation, in exaggerated form, of the values, attitudes, standards, and characteristics of persons who are anxiety provoking, as when a child punishes herself for being bad.

regression—a retreat to an earlier stage of development because of fear. Any flight from controlled and realistic thinking may constitute a regression.

fixation—the tendency to remain at one level, interrupting the normal plan of psychological development. It is generally a defense against anxiety and results from the fear of taking the next psychological step of development.

In general, defense mechanisms are irrational methods used by the ego to deal with anxiety. They tend to distort, hide, or deny reality and hinder psychological development. They are essential to the infantile ego because of the lack of ego strength; however, they will persist when the ego has not matured sufficiently. One goal of therapeutic counseling, from the perspective of psychoanalytic theory, is to foster the healthy development of the ego.

Criticisms of Psychoanalytic Counseling

Traditional psychoanalytic counseling has been criticized on a number of grounds, many of which relate to its deterministic philosophy and inflexible closed-system approach:

1. The expense and time involved in psychoanalytic treatment are considerable, requiring lengthy training for the counselor and treatment for the client that could run into years.
2. It is not useful as an approach for treating large numbers of people who require counseling services.
3. There is an overemphasis on the role of insight and very little emphasis on making life changes.
4. The approach is based on experiences with neurotic rather than normal populations and may be skewed in the direction of sickness instead of health.
5. The concepts of psychoanalytic theory are difficult to research and support empirically.
6. Traditional Freudian psychoanalysis places excessive emphasis on basic instinctual desires and forces, ignoring the effects of social and cultural factors.
7. It is not useful for persons in crisis who require immediate relief of symptoms.

It has become so fashionable to criticize Freud's ideas, especially the rigidity with which some psychoanalysts function, that many valuable therapeutic concepts have been discarded in the backlash. In part to answer their critics and in part to make the treatment more realistic, the core of psychoanalytic thinking has been preserved by some theorists in a new short-term form of therapeutic counseling. More focus is placed on specific problem areas (Bauer & Kobos, 1984). The treatment is more individually designed, and the counselor confronts resistance more directly (Bennett, 1984). Efforts are made to establish time limits for both the length of treatment and specific goals (Dasberg & Winoker, 1984). Finally, the clinician plays a more active role in interpreting transference issues and in linking them to previous relationships (Davanloo, 1978).

Personal Applications

One of the distinguishing features of psychoanalytic theory is the strong emphasis placed on applying the concepts and techniques to one's own life. In a revealing letter to a friend, Freud remarked on his own painful struggles with self-analysis, which eventually led to further refinements of his ideas:

15. 10. 97.
IX. Bergasse 19

My dear Wilhelm,

My self-analysis is the most important thing I have in hand, and promises to be of the greatest value to me, when it is finished. When I was in the very midst of it it suddenly broke down for three days, and I had the feeling of inner binding about which my patients complain so much, and I was inconsolable. . . .

It is no easy matter. Being entirely honest with oneself is a good exercise. Only one idea of general value has occurred to me. I have found love of the mother and jealousy of the father in my own case too, and now believe it to be a general phenomenon of early childhood . . . [Freud, 1954, pp. 221, 223].

The theory and techniques of psychoanalysis naturally lend themselves to personal experimentation; it was that exact method that Freud employed in their invention. Interpreting dreams is an especially fruitful method of understanding our unconscious desires and avoiding resistance, since even our defense mechanisms sleep at night. Other techniques designed to unlock the secrets of the soul include hypnosis and free association. In applying any of these strategies to ourselves, it is crucial to follow Freud's imperative that we be entirely honest about our desires, wishes, and motives.

GESTALT COUNSELING
Originators and Basic Concepts

Gestalt counseling has distinguished roots that go back to the very beginning of psychology as a discipline. Scientists interested in the process of learning and perception noted that problem solving is less a gradual phenomenon than it is a critical moment of insight. Kurt Koffka (1935) and Wolfgang Köhler (1929) spent considerable time between the world wars creating certain laws of behavior that could be used to explain the process of learning. For example, they noted that we tend to perceive things grouped together as clusters, according to their proximity to one another, and that we learn to focus our attention selectively on those events, situations, or stimuli that provide internal psychological equilibrium, even though we may thereby distort reality.

The basic goal of Gestalt theory is to describe human existence in terms of awareness. Gestalt counseling has been influenced philosophically by existentialism and psychologically by humanism. Each of these influences has reinforced experience as the central concept upon which awareness is built. Gestalt therapy focuses on the *what* and *how* of behavior and on the central role of unfinished business from the past that interferes with effective functioning in the present. By helping individuals more fully to experience the present—the "here and now"—Gestalt counselors facilitate greater self-awareness and understanding.

Gestalt counseling is most closely associated with Fritz Perls (1969a), who organized the contemporary Gestalt movement in California and was its central figure until his death in 1970. Gestalt counseling is essentially experiential rather than theoretical and to a large extent is strongly influenced by the character and person of the practitioner. This was certainly true in the case of Perls, who was a charismatic personality.

Gestalt counseling stresses the role of personal responsibility in the development of awareness and experiencing of feelings. *Unfinished business* from the past is brought into the present, and the impasse it represents is dealt with therapeutically. *Being "stuck"* is a term used to describe the inability to resolve

Fritz Perls (1893–1970), originator of gestalt counseling.

issues and thereby avoid dealing with the "now." *Polarization* is another key Gestalt concept; it refers to the various parts of the self that are in conflict. In his autobiography Perls interrupts the flow of his narrative to conduct an internal dialogue between his polarized, conflicted selves:

TOPDOG:

Stop, Fritz, what are you doing?

UNDERDOG:

What do you mean?

TOPDOG:

You know very well what I mean. You're drifting from one thing to another. . . .

UNDERDOG:

I still don t see your objection.

TOPDOG:

You don't see my objection? Man, who the hell can get a clear picture of your therapy?

UNDERDOG:

You mean I should take a blackboard and make tables and categorize every term, every opposite neatly?

TOPDOG:

    That's not a bad idea. You could do that. . . .

UNDERDOG:

    So what do you want me to do? Stop letting the river flow? Stop playing my garbage bin game?

TOPDOG:

    Well, that wouldn't be a bad idea, if you would sit down and discipline yourself. . . .

UNDERDOG:

    Go to hell. You know me better. If I try to do something deliberate and under pressure, I get spiteful and go on strike. All my life I have been a drifter . . . [Perls, 1969b, pp. 117-118].

Techniques of Gestalt Therapy

There are literally hundreds of techniques that have been developed for Gestalt work. A few of the more common ones are the following.

Hot Seat. This technique requires an individual to be the focus of attention and answer all questions with complete honesty and sincerity. The participant is challenged to be the "here-and-now" self at all times, a task that is quite difficult, considering the intensity of questions that could be posed: "What is your most common fantasy?" "What in your life are you most ashamed of?" "Which person in the group are you most attracted to and why?" "What question are you afraid we might ask?"

Resentment Expression. Perls believed that it was essential to express resentments, which, if unexpressed, are converted to guilt. To take an example: make a list of all the things about which you consciously feel guilty. Now change the word guilt to resentment. "I feel guilty because I do not spend enough time with my children" becomes "I resent having to spend time with my children." Exploring and expressing the resentment can help a person become unstuck and work through unfinished business.

Double Chairing. This technique is designed to help persons to experience the opposite poles of the self. The counselor explores a problem with a client and identifies the opposing feelings. Two chairs are then set up, and the client is instructed to take one and talk to the empty chair from one (specified) pole of the issue. On instruction from the counselor, the client moves to the second chair and talks from the opposite perspective. For example: "I can't stand the way my wife puts me down for everything, and I won't take it. I won't spend another minute in that house. I'm going to ask for a divorce and stick with it. Being alone is better than this misery." From the opposite pole: "Even though I feel very dissatisfied and maybe even angry with my wife, I really need to try harder to make this marriage work. We have a lot of years invested, our kids deserve an intact home, and I really don't like the idea of being alone and starting over. Besides, I'm not the easiest guy to live with." The purpose of this technique is to increase the awareness of feelings, resentments, fears, and issues from each pole of the individual's experience.

Owning the Projection. In this exercise the client is encouraged to apply his or her projections to himself or herself to demonstrate how we sometimes avoid our negatively perceived qualities and traits by putting them onto others. For example, a client says to a group member "I think you are manipulative" and then says "I am manipulative." Or, "I don't think you are trustworthy" and then "I don't think I am trustworthy."

Criticisms of Gestalt Counseling

As is immediately evident from this brief presentation, Gestalt counseling is considerably different from the other insight theories in that little attempt has been made by its creators to explain concepts and more emphasis has been placed on experiential aspects. Consequently, the Gestalt approach is rich in strategies to help the client and counselor stay in the "here and now" and work toward greater integration of the self's polarities.

However, Gestalt counseling has been soundly criticized for its lack of a clearly articulated theory and its limited empirical base. Among other criticisms are these:

1. There is a tendency for counselors to be overly manipulative and controlling.
2. Gestalt counseling is sometimes viewed as anti-intellectual because cognitive/thinking factors are greatly deemphasized.
3. Gestalt counseling is sometimes viewed as gimmicky and having a high potential for abuse.
4. It sometimes encourages a "do your own thing" attitude, which can create a sense of irresponsibility.
5. There is very little emphasis on acquiring behaviorally useful life skills.

HONORABLE MENTIONS

Because of space limitations and the vast array of theoretical orientations, only a few counseling approaches could be described in any detail. We would, however, like to mention several other insight-focused therapies that have been influential in the field. Our decision not to give them as much space as the ideas discussed above is based solely on our perception that they *currently* exert less influence on the field than those previously mentioned. That is not to say that these theories are not potentially as valuable or useful as the ones we have chosen to present; it is more a matter of our personal opinion about what is most appropriate for beginning students.

Transactional Analysis

Transactional analysis was developed by Eric Berne (1961), a San Francisco psychiatrist, in the 1950s and 1960s and has grown rapidly since that time. More commonly known as TA, it was developed as one of the first therapies for the lay public and used group treatment as its primary modality. It has enjoyed wide appeal and great popularity, and several TA books have become bestsellers: *Games People Play* (Berne, 1964), *I'm OK—You're OK* (Harris, 1969), and *What Do You Say after You Say Hello?* (Berne, 1972).

Transactional analysis adopts an antideterministic view of human behavior, believes that persons who suffer from emotional problems are intelligent and capable, and believes that all people can remake old decisions that have led to problems. Berne believed that humans are motivated by those basic psychological needs that he termed *stimulus hunger, structure hunger,* and *position hunger.*

Stimulus hunger is the need to be acknowledged or affirmed by others, both psychologically and physically. This need is satisfied by strokes, or the recognition of other people, which Berne believed were essential to life. Strokes can be either positive (smiles, hugs) or negative (frowns, slaps) and constitute the basic units of human interaction.

Structure hunger refers to the ways in which we use time to maximize the number of strokes received. Berne (1972) identified several options that people have:

1. Withdrawal: escape into the safety of the self to avoid risk. In this mode it is necessary to live on "stored" strokes or to fantasize "artificial" strokes.
2. Rituals and pastimes: interactions based on greetings, pleasantries, and other low-risk, noninvolving social conversations.
3. Activities: time, structured in goals, work, and hobbies, that typically brings strokes from others.
4. Games: interaction based on unwritten rules designed to create a payoff. Games are usually dishonest and covert and generate negative payoffs. They are the most common disturbance in interpersonal behavior.
5. Intimacy: a method of structuring time that, unlike the other four, is designed to bring people together, not keep them apart. It is based on honest, open, and mutual relationships, which carry the highest risks but also offer the greatest rewards of all interactions.

The issues of time structuring in our lives are personalized by James and Jongeward (1971). Consider their questions for yourself:

- What did your parents say about time? Did they use phrases such as: "You only live once"; "Enjoy it while you may"; "Don't waste your time"; "What are you going to do, sit around all day? Get going"; or "Relax, honey, there's always another day"?
- Are you fighting time? Killing it? Using it? Enjoying it?

- Now select an average weekday and try to determine what percentage of your time is structured with rituals, pastimes, withdrawing, activities, games, and intimacy [p. 66].

Position hunger is the need to have decisions affirmed; to be told we're OK. It is a reflection of intrinsic self-worth. Early in life one makes basic decisions about the self: either "I'm OK" or "I'm not OK." Once this decision about the self has been made, it provides a script for the ways in which a person structures time and seeks strokes.

Another aspect of transactional analysis refers to the three ego states of the personality structure: the Child, the Adult, and the Parent:

The *Child* is composed of the feelings and behaviors that were experienced in childhood. It contains spontaneous and natural feelings.

The *Parent* reflects the incorporation of attitudes, feelings, and behaviors from significant other adults during childhood. The parent ego state can be both nurturing and critical.

The *Adult* develops over time and reflects the ability to evaluate the reactions of the Child and Parent in an objective and factual manner. The Adult ego state develops throughout the life of the individual, whereas the Child and Parent remain static after 6 or 7 years of age.

The basic unit of communication in TA is the transaction, which consists of an exchange of strokes. Transactions can be complementary (that is, between equivalent ego states: Parent/Parent, Child/Child, or Adult/Adult) or crossed (that is, between nonequivalent ego states: "What time is it?" [Adult]; "How should I know?" [Child]).

The person in transactional analysis analyzes various interactions and attempts to increase personal autonomy and decrease the impact of self-defeating scripts and manipulative game playing. The person is freed from the contaminating and troublesome aspect of Child/Parent in order to experience choices in the present without the limitations of the past.

Adlerian Counseling

Alfred Adler, another of Freud's disciples who went his own way, developed a remarkably integrative theory for his time—one that combined some of the premises of psychoanalysis with a more pragmatic approach that emphasized such ideas as: (1) the social context for human behavior, (2) the interpersonal nature of client problems, (3) the cognitive organization of a client's style of thinking, and (4) the importance of choice and responsibility in making decisions.

Adlerian counselors, while subscribing to the tenets above, are quite flexible in their style of practice. After all, they hold much in common with some of the existential practitioners (the emphasis on personal responsibility), the cognitive therapists (the focus on the subjective perception of reality), the psychoanalysts (attention to dreams and the unconscious), and even the behaviorists (the focus on specific tasks to be completed).

A resurgence of interest in Adlerian approaches has been evident in recent years, due in part to the systematic organization and explication of Adler's ideas by authors such as Lundin (1989), Sweeney (1989), and Dinkmeyer, Dinkmeyer, and Sperry (1987). Prior to these contemporary spokespeople, it was primarily Rudolf Dreikurs who popularized Adler's work. Dreikurs (1950) formulated five basic norms of Adlerian theory:

1. Socially embedded: All problems are basically social problems and emerge from the need to "belong" and find a place in the group. A well-adjusted person is oriented to and behaves in line with the needs of the social situation. A maladjusted person has faulty concepts, feelings of inferiority, and mistaken goals and is overly concerned with what others think of him or her and/or with "what is in it" for him or her.
2. Self-determining and creative: Adler believed that life is movement and that individuals have the power to change interactions by what they do. The belief that individuals can change and are active participants in their lives is the basis for such optimism.
3. Goal directed: Behavior, according to Adler, is directed toward goals that are inferred from the consequences of behavior. Looking for "causes" of behavior is unproductive because they are unknowable and, even if known, cannot be changed. Goals, once recognized, can be modified and represent a behavioral choice.
4. Subjective: Reality is as we perceive it and is not absolute. Adler further believed that it is not what happens to us that matters, but how we feel about it. As a result, Adler emphasized interactions and movement in all relationships as the units of analysis.
5. Holistic: Human beings are integrated, whole, and incapable of being reduced to discrete units. One must deal with the entire person.

In Adlerian psychology, feelings of inferiority are the basis of anxiety and are destructive to clients. Inferiority feelings are not "feelings" in the usual sense but are a belief system or a reasoning process about how one should be. One's response to inferiority feelings is the basis for character formation.

Adler (1958) believed that the purpose of counseling is to restore faith in the self to overcome these feelings of inferiority. The process of counseling contains four steps for the individual:

1. Become aware of our own prejudice. Recognize that as children we learned that we were not good enough as we were; thus, we were urged to do better.
2. Stop being afraid of making a mistake. Overconcern with error encourages more, not fewer, mistakes. Further, it is human to make mistakes; do we expect ourselves to be superhuman? Mistakes reflect an opportunity to learn if they are accepted and if we avoid discouragement.
3. Cultivate the courage to be imperfect. Working to resist self-evaluation and to do our best to respond to the needs of a situation is preferable to feeling

inadequate because we could improve performance. We don't have to be any better than we are.

4. Enjoy the pleasure in an activity. It is important not to reduce pleasure in life by being overly concerned with success, failure, or prestige. Learning to do one's best and accepting the outcome increase the pleasure in life.

The Adlerian approach is concerned with helping individuals develop a lifestyle that is socially responsible and personally fulfilling, one that allows for growth and a holistic integration. A person who is psychopathological is discouraged and has lost faith in the ability to change.

Character Analysis

Character analysis was initially developed by Karen Horney (1939) in response to Freud's theory of instincts. She believed that the core of neurosis emerged from cultural conditions and human relations rather than from instinctual energy. In character analysis, individuals are seen as one of three types: (1) the compliant type, (2) the detached type, and (3) the aggressive type. A compliant character type tends to move toward people, is somewhat dependent, and has prominent needs for love and approval. A detached character type does not create emotionally close relationships and is distant from self and others. An aggressive type has a strong need for power and control and often moves against people.

Horney believed that basic anxiety comes from the disturbed elements of a parent/child relationship and reflects the child's feeling of isolation and helplessness in a hostile world. Anxiety is produced by anything that disturbs a child's basic security in intimate family relationships. As an adult, the neurotic needs emerge as ways of dealing with anxiety. They include:

1. the need for affection and approval
2. the need for a partner to take over one's life
3. the need to restrict one's life to narrow borders
4. the need for power
5. the need to exploit others
6. the need for prestige
7. the need for personal admiration
8. the need for personal achievement
9. the need for self-sufficiency and independence
10. the need for protection

These needs are classified as neurotic because they are compulsive, reflect instability, and are unrealistic in their nature and expectations. Character analysis represents an analytic orientation to counseling that substitutes an exploration of social and cultural issues for Freud's analysis of instinctual drives. As an analytic or neo-Freudian approach, it shares both the advantages and the limitations of the psychoanalytic model.

SUMMARY

In this chapter we have presented some of the more prominent insight-oriented theories that influence therapeutic counseling. There are, of course, many we have neglected, such as the other psychodynamic approaches of Jung, Alexander, Bordin, Sullivan, Reich, and Fromm. Part of the task of developing into a mature therapeutic counselor is coming to terms, on a personal and intellectual level, with the many options available.

Each of the insight approaches presented offers the counselor a framework for understanding the client's world and a methodology for promoting greater self-awareness and self-understanding. It is assumed that such exploration and knowledge will lead a client toward making desired life changes. It is also believed that the presence of the counselor and the relationship between counselor and client provide nonspecific curative effects that are helpful in the process of being and becoming.

SUGGESTED READINGS

Adler, A. (1969). *The practice and theory of individual psychology*. Paterson, NJ: Littlefield, Adams.

Corey, G. (1991). *Theory and practice of counseling and psychotherapy* (4th ed.). Pacific Grove, CA: Brooks/Cole.

Freud, S. (1952). *A general introduction to psychoanalysis*. New York: Washington Square Press.

Jung, C. (1961). *Memories, dreams, reflections*. New York: Vintage Books.

May, R. (1983). *The discovery of being*. New York: W. W. Norton.

Perls, F. (1969). *In and out of the garbage pail*. Lafayette, CA: Real People Press.

Rogers, C. (1980). *A way of being*. Boston: Houghton Mifflin.

Strupp, H. H., & Binder, J. L. (1984). *Psychotherapy in a new key: A guide to time-limited dynamic psychotherapy*. New York: Basic Books.

Van Deurzen-Smith, E. (1988). *Existential counseling in practice*. Newbury Park, CA: Sage.

Yalom, I. (1989). *Love's executioner and other tales of psychotherapy*. New York: Basic Books.

CHAPTER SIX

ACTION-ORIENTED COUNSELING APPROACHES

BEHAVIORAL COUNSELING
    Conceptual Perspective
    Behavioral Technology
    Criticisms of the Behavioral
        Approach
RATIONAL-EMOTIVE
    COUNSELING
    Originators
    Basic Points of RET
    Therapeutic Techniques
    Criticisms of RET
    Personal Applications
STRATEGIC COUNSELING
    Origins
    Strategic Interventions
    Criticisms of Strategic
        Counseling
    Personal Applications

MULTIMODAL COUNSELING
    Originators
    Basic Concepts
    Premises of the Multimodal
        Approach
    Some Multimodal Techniques
    Criticisms of the Multimodal and
        Other Eclectic Approaches
HONORABLE MENTIONS
    Reality Therapy
    Expressive Therapies
SUMMARY
SUGGESTED READINGS

The theoretical perspectives presented in Chapter 5 emphasized the importance of self-awareness and understanding in the counseling process. The primary medium used in insight-based approaches is verbal intervention designed to promote the client's exploration of presenting complaints. In this chapter we will examine theories that stress not insight but interventions leading more directly to relief of symptoms. These approaches blend an emphasis on action with verbal processing to accomplish specific therapeutic goals.

Action-oriented approaches to counseling are generally characterized by their reliance on behaviorally specific interventions and outcome measures. The counselor in these approaches works actively to structure sessions so that concrete, observable, and measurable goals can be established and accomplished. The role of the counselor tends to be active and directive, working with the client to structure the sessions. Action-oriented counseling gives less attention than insight theories to the therapeutic relationship and to process, interpretation, and insight. Instead, its proponents emphasize a more objective and scientific approach to counseling that makes use of a variety of techniques and structures.

BEHAVIORAL COUNSELING

Aliases: Behaviorism, Behavior Modification, Behavior Therapy

Conceptual Perspective

The influence of behaviorism on counseling has come a long way since B. F. Skinner and his rigid prescriptions for human control and manipulation (Skinner, 1938, 1953). Once viewed as a radical counterpoint to the humanism of Carl Rogers and Abraham Maslow, behavioral principles have been assimilated into the mainstream of therapeutic counseling to the extent that even insight-oriented counselors regularly use many of the behavioral techniques such as thought stopping, goal setting, assertiveness training, relaxation training, systematic desensitization, and other methods of skill acquisition.

There are now so many different kinds of behavioral treatments currently in practice that it is difficult to lump them all together into a common camp. Some emphasize cognitive features; others stress reinforcement or modeling or self-control or behavioral analyses. Nevertheless, most behavioral approaches have the following elements in common: (1) an emphasis on the present rather than on the past, (2) attention to changing specific dysfunctional behaviors, (3) reliance on research as an integral partner for developing and testing interventions, and (4) a preference for carefully measuring treatment outcomes (Burke, 1989). It must be noted that these factors common to behavioral approaches are now more and more being integrated into many other counseling styles.

The term *behavioral counseling* was first introduced by John Krumboltz in 1964. He suggested that counselors should remind themselves that the purpose of their activity is to foster *behavioral* changes in clients; thus all counseling is ultimately behavioral (Krumboltz, 1965). From a behavioristic perspective, counseling can be viewed as the systematic use of procedures to reach mutually established therapeutic goals that will resolve client concerns and conflicts (Thoresen, 1969). The behavioral approach therefore views counseling less as a philosophy of life and more as a set of principles to be used in a targeted and situationally specific manner.

Although there are many variations on the behavioral approach to counseling, most proponents agree that clients' problems are the result of maladaptive learning patterns; treatment thus takes the form of learning new life skills. Concepts central to the work of a behavioral counselor include reinforcement (both operant and classical), social modeling, environmental changes, specific identification of problems and goals, and, especially, objective measurement of changes over time. In many ways behavioral counseling is viewed as an educational process that borrows heavily from learning theory and emphasizes the acquisition of more adaptive ways to act.

The work of Ivan Pavlov, with his salivating dogs and their responses to the ringing of dinner bells, John Watson's discovery that neurosis can be induced by scaring infants, and B. F. Skinner's fascination with teaching pigeons to play Ping-Pong are important milestones in the development of behaviorism. Those early research efforts were translated into action techniques for promoting systematic client change (Garfield & Bergin, 1986; Kanfer & Goldstein, 1991).

John Dollard and Neil Miller (1950) attempted to combine psychoanalytic insights and practical learning principles into a science of human behavior. Joseph Wolpe (1958, 1969) worked to apply Pavlov's classical conditioning to systematic desensitization. Julian Rotter and Albert Bandura worked independently on a behavioral approach that stressed the impact of social learning and modeling concepts, in which context behavior is shaped by the interactions of an individual personality with significant others. Kanfer and Phillips (1970) used Skinner's operant model as a basis for developing the methods we now know as "behavior modification." Within the counseling literature, significant contributors such as John Krumboltz (1966), Carl Thoresen (1969), and Ray Hosford (1969) have been active in translating learning-theory principles into therapeutic practice.

The theory of behavioral counseling is deceptively simple. We are born into the world basically empty headed, with a few reflexes. All our values, attitudes, preferences, emotional responses, thinking patterns, personality styles, and problems are the result of learned behavior. We are shaped by our environment, reinforced and molded by the world around us. A systematic and scientific approach is used to (1) identify specific behaviors in need of elimination or acquisition, (2) set objectives that are reasonable and desirable, (3) collect data on the client's functioning levels, (4) design and engineer initial change efforts, (5) isolate and diminish client resistance, (6) modify distracting variables, (7) monitor and assess the impact of planned interventions, and (8) make alterations as needed in the treatment plan (Gottman & Leiblum, 1974).

Behavioral Technology

One valuable tool of the researcher in general, and of behaviorists in particular, is the use of time-series charts for graphic portrayal of client change. This method helps the counselor to study a single case intensively, plotting baseline data and the results of therapeutic interventions. It aids in quantitatively and specifically describing the behaviors targeted for changes, as well as in noting the effects of any action. In Figure 6-1, the counselor has available at a glance a summary of the client's presenting problems and the results of several attempts to change the behavior.

A strength of the behavioral approach consists not only in its assessment procedures but in its wide variety of treatment strategies. Its technology of helping is consistently and reliably applied to produce observable client changes, which the behaviorist is skilled at identifying, measuring, and changing. Many behavioral methodologies, succinctly organized by Groden and Cautela (1981), are now part of the repertoire of every therapeutic counselor.

Operant-conditioning Procedures. Operant-conditioning procedures, including those based on the work of B. F. Skinner (1953) and other researchers, are methods in which the frequency of behavior may be increased or decreased according to the type and timing of stimuli presented. In positive reinforcement strategies the counselor hopes to increase behavior by rewarding the client. Implicitly, the most subtle head nods, "uh-huh's," smiles, and twinkling eyes positively reinforce the client's talking, trusting, and opening up. Operationally, this methodology is used in token economies with a variety of normal and maladjusted client populations, often in classroom settings, to spell out and encourage acceptable behavior as it spontaneously or deliberately occurs. Participants receive rewards in the form of points or privileges in exchange for their cooperation and lose points for obstructing progress.

The counselor's task is to (1) identify the specific target behaviors in need of upgrading, (2) discover situation-specific, individually designed rewards that motivate a given client, (3) administer the reinforcement soon after the target behavior is displayed, and (4) slowly wean the client from any dependence on the external motivation in favor of internalized, self-administered reinforcers. These same principles would hold true for any other operant procedure.

Negative reinforcement also produces an increase in desired target behaviors such as assertiveness but does so by removing a stimulus that the client perceives as aversive. Resistant clients, for example, can rid themselves of the inconvenience and discomfort of their counseling sessions only by being more cooperative and working faster to change.

Punishment strategies are used to reduce the frequency of a client's behavior by presenting an aversive stimulus. Unfortunately, many parents and teachers rely too heavily on this strategy because of its seeming convenience, even though it usually produces negative side effects in the child such as withdrawal, aggression, and generalized fears. Another problem with punishment is that its

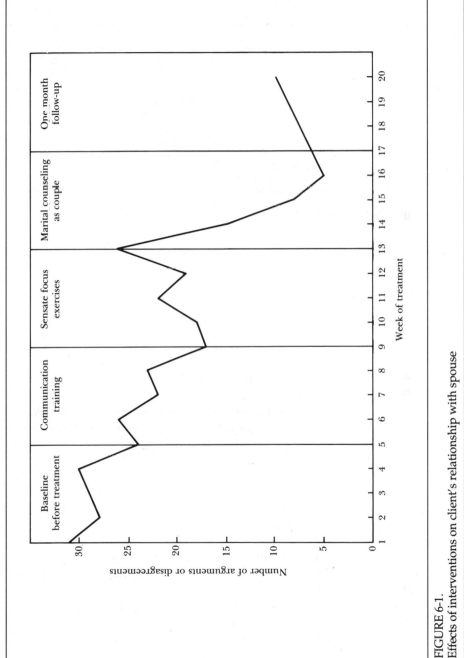

FIGURE 6-1.
Effects of interventions on client's relationship with spouse

effects are brief and the behavior that is stopped often reappears at a higher level of frequency. Punishment may be used in conjunction with other operant procedures, such as in a weight-loss program in which the client writes a self-contract like the one shown in Table 6-1:

TABLE 6-1.   Contract

Goals:	To lose 15 pounds in 60 days. To change my eating habits to include more fruits and vegetables and less chocolate. To exercise 3 times per week for no less than 20 minutes.
Procedures:	I will limit myself to 1500 calories per day and restrict all eating activities to the dinner table. Snacks and in-between meals are strictly forbidden.
Consequences:	Daily reward: For each day I am able to stay within my calorie limit I am permitted to play my tuba for 2 uninterrupted hours.
	Daily punishment: For each day I violate my calorie limit I will set my alarm for 3 A.M., wake up, and vacuum and clean the house from top to bottom.
	Contract reward: If I am successful in losing 15 pounds within 2 months, I will treat myself to a 4-day skiing weekend and buy myself a new outfit in a smaller size.
	Contract punishment: If I am unsuccessful, I will agree to do all housekeeping chores for a month.

Signed _____   Date _____

Witness _____

_____

The behavioral counselor has a variety of other standard techniques that have developed from laboratory research on conditioning processes.

Extinction involves the removal of the reinforcement for a given behavior, such as ignoring a child's temper tantrum. Two factors should be kept in mind when using extinction: (1) during the initial phase, after the reinforcer has been removed, the target behavior increases dramatically; during the second phase, the behavior decreases; and (2) extinction, once implemented, must be applied systematically and consistently.

Covert reinforcement uses mental images that function as reinforcers and can be generated by the client. The client is asked to imagine a situation in which he or she might refrain from an undesirable behavior. The counselor then instructs the client to visualize the reinforcing image.

Contingency contracting is the use of a behavioral contract that defines the necessary contingencies upon which a reinforcer will be presented. Clients decide how often and at which levels they desire the reinforcer, thus shaping their own behavior.

Shaping is a process in which complex terminal behaviors are reinforced in approximate successive stages. The client receives consistent reinforcement in small steps as movement is made toward the ultimate goal.

Classical-conditioning Procedures. In classical or Pavlovian conditioning, a presented stimulus elicits automatic responses. Systematic desensitization, an example of classical conditioning developed by Joseph Wolpe (1958, 1982), is the most common of these methodologies; clients are taught to substitute relaxation responses for anxiety when confronted by previously frightening situations such as tests or social events. Anxiety is thereafter inhibited. Two basic principles underlie systematic desensitization: (1) one emotion can be used to counteract another, and (2) it is possible to adapt to a perceived threat.

Systematic desensitization initially involves teaching the client how to relax. Next a hierarchy of perceived threat is developed in which the client lists minimally stressful scenes (for example, watching a film of someone receiving an injection) and works toward progressively fearful images (receiving a flu shot in the arm).

The counselor will usually use a hypnotically calm, relaxing voice, even pacing the words . . . to . . . the . . . rise . . . and . . . fall . . . of . . . the . . . client's . . . breathing. The client is instructed to relax each muscle in the body, to imagine all tension draining away, to visualize a floating, drifting scene on the beach, perhaps feeling the warm sun and cool sand, hearing the waves crash against the surf, seeing birds sailing high above. After the client reaches a state of total relaxation, she or he is asked to work through the fear hierarchy, systematically reducing any tension with learned relaxation responses. After a few practice sessions almost anyone can learn to inhibit his or her anxiety.

In flooding, an opposite strategy is employed to erode the stimulus/ response sequence. A phobia, fear, or bad habit can be extinguished by bombarding the person with the stimulus until fatigue sets in or until (in the case of a habit) the stimulus loses its pleasurable value. While lecturing on this subject, one of the authors was confronted by a disbelieving student who aggressively asked "If this stuff works, how could I use it to stop smoking?" The instructor flippantly replied "Lock yourself in the closet with a pack of Camels, and don't come out until you're done smoking them all," never once considering that the student might actually follow the advice. A week later the student showed up in class again to report his story:

> I wasn't sure if you were kidding or not but I decided to try this behavior stuff anyway. I bought a pack of unfiltered cigarettes, went home, told my mother I was doing an experiment for school, and proceeded to lock myself in the bathroom. Since I usually smoke filtered menthols, I was, at first, a little surprised that I actually enjoyed the first two cigarettes. I even thought to myself, not only is this not going to work but now I'm going to be addicted worse. By the fifth cigarette I noticed I was feeling a little dizzy, and by the seventh the smoke was starting to burn my eyes. I finally started to get really sick by the tenth. I guess I must have passed out because the next morning I woke up in a pool of vomit with a cigarette burn on my leg. Not only will I never smoke again but I can't even stand being in the same room with someone else who is.

This student's experience illustrates not only the effectiveness of behavioral strategies but also the importance of carefully monitoring their application so that abuse and harm can be avoided. Because the counselor has a more forceful role in behavioral counseling, the client's rights and freedom of choice are jeopardized unless great caution is taken to ensure that the ends justify the means and that the client is fully informed about the implications, dangers, and limitations of a given procedure (Van Hoose & Kottler, 1985).

Criticisms of the Behavioral Approach

Behaviorism has been criticized most often because of its narrow focus on observable human behavior and its lack of attention to feelings and thoughts, which also make up a significant part of a person's functioning. In addition, the behavioral approach works only with the presenting complaint, which could be a symptom of underlying intrapsychic conflicts. Many insight-oriented theorists therefore believe that symptoms thus cured will inevitably be replaced by others, since the internal condition of the client has not been altered.

As an action-oriented approach, behaviorism has also been criticized as mechanistic, manipulative, and impersonal because it downplays the role of the therapeutic relationship and all but ignores the value of self-understanding in the change process. Because it also works toward empiricism (that is, specificity or quantification), prediction, and control, it often sacrifices the values of intuition and artistry in change endeavors.

RATIONAL-EMOTIVE COUNSELING

Aliases: Rational-Emotive Therapy, RET, Cognitive Behavior Therapy, Rational Behavior Therapy, Cognitive Therapy

Originators

Feeling confined and bored by the rigid structures of traditional psychoanalysis, Albert Ellis (1962) developed a system of counseling based on principles of logic and rational analysis. Ellis has written hundreds of books and articles—even song and coloring books—to further refine and popularize his theory of rational-emotive therapy (RET). He has remained remarkably (perhaps even rigidly) consistent through the years, attempting to live his life as a model of rational functioning. In the past decade he has devoted himself to collaborating with researchers (Ellis & Grieger, 1986; Ellis & Whiteley, 1979; Ellis & Dryden, 1987) to establish a more solid empirical base for the theory.

There have been many offshoots of RET that put more emphasis on the rational-educational process (Maultsby, 1984) or the cognitive-behavior components (Beck, 1976; Mahoney, 1974; Meichenbaum, 1977; Cormier & Cormier, 1991). All the proponents of the rational-cognitive-behavioral-emotive approach are in basic agreement that the legitimate focus of counseling ought to be modification of the way people think.

Albert Ellis (1913–), originator of Rational Emotive Therapy.

Basic Points of RET

A thunderstorm, missed appointment, critical comment, failing grade, and flat tire are all examples of daily occurrences that can make us feel upset, right? Not so, according to Ellis and company.

> My approach to psychotherapy is to zero in, as quickly as possible, on the client's basic philosophy of life; to get him to see exactly what this is and how it is inevitably self-defeating; and to persuade him to work his ass off, cognitively, emotively, and behaviorally, to profoundly change it. My basic assumption is that virtually all "emotionally disturbed" individuals actually think crookedly, magically, dogmatically, and unrealistically [Ellis, 1988, p. 58].

Nobody or nothing outside of ourselves can *cause* us to feel anything. There is no "bad-temper button" on our foreheads that anyone else can push to make us angry on demand. Granted, there are many things that people do or events that occur that are very conducive to our upsetting ourselves. Nevertheless, it is our choice, due to years of lazy negligence and wallowing in our irrational beliefs, to interpret the world negatively and consequently to feel depressed, anxious, guilty, or frustrated.

It is the primary goal of RET to help clients identify their patterns of irrational thinking, those habitual beliefs that lead one to misperceive reality, and subsequently learn alternative tools of thinking that are, in real-world terms, more logical, consistent, rational, and scientific. According to the ABC theory of emotions (see Table 6-2), it is evaluative thoughts (B) rather than the traumatic situation itself (A) that will primarily determine the emotional reaction (C). This response will be an extremely negative emotion unless the person vigorously challenges the validity of assumptions, thereby disputing irrational beliefs (D) and making a new, more desirable emotional response (E) more likely.

TABLE 6-2.   ABC Theory of Emotions

A	B	C
Activating Experience	*Belief or Interpretation of Experience*	*Emotional Consequence*
Reading chapters on counseling approaches that present a dozen complex theories	"I feel so stupid that I can't understand all this stuff." "This is terrible. I'll *never* be a good counselor since I already feel lost." "I *should* be able to pick this stuff up faster."	Confusion Frustration Anxiety Anger

	D	E
	Disputing Irrational Beliefs	*Emotional Effect*
	"Of course I feel overwhelmed—that is what an introductory student is *supposed* to feel when presented with an overview of the field in but a few weeks." "Just because I don't understand everything about these theories doesn't make me a stupid person—just a person who will have to work a little harder and have more patience." "This isn't a terrible situation—it's only difficult and slightly uncomfortable."	Relief Mild tension Mild annoyance Excitement

---

Thoughts or behaviors are viewed as irrational if they create significant emotional conflicts with others, block constructive goals, do not adhere to objective reality, or needlessly threaten life. Originally Ellis proposed 11 separate irrational beliefs (Ellis & Harper, 1975), which he later simplified to four basic ideas (Ellis, 1977).

Awfulizing. "Awfulizing" is the habitual exaggeration of reality by "disaster-izing" about the future, focusing on the worst possible outcome:

- "OK, I'll study to take the dumb test again, but I'll probably never pass it."
- "It's just *terrible* that we have to live through this divorce."
- "I can't believe this *catastrophe:* can you just imagine my shame when I found out he was already *married?*"
- "Yeah, sure, my speech went well, but what a *total flop* when those people in the back left early."

Since it can never be proved that anything is totally bad and since things can always turn out worse than they actually did, awfulizing makes a major emotional tailspin out of a minor disappointment. By keeping expectations to a minimum and countering exaggerations with more appropriate, realistic interpretations of life's unexpected events, such irrational beliefs can be neutralized.

"I can't stand it." As a corollary and companion to the irrational belief represented by awfulizing, this belief also distorts the relative significance of things when they don't go our own way. For those people with a low tolerance for frustration, life's normal setbacks take on gargantuan proportions of pain.

In reality, we can stand everything but death—up to and including having to go to the bathroom desperately with no facility around. Indeed we grit our teeth, cross our legs (unless walking quickly), and bear the pain until we can find release. This metaphor is typical of those a counselor might use to illustrate humorously the childish foot stomping we resort to when confronted with disappointment.

Musterbating. A close relative of masturbation in its potential for self-abuse, the use of "musts," "shoulds," and "oughts" is, Ellis believes, the cornerstone of all emotional disturbance. The use of these words, and the underlying thoughts they represent, implies that a person expects special treatment and that the forces of the universe have to cooperate to provide what is demanded:

- "I *must* do well in all situations and circumstances, and, when I don't, it's *awful.*"
- "I *must* be loved and approved of by everyone to feel worthwhile."
- "They *ought* to have given me the job. I deserved it. It just isn't fair."

There is nothing inherently fair and equitable about the world we live in. In spite of our expectations and demands that we get what we want and feel we deserve, rarely does the world cooperate. To expect it to do so is irrational.

Self-judgments. Evaluating oneself or others in absolute terms of good, bad, right, or wrong, and therefore condemning less-than-desirable performance, represents the fourth kind of irrational belief.

- "I completely blew the whole interview; I'm a horrible counselor."
- "I'm just not comfortable at parties because I make such a fool of myself."
- "You're not a very good mother to let your kids have so much freedom."
- "He's a real idiot and can't do anything right. If *I* were in his place. . . ."

It is irrational to expect perfection of oneself or others, on any level, since such a goal is impossible. Treatment of this irrational belief involves teaching clients to rate their behavior rather than their personhood and not to permit themselves to dislike other people but only to disapprove of things they might do (or not do).

According to the tenets of RET, all human beings have each of the irrational beliefs in varying quantities, although their effects, intensity, and destructive potential will depend on the individual. Essentially, the counseling strategy involves defining, discriminating, debating, and disputing the client's irrational thinking patterns while substituting alternative thoughts that are more appropriate and logical. So the reasoning goes: if we can change how we think, we can change how we feel and therefore how we behave.

Therapeutic Techniques

Since RET is action oriented in its application of insight, a rich variety of techniques is available to the practitioner in his or her quest to confront irrational thinking.

Disputing Irrational Beliefs. The counselor, in a role that is active, directive, and confrontive, probes the client's unique irrational beliefs by acting as a logical springboard of ideas. The focus is usually in the present, and client and counselor verbalizations normally have about equal shares of time. The content is, of course, cognitive in nature, concentrating on how the client characteristically thinks. The following are examples of interventions:

- *"Where is the evidence* that you are a loser just because this one relationship has ended?"
- "Who said the world was fair? Oh, *you* did. Well, it's *your* rule!"
- "What are you telling yourself to make yourself feel upset?"
- "Is it really *terrible* that things aren't working out the way you would like, or perhaps only a little inconvenient?"

Rational-emotive Imagery. As an action-oriented modality, RET provides opportunities for safe rehearsal of new ways of thinking. This mental practice creates more positive habits, which lead to greater internal control of emotions. An imagery exercise might take the following form:

> Just relax and lean back. Let all your muscles go loose and your mind feel free. Now imagine that situation you so dread. You are walking down the street and you meet your ex-wife. How do you feel right this moment? scared? angry? and depressed too? OK, now practice what we have been discussing. Change the fear to mild apprehension, the anger to mild irritation, and the depression to sadness. Signal when you've done that—OK, now, what did you tell yourself to change your feelings? Which thoughts did you change?

The client is thus helped to practice a new, more constructive way of thinking, both in the sessions and as systematic homework between counseling meetings.

Psychological Homework. As do other behavioral methods, RET relies on regular assignments between sessions to reinforce new ideas and provide opportunities to test skills in the outside world. Homework may be individually designed and may include reading assignments and specific risk-taking activities, or it may be of a more general nature that requires the client to practice new skills by rehearsing the ABC theory of emotions in real-life situations.

Self-talk. A client is taught to think differently by talking differently to himself or herself. This strategy involves closely monitoring the choice of words such as "should," "must," "ought," and "can't" and substituting other words more consistent with rational thinking. The counselor listens carefully to the language patterns used by the client, confronting irrational self-statements and helping the client to rephrase. Increasing client awareness of the insidious reinforcing nature of irrational thinking is an objective of this technique. Clients often spend time monitoring television, radio, and the conversations of others, as well as their own speech patterns, to improve their proficiency in recognizing irrational statements.

Criticisms of RET

1. Human beings are multifaceted, with feelings as well as thoughts. Critics suggest that RET puts undue emphasis on thought processes to the exclusion of many legitimate feelings, thereby contributing to repression and denial of feelings.
2. RET is probably less effective with some kinds of clients—those who already have problems with overintellectualizing or who don't have the capacity to reason logically (young children, schizophrenics, some clients with character disorders, or clients with minimal intelligence).
3. Many RET counselors complain of boredom and burn-out from continuously repeating the same arguments and processes with all clients.
4. RET is difficult for some professionals to practice if they are not outgoing and combative and don't enjoy vigorous debate and confrontation.
5. Because the counselor's role is so verbal, active, and directive, the client may feel overpowered, dominated, not responsible for the outcome.

Personal Applications

Among counseling approaches, RET lends itself particularly well to personal adoption by the professional. Ellis has said repeatedly that, by talking our clients out of their crazy beliefs, we cannot help changing our own in the process. Other RET practitioners report that they have noticed themselves becoming more psychologically healthy as they become more experienced clinicians.

Personally useful ideas from RET include the following:

1. The idea that, because we create our own emotional misery through distorted thinking, we can potentially change these negative feelings by changing the way we think about our situations. A flat tire, highway accident, critical comment, and missed appointment can all be viewed as inconveniences or disasters, depending on our point of view.
2. The technique of carefully monitoring our language for words such as "should," "must," and "ought," which may imply irrational beliefs. As we

become more aware of illogical language, we start to hear faulty phrases in others and ourselves: "She makes me so angry" (how can anyone make you feel anything without your consent?); "This weather is so depressing" (rain is just rain—it's your interpretation that makes it seem depressing; "It just frustrates me so much" (don't you mean "I frustrate myself over what I perceive is happening"?).

3. The structure of mentally rehearsing difficult tasks for the future or painful events of the past to relieve anxiety and work through unsolved irrational beliefs. These imagery techniques are helpful, for instance, in allaying fears for an upcoming interview in which penetrating questions can be asked: "What's the worst that could happen? Even if I mess up the interview and perform less than perfectly, does that mean I'm not a good counselor and will *never* be competent? And even if *that* were so, what does that have to do with my 'goodness' as a human being?"

STRATEGIC COUNSELING

Aliases: Strategic Family Therapy, Structural Family Therapy, Neurolinguistic Programming, Ericksonian Therapy, Problem-Solving Therapy, Brief Therapy, Tactical Therapy, Ordeal Therapy

Origins

Perhaps the most exciting change in the direction of therapeutic counseling to occur in many years, strategic counseling combines the methods and theory from a number of disciplines into a dramatic action-oriented helping model that often requires but a few sessions to rid clients permanently of their presenting complaints. Milton Erickson—psychiatrist, hypnotist, wizard—grew up physically handicapped. He discovered ways of getting other people to do things for themselves or for him without having to ask. As a professional adult, Erickson developed new ways of helping people through the uses of metaphor, paradoxical instructions, hypnotic suggestions, and other elaborate and sophisticated communication devices (Haley, 1973).

Richard Bandler and John Grinder systematized what Erickson did intuitively by creating a communication model of counseling that diagnoses a client's personal style and then matches the helper's mode to ensure greater rapport and influence. The efforts of a Gestalt therapist and a linguistics professor were thus merged to create neurolinguistic programming, a system of eye-watching and language patterning that allows counselors to persuade clients to change on conscious and unconscious levels (Bandler & Grinder, 1979).

Jay Haley and Cloe Madanes were also strongly influenced by Erickson but moved in another direction, one that emphasized symptoms in the context of family systems. In collaboration with the "Palo Alto Group," Haley, his mentor, Gregory Bateson, and a host of skilled researchers, theoreticians, and clinicians in sociology, education, medicine, anthropology, and psychology, combined forces to revolutionize strategic counseling with families.

Haley and his associates sought to examine individual problems as metaphors for patterns that exist in the family. A child who develops problems in school has found a way to distract the parents from their own troubles. As long as they focus on the child's delinquent activities, they function as a cohesive team. Once the child recovers, the parents begin their bickering anew. Haley (1976) sought to break the destructive chain by analyzing and changing the patterns of communication among family members. He was later to refine his theory into a form of "ordeal therapy" in which the goal is to present a therapeutic problem more difficult than the client's presenting concerns (Haley, 1984).

While Haley and other family therapists such as Virginia Satir and Salvador Minuchin were laboring on the East Coast, the Palo Alto Group continued to flourish, culminating in the publication of two works that describe the art and science of doing counseling briefly and strategically. In *Change: Principles of Problem Formation and Problem Resolution* (1974), Watzlawick, Weakland, and Fisch described a new way of looking at problems: as a vicious-cycle process in which the client's attempted solutions only maintain the problem. In *The Tactics of Change*, Fisch, Weakland, and Segal (1982) give an example: "The husband withdraws 'because my wife nags' while the wife nags 'because my husband withdraws'" (p. 13) . The authors argue that the only efficient way for a therapist to intervene in such a system is to assume a "maneuverable" position having maximum flexibilities while limiting the client's avenues of escape. They provide specific descriptions of various tactics that effectively change the ways a client can respond, thereby forcing the client to choose other, more self-enhancing, responses.

Strategic Interventions

The strategic practitioner follows an orderly sequence of steps: understanding the dynamics of the client's relationships, identifying the sources of conflict, and planning a strategy for change (Madanes, 1984). The principal strength of this approach, however, lies not with its innovations in theory but, rather, with its creative, often radical, prescriptions for change.

The great majority of the contributors to strategic counseling would agree on the basic assumptions that (l) the counselor's role is highly active and directive, (2) counseling need not take a lot of time to be effective, (3) analyzing family and individual communication patterns is crucial to understanding the client's problems, (4) intervention efforts are action oriented, with insight largely ignored, (5) strategies are all individually designed to match the client's personal style and situation, and (6) if one strategy doesn't work, try something else (Gentner, 1991).

Bandler and Grinder (1979) eloquently summarize the important issue of flexibility in counseling:

One of the operating procedures of most disciplines that allows a field to grow and to continue to develop at a rapid rate is a rule that if what you do doesn't work, do *something else.* If you are an engineer and you get the rocket all set up, and you push the button and it doesn't lift up, you alter your behavior to find out what you need to do to make certain changes to overcome gravity.

However, in the field of psychotherapy, if you encounter a situation where the rocket doesn't go off, it has a special name; it's called having a "resistant client" [p. 13].

Strategic methods are controversial. They tell us to do everything that just a few years ago we learned not to do: be active, directive, controlling, and mysterious. The counselor, as an expert, accepts responsibility for designing treatment methods that are effective. The task of getting clients to respond differently to their life situations requires artistry and skill in persuasion, motivation, and influence, as well as a sense of humor and of the absurd (Haley, 1984; Madanes, 1990). Here is a sampling of some flexible, unusual, and ingenious strategies.

Pretending is a strategy that Madanes (1984) prefers when working with children who have disruptive symptoms irritating to their parents. After the child has been deliberately directed to engage in the symptoms, they lose their controlling power. Other forms of directive intervention involve shifting the power in a family, changing the family members' style of interaction, and posing paradoxical tasks: the client is given instructions that the counselor hopes she or he will disobey. With clients who wished to lose weight, for example, Milton Erickson was fond of ordering them to gain five pounds before the next session. If they complied, they demonstrated the potential control they had over their weight—the ability to increase (and, by implication, decrease) it at will. More likely, however, they would think Erickson crazy, deliberately disobey the order, and lose weight, thereby following the road to recovery.

Many other strategic interventions, such as metaphorical directives, power shifts, and reframing, will be described in the chapter on marital and family counseling. The action orientation of the strategic approach is already evident: counselors seek to influence behavior dramatically by disrupting existing life patterns. Since much of strategic counseling is intuitive and creative, *it requires a solid base of clinical experience and supervision before it can be safely and effectively used.* This approach to helping tends to work best with complex family systems and with individuals who have strong commitments to maladaptive behavior.

Criticisms of Strategic Counseling

Although strategic interventions can be quite dramatic and effective in helping clients, especially those who are resistant or who feel stuck, there are also a number of problems associated with their use:

1. The client is not given primary responsibility for the content or focus of the session; it is clear that the counselor is the authority in charge.

2. The process is deliberately mysterious, so the client never understands what has happened or why.
3. Insight is unnecessarily downgraded or totally ignored as a distracting variable, even though self-understanding is an important goal of many clients.
4. Ethical problems are potentially associated with such explicit influence and control. There is some danger if directives are misinterpreted or used irresponsibly.
5. Many of the strategies are intuitively constructed and are therefore difficult to learn and apply reliably.
6. The influence of the counselor is crucial to the success of these techniques and may therefore minimize the curative effects of the therapeutic relationship.
7. There is a limited empirical base for these approaches, and by their nature they prove difficult to research.

Personal Applications

Strategic counseling emphasizes a flexible, pragmatic approach to solving problems. As such, it helps the practitioner to be quite creative, inventive, and even playful in his or her outlook. Many of the therapeutic principles applied to client issues are equally helpful in working through conflicts of your own, especially when following a few rules:

1. When you try something and it doesn't work, *don't* do the same thing; try anything else other than what you are doing. For example, if you repeatedly push on a door to get out of a room, and nothing happens, pushing harder is not likely to work either. Operating strategically would have you do the opposite: try pulling. Although there is no guarantee that this will be any more successful, at least it gets you out of a situation in which you are stuck repeating the same thing over and over.

2. When you are facing a problem that feels insurmountable, reframe it in a way that makes it more manageable. Imagine, for example, that you are feeling discouraged because you keep "failing" at something that is important to you. Morale can be substantially improved by casting the term "failure" in a different light: not succeeding at something is simply a means of gaining greater experience and practice.

3. Typical of the innovative ways that strategic counselors tackle difficult problems, O'Hanlon and Weiner-Davis (1989) describe a dramatic method of change called "time travel." Assume that you are a client who feels stuck. First, you are asked to practice traveling into the past and future through the use of fantasy. Once you can easily move forward or back at will, you are asked to travel into the future to a time when your problem is resolved. Are you there yet? OK, then, what did you do to fix your problem? You can then retrospectively "look back" from your perch in the future and tell yourself what you need to do.

MULTIMODAL COUNSELING

Aliases: Eclectic Counseling, Pragmatic Counseling

Originators

Arnold Lazarus is one of several action-oriented practitioners who have sought to combine features from several theories into a flexible system for analyzing and treating clients' problems. Originally a behaviorist, Lazarus was influenced by the behavioral therapy of Joseph Wolpe and, later, by the cognitive therapy of Albert Ellis. He has endeavored to create an approach to counseling that is behavioral in its systematic analysis, comprehensive in its scope of exploring the total person, and pragmatic in its selection of techniques.

Other attempts to integrate existing theories into a multidimensional model include Thorne's (1967) eclectic system, the tactical approach of Watzlawick, Weakland, and Fisch (1974), Bandler and Grinder's (1975) neurolinguistic programming, and Prochaska and DiClemente's (1984) transtheoretical model, as well as others by Norcross (1986), Wachtel (1987), Millon (1988), and Kottler (1991).

Basic Concepts

This theory is called "multimodal" because it seeks to understand and intervene at the levels of all seven modalities of the human personality. People are capable of experiencing sensations, feelings, thoughts, images, observable behavior, interpersonal responses, and biochemical and neurophysiological reactions. These human components are conveniently organized into the acronym BASIC ID, in which each letter represents a different modality that can be used to explore and change behavior. In Table 6-3, each component is accompanied by examples of client symptoms and counselor interventions at a compatible level. Multimodal assessment thus permits the practitioner to understand at a glance (1) how the client characteristically functions; (2) how, where, and why the presenting problem manifests itself; and (3) how specifically to use the profile as a blueprint for promoting change.

Premises of the Multimodal Approach

Each of the following principles represents an attempt to integrate several action-oriented theories into an eclectic, flexible position. Even for those without a multimodal orientation, many of the concepts are valid and useful.

1. Avoid formal diagnostic labels because of their poor reliability and validity in favor of the BASIC ID profile for describing clients' problems.
2. Eliminate psychological jargon from the descriptions of theory and technique, relying instead on a precise everyday vocabulary. The language of the system includes only basic terms such as *nonconscious process* (in lieu of

the more complex "unconscious" and "defense mechanisms"), *defensive reactions, private events,* and *vicarious processes.*

3. Focus on resolving the presented problem, the symptoms that the client wishes to change, rather than on some underlying conflict.
4. Shape the human personality by classical and operant conditioning (behavioral theory), social learning (modeling theory), irrational ideas (rational-emotive theory), nonconscious processes (psychoanalytic theory), and biological factors (neurophysiological theory).
5. Design individualized treatment strategies for each client and BASIC ID modality profile. Match language and approaches to the particular circumstances.
6. Track interactive effects between the various modalities to establish the client's sequential firing order. For example, one person will feel sick (sensation), imagine that he is dying (imagery), tell himself that he will never see his children again (cognition), feel anxious and scared (affect), scream at a salesclerk (interpersonal), hurriedly leave the store (behavior), and, finally, take five milligrams of Valium to calm the panic (drug). Firing order: S I C A I B D. The treatment strategy would therefore be matched to attack the sensations (body-awareness exercises), images (emotive imagery techniques), and cognitions (disputing of irrational beliefs).
7. Use follow-up questionnaires as an integral part of treatment to monitor client progress years after sessions have ended.
8. The choices of techniques available are virtually unlimited and may be borrowed from *any* approach.

TABLE 6-3.   Sample Structural Profile of BASIC ID in Multimodal Assessment

	Modality	Client Symptoms	Counselor Interventions
B	Behavior	Inability to work, sexual impotence, pouting and withdrawal	Role-play of job interviews; sex therapy; assertiveness training
A	Affect	Helplessness, depression, uselessness and apathy, anger	Sharing of feelings about control; awareness of anger; release of frustrations
S	Sensation	Tension, tiredness, laziness	Relaxation training
I	Imagery	Fantasies of being a famous artist, image of dying young, revenge fantasies to "get" former employer	Positive imagery
C	Cognition	"I deserve a good job," "They all think I'm strange," "I'm a loser," "I'll never make it"	Bibliotherapy; systematic self-talk to dispute irrational thoughts
I	Interpersonal	Rejecting and indifferent to spouse; lonely and isolated from friends; bad tempered with child, superficially cooperative during sessions	Marital counseling to improve communications; paradoxical strategies
D	Drugs	Sleeps a lot; lacks appetite; does not exercise, uses marijuana daily	Begin exercise routine to stimulate energy and appetite; consider vitamin supplements; refer to physician for physical exam

Some Multimodal Techniques

Fantasy Exercise. Use your imagination and creativity to picture yourself on a deserted island, where you will spend six uninterrupted months. Survival will not be a problem, for there are plenty of provisions. While you are gone, the rest of the world will remain frozen in time waiting for your return.

Before you leave, you have the choice of going alone or with someone. Which would you prefer?

OK. You have now arrived. You have shelter and shade, a beach, food, and water. Your companion (if you choose one) welcomes you. She or he is attractive and friendly.

How will you spend your time?

What happens, and how does it develop?

Imagery. A client visualizes a scene or an experience for therapeutic benefit. To be effective, (1) imagery should be concrete and specific in detail, with evidence of sight, sound, touch, and smell; (2) the client should be a participant in the scene, not an observer; (3) the client should be able to switch the scene off; and (4) the client should be able to maintain the scene without drifting.

Behavior Rehearsal. The term refers to the technique of practicing or rehearsing new behaviors either in a group or in individual session. The purpose is to increase comfort with the new behavior and to receive feedback on performance.

Self-monitoring. Clients observe and record specific things about themselves. The purposes of self-monitoring are (l) to develop a baseline for behavior change, (2) to gather information so as to improve and clarify problem definition, (3) to increase the client's self-awareness and sensitivity to problem situations, and (4) to identify antecedents and consequences of problem behavior.

Problem Solving. Problem solving is the systematic process of responding to personal decision making about problematic situations. The elements of problem solving include problem definition, brainstorming, determination of courses of action, analysis of alternatives, selection of preferred options, and implementation. Problem solving is useful in multimodal approaches because it provides a rational and cognitive context in which to state concerns.

Criticisms of the Multimodal and Other Eclectic Approaches

1. The multimodal approach could be considered to be *too* routine and systematic. All clients are assessed according to their BASIC ID profiles, and then the counselor operates as a glorified technician, selecting interventions from the "fix-it manual."
2. It is difficult enough for counselors to master the theory and techniques of

one system without trying to learn the technology of all systems. The result of such an effort could be mediocrity: the work of an inept generalist who can do a little of everything but none of it very well.
3. The technician's approach may cause the counselor to see clients as problems rather than as persons. An excessively clinical approach can neutralize relationship aspects and may create an overly structured relationship.
4. There may be a tendency to use a shotgun approach and to become unduly concerned with symptom alleviation at the expense of helping the client to resolve underlying problem areas.

HONORABLE MENTIONS

Here we present briefly several other action-oriented theories to familiarize you with some of their basic concepts and unique contributions.

Reality Therapy

William Glasser (1965) is credited as the founder of reality therapy, which reflected his dissatisfaction with contemporary psychoanalytic theory. It is an essentially didactic approach that stresses problem solving, personal responsibility, and the need to cope with the demands of a person's "reality." Reality theory is based on the assumption that all individuals need to develop an identity, which can be either a "success identity" or a "failure identity."

The counselor's job is to become highly involved with the client and to encourage motivation toward a plan of responsible action that will lead to constructive behavior change and a "success identity." The reality-therapy approach is active, directive, and cognitive, with a strong behavioral emphasis that makes use of contingency contracting. The counselor assumes simultaneous supportive and confrontative roles with clients.

Reality therapy is a short-term treatment that has been widely used in schools, institutions, and correctional settings. It is a fairly simple therapeutic approach and can be mastered without lengthy training and supervision. The disadvantages of reality therapy include its tendency to reward conforming behavior, the danger of the therapist's imposing personal values of reality, and its tendency to treat symptoms rather than possible underlying causes.

Expressive Therapies

Expressive therapies include a variety of therapeutic approaches that, although loosely integrated, all rest on the assumption that primarily nonverbal media are effective in the release and resolution of clients' problems. Expressive therapies tend not to rely on language and thus are able to bypass much resistance and to intensively explore underlying conflictive and dysfunctional issues.

Frequently the use of expressive therapy is not theoretically isolated but occurs as an adjunct to other theoretical modalities. We offer several examples of these alternative approaches to balance the more traditional modalities that we have previously explored.

Art Therapy. Art therapy has long been a form of treatment for children, helping them to express feelings actively as well as to talk through images represented in their drawings. The *Journal of Art Therapy* contains suggestions for using materials to promote better cooperation in children, for gathering data, for diagnoses, and, especially, for helping people become more creative and emotionally expressive. Practitioners resort to such alternative therapeutic media as musical instruments, games, sculpture, drawing, writing, puppetry, and drama when verbal strategies are ineffective. Resistances and emotional blocks can therefore be bypassed through treatment strategies that are primarily nonverbal.

Biofeedback. Another action method that can be used to improve client control, biofeedback gives clients accurate information about their psychophysiological responses. Readings can be taken of bodily functions such as brain activity, heart rate, muscle movement, blood pressure, and skin responses to improve muscular and neurological control. Katkin and Goldband (1980) suggest that biofeedback may be applied to teach relaxation skills and thereby to reduce general tension, to control migraine headaches, to modify vascular disorders such as hypertension, to better tolerate chronic pain, to relieve sexual dysfunctions, to control seizure disorders, or to prevent stress-related problems.

Play Therapy. Most counseling with children employs some kind of play, whether it involves drawing, playing cards or games, building structures, dressing up in costumes, or playing catch with a ball. Beginning from about age 2 until the teen years, but especially during the early childhood and elementary school years, play is the primary form of expression for children. The counselor seeks to establish trust with the child, as well to facilitate communication and even solve problems, through the interactive nature of play. It is recommended that counselors interested in working with children receive specialized training and supervision in this valuable treatment approach.

Bioenergetics. According to some practitioners in the field, stress, tension, and most forms of emotional turmoil accumulate in the body. Muscles become tight, especially in the neck and shoulders. Blood flow becomes restricted. Posture and gait become affected as do many other aspects of physical functioning. The qualified and specially trained bioenergetic practitioner seeks to release negative emotional energy through a series of massage and physical exercise techniques.

Hypnotherapy. Another area that requires additional training and certification for counselors is hypnotherapy. Hypnosis has been applied widely in therapeutic situations since Freud's day—by behavioral counselors who wish to intensify systematic desensitization techniques, by psychoanalysts to access the unconscious, and by many other clinicians who use imagery, rehearsal, and fantasy techniques. Whereas hypnosis has most commonly been integrated into weight-loss and smoking-cessation programs, its methods of inducing relaxation and hypersuggestibility are also useful in working through many forms of client resistance.

Exercise. Other more natural forms of handling stress have evolved through the popularity of structured exercise programs. Many people have discovered the therapeutic benefits of activities such as running, walking, bicycling, rowing, aerobic dance, swimming, weight lifting, and the martial arts.

It is only recently that mental health and medical experts have begun to recognize the potential benefits of exercises such as running to improve creativity, confidence, self-control, and well-being, as well as to reduce negative addictions, boredom, anxiety, and depression (Sachs & Buffone, 1984). Running and similar activities have thus become integrated into many therapeutic programs as adjuncts to treatment, as transitional support systems after counseling has ended, or even as a sole means of psychological and spiritual rejuvenation. Some therapists, such as Glasser (1976), recognized a while ago that positive addictions like running can combat self-destructive patterns and be a form of self-medication for stress.

SUMMARY

Chapters 5 and 6 have reviewed most of the major therapeutic systems moving from the formal insight-oriented theories to the precise action-oriented approaches that place more emphasis on the technique and technology of change. At this juncture, your state of confusion is probably unavoidable, if not desirable. It *is* overwhelming to study so many different explanations of how best to do counseling, especially when each system appears to have attractive components.

On an unconscious if not deliberate level, your mind is already sifting through the vast array of new ideas and making decisions about what to reserve for further study and what to throw out because of apparent clashes with your values, personality, skills, and interests. In the next chapter you can carry on with the task of building a tentative personal theory of counseling; this is a process that will continue throughout the balance of your life. We urge you to keep an open mind.

SUGGESTED READINGS

Bandler, R., & Grinder, J. (1975). *The structure of magic* (Vol. 1). Palo Alto, CA: Science and Behavior Books.

Bergin, A. E., & Garfield, S. L. (Eds.) (1986). *Handbook of psychotherapy and behavior change* (3rd ed.). New York: Wiley.

Ellis, A., & Dryden, W. (1987). *The practice of rational-emotive therapy*. New York: Springer.

Fisch, R., Weakland, J. H., & Segal, L. (1982). *The tactics of change*. San Francisco: Jossey-Bass.

Haley, J. (1984). *Ordeal therapy: Unusual ways to change behavior*. San Francisco: Jossey-Bass.

Kanfer, F. H., & Goldstein, A. P. (1991). *Helping people change* (4th ed.). New York: Pergamon Press.

Lazarus, A. A. (1985). *Casebook of multimodal therapy*. New York: Guilford Press.

O'Hanlon, W. H., & Weiner-Davis, M. (1989). *In search of solutions: A new direction in psychotherapy*. New York: W. W. Norton.

CHAPTER SEVEN

DEVELOPING A PERSONAL STYLE

A PERSONAL JOURNEY

GRABBING TRUTH BY THE TAIL

A PERSONAL THEORY
    Criteria of Effectiveness
    Guidelines for Usefulness

STAGES IN DEVELOPING A
    PERSONAL THEORY
    Entry
    Mentorhood
    Eclecticism
    Experimentation
    Pragmatism

SUMMARY

SUGGESTED READINGS

A fter a brief (or even prolonged) study of the various counseling theories, a reasonable reaction is to be both impressed and confused. Each theory seems to be useful in understanding people and behavior and appears helpful in promoting lasting change. Yet the theorists seem to contradict one another, and each stands on propositions that directly refute what another holds as sacred. How is it possible that Rogers helps people when he is actively listening, whereas Ellis is aggressively disputing, Freud is wisely interpreting, Perls is integrating, Lazarus is defining, and the rest are analyzing, diagnosing, clarifying, and counseling in their own unique ways? It is clearly difficult for the practitioner to make any sense of the conflicting opinions and the passionate dogma presented by the various theorists.

A PERSONAL JOURNEY

A sketch of the authors' own professional development illustrates the process of acquiring a personal counseling style. Our first introduction to counseling theory occurred with our exposure as undergraduates to the idea that there were different theories that attempted to explain the human condition. It was comforting to learn that we were experiencing developmental growth and that our confusion was to be expected. According to Erik Erikson, crisis and the resolution of opposing polarities are central to personal and social development. It appears that this principle is no less true for the development of a personal theory of counseling than it is for lifespan development.

In our next phase of professional development, we became personally involved as clients in counseling. The counselor we selected was sensitive, helpful, and Freudian. Naturally, Freud's became the next theory to explore. Freud was wonderful! He wrote so well. The analytical model offered many interesting possibilities. A Freudian analyst can be detached, knowledgeable, mysterious, and best of all, omnipotent. Joining the Freudian theory group was like being part of a club, or maybe even a religion. People were zealous in their belief in Freud, his theory, and his teachings. At that early point in professional development, however, it seemed to us too confining to choose such an encompassing theoretical model.

In graduate school we found Rogers's theory a refreshing change. As Rogerian counselors we were instructed to be kind, to smile, and to develop an accepting environment for clients. Reflecting feelings was effective, but the way we were working felt stale and restrictive. Perhaps our own inner voices were urging us to not become satisfied with what had become easy.

Impatient with some of the limitations of dealing only with feelings, we next sought out skilled professionals to teach us other alternatives. We imitated them until we recognized that we were ready to add more to our professional skills. We practiced rational-emotive techniques and found them extremely useful. Moving on to existential theory, we added some new understanding and searching techniques to our repertoire, but they also aided our tendency to

As each person finds his or her own form of self-expression, each counselor constructs a personal theory of practice.

intellectualize. We therefore welcomed the relief of Gestalt theory's apparent simplicity but then realized that it was a lot more complex than we had patience for.

To develop our skills further, we attended many workshops, discovering strategic counseling, family counseling, group counseling, and other approaches. By that time we had begun to integrate meaningful parts of the various theories and refine our own techniques through our work with clients. Then we began to teach counseling theory and help students to work toward integration. In the struggle to develop our own opinions, we had to sort through everyone else's, saving what seemed useful and fit each of our unique styles. It is at this stage that you are now encountering us. We are still exploring new ideas and developing models to help our clients. And we are sometimes still confused.

This autobiographical case study typifies the progression of professional development for many counselors as they develop a personal theory. Initially, it is easy to imitate and follow specific rules; later, it is important to integrate these techniques into a style that is personally congruent.

Most of the theories mentioned in the previous chapters, and those you will study more closely in later courses, are not meant to represent a finite selection of absolute approaches; rather, they may be viewed as historical referents that form the basis for effective clinical practice. Our profession is clearly headed in the direction of theoretical integration rather than allegiance to a single approach (Kelly, 1991; Simon, 1991; Kottler, 1991). It is also encouraging to realize that, in several recent surveys of counselors and therapists, over half describe themselves as eclectic in orientation and refuse to affiliate themselves with any single theory of practice (Smith, 1982; Watkins, Lopez, Campbell, & Himmell, 1986; Norcross, Prochaska, & Gallagher, 1989).

Some writers, such as Simon (1991), believe it is a professional obligation to pursue an individualized form of theoretical eclecticism. This means that the movement toward developing a personal style of counseling will only continue to flourish, requiring you not only to be intimately familiar with several counseling approaches but to integrate them in an individually designed way that is best suited to your personality, clients, and setting.

GRABBING TRUTH BY THE TAIL

The past century in psychology, since the days in Wilhelm Wundt's laboratory, William James's classrooms, and Sigmund Freud's consultation chambers, might well be called the "Hundred Years' War." There is no doubt that the proliferation of significant research, the advances in theory, the development of technology, and the growth of therapeutic counseling as a profession have been spectacular during modern times. The scholarly debates, round-table discussions, and controversial dialogues in the literature are in fact necessary for the continued progress of any field. Only through dispassionate analysis of conflicting points of view may we ever hope to improve the quality of our theories in explaining complex phenomena and the effectiveness of our interventions in promoting constructive change. However, in many ways the history of counseling theory shows a spotted record of petty skirmishes, insignificant fights, and self-serving platforms.

Professional counselors who, above all else, stand for the values of flexibility, openness, genuineness, sensitivity, and aggressive truth seeking have often been guilty of levels of rigidity and resistance to change that would make even our clients blush in embarrassment. The field of counseling, which is, after all, the perfect marriage of philosophy and science, has actually evolved into forms of tribalism, denominationalism, and parochialism. We have different sects under the guise of scholarly theories. Each therapeutic approach, whether psychoanalytic, behaviorist, Gestalt, rational-emotive, nondirective, existential, strategic, or whatever, has developed a passionate following of disciples. Each theory claims to be the heir to "truth" and has an impressive body of evidence to support that belief.

Unfortunately, the main attribute of tribalism, in the wilds of Africa or Academia, is a single-minded determination to preserve the status quo and repel outside agitation. With all his wisdom and far-sighted perspectives, Freud set this precedent by ostracizing those of his disciples who were troublemakers—independent thinkers—expelling the apostles who dared question the sacred word of the master. Thus Jung, Rank, and Adler, to name but a few, left the camp in exile, only to begin their own tribes.

Freud set up a brilliant psychological defense mechanism to protect his ideas—his children—from mutilation. To legitimately criticize his theory, Freud felt, one first had to undergo psychoanalysis. If, after completing the treatment, the critic still persisted in attacks, obviously the psychoanalysis was unsuccessful and further work was indicated. Our intent here is not to criticize Freud, who unfortunately has been the scapegoat for a century of attacks, but rather to point out the precedent he established as the protective creator of ideas he did not wish to see deviate from his intent or control.

The history of counseling, which is the applied study of personality, is itself a chronicle of the influences of a number of formidable personalities. New schools of counseling are generally not discovered in the laboratory, nor are they usually the result of formal experimentation; they are, rather, the insights and conclusions of a single clinician, or a small group of practitioners, who has found a particular set of assumptions and techniques to be reliably helpful with clients. In each case the theory is the result of a life's unique experience and a personality's individual expression. It can be no coincidence that traditionally trained former psychoanalysts such as Albert Ellis, Eric Berne, and Fritz Perls branched off to create new approaches that reflect their unique attributes and values. Carl Rogers, the embodiment of a congruent, genuine, warm human being, constructed a theory that was an extension of his personality. Similarly, Albert Ellis, a logician, a clear thinker, a convincing debater, developed an approach branded with his unique assets. Can we do less for our clients, who are *our* responsibility and respond to *our* unique personalities, than to construct a personal theory of action that has been pragmatically designed for our particular situation?

As Ivan Turgenev explained to Leo Tolstoy in 1856, "The people who bind themselves to systems are those who are unable to encompass the whole truth and try to catch it by the tail; a system is like the tail of truth, but truth is like a lizard; it leaves its tail in your fingers and runs away knowing full well that it will grow a new one in a twinkling" (Boorstein, 1983, p. 81).

A PERSONAL THEORY
Criteria of Effectiveness

Theories are not designed to help clients; rather, they are developed to reduce the *counselor's* anxiety in dealing with the complexities, the ambiguities, the uncertainties of the therapeutic process (Yalom, 1989). In exploring why a particular counseling theory may or may not be helpful in one's work with clients, Boy and Pine (1982) identified several influential factors. The effectiveness of any such model will depend on the following:

1. The quality of the therapeutic relationship. Any theory is functionally

impotent without the cooperation, trust, and motivation of the client—circumstances that can be created and maintained only by a supportive, nurturing relationship.

2. The perception of shared power. Without approximate equality of responsibility between counselor and client, the encounter is likely to be devoid of commitment, freedom, and independence. Milton Erickson has been credited with this definition of counseling: two people sitting down and trying to figure out what one of them wants. Sometimes there is the illusion of equality, since both counselor and client understand their respective roles—one to cooperate, the other to imitate.

3. The counselor's understanding of theory. Before one can use an idea effectively, one must understand its subtle complexities. Far beyond imitating one's professors, mentors, supervisors, or colleagues, the counselor should explore the body of knowledge, research, and skills associated with the chosen theory—its history, influences, antecedents, process, goals, outcomes, strengths, and weaknesses.

4. Intellectual and attitudinal commitment. Credibility and enthusiastic application depend, to a large part, on the counselor's personal commitment to the theory. This loyalty springs from more than either an emotional allegiance of one's beliefs (as in a religious system) or an alignment of one's intellect. A balance is necessary between the two so that the counselor may believe in the power and value of a theory—but as a passionate scholar rather than as a zealot.

5. Flexible integration with institutional requirements. Boy and Pine's final criterion for effective theory application brings in an important aspect of reality—counselors do not work in a vacuum. There are powerful pressures from administrators and colleagues, diluted roles, and institutional policies that often make pure application of one's theory impossible. A theory should look good not only on the drawing board or when a counselor is functioning in a pure, unencumbered way but also when the counselor is conflicted, distracted, hurried, and pressured. The theory should be useful in reality.

Guidelines for Usefulness

The criteria just listed are optimally useful when adapting an existing theoretical structure for personal use. For those who are motivated (by growth, curiosity, or the desire to be more flexible and effective) to construct their own theory from the abundance of diverse ideas, there are many other guiding concepts to consider. For instance, one helpful approach is to identify potentially valuable ideas in existing theories. The key to progress is to improve on what has already been done rather than starting over and over again. The impetus to create a new theory comes from the rebellious internal drive to wear one's *own* clothes instead of hand-me-downs from an older sibling. The critical attitude of doing it oneself can lead one to overreact to the limitations of the status quo and thereby reject everything, instead of just those parts that are inhibiting. Freud, Adler, Rogers, Perls,

Ellis, and all the rest had something valuable to say, some idea that is salvageable for a new theory, some concept or technique that could still be useful in a slightly altered form.

Often the complaint of the counseling student is that theories tend to be needlessly complex, with jargon and language that are abstract, ambiguous, and incomprehensible. Considering for a moment how difficult it is to explain and understand a phenomenon as complex as the human organism in its process of psychological change, one can see that a simplistic theory is unlikely to suffice. Nevertheless, that is not to say that in your own theory building you cannot work toward clarity, precision, and simplicity of language without sacrificing utility.

Patterson (1986), in his book on counseling theory, reviews more formal criteria that might be considered in evaluating or creating a theory. A theory should be (1) important, in the sense that it is relevant and applicable to a variety of circumstances, and (2) comprehensive in its attempt to include all known information. It should be both (3) parsimonious and (4) precise, including the fewest possible assumptions and the clearest possible hypotheses and predictions. It should also be (5) operational, with its concepts specifically stated so as to be testable and (6) empirically verifiable. It ought to be (7) practical as well as fruitful; a useful theory leads to predictions, which lead in turn to experimentation and thus to further knowledge and other theories.

STAGES IN DEVELOPING A PERSONAL THEORY

The process of developing a personal theory of counseling can seem overwhelming, especially to the beginning student, but it is more manageable when broken down into steps. Each of the stages describes a plateau on the road to developing a personal theory and represents a series of questions that can be answered on a personal level and from which generalizations must emerge. A personal theory evolves ultimately from two major sources of knowledge: the techniques and theories of counseling and the richness and realities of life itself. Minuchin and Fishman (1981), two leading family therapists, admonish the beginner to "disengage from the techniques of therapy and engage with the difficulties of life" (p. 10). Developing a valid and useful personal theory of counseling depends on knowing yourself well and participating in the experience of life.

The stages you will encounter en route to your own theory are laid out in Figure 7-1.

Entry

The counseling student begins the task of theory building by learning an overview of theories. Even those students with substantial practical experience choose a formal counselor education program to legitimate their status as well as to refine skills and acquire additional knowledge. The course of study normally begins with an introductory course, using a text similar to the one you are reading.

Decision to enter program

Critical incident, career change

Formal course work

Soak in overview and follow progression

Eclecticism

Practicum/internship experience leads one
to abandon formal theory temporarily to get
through the experience

Theory hopping

Interaction with colleagues leads to greater
flexibility and experimentation

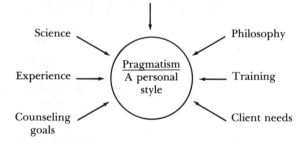

Science   Philosophy

Pragmatism
Experience   A personal   Training
style

Counseling   Client needs
goals

FIGURE 7-1.
Stages of personal theory building

The first stage of professional theory development is usually confusing. Within a short period of time the beginning student is exposed to a variety of approaches to counseling. Their conflicting points of view can be disorienting enough, but the student is also learning about relevant theories in other courses. Just when the names and terms of basic theories are beginning to make sense, additional input from these other courses renews the confusion. Learning about the history of counseling includes the study of various theories of education, philosophy, and psychology. To the list of names such as Ellis, Perls, Freud, and Rogers are added influential philosophers like William James, John Locke, Jean-Paul Sartre, and Jean Jacques Rousseau, as well as important educators like Robert Gagne and Jerome Bruner.

The introduction to human development includes the theories of Erikson, Piaget, Maslow, and Havighurst; theories of learning include those of Skinner, Pavlov, Watson, Guthrie, Thorndike, Lewin, and Mowrer. A study of personality theories such as those of Sullivan, Allport, Kelly, Cattell, Hilgard, and Eysenck is included to help the student better understand people. It is no wonder, then, that the first stage in a beginning counselor's attempts to construct a personal blueprint for guiding behavior is marked by swings from enlightenment to frustration.

Eventually most new students, out of a sense of self-preservation, decide to suspend judgment temporarily and try to understand all the theories, deferring evaluation until later. It is difficult, if not impossible, to organize information at this point because all the information is so new that it is hard to know what questions to ask.

The slightly stressful job of the learner is occasionally interrupted by an inevitable question that will push the student onward to the next stage of theory building. The query is "What are you?" Students' responses reveal the first of their many alliances to a particular theory.

Mentorhood

When you attempt to answer that deceptively simple question, consider the consequences of declaring your primary theoretical affiliation. Since "I don't know," "What do you mean?" and similar responses may make you appear nonstudious or less mature than your classmates, you will probably prefer to name a particular theory that sounds good and that you understand to some degree. Now you have catapulted yourself into the second stage of theory construction and will experience added pressure to find a label to describe the way you think (even though you are not yet certain about your choice).

During this phase a student is sometimes impressionable and susceptible to hero worship. Professors or supervisors who are good at their work and skilled at helping others learn are good candidates for this role. These mentors and modeling influences are particularly important to later development, for they provide guidance and a behavioral model. It becomes relatively easy to affiliate yourself with the point of view of a model whom you admire and even to convince yourself that this is the model that will work best for you.

You now have reason to study one theory thoroughly and intensively. An unfortunate side effect of concentrated interest can be a mental block to examination of other theories that increase cognitive dissonance. Some practitioners never progress beyond their allegiance to one counseling approach. Many of them become extraordinarily knowledgeable and skilled at applying its concepts; they can devote time and energy toward improving themselves as specialists in a particular style. With such a commitment comes an increased acceptance of one's mentor and of the support system of other like-minded practitioners. There are special books, journals, meetings, and conventions, all intended to help counselors grow in their chosen affiliation. The result can be immunization against others from outside the "club" who could lead a confused sheep astray.

For many students, participation in the practicum or internship helps to shatter the illusion that only one theory works. The temporary sanctuary of mentorhood is left behind as the student continues on to the next stage.

Eclecticism

Held (1984) distinguishes between technical and prescriptive eclecticism. In the former, the counselor is a technician, a skilled master of technique who may be successful on a practical level without a well-articulated guiding philosophy. Prescriptive eclecticism rests more firmly on a solid theoretical base and places more emphasis on prediction and explanation of phenomena. Flexibility is the hallmark of both eclectic approaches, in which professionals subscribe to parts of many different theories.

Renewed flexibility is the logical result of your first actual experience as a counselor. You soon realize that imitating a mentor is hollow without an integrated understanding of the theory. You may have temporarily abandoned organized theory in your attempts to get through the practicum experience, experimenting with a variety of ideas to alleviate personal anxiety while helping a client. Adventurous students will even try out a few of their own ideas, but such behavior may be risky unless it is successful. You are wise to be conservative and cautious in trying out the range of theories as you have personally interpreted and integrated them. When in doubt, you can always fall back on the ideas of your mentors—who, after all, have spent decades developing and practicing the techniques—or revert back to a previous theory of your own. When not under pressure, you can find another favorite to study. Ever so slowly your own personality and preferences begin to demonstrate a unique style.

Experimentation

School is over. The counselor, as an employed professional, has the opportunity to test the theories and techniques that were presented in the classroom. Refinement of theory is encouraged by colleagues and supervisors, who have firm ideas of their own regarding the best ways to help clients. The fundamental concepts favored in the textbooks and classroom are sometimes downplayed by the seasoned professionals, who warn: "Forget relying on theory. Around here we do things our own way." Of course, the supervisors are really presenting theories of their own choice.

This particular stage of professional development is often marked by experimental theory hopping, trying out attractive concepts, listening to more experienced peers, and remembering the wise words of mentors. Books play an influential role as the ex-student revels in new freedom while feeling eager for the excitement of new ideas. Because there is so little time and structure to reinforce learning, classic books become the mainstay of further theory development.

Pragmatism

Not all counselors reach the stage of pragmatic flexibility; nor do they want to. Many practitioners remain satisfied and quite effective at applying the concepts of their favorite theory. The principal advantage is a sense of comfort and familiarity with the theory and its accompanying techniques. The counselor becomes increasingly more experienced and eloquent at personalizing and adapting the preferred theory in his or her work with clients.

For others, single-theory allegiance feels conforming, limiting, boring, and routine. Some choose to move beyond mere eclecticism, or a stance of technical proficiency in many techniques, to a philosophy of pragmatism.

As originally conceived by the first psychologist, William James, "Pragmatism unstiffens all our theories, limbers them up, and sets each one at work" (James, 1907, p. 46). The pragmatic counselor is concerned with integrating the body of knowledge from all relevant disciplines into a personalized and pluralistic philosophy that is empirically based and can be practically applied to specific situations.

Some other assumptions of a pragmatic approach include the following:

1. Counseling deals with relative rather than absolute concepts—values that change depending on the circumstances and needs of the individual client.
2. Counselors are concerned primarily with useful knowledge, meaningful research, and applied theory that will make a difference with a particular case.
3. Counseling relies on functional diagnoses that help to conceptualize a client's behavior so that it can be understood and changed.
4. Counseling combines the best of art and science, humanism and behaviorism, intuition and empiricism.
5. The goal of counseling is to help clients make constructive changes through the use of reliable interventions that have empirical support and a defensible rationale. Prior to any therapeutic action, a counselor should ask several internal questions:

   a. Exactly what appears to be happening?
   b. What do I wish to accomplish?
   c. How will this intervention meet the desired goal?

If the counselor is unable to answer these questions in a clear and cogent manner, depending instead on intuitive hunches such as "I have a gut feeling that this will work," then it may be necessary to examine personal motives. A detailed analysis of "gut feelings" will aid the counselor to understand more precisely the underlying rationale for intervention choices and will also help to stifle counselor self-indulgence. Before using confrontation, for example, the counselor can ask himself or herself: "Am I confronting this client because he is genuinely disrupting the process or because he is irritating to me?" Beyond eliminating inappropriate verbalizations, defining the rationale for actions helps the counselor to develop for future use a repertoire of strategies that have been found to be effective in similar circumstances.

Pragmatism is a useful philosophical stance for counselors because it encourages us to view the profession in a broad interdisciplinary context, integrating approaches and techniques from a variety of theoretical perspectives. It also encourages the counselor to avoid an overdependence on a single theoretical construct as heir to truth and facilitates the mechanisms of personal theory building so that relevant principles may be systematically collected from the universe of available knowledge. Perhaps Pablo Picasso best summarized the simplicity of a pragmatic philosophy: "When I haven't any blue, I use red."

SUMMARY

Theory is not the enemy. It should not constrict one's freedom and movement. In the words of Leona Tyler, one of our profession's most eminent theoreticians, "If by theory one means a tightly organized set of postulates from which rigorous inferences can be drawn, I certainly do not have one. Furthermore, I do not even want one. . . . If by theory, however, one means simply the organized set of concepts by means of which one attempts to fit experience into a meaningful pattern, then I may call myself a theorist" (Tyler, 1970, pp. 298–299). To Tyler, theory is no more and no less than the search for personal meaning, the organization of ideas, a way of thinking about a part of the world.

The preceding chapters on theory have given you a foundational base to understand the variety of approaches to counseling. It is advisable to study the concepts exposed to you in class and in texts, to practice new skills you see demonstrated, and to learn the techniques described in the various theoretical orientations. However, only after you have mastered, summarized, and mimicked these approaches should you then strive to personalize them. Store away your books, lecture notes, and images of how your professors do counseling. Only then can you *become* a therapeutic counselor, an effective agent of change.

The teaching of skills, knowledge, and techniques is the task of a good teacher; integrating them is the task of the student. To be a true man or woman of knowledge, the student should follow the wisdom of Castaneda's (1971) Don Juan: to choose a path with the heart and to follow it, to look, rejoice, laugh, see, to *see*, and finally to know.

SUGGESTED READINGS

Beutler, L. E. (1983). *Eclectic psychotherapy: A systematic approach*. New York: Pergamon Press.

Corsini, R. J. (1989). *Current psychotherapies* (4th ed.). Muncie, IN: Accelerated Development.

Kottler, J. A. (1991). *The compleat therapist.* San Francisco: Jossey-Bass.

Norcross, J. C. (Ed.) (1986). *Handbook of eclectic psychotherapy.* New York: Brunner/Mazel.

Rosenbaum, R. (1988). Feelings toward integration: A matter of style and identity. *Journal of Integrative and Eclectic Psychotherapy, 7*(1), 52–60.

Saltzman, N., & Norcross, J. C. (Eds.) (1990). *Therapy wars: Contention and convergence in differing clinical approaches.* San Francisco: Jossey-Bass.

Wachtel, P. C. (1987). *Action and insight.* New York: Guilford Press.

CHAPTER EIGHT

THE ASSESSMENT PROCESS

WHAT IS ASSESSMENT?

THE ROLE OF TESTING IN
THE ASSESSMENT PROCESS

THE VALUE OF TESTING

STANDARDIZED MEASURES
Tests of Ability
Tests of Aptitude
Tests of Achievement
Tests of Typical Performance
Selecting Tests

NONSTANDARDIZED MEASURES
Observational Assessment
Rating Scales
Self-Assessment

USING ASSESSMENT
IN COUNSELING
Test Interpretation
Summary of Assessment
Principles

FORMAL AND FUNCTIONAL
DIAGNOSIS
Psychiatric Diagnosis
Ethical Concerns
Behavioral Diagnosis

SUMMARY

SUGGESTED READINGS

W hether therapeutic counselors subscribe to insight-oriented theories, action-oriented approaches, or individually designed personal models, there is virtually universal endorsement of an assessment process in helping. This can take the form, for some practitioners, of an elaborate set of testing instruments and procedures; for others it may simply constitute an informal conversation about what is going on (and has been occurring) in the client's life.

In whatever form it is structured—as paper-and-pencil tests, detailed background questionnaires, structured interviews, or lengthy conversations—an assessment process is crucial to accomplishing several important tasks: (1) familiarizing yourself with the client's world and characteristic functioning; (2) learning about past events and developmental issues that have been significant; (3) studying family history and the current living situation; (4) assessing the client's strengths and weaknesses with regard to intellectual, academic, emotional, interpersonal, moral, and behavioral functioning; (5) identifying presenting problems; (6) formulating a diagnostic impression; and (7) developing a treatment plan to reach mutually agreed-upon therapeutic goals.

WHAT IS ASSESSMENT?

Assessment is a multifaceted process that involves a variety of functions, such as testing and evaluation, in an effort to determine an individual's characteristics, aptitudes, achievements, and personal qualities. Assessment can be viewed as an integrative process that combines a variety of information into a meaningful pattern reflecting relevant aspects of an individual. Assessment never depends on a single measure; nor does it emphasize one dimension at the expense of another. For an assessment profile to be meaningful and useful, it must provide a means of understanding the individual from as broad and integrative a perspective as possible.

The major obstacle to true knowledge about people, laments anthropologist J. Konner, is not a dearth of information but rather too much disorganized data. For information about a culture, or individual client, to be useful, it must be systematically collected and meaningfully organized. "So there are two tasks, really: first, the assessment of what we know, the assembly of the pieces; second, the discernment of a human face" (Konner, 1982, p. xiii).

Only with maximum accurate information can an assessment be appropriately used in counseling. An assessment of a candidate's suitability for entrance into a graduate counseling program might include a standardized test score, a measure of past academic performance, a review of related experiences and accomplishments, recommendations from knowledgeable observers, and a self-statement of goals and objectives. Each of these segments would provide information from which to construct an integrated portrait. Assessment thus attempts to build a comprehensive composite of an individual's characteristics, qualities, or aptitudes from as broad a vantage point as possible, sampling all pertinent sources of information.

Conducting an assessment requires that a wide range of information be gathered to illuminate as many relevant aspects of the person as possible. Information sources can be divided into two general categories. Standardized measures include tests that have been designed to ensure uniformity of administration and scoring and for which norms are generally available. Nonstandardized measures, which do not ensure uniformity of measurement and tend to be subjective, take a more general and diverse approach and do not provide normative data.

THE ROLE OF TESTING IN
THE ASSESSMENT PROCESS

Although it certainly is not the only way to collect useful information and assess client functioning, testing is one of the most common methods that counselors employ. It should also be noted that the history of our profession is very much interwoven with the parallel evolution of the testing movement.

At the beginning of this century, James Cattell, one of the first experimental psychologists, coined the term "mental test" to describe his attempts to measure the intellectual ability of students. Building on the work of Sir Francis Galton and his development of rating scales, questionnaires, and statistical methods, Cattell began the science and industry of testing, along with researchers in Europe—Kraepelin, who made assessments of the mentally ill, and Binet, whose scales measured children's mental abilities. Although Binet's (and later Terman's) intelligence tests for screening schoolchildren were the first widely accepted tests, it was the development of group intelligence testing during World War I that gave real impetus to psychological and educational testing as we know it today. The Army Alpha and Beta were the first group intelligence tests used to screen those who might be unfit to serve. Army psychologists also worked to develop group personality tests to screen recruits for potential problems.

The Army's experience with group intelligence and personality testing provided the basis for a significant expansion of the assessment process in the 1920s. Between 1920 and 1940 many other tests were developed to measure a wide range of characteristics, including intelligence, aptitude, ability, attitude, personality, and interests. The number of tests expanded to the point at which a catalog of instruments was needed just to familiarize the practitioner with all the options that were available. Originally published by Oskar Buros, this publication still exists today as the *Mental Measurements Yearbook*.

The second major acceleration in the development and use of testing occurred in the years around World War II, for many of the same reasons mentioned earlier—to find more efficient ways to screen personnel and to use their talents in optimal ways. Tests such as the WAIS (Wechsler Adult Intelligence Scale) and the MMPI (Minnesota Multiphasic Personality Inventory) were first developed and extensively used during this time.

Testing has, historically, been poorly understood and severely criticized (Cronbach, 1975; Haney, 1981). In recent years, though, testing has come under increased criticism, primarily because of concerns that intelligence tests, in particular, are culturally and ethnically biased. These problems have led to a number of restrictions on the use of tests and to some professionals' disenchantment with them.

Nevertheless, testing and the use of tests to make predictions about people have continued to expand. Computers have greatly simplified the process of test development, scoring, and interpretation. The current explosion in the availability of microcomputers is likely to increase the use of tests still further. These recent developments and innovations renew concerns about bias, privacy, and confidentiality (Sampson, 1983).

THE VALUE OF TESTING

Perhaps a useful way to begin a study of testing and assessment is to explore why it is important in the first place. The process of counseling involves decision making at many levels to help the client resolve concerns, effect change, and plan for contingencies and opportunities. For decision making to be maximally effective, it must be based on self-understanding, awareness of various options and alternatives, and a fund of relevant information. We have already described a number of widely accepted techniques used in therapeutic counseling to provide information for decision making. Verbal and nonverbal techniques, in particular, have been presented as basic counselor-offered conditions that facilitate counseling and help the client integrate a variety of information about self and relevant counseling issues. Testing, as part of an appraisal process, is an additional source of useful information about clients that can affect the decision-making process. In fact, tests offer a type of information not readily available through nontest methods: they gather information that highlights the ways in which clients are alike and different. The results of a test or series of tests can provide clients with information about themselves and illustrate how they compare with others who are similar to them. This information can help clients understand themselves and can be an asset in exploring alternatives during decision making. It also helps counselors to describe people and predict their behavior (Wiener & Stewart, 1984).

The information provided by testing is not always consistent; therefore the counselor must be skilled in appraisal technology so that discrepancies in test data can be resolved in an exploration of the information. To help clients have the broadest possible source of information about self, the counselor must be knowledgeable about the selection, use, and interpretation of tests. To be uninformed about testing and assessment is to arbitrarily delete a potentially valuable source of data that could improve the quality of decisions about change of lifestyle, work, or behavior patterns.

Testing and assessment depend to a large extent on quantitative methodology and statistical analysis, features that are often troublesome to students
and can present a barrier to developing skill and expertise in the process.
Many students who enter the field of counseling have limited backgrounds in
mathematics, quantitative processes, and systematic analysis. Their reactions
often range from anxiety to overt hostility when they are confronted with the
need to master subjects utilizing those techniques. Remer (1981) has reviewed
the resistance of students to analytical courses and has attempted to point out
why it is necessary to engage in quantitative study:

1. Analytical courses help students to create a balance between the experiential
   and the cognitive aspects of counseling.
2. Analytical courses help students to expand themselves and become aware of
   new alternatives and perspectives.
3. Analytical courses help students to learn the language of research and thus to
   have the necessary skill to understand and use research in the field.
4. Analytical courses help students to be more disciplined, to organize information more rigorously, and to generate hypotheses more fully and creatively.
5. Analytical courses help counselors to discharge their ethical responsibility to
   be aware of the limits of their techniques and practices.
6. Analytical courses help counselors to develop the necessary skills to use and
   interpret tests accurately, fully, and ethically.
7. Analytical courses help students and counselors to become familiar with
   research so they can make informal judgments about various counseling
   techniques, theories, and practices.

It may be necessary to confront personal biases against analytic methodology and to challenge oneself to grow beyond personal resistance. To do so
requires an openness to experience, a willingness to confront personal resistance, and the development of a support system to aid in the process of
understanding the quantitative knowledge required for the use of tests and
other assessment techniques. This knowledge is not only crucial to collecting
meaningful information from the client but is also helpful in formulating a
plan with which to begin therapeutic efforts.

STANDARDIZED MEASURES

A test is nothing more or less mysterious than an attempt to measure a sample
of behavior objectively and consistently (Anastasi, 1988). Whether the issue is a
client's career preferences, mathematical skill, verbal reasoning ability, personality characteristics, or potential for success, tests are a convenient basis for judg-
ing the strength, utility, or desirability of various human qualities.

Tests are used to match the most capable and well-suited individuals with a
particular program, position, or job. They have value as predictive devices for
hypothesizing about a person's future performance or action. And certainly tests

help counselors in their overwhelming task of understanding clients—their characteristic behavior patterns, their strengths, deficiencies, values, aptitudes, mastered skills, and, most important, their potential and capacity for growth. For a
test to be useful, however, there must be evidence that it is a valid and reliable
measure of behavior. Reliability refers to the consistency or accuracy of a test
score, whereas validity refers to the extent to which tests actually measure what
they purport (Anastasi, 1988). Although no test is absolutely valid or perfectly
reliable, any assessment instrument or methodology that a counselor uses must
meet these criteria for the specific group and context in which it is employed
(Groth-Marnat, 1990).

Despite being scientifically designed to be fair, objective, reliable, and
appropriate, testing procedures have many problems. They are not unbiased
instruments; indeed, they reflect the values and socioeconomic and cultural
backgrounds of their authors. In his review of the *Standards for Educational and
Psychological Testing*, Wagner (1987) encourages counselors "to go beyond traditional roles in testing and advisement and to consider client backgrounds in
terms of age, sex, and ethnicity in determining the appropriateness of tests and
the interpretation of results" (p. 203).

Shertzer and Linden (1979) review several other criticisms and cautionary
factors involved in testing procedures:

1. Tests create classificatory categories that are potentially harmful to
clients. Application of labels such as "retarded," "mentally ill," "underachiev-
ing," and "passive-dependent" often follows test interpretations. And even
though sticks and stones will break your bones, names will *also* hurt you.

2. Test construction is an imperfect science leading to results not necessarily accurate or useful. Test validity and reliability statistics are not impressive. For instance, when a mother brags that her son has an "IQ" of 116, she is
certainly exaggerating appropriate levels of confidence in that magical number.
To be honest, she would actually have to state the result in a considerably more
cautious way: "There is a 68.4% probability that my son's *real* IQ falls some-
where between 110 and 122."

3. Charges of sexual and racial bias have been directed against many standardized instruments because the questions and norming procedures reflect the
language and customs of the white middle-class majority.

4. Testing is often used as an excuse to guide clients in specific directions,
often limiting their future vision and potential. A fifth-grader who shows early
promise as a math wizard may never have the opportunity to develop latent
artistic and writing talents.

5. Tests often reveal hidden and disguised information (one of their functions) and therefore may be construed as an invasion of privacy. They reveal
aspects of the self a client may not wish others to know.

Their limitations and ethical problems notwithstanding, standardized tests
have several useful functions that cannot be duplicated by alternative assessment strategies such as the clinical interview and other nonstandardized proce-

dures. First of all, the fact that tests are standardized means that attempts are made to ensure uniformity of administration and evaluation for all clients. No matter where the test is being administered, at what time, by whomever, to whomever, subjective factors will tend to be minimized. The concept of standardization also refers to the common practice of providing "norms," or measures of normal performance, so that any individual's sample behavior may be compared with that of a large group of others.

Standardized assessment procedures provide a database for making predictions about a client's future behavior. In making clinical judgments about whether a client is a likely candidate for suicide, a good prospect for a particular job opening, or a potentially responsive client for counseling, the interpretation of results from tests is invaluable. Tests can also be used to evaluate the effects of various counseling methods to determine if supplemental interventions are necessary. They are often used as selection and classification tools as well, helping in the complex process of matching the right jobs with the best people. Finally, tests are simply an additional source of information for clinicians, a concise summary of the client's typical behavior.

Whether administered in groups for the sake of efficiency and economy or given individually, tests come in every conceivable size, shape, and purpose. There are instruments for measuring ability, aptitude, achievement, personality, and interests.

Tests of Ability

Defining intelligence has been a difficult task surrounded by controversy and strong debate. Although the dialogue is likely to continue for some time among experts, it is now generally agreed upon that intelligence consists of several factors: (1) abstract thinking, (2) problem solving, (3) capacity to acquire knowledge, (4) adjustment to new situations, and (5) sustaining of abilities in order to achieve desired goals (Snyderman & Rothman, 1987; Groth-Marnot, 1990).

In spite of the difficulty in defining intelligence, there are a number of instruments that attempt to assess an individual's general mental ability or stable intellectual capacity to reason and apply knowledge. Tests that attempt to measure intelligence are most likely to reflect a person's scholastic/ academic learning potential, especially with conceptually difficult or abstract material. Most of these tests also include a set of tasks that require a client to demonstrate memory, pattern recognition, decision making, verbal and analytic skills, general knowledge, and the ability to manipulate the environment.

Two of the most popular intelligence tests are the Stanford-Binet, which is considered to be the most accurate measure of verbal intelligence, and the Wechsler Scales, which include specific instruments designed for adults (Wechsler Adult Intelligence Scale—WAIS-R), children (Wechsler Intelligence Scale for Children—WISC-III), and preschoolers (Wechsler Preschool and Primary Scale of Intelligence—WPPSI). Both the Wechsler Scales and the Stanford-Binet are examples of individually administered intelligence tests that attempt to measure IQ (intelligence quotient) as a general underlying composite of intelligence, often with an emphasis on verbal and nonverbal problem solving. Administering these tests requires special training and often a state license.

There are also group ability tests, such as the Otis-Lennon Scholastic Ability Test, that tend to measure intelligence as scholastic aptitude and are more dependent on previous learning experiences. These group tests, however, do not have the same administrative requirements as the individual tests and are often used in educational settings.

Tests of Aptitude

Aptitude tests are concerned primarily with prediction of a person's performance in the future. All of us have, at one time or another, run the gauntlet of tests to determine if we are good candidates for an available slot. It is likely that you have had experience with the SAT (Scholastic Aptitude Test) or the ACT (American College Test) for admission to college or the GRE (Graduate Record Exam) for entrance to your graduate counseling program.

The Law School Admission Test (LSAT) is another example of a test used to predict success in programs of advanced study. At the level of state employment agencies, aptitude tests such as the General Aptitude Test Battery (GATB) are used for job placement, and school systems rely on instruments like the Differential Aptitude Test (DAT) for assessing academic aptitude and educational placement of children.

Tests of Achievement

Often called proficiency tests, achievement tests are used to measure learning, acquired capabilities, or developed skills. They are widely used and can be adapted to almost any type of task from measuring course content (a typical exam) to administering the road test for a driver's license. Results can be used as diagnostic tools, as demonstrators of accountability, and, since past performance is the best measure of future performance, as predictors. Commonly used tests in this category are the California Achievement Tests and the Metropolitan Achievement Test.

Tests of Typical Performance

Tests designed to measure an individual's day-to-day behavior or performance are interested not in what a person *can* do (ability) but in what a person *does*. Although motivation is important in this type of test, it is less so than in ability testing. Two common categories of typical-performance testing are personality and interest inventories.

Personality Inventories. These tests are designed to gather information on an individual's preferences, attitudes, personality patterns, or problems. Results are expressed by comparison with a specific reference group. A concern with personality inventories is the possibility of faking responses, but most instruments of this type have a scale to detect a tendency to present an overly favorable profile (see Table 8-1). Examples of personality inventories include the Edwards Personal Preference Schedule (EPPS), the Personal Orientation Inventory (POI), and the Minnesota Multiphasic Personality Inventory (MMPI-2). Another type of personality measure is the projective type, which does not use a pencil-and-paper format but is individually administered. This type of test requires a client to respond to unstructured stimuli such as an inkblot or an incomplete sentence. A qualified examiner then interprets these responses as reflective of underlying personality organization and structure. Examples include the Rorschach and the Thematic Apperception Test (TAT).

TABLE 8-1.   MMPI Scales and Simulated Items

Validity (or Test-Taking Attitude) Scales

? (Cannot Say) Number of items left unanswered.

L (Lie) Fifteen items of overly good self-report, such as, "I smile at everyone I meet" (answered true).

F (Frequency or Infrequency) Sixty items answered in the scored direction by 10 percent or less of normals, such as, "There is an international plot against me" (true).

K (Correction) Thirty items reflecting defensiveness in admitting to problems, such as, "I feel bad when others criticize me" (false).

Clinical Scales

1 or Hs (Hypochondriasis) Thirty-two items derived from patients showing abnormal concern with bodily functions, such as, "I have chest pains several times a week" (true).

2 or D (Depression) Fifty-seven items derived from patients showing extreme pessimism, feelings of hopelessness, and slowing of thought and action, such as, "I usually feel that life is interesting and worthwhile" (false).

3 or Hy (Conversion Hysteria) Sixty items from neurotic patients using physical or mental symptoms as a way of unconsciously avoiding difficult conflicts and responsibilities, such as, "My heart frequently pounds so hard I can feel it" (true).

4 or Pd (Psychopathic Deviate) Fifty items from patients who show a repeated and flagrant disregard for social customs, an emotional shallowness, and an inability to learn from punishing experiences, such as, "My activities and interests are often criticized by others" (true).

5 or Mf (Masculinity-Femininity) Fifty-six items from patients showing homoeroticism and items differentiating between men and women, such as, "I like to arrange flowers" (true, scored for femininity).

6 or Pa (Paranoia) Forty items from patients showing abnormal suspiciousness and delusions of grandeur or persecution, such as, "There are evil people trying to influence my mind" (true).

7 or Pt (Psychasthenia) Forty-eight items based on neurotic patients showing obsessions, compulsions, abnormal fears, and guilt and indecisiveness, such as, "I save nearly everything I buy, even after I have no use for it" (true).

8 or Sc (Schizophrenia) Seventy-eight items from patients showing bizarre or unusual thoughts or behavior, who are often withdrawn and experiencing delusions and hallucinations, such as, "Things around me do not seem real" (true), and "It makes me uncomfortable to have people close to me" (true).

9 or Ma (Hypomania) Forty-six items from patients characterized by emotional excitement, overactivity, and flight of ideas, such as, "At times I feel very high or very low for no apparent reason" (true).

0 or Si (Social Introversion) Sixty-nine items from persons showing shyness, little interest in people, and insecurity, such as, "I have the time of my life at parties" (false).

Interest Inventories. Interest inventories attempt to develop a profile of an individual's career-interest areas through a series of questions about preferences, jobs, hobbies, and other activities. The pattern of responses is then compared to the responses of persons successfully engaged in a variety of occupational areas. Profiles are constructed by matching high and low scores in occupational clusters. A limitation of these inventories is that, because interest does not reflect ability, it is possible for a person to dislike a career area in which he or she has earned a high score. Commonly used interest inventories are the Strong-Campbell Interest Inventory (SCII) and the Kuder Preference Record.

Selecting Tests

One of a counselor's important responsibilities is to select tests from the myriad of available choices. The selection of a test is complex, because a number of competing factors must be analyzed and evaluated. Among the resources frequently consulted in the effort to evaluate and select tests, here are three important ones:

1. *Buros Mental Measurements Yearbook* (Conoley & Kramer, 1989) contains reviews of major tests by experts in the field, who evaluate them critically, emphasizing shortcomings and strengths. It is a reasonably objective source of information about tests and should be consulted in the process of making selections.

2. Test manuals accompanying published tests compile relevant data on theoretical base, development, standardization, validity, reliability, and other technical features. This information can assist the potential test user to evaluate a test's suitability for a target population.

3. Test reviews often appear in professional journals, which also publish articles reporting technical data.

Each of these sources can provide useful information to the counselor, who must then relate these data to the characteristics of the population to be tested. Ideally there should be a high degree of correspondence among the test objectives, the standardization sample, and the population to be served. In collecting test-evaluation data, the counselor should consider a number of factors:

1. Validity, the most important single factor in test selection, refers to the extent to which the test measures what it claims to measure. Evidence supporting validity claims of tests must be carefully analyzed to determine if the test is appropriate for the ways in which it will be used.

2. Reliability refers to the consistency of scores and freedom from error of measurement. Evidence supporting reliability should be carefully evaluated for relevance to the target population.

3. Usability takes in factors such as convenience, cost, and ease of interpretation, which need to be carefully considered, along with things like reading level, suitability of content, design of the booklet, ease of administration, scoring procedures, examiners' qualifications and required training, and reviewers' comments.

In selecting tests, it is helpful to remember that no one test will be ideal for a given task; there are always tradeoffs. It is the counselor's responsibility to select tests that have the highest possible relevance for the purposes at hand, recognizing their limitations and imperfections.

NONSTANDARDIZED MEASURES

Nonstandard assessment tools are widely used to gather information about clients. They represent a "nontest" approach and are especially useful in gathering data that do not lend themselves to numerical reduction. Combining the results of standardized and nonstandardized measures often creates an optimal base for developing a truly multifaceted assessment process. Some of the more common types of nonstandardized measures are the following.

Observational Assessment

Observational measures are commonly used to gather information that is often unavailable through other means. Observational procedures can be classified in a number of different ways, according to type (systematic, controlled, or informal), setting in which they take place (natural or contrived), or methods used (interview, direct observation). For example, one direct and systematic means of observation in a natural setting might involve counting the number of times a client averts his eyes whenever an emotional topic is introduced in counseling. Another more contrived and controlled method of observation would be to use a standardized interview technique to ask a series of questions and note responses.

The interview is the most commonly used observational technique in counseling; however, other methods are also used. Anecdotal data, for example, often form the basis for progress notes, and role-playing structures might be seen as situational tests. It is important to emphasize that observational methods lack the normative data available from well-defined populations, a characteristic of standardized assessment tools, and are therefore more susceptible to biases. They have also been criticized because subjects can change their behavior if they know they are being observed, and the relatively limited range of situations available for observation may not produce an adequate sample of behavior.

Rating Scales

Rating systems provide a common basis for collecting certain types of observational data. They differ from observation in that observation is only the recording of behavior, whereas rating involves both recording behavior and simultaneously making an evaluation of specified characteristics, which are usually tabulated on a scale. The value of ratings depends primarily on the care taken in the development of the rating form and the appropriateness with which it is employed.

Self-Assessment

Self-assessment is a valuable nonstandardized assessment tool that is often underutilized in appraisal programs (Osberg, 1989; Hermans et al., 1990). Self-assessment reinforces self-determination and recognizes that the individual is truly the "expert" on himself or herself. It further enhances the participatory aspect of assessment. There are a number of self-assessment devices, many of which are based on the logic of the Self-Directed Search (Holland, 1972) and Goal Attainment Scaling (Paritzky & Magoon, 1982), available for use in assessment programs.

USING ASSESSMENT IN COUNSELING

Ideally, in conducting an assessment, a counselor would choose options among both standardized and nonstandardized measures to ensure the broadest possible base of information on which to plan intervention techniques. Although it is not always possible to develop a comprehensive base for each client assessment, counselors should strive for the fullest range of information and acknowledge the limitations of overrelying on a single measure.

Test Interpretation

There has been much criticism of assessment, and especially of testing, in counseling (Goldman, 1972); however, if properly interpreted, tests and assessment results can be very useful in stimulating exploration and helping clients to plan, develop self-understanding, improve decision making, and set appropriate goals.

A prerequisite of effective interpretation of tests and other assessment results is a thorough understanding of their technical aspects, including limitations of the assessment data. Further, the ability to integrate information into meaningful patterns, as in the case-study method, is a crucial skill. Undergirding these skills, however, is the necessity of applying counseling methods in both individual and group interpretations. Microcomputer technology is likely to serve as an aid to the counselor in the process (Sampson, 1983), but it is unlikely to replace the need for trained counselors to work in face-to-face situations with clients exploring assessment results.

The interpretation of assessment data should fully engage the client in thinking about the implications of the assessment results for his or her own problem solving and self-awareness (Biggs & Keller, 1982). Clients should not have interpretations done *to* them but must be directly involved in the process (Tinsley & Bradley, 1986). The following factors should be considered in interpreting test results to clients (Miller, 1982):

1. Engage the client in a discussion of feelings about the test experience.
2. Review the purpose of the testing procedures, and discuss how the results

will be presented. Ensure that the client understands concepts such as norms, percentiles, stanines, ranks, and other relevant measures, including the use of profiles.

3. Present the test scores, and examine the actual test. Discuss what the scores actually mean to the client.
4. Integrate the test results with the client's other self-knowledge, helping the client to see the relationship between the scores and the self.
5. Assist the client to develop a plan for operationalizing the results of the testing experience, using the test scores and other self-knowledge.

Summary of Assessment Principles

1. Never use an assessment device without having a specific purpose and use for the results.
2. The results belong to the test taker, who has a right to have them explained in understandable terms.
3. The test user is responsible for preparing clients to take the test under optimal conditions (pretest orientation).
4. No set of numerical test results captures the essence of a human being.
   a. It's possible and desirable to describe things nonnumerically.
   b. Numbers have no meaning in themselves; only *people* experience meaning. Thus there is no such thing as objectivity.
   c. Numbers as labels imply static beings. Humans are dynamic.
5. Things that can be measured precisely tend to be relatively unimportant.
6. Assessment must be carried out with techniques that:
   a. are suitable for the test taker;
   b. are of high validity and reliability;
   c. engage the participation of the assessed person as much as possible;
   d. are supported by multiple observations.
7. Interpretation should focus on strengths, on possibilities, and on remedies. Healthy optimism is a key to helpful interpretation.

FORMAL AND FUNCTIONAL DIAGNOSIS

As the client enters the office, furtively glances around for a place to sit, briefly locks eyes with the counselor, and, finally, with an inward sigh, burrows deeply into the couch, the mutual assessment process has already begun. While the client nervously checks out the furniture, books, and framed diplomas, and wonders what sort of image she or he is projecting, the counselor casually yet systematically makes careful observations. The client's dress, posture, and bearing are noted, as well as where and how she or he has chosen to sit. Facial expressions, gestures, body language, and other nonverbal behavior also give valuable cues regarding the client's style.

The interview progresses. Information about the presenting complaint, the solutions that have already been tried, and the current life situation is gathered. The counselor is searching for a summary statement of the client's problem, a formal diagnosis to describe the general pattern of behavior, and a behavioral label to describe meaningfully and individually what the client is doing, feeling, and thinking. Making these distinctions is important. In the assessment process, diagnoses are significant because they have implications for selecting a treatment strategy and because they are often required by the system. For example, the diagnosis of "cyclothymic disorder" might imply a condition involving dramatic mood swings that have been chronic throughout the client's life and may be biochemically triggered, thus suggesting the importance of medical consultations on the case. The diagnosis, however, gives us very little meaningful information about what the client is like as a person. Although useful in the general understanding of a behavioral syndrome, in formulating goals, predictions, and prognoses for the case, and in creating a few working hypotheses for designing a treatment strategy, a diagnosis alone is not enough for beginning treatment (Beutler, 1989).

There are many diagnostic decisions that counselors must continuously make, revising them as they gather more information. Imagine, for example, that a severely depressed teenager enters your office. Dozens of diagnostic questions will likely flash through your mind:

- Is this client a good candidate for counseling?
- Is this client most suitable for individual, group, or family treatment?
- Which counseling interventions are likely to be most helpful?
- Is antidepressant medication indicated in this situation? Should I ask for a psychiatric consultation?
- Is this client actively suicidal?

It is important to realize that, during an assessment process such as this, there rarely is a single correct diagnosis that accurately summarizes what is happening for a client. The question, more appropriately, should be not whether your diagnostic impression is correct but whether it is useful. "A useful diagnosis is one that offers us a treatment plan that is (1) easy, (2) efficient, and (3) effective" (Weltner, 1988, p. 54). By this the author means that, when assessing where clients are at, what their problems are, and what is causing them, it is important to be pragmatic and flexible. Since there is probably no single correct diagnosis of a situation, Weltner believes, the best we can do is generate as many definitions as possible. For each one you can then develop a different treatment plan, systematically trying them all until you get desired results.

For example, suppose you are called upon to help a 9-year-old boy who is referred to you by his teacher because he appears withdrawn. Although he is a cooperative and likable young man, as well as a good student, the teacher has expressed some concerns because he doesn't interact much with other children. He stays pretty much to himself or clings to the teacher.

The boy, who has only recently moved to the school district, is an only child. After meeting with him for a very brief period of time, you readily agree that he does indeed appear to be unhappy. How, then, would you proceed in your counseling efforts?

There are, of course, a number of directions in which you might head, depending on which part of the problem draws your attention. Although you would certainly want to collect quite a bit more background information before you formulated a reasonable plan, we use this case to illustrate that a number of diagnoses, and corresponding treatments, are possible. Each of the definitions of the problem and courses of action shown in Table 8-2 are based on reasonable assumptions drawn from the limited clinical data provided and the various theoretical approaches presented in the previous chapters.

TABLE 8-2.   Definitions of the Problem and Possible Courses of Action

Diagnosis	Treatment Plan
He is lonely and isolated because of a deficiency in social skills.	Provide structured practice for initiating relationships.
He is holding in feelings that he has been unable to express.	Reflect his underlying feelings of inadequacy.
He is discouraging himself by repeating self-defeating thoughts.	Use cognitive restructuring to help him think differently.
He is emotionally underdeveloped due to unresolved issues in the past.	Use play therapy to help him come to terms with unexpressed rage and resentment.
He is depressed in response to unresolved conflicts between his parents.	Begin family counseling or parallel marital counseling to help the parents.
He is going through a normal adjustment and grieving process that is part of a major life transition.	Offer reassurance and support until he acclimates himself to his new situation.

The point of this summary is not to overwhelm you with all the options that are possible but, rather, to acquaint you with the intrinsically elastic properties of the assessment process. Before we move into some of the more traditional forms of diagnosis and assessment that are part of the helping professions, we want you to understand how subjective this process can sometimes be.

There are currently four major diagnostic models that are used by practitioners in the various helping professions. Depending on their professional identity, training, and treatment philosophy, counselors or therapists may rely on a medical, developmental, phenomenological, or behavioral model. Each of these diagnostic systems is based on different structures, assumptions, and research data and has distinct advantages and disadvantages (see Table 8-3).

Although it is a good idea to become familiar with each of these models so that you may converse intelligently about your cases with a variety of helping professionals, the developmental and medical/psychiatric models are the ones most commonly used by those in the counseling profession. The developmental

TABLE 8-3.   Diagnostic Models

Model	Primary Structure	Sources of Information	Advantages	Disadvantages	Treatment Implications
Medical	Discrete categories of psychopathology	Data based on quantitative research	Organization of etiology, symptom clusters, and prognoses	Categories not as discrete and reliable as needed; individual reduced to a label	Application of treatment to diminish symptoms and cure underlying illness
Developmental	Predictable stages of normal development	Case studies; qualitative and quantitative research	Ease of prediction; emphasis on healthy functioning	Stages overlap and are difficult to assess; system not universal	Identification of current level of functioning so as to stimulate growth to next stage
Phenomenological	Complex descriptions of the person with minimal use of labels	Qualitative research and personal experience	Focus on capturing of essences; flexibility	Model is subjective, subject to biases and distortion	Use of self as instrument to establish relationship and understand client's world
Behavioral	Specific description and identification of behaviors and reinforcers	Direct observation and quantitative measurement	Ability to be very specific and descriptive	Misses complexity of human experience	Establishment of specific goals to increase or decrease target behaviors

model has been used traditionally in educational settings and is part of our identity as therapeutic counselors. As opposed to a medical model (described in the next section), developmentally based diagnosis describes client symptoms and behavior in terms of their adaptive functions and focuses primarily on levels and stages of present functioning (Ivey, 1991). This is a quite different way of thinking about assessment than the diagnostic system favored by psychiatrists and many psychologists.

Psychiatric Diagnosis

Therapeutic counselors in community agency settings are expected to have a working knowledge of a diagnostic system. Two models in wide use today are the *Diagnostic and Statistical Manual of Mental Disorders*, 3rd Edition, Revised (DSM-III-R), and the *International Classification of Diseases*, Clinical Modification, 9th Edition (ICD-9-CM). Both of these diagnostic systems have been developed primarily by psychiatrists employing a "medical model" of conceptualizing mental illness (Downing & Paradise, 1989).

Currently the DSM-III-R is considered to be the bible of the mental health professions, containing authoritative information and "official opinions" about the range of mental problems. Counselors rely on the DSM-III-R (1) as a source of standardized terminology in which to communicate with other mental health specialists, (2) for satisfying the record-keeping requirements of insurance companies or credentialing agencies like the Joint Commission on Accreditation of Hospitals, (3) for classifying clientele in statistical categories, as is necessary for research and accountability, (4) for predicting the course of a disorder and the progress of treatment based on available evidence, and (5) for constructing a treatment plan that will guide interventions (Seligman, 1990).

The actual process of differential diagnosis with the DSM-III-R is complex, and mastery of the system requires considerable study and supervised clinical experience. Diagnostic information is obtained during a clinical interview that is primarily symptom oriented, focusing on significant behavioral and psychological patterns associated with a presenting complaint (Othmer & Othmer, 1989).

One example of the criteria used in the DSM-III-R for making diagnostic decisions is illustrated in Table 8-4. You can see from examining this chart that each psychological disorder (in this case, "Generalized Anxiety Disorder") is described in terms of specific symptoms that can be compared to a client's presenting complaints and behavior. In addition, information is provided about the disorder's essential characteristics, frequency of occurrence, predisposing factors, and suggestions of other problems that have similar features.

The process by which the interviewer uses the DSM-III-R involves making a series of decisions about the client's functioning in five different areas, called *axes*. These are described as follows:

Axis I—Mental disorders, addictions, and adjustment reactions are described.

Axis II—Personality features and developmental disorders are described.

Axis III—Physical conditions are described.

Axis IV—The severity of stress in the client's life is rated on a scale from 1 (no stress) to 6 (catastrophic events).

Axis V—The client's functioning level is rated on a scale from 1 (dangerous to self and others) to 90 (high functioning).

TABLE 8-4.   Diagnostic Criteria for 300.02 Generalized Anxiety Disorder

---

A. Unrealistic or excessive anxiety and worry (apprehensive expectation) about two or more life circumstances—e.g., worry about possible misfortune to one's child (who is in no danger) and worry about finances (for no good reason), for a period of six months or longer, during which the person has been bothered more days than not by these concerns. In children and adolescents, this may take the form of anxiety and worry about academic, athletic, and social performance.

B. If another Axis-I disorder is present, the focus of the anxiety and worry in A is unrelated to it— e.g., the anxiety or worry is not about having a panic attack (as in Panic Disorder), being embarrassed in public (as in Social Phobia), being contaminated (as in Obsessive Compulsive Disorder), or gaining weight (as in Anorexia Nervosa).

C. The disturbance does not occur only during the course of a Mood Disorder or a psychotic disorder.

D. At least 6 of the following 18 symptoms are often present when anxious (do not include symptoms present only during panic attacks):

Motor tension
1. trembling, twitching, or feeling shaky
2. muscle tension, aches, or soreness
3. restlessness
4. easy fatigability

Autonomic hyperactivity
5. shortness of breath or smothering sensations
6. palpitations or accelerated heart rate (tachycardia)
7. sweating, or cold clammy hands
8. dry mouth
9. dizziness or lightheadedness
10. nausea, diarrhea, or other abdominal distress
11. flushes (hot flashes) or chills
12. frequent urination
13. trouble swallowing or "lump in throat"

Vigilance and scanning
14. feeling keyed up or on edge
15. exaggerated startle response
16. difficulty concentrating or "mind going blank" because of anxiety
17. trouble falling or staying asleep
18. irritability

E. It cannot be established that an organic factor initiated and maintained the disturbance—e.g., hyperthyroidism, Caffeine Intoxication.

SOURCE: Reprinted with permission from the *Diagnostic and Statistical Manual of Mental Disorders, Third Edition, Revised*. Copyright 1987 American Psychiatric Association.

It can be seen that the major strength of this diagnostic system is that it captures the essence of the client's symptomology, personality style, and functioning in a brief descriptive summary. It allows the counselor to communicate information about clients in a standardized format. For example, in a case suggested by Spitzer, Skodol, Gibbon, and Williams (1981), we look at how the diagnostic process would be applied to a young woman.

Phoebe is a 17-year-old high school junior who became agitated during the funeral of her father, who had died suddenly of a heart attack. She complained of stomach problems that turned out to be stress-related gastritis. She also developed bizarre delusions that the devil was coming to get her and spent hours each day rocking in the corner of her room. There was no previous psychiatric history and Phoebe was well adjusted before her father's death and a good student in school. Sometimes, she was described as "overreacting" to things in her life.

DSM-III-R Diagnosis for Phoebe:

Axis I—*Brief Reactive Psychosis*
> Psychotic symptoms of less than two weeks in reaction to father's death.

Axis II—*Histrionic traits*
> Her personality style is prone to "overreacting."

Axis III—*Gastritis*
> She developed physical symptoms in response to her father's death.

Axis IV—*Severity of Stress:* 5, extreme
> Her father's death is a fairly severe incident in an adolescent's life.

Axis V—*Highest level of functioning during the past year:* 80, Very Good
> Prior to this episode Phoebe was generally high-functioning.

There is a thinking process that accompanies the use of the DSM-III-R in which a client's symptoms are clearly defined and described, compared and differentiated from other similar kinds of disturbances, and then progressively narrowed in focus from the general to more specific diagnostic categories. In an appendix to the manual, flowcharts are presented that illustrate the process of diagnostic decision making. In the case of Phoebe, for example, the following questions might be asked:

Diagnostic Questions	*Behavioral Evidence*
Is there evidence of psychotic symptoms?	Yes, bizarre delusions.
Are there organic factors operating?	No, symptoms appear reactive.
Duration of symptoms?	Less than one week.
Recurrent episodes?	No, first episode.
Major mood disorder present?	No.
Ongoing personality disturbance?	A dramatic style, but no disturbance.

This series of questions would then allow the diagnostician to differentiate Phoebe's brief psychotic episode from other possibilities such as schizophrenia, a schizoaffective disorder, or a mood disorder. Although counselors are rarely called upon (or trained) to work with severe emotional disturbances, it is important for them to understand the diagnostic process and procedures that other mental health professionals use in their work.

Counselors also find it valuable to apply differential diagnostic thinking when working with less severe presenting problems such as adjustment reactions. For example, if a client were to come to you complaining about feeling anxious, it would be important for you to be able to distinguish among an anxiety disorder, an adjustment reaction with anxious mood, panic disorder, or agoraphobia. There are features common to all these diagnoses, yet the treatment strategy would probably vary with each one. One of the hallmarks of effective practice is adapting what you do with clients, depending on their presenting complaints and individual needs.

Ethical Concerns

Diagnosis, in and of itself, creates its own ethical problems, not through its use but through its abuse and imperfections. First of all, it has less-than-perfect reliability: when several clinicians view the same client in action, they may be unable to agree on the proper category. Diagnoses are often inconsistently applied and err in the direction of pathology rather than health. Counselors often find this last point to be particularly restricting, since much of our orientation views client symptomatology from a developmental rather than a psychopathological perspective; that is, rather than trying exclusively to find out what is wrong with clients, we attempt to focus on their internal strengths, capacity for self-healing, and resources for resolving normal life crises.

Other sources of error that affect the accuracy and validity of a psychiatric diagnosis include the counselor's expectations, theoretical orientation, and observational skills, as well as the client's inconsistent behavior, attitudes toward treatment, similarity to the counselor in basic values, and socioeconomic background (Stuart, 1970). Poor people are more often diagnosed as crazy, whereas rich people are labeled eccentric.

There is nothing magical about the classification scheme currently in use. There is no overwhelming evidence or research data to support the discrete categories that make up the various DSM-III-R diagnoses. Kroll (1988) has pointed out that this is especially true with the "personality disorders," which are supposed to be stable, relatively permanent traits that are part of a person's characteristic style of functioning. Although there are an even dozen such diagnostic classifications—paranoid, schizoid, schizotypical, histrionic, narcissistic, antisocial, borderline, avoidant, dependent, compulsive, passive-aggressive, and atypical—they are not necessarily mutually discrete groups; nor do they represent an exhaustive list. Kroll points out that, although there is no diagnosis for "macho" or "pedantic" personality disorder, he certainly knows people who would fit. Likewise, although borderline, narcissistic, and histrionic personalities are supposed to be different entities, there are some clients who meet the criteria for all three. To complicate matters further, traditional diagnostic systems such as the DSM-III-R can be easily abused in that they encourage practitioners to look at people as labels.

Application of the medical model to therapeutic counseling has been eloquently and passionately denounced as morally unacceptable by such influential writers as Thomas Szasz, R. D. Laing, Erving Goffman, Theodore Sarbin, and even Chief Justice Warren Burger (Edwards, 1982). Critics warn that the diagnostic scheme developed from the medical model is not useful for therapeutic practice because its concepts are descriptive rather than normative, exhibit physical symptoms instead of behaviors, rely on known physical causes, use physical treatment interventions, and define the client as "sick" or "diseased."

Moreover, diagnoses can be dehumanizing in that they pigeonhole human beings into slots that can be difficult to escape. Some clinicians are especially concerned with the overuse of terms like "minimal brain dysfunction," "hyperkinetic," and "retarded" to describe children who are disruptive, active, or easily distracted. Although in some cases these labels denoting disturbances of conduct or organic problems may be justified, there are other instances in which the child's behavior is the logical response to a teacher's or parent's confusing messages. Meanwhile, the labels remain forever imprinted in the minds of others and in the records that follow the child wherever he or she may go. It is for this very reason that it is so important to use the least stigmatizing label possible that is consistent with accurate reporting (Cohen, Montague, Nathanson, & Swerdlik, 1988).

There are alternatives to diagnostic systems based on the medical model, which equates client problems with pathological processes. Boy (1989), for example, describes a diagnostic method based on a client-centered model that emphasizes a person's individuality and uniqueness rather than trying to put him or her into a particular box. You have also read about how strategic counselors prefer to use diagnoses that are descriptive and phrased in such a way that they imply that a solution is likely.

Behavioral Diagnosis

Functional behavioral labeling is another alternative assessment and diagnostic strategy. In this process a client's specific behaviors are described in meaningful, illustrative, individualized language, not only to help the counselor to understand exactly which concerns are to be addressed but to aid the client's understanding of how, when, where, and with whom the self-defeating patterns are exhibited. There are thus therapeutic advantages to functional behavioral labeling:

1. Clients learn the methods of identifying and describing complex, abstract, ambiguous processes in specific, useful terms.

   Before:

   "Ah, I don't know exactly. I just can't seem to concentrate anymore."

   After:

   "I have difficulty structuring my study time on the weekends I spend at home, particularly when I allow the distractions of my brother and girlfriend to interfere."

2. Clients understand that they are unique individuals with their own characteristic concerns.

   Before:

   "I've been told that I'm a drug addict."

   After:

   "I'm a person who tends to overindulge in cocaine and marijuana when I feel school pressures building up."

3. Clients describe their behavior in such a way that it can be changed. Whereas a *personality* characteristic is stable, invariant, and permanent, a *behavior* can be changed.

   Before:

   "I'm shy. That's the way I've always been."

   After:

   "I sometimes *act* shy when I meet a new guy I find attractive."

4. Clients label their behavior in the specific situations in which they have difficulty.

   Before:

   "I'm depressed."

   After:

   "I feel depressed in situations like my job and marriage, in which I feel powerless to do anything to change."

5. Clients accept responsibility for their destructive behaviors rather than blaming them on something beyond their control, like bad genes.

   Before: "I'm passive. Everyone is my family is. What do you expect?"

   After: "I act passively in some novel situations because I have learned to let others take charge. Yet in other situations, in which I feel more comfortable, I don't act passively at all."

Within the context of the assessment process are several methodologies that may be used to collect valuable data, formulate workable diagnoses, and create specific behavioral assessments. We have mentioned how standardized testing is helpful in that regard. We wish to remind you, however, that all assessment efforts and testing practices are effective only in the context of the therapeutic relationship and initial interview process (see Chapter 4).

SUMMARY

In this chapter we have presented a brief overview of the major themes involved in testing and assessment. The field is broad, the focus controversial, and the need for technical expertise and cogent thinking great. Assessment cannot ethically be avoided by counselors; it's their job to observe, evaluate, diagnose, and intervene. It is our contention, and we hope your growing awareness, that using as broad a range as possible of relevant assessment devices, including standardized instruments, provides to both the client and counselor the maximum amount of potentially useful information. Assessment will be done; the only question is, will it rest upon a defensible base?

SUGGESTED READINGS

American Psychiatric Association (1987). *Diagnostic and statistical manual of mental disorders* (3rd ed., rev.). Washington, DC: Author.

Anastasi, A. (1988). *Psychological testing* (6th ed.). New York: Macmillan.

Cohen, R. J., Montague, P., Nathanson, L. S., & Swerdlik, M. (1988). *Psychological testing: An introduction to tests and measurements.* Mountain View, CA: Mayfield.

Fischer, C. T. (1985). *Individualizing psychological assessment.* Pacific Grove, CA: Brooks/Cole.

Groth-Marnat, G. (1990). *Handbook of psychological assessment* (2nd ed.). New York: Wiley.

Hood, A. B., & Johnson, R. W. (1991). *Assessment in counseling: A guide to the use of psychological assessment procedures.* Alexandria, VA: American Association for Counseling and Development.

Ivey, A. E. (1991). *Developmental strategies for helpers.* Pacific Grove, CA: Brooks/Cole.

Meyer, R. G. (1989). *Cases in developmental psychology and psychopathology,* Boston: Allyn & Bacon.

Reid, W. H., & Wise, M. G. (1989). *DSM-III-R training guide.* New York: Brunner/Mazel.

Snyderman, M., & Rothman, S. (1987). Survey of expert opinion on intelligence and aptitude testing. *American Psychologist, 42,* 137–144.

PART THREE

APPLICATIONS
OF
COUNSELING

CHAPTER NINE

GROUP COUNSELING

SURVEY OF GROUPS
  Encounter Groups
  Guidance Groups
  Counseling Groups
  Therapy Groups
SOME CONSIDERATIONS IN THE
  USE OF GROUP MODALITIES
COUNTERACTING POTENTIAL
  LIMITATIONS
ADVANTAGES OF GROUP WORK
  Cost Efficiency
  Spectator Effects
  Stimulation Value
  Opportunities for Feedback
  Support
  Structured Practice

BASIC ASSUMPTIONS ABOUT
  GROUPS CUES FOR
  INTERVENTION
  Abusive Behavior
  Rambling and Digressions
  Withdrawal and Passivity
  Lethargy and Boredom
  Semantic Errors
SPECIALIZED SKILLS OF
  GROUP WORK
SUMMARY
SUGGESTED READINGS

I n some ways group counseling is not unlike the therapeutic experience of individual sessions. In both settings a systematic helping procedure is used to further the work of individual clients toward improving their personal functioning: identifying specific behaviors clients wish to change, understanding the underlying causes of problems, and designing strategies for making constructive changes. Although individual and group counseling modalities share similar theoretical heritages, basic strategies, and desired outcomes, there are indeed some fundamental differences between them that warrant closer inspection. There is no doubt that counseling in groups is more complex, requires more leader training, and has the potential to do more good or harm than similar helping efforts in individual counseling. It is for these reasons that students are given additional training in group modalities, as well as cautioned in their judicious use.

SURVEY OF GROUPS

We live in a world of groups: social groups, family groups, ethnic groups, athletic groups, fraternities and sororities, neighborhood groups, professional groups, religious groups. The only time we are ever really alone is in the car or the bathroom, and even then we are often invaded.

The composition of any group, whether for social, business, or therapeutic purposes, involves a collection of persons gathered together for compatible goals. Although they may (and usually do) have personal motives and objectives that they wish to satisfy as a result of their participation, group members agree on a set of basic governing principles to guide their collective behavior. These norms and roles implicitly or explicitly specify leader actions as well as appropriate member behaviors (Baird & Weinberg, 1981).

Groups have many different labels that have been somewhat arbitrarily used, leaving the public as well as some professionals a bit confused. Some of the most common types are illustrated in Table 9-1.

Just as there are differences in the various modes of group work, there are also a myriad of leadership styles that can be applied, each with its own set of goals. "Should the leader be a facilitator? a therapist? a teacher? a catalyst? just another, albeit more experienced, group member? a technician? a director? an evaluator? some or all of these?" (Corey, 1990, p. 517).

Whereas some approaches focus on the group goal of building greater trust, intimacy, and interpersonal openness, other approaches deemphasize group goals altogether, instead helping each individual member to commit him- or herself to reaching personal objectives. Some of the most popular of these group methods are summarized in Table 9-2 (see p. 185), a comparative chart developed by Corey (1990).

We will now take a closer look at four of the most common types of groups: encounter groups, guidance groups, counseling groups, and therapy groups.

TABLE 9-1. A Continuum of Group Work Styles

Discussion Group — Group Guidance — Human Potential Group — Counseling Group — Group Therapy with Neurotics — Group Therapy with Psychotics

EDUCATIONAL MODEL	MEDICAL MODEL
Cognitively oriented	Affectively oriented.
Task oriented	Process oriented
Short term	Long term
For normal functioning persons	For those with problems in reality testing
Identification of goals	Use of differential diagnosis
Focus on upgrading skills or knowledge	Focus on personality restructuring
Use of readings and homework as adjunct structures	Use of medication and individual therapy as adjunct structures

SOURCE: Kottler, J. A. (1983). *Pragmatic group leadership.* Pacific Grove, CA: Brooks/Cole.

Encounter Groups

The most ambiguous category of groups includes names such as Human Relations Group, Human Potential Group, T-Group, Training Group, Encounter Group, and Growth Group. All of these groups developed from the early work of the National Training Laboratory (NTL), Esalen Institute, and the writings of Carl Rogers and Kurt Lewin.

There are substantial differences in the quality and execution of these experiential-type groups, depending on the leader's training and experience, but they all have a free-flowing flavor within an educational model. They are designed for relatively normal persons and usually have a fairly loose structure, and the leader is viewed primarily as a facilitator/participant rather than as an expert (Rogers, 1970).

An Encounter Group in Action

The silence has lasted four minutes by the clock, but it feels like an hour. Everyone looks to the leader, who merely smiles and waits. Finally, one woman, in exasperation, screams out "I'm tired of this crap! When are we going to *do* something?"

The leader meets her eyes squarely and responds softly "This is *your* group. What do *you* intend to do?"

Another participant chimes in, then another, all voicing their frustration at the aimless direction in which they have been moving: "What are we supposed to be doing here?"

The leader answers "I feel frustrated too, but isn't this a bit like our lives? It is up to us to create structure. Maybe a good place to start would be for us to tell each other how we feel about one another. For instance, Martha, in the beginning I thought, I mean I *felt*, that you were real tight and inhibited, until you were the first to speak up. I wonder if anyone has any feelings about me?"

Guidance Groups

In contrast, guidance groups, although sharing an educational emphasis, tend to be didactic and instructional rather than experiential and focused on feelings. They often have planned, structured activities and fairly definite goals that are identified by the leader, who operates in an instructor/facilitator role. Guidance groups are often found in school settings, where counselors attempt to provide relevant information on careers, sex, job possibilities, colleges, and other topics that might be of interest. Generally, they focus on preventing problems in the future by encouraging developmental growth, aiding the decision-making process, teaching valuable life skills, and providing useful information. Guidance groups are particularly well suited for many structured interpretations that facilitate self-awareness and values clarification.

A Guidance Group in Action

"You have all had time to study various careers, visit job sites directly, and hear some interesting talks by representatives of various professions. Still, many of you are confused as to which direction to move in and are even more uncertain as to what you are uniquely suited to do. Although just beginning your lives, you already are aware of things you like and dislike as well as those things you can easily do or not do. Perhaps it might be helpful for you to get some honest feedback from your friends in this group who know you so well. Tina, you had mentioned earlier that you could never be in a medical profession because you can't stand sick people. Based on what the rest of you know about her, what careers do *you* think she'd be good at?"

Counseling Groups

Group counseling is the modality most appropriate for students using this text. The techniques and strategies are all designed to help resolve interpersonal conflict, promote greater self-awareness and insight, and help individual members work to eliminate their self-defeating behaviors. Most often, the clientele have few manifestations of psychopathology; they simply wish to work on personal concerns in daily living.

Group counseling is usually focused in the present rather than dwelling on the past. It is relatively short term, spanning a period of weeks or months, and stresses relationship support factors to resolve stated conflicts. The leader is always a trained expert who is prepared to protect individual clients' rights while stimulating constructive interpersonal action. Clients are usually helped to work toward individually designed goals, although there is a common interest in becoming more intimate, trusting, accepting, empathic, and interpersonally effective.

A Counseling Group in Action

COUNSELOR:
Who wants to use group time today? We've cleared up some loose ends from last week and got progress reports on what has happened during the week, so let's move on.

KILE:
Well, if nobody else wants. . . .

SARAH:
Damn it, Kile. You talk too much. Why don't you give someone else a chance?

KILE:
But I was only. . . .

COUNSELOR:
Sarah, you seem unusually frisky today. I don't think you're as angry at Kile as at yourself for letting things slide so long. But there's plenty of time for both of you. And I remember that you, Nicolas, had a concern you wanted to work on as well. Let's budget our time accordingly.

KILE:
Sarah, I know you're not angry at me and I'm glad you finally want to work on something. I only need about ten minutes anyway. Two weeks ago you guys helped me a lot—and things are much better with my girlfriend. The only thing is that I'm having second thoughts about getting married. I just wanted to get some

feedback from the rest of you as to how *you* felt before you got married and how *you* feel about your situations now.

Therapy Groups

In practice there is often very little difference between group counseling and group therapy, whereas in theory the goals and purposes are miles apart. Psychotherapy in groups most often takes place in hospital, medical, or clinic settings with patients who are diagnosed as having some form of psychoneurosis, personality disorder, or psychosis. These severe disorders require longer treatment, intensive analysis, and structural personality changes.

The content of most counseling programs does not adequately prepare students to deliver group psychotherapy services. Often counseling practitioners may find themselves, by choice or circumstances, functioning as group psychotherapists and so often seek to supplement their training with further study in psychodynamic methodologies, psychopathologic process, psychodiagnosis, psychophysiology, and psychopharmacology.

A Therapy Group in Action

The therapy group has been meeting weekly for two years. The support has been crucial for many of the participants, who include an alcoholic, a spouse abuser, a man with severe depressive episodes, a woman with an eating disorder who indulges in periodic binges, another woman fearful of crossing bridges, a man with chronic anxiety and insomnia, and a man who won't admit he has any problems, although his behavior is passive-aggressive. There are two leaders: a psychiatrist who monitors medication and a psychologist who works with them in testing. Both have a psychoanalytic perspective and have been working to help each patient minimize his or her symptoms, understand past actions, and function more normally in their worlds. The sessions are usually quite emotionally charged, requiring all the skills and training of the two leaders to reduce manipulation, resistance, and game playing and to avoid casualties. The group has acted as a buffer, a transitional step between the members' intensive individual therapy sessions and a gradual tapering off of treatment that will eventually lead to a monthly checkup and support system.

SOME CONSIDERATIONS IN THE USE OF GROUP MODALITIES

There has been considerable debate in the literature about whether group counseling is essentially safe and successful as a treatment modality or whether it produces too many casualties and is a waste of time. Some proponents (Bergin & Garfield, 1978; Ohlsen, Horne, & Lawe, 1988) claim that therapeutic groups hold the future of our field because of their tremendous influencing power and efficiency. Critics (Corazzini & Anderson, 1980; Lieberman, Yalom, & Miles, 1973) believe that group therapies are faddish and possibly detrimental.

TABLE 9-2.   Comparative Overview of Group Goals

Model	Goals
Psychoanalytic	To provide a climate that helps clients reexperience early family relationships. To uncover buried feelings associated with past events that carry over into current behavior. To facilitate insight into the origins of faulty psychological development and stimulate a corrective emotional experience.
Adlerian	To create a therapeutic relationship that encourages participants to explore their basic life assumptions and to achieve a broader understanding of lifestyles. To help clients recognize their strengths and their power to change. To encourage them to accept full responsibility for their chosen lifestyle and for any changes they want to make.
Psychodrama	To facilitate the release of pent-up feelings, to provide insight, and to help clients develop new and more effective behaviors. To open up unexplored possibilities for solving conflicts and for experiencing dominant sides of oneself.
Existential	To provide conditions that maximize self-awareness and reduce blocks to growth. To help clients discover and use freedom of choice and assume responsibility for their own choices.
Person-centered	To provide a safe climate wherein members can explore the full range of their feelings. To help members become increasingly open to new experiences and develop confidence in themselves and their own judgments. To encourage clients to live in the present. To develop openness, honesty, and spontaneity. To make it possible for clients to encounter others in the here and now and to use the group as a place to overcome feelings of alienation.
Gestalt	To enable members to pay close attention to their moment-to-moment experiencing, so they can recognize and integrate disowned aspects of themselves.
Transactional analysis	To assist clients in becoming free of scripts and games in their interactions. To challenge members to reexamine early decisions and make new ones based on awareness.
Behavior therapy	To help group members eliminate maladaptive behaviors and learn new and more effective behavioral patterns. (Broad goals are broken down into precise subgoals.)
Rational-emotive therapy	To teach group members that they are responsible for their own disturbances and to help them identify and abandon the process of self-indoctrination by which they keep their disturbances alive. To eliminate the clients' irrational and self-defeating outlook on life and replace it with a more tolerant and rational one.
Reality therapy	To guide members toward learning realistic and responsible behavior and developing a "success identity." To assist group members in making value judgments about their behaviors and in deciding on a plan of action for change.

SOURCE: Corey, G. (1990). *Theory and practice of group counseling* (3rd ed.). Pacific Grove, CA: Brooks/Cole.

Still other writers question whether group counseling is really any different from individual or family counseling, since all the treatments make use of essentially the same therapeutic variables (Hill, 1990).

It may, therefore, be helpful to review some considerations in the use of groups so that you, as a student, may realistically assess the potential and dangers of this helping procedure. If you choose to work in groups—as a leader of a counseling group, as an administrator conducting meetings, as an instructor in the classroom, as a public figure in the media, or as a consultant in the field—you would be well advised to study the contraindications of group methods carefully so that you may adequately prepare needed safeguards as well as face your critics. Similarly, you can capitalize on the therapeutic variables that operate in groups only if you are well aware of what can and cannot be effectively accomplished.

The history of group work is checkered with the contributions of many distinguished professionals as well as the practices of charlatans and witch doctors. Recall that, throughout human history, group hysteria has accounted for more havoc and death than all contagious diseases. After all, what is war but an organized form of group work, in which one team, led by leaders who are masters of group dynamics, attempt to obliterate the other team in the name of abstractions like territorial boundaries? In our recent history we have witnessed the dramatic influencing capabilities of self-serving group leaders who could induce murder or suicide with their persuasive tongues and intricate knowledge of the power of group forces. Adolf Hitler, Charles Manson, and Reverend Jim Jones are but a few of the more skilled group tacticians of this century who could warp group dynamics to suit their own needs.

It is no wonder that therapeutic groups are often viewed with suspicion by the public and by some clinicians. Only in the past few years have standards for acceptable practice been developed and systematic training programs implemented (Patterson, 1972). For these reasons, new graduates sometimes experience frustration when trying to begin group work in their schools or agencies. They get opposition from their clients, who resent the pressure to participate in an uncomfortable setting and who thus resist the coercion. Further, clients are often more inhibited in groups, less willing to disclose because of fears—some of which are justified. How, after all, can confidentiality ever be enforced and guaranteed in a group? Who can promise never to let secrets slip out inadvertently or never to talk about private things outside the group? And who would believe such promises?

There are also complaints from parents and spouses: "What's this? I heard that you stuck my son in one of those touchy-feely groups. I'll not have a child of mine in one of your orgies!" Or, "I notice my wife is different since she's been hanging around with those dingbats in that group. How dare you people interfere in my life!"

There is also resistance to implementing group strategies from some senior colleagues in administration or counseling who never received group training. Many counselor/therapist education programs added their first course in the techniques of group work only in recent years. And the majority of group counseling classes currently focus as much on theory as on any practical considerations for how to organize, market, begin, run, and end a therapeutic group.

In group work, clients receive less time than they would in individual sessions and have less privacy. Groups require more sophisticated training on the part of leaders and are generally not suited for people who are easily intimidated or manipulative or who talk incessantly.

Why, then, would we ever choose to work in group settings? Why indeed?

COUNTERACTING POTENTIAL LIMITATIONS

It has been our own experience as counselor educators and practitioners, as well as specialists in group work (and we are therefore a little biased), that several of the distinct disadvantages, such as those just mentioned, can be controlled or minimized through sufficient caution and training. Lieberman et al. (1973), for example, have reviewed the issue of client casualties in encounter groups and offer the following guidelines to group leaders:

1. Evaluate the normative structure of the group, and assess members' expectations about the forms and structures the group will assume. This is most effectively done in a pregroup interview.
2. Evaluate the psychosocial relations in the group, and pay particular attention to members with minimal interaction.
3. Recognize the importance of cognitive factors on positive group outcome.
4. Organize the group experience around a theoretical framework, and plan activities and interventions accordingly. The choice of an intellectual posture is less important than the consistent use thereof.
5. Monitor carefully the ratio of confrontation to support, and avoid over-stimulating the group members. Too much stimulation, especially confrontation, can lead to casualties, whereas too little can result in apathy and high group dropout.
6. Be aware of the leader's impact on the group members through the transference process, and temper interactions with timing and patience. Avoid the temptation to use transference to force member "breakthroughs."
7. Accept responsibility for the constructive emotional climate of the group.
8. Allow members to "exit" an experience without censure if the focus or experience becomes uncomfortable or too intense for the participant. Follow up on dropouts to resolve any lingering negative effects.
9. Understand the dynamics of the change process, and help members to create more adaptive structures for implementing change beyond the group experience.

Issues such as the suitability of certain personality types (passive-dependent, sociopathic), appropriateness of the group for individual problems, and level of psychological functioning (borderline personality, psychotic) can be handled through screening procedures that would permit participation only by those who are reasonably respectful of others' rights and who seem to be good candidates for groups (however that may be operationally defined).

There are other issues that may not be so readily dismissed. Confidentiality cannot be strictly guaranteed, and it is true that clients receive less attention than in private counseling. With these limitations in mind, the leader must take extra care to ensure that time is spent equitably and that adequate safeguards are planned to prevent anticipated problems. Taking these conditions as givens, we can more realistically survey some of the powerful advantages implicit in therapeutic groups.

ADVANTAGES OF GROUP WORK
Cost Efficiency

It would take a counselor two full working days to see a dozen clients in individual sessions; the same number could meet in a single group session for two hours. The counselor is thereby able to reach more prospective clients in a considerably shorter period of time, and at significant savings to the institution and clientele. Most counselors and agencies are already so overburdened with work demands that group modalities allow for the most cost-efficient means to help the largest needy population.

Spectator Effects

While one person is receiving help in a therapeutic group—struggling, confronting, exploring, growing—a dozen other clients are carefully observing the process. They are internalizing the therapeutic messages, personalizing and adapting the content to their own lives. As one client complains about conflicts with a roommate, all others in the group (and those who are now reading these words) must ask themselves: How am I getting along with my spouse/ friend/roommate? What things in this relationship am I willing to fight for, and which freedoms am I prepared to sacrifice? How much do I value my privacy? Do I want to live alone? How could we better settle our arguments?

Group work has the distinct advantage of permitting others to learn by observation. Clients are able to monitor the leader's behavior, imitating the actions that they admire: how to speak with confidence, how to create metaphoric language, how to take risks. The clients also scrutinize one another. When one member experiences success, the rest will live it vicariously. When a member is censured for monopolizing too much time, the others note the lesson as well.

The learning effects become contagious as an active participant is silently or not so silently cheered by the enthusiastic spectators. Each time a client opens up, takes a risk, or tries out a new behavior and *doesn't* die as a consequence, the other clients will feel more ready to test themselves.

Stimulation Value

It is no surprise that the quantity and quality of ideas generated through group interaction are significantly more enriched than the results of solo brainstorming

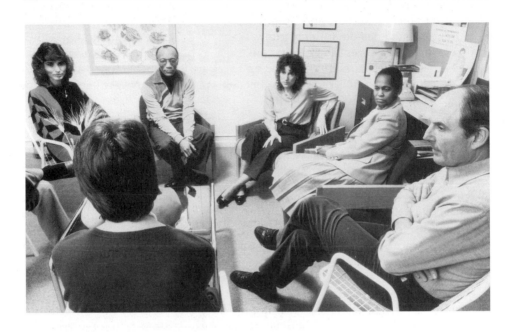

Counseling groups provide opportunities for feedback, authentic interaction, support, belongingness, and supervised practice of new behaviors.

(Meadow, Parnes, & Reese, 1959; Brilhart &Jochem, 1964). Discovery of this fact revolutionized industrial product design: experts from compatible fields learned to pool their problem-solving efforts.

The atmosphere of a therapeutic group is a virtual utopia of emotional and cognitive stimulation, with its emphasis on freedom of expression, honest feedback, interchange of novel ideas, acceptance of individual differences, prizing of creativity and spontaneity, experimentation without fear of failure, and focus on risk taking, sharing, and giving. In such an environment it is impossible to be bored or to repeat an experience in exactly the same way.

Group sessions provide an exciting and fertile atmosphere for change because of the collective energy available. The whole is greater than the sum of its parts. Giggles quickly become contagious. As new ideas are passed around, they grow with each input, contribution, refinement. You can feel the hearts beating in a group. You can smell the sweat and sense the nervous shuffling. You can hear the pounding in your brain as it tries so hard to understand. And the sights are a visual Disneyland—nonverbal behavior to monitor, facial expressions, territorial imperatives, positionings and status hierarchies, insight in action, gestures of defiance, respect, or affection. A group is alive with ideas and emotion and change. It is stimulation itself. It is a dozen people struggling to understand themselves and one another.

Therapeutic groups not only prevent burnout in the counselor, who must

constantly stay on top of things, but energize the clients through lively interactions, spontaneous humor, and abundance of stimulation. Many practitioners
with hectic schedules often deliberately plan group sessions to help both their
clientele and themselves. The groups are often so professionally rewarding that
the leader, although carefully monitoring his or her own behavior to avoid self-
indulgence or meeting his or her own needs in the session, nevertheless, cannot
help growing.

Opportunities for Feedback

Where can you go for truth? Ask your mother or your best friend for an opinion
on your new shoes or what you should change about yourself. They will lie, or
at least hedge, to water down an unpleasant truth. Where can you go to find out
what people really think of you?

A counseling group provides the opportunity for participants to receive
straightforward, honest, and constructive reactions to their behaviors, both
attractive and unattractive. After role playing or risk taking, a client gains feedback from astute observers that helps in making needed adjustments, identifying areas that could be upgraded, and providing reinforcement by acknowledg-
ing progress. When feedback is diplomatically confrontive, honest without
being destructive, expressive but devoid of clichés, sensitive but not overly evasive, concise by boiling down the essence of a person's behavior into a memo-
rable image, it becomes one of the most powerful of therapeutic devices for promoting change.

In one introductory exercise used to open groups, for example, the leader
encourages an exchange of first impressions among participants. Early in the
therapeutic experience, the exercise helps them to give one another the gift of
honest reactions. After members are instructed about the purposes of such an
exercise—to encounter one another in a personal way, to collect information on
possible areas of needed growth, to hear (perhaps for the first time) of the effect
they have on others—they are then educated in the requirements of effective
feedback. They are reminded to avoid stereotypes and clichés, to be brief rather
than long-winded, and to be honest, helpful, and constructive by including both
effective and ineffective behaviors. To give the exercise structure and direction,
which are often necessary in initial sessions until members learn rules and roles,
the leader asks the members to write down the name of the animal that each
person in the group brings to mind. Using their observations of each person's
gestures and appearances, their own intuition, and any other data available, trying to be creative in their thinking, clients send feedback to one another by disclosing the animals of which they are most reminded and the reasons why.

Angela, a shy, withdrawn girl, learns that some of the others see her as a
turtle because "she loves to swim beneath the surface where no one can see" or
a golden retriever "because she appears loyal, affectionate, and maternal" or an
opaline gourami (the speaker is a fish expert) "because she's cautious when people are around but prances when alone; she has a beautiful display of colors and

grace, yet she hides behind the plants even if she sees a tasty morsel to eat; she prefers to wait for things to come to her." Other members learn from the feedback on first impressions that they may resemble a Colorado River mule, because they are survivors, are self-sufficient, and have a flexible diet; or a Hobbit, because of their playfulness, innocence, perceptiveness, and love of adventure; or a queen bee, because they are good organizers but manipulative and overdemanding.

Any and all feedback in a group is aimed at providing experiences that are rarely available in the "outside world"—direct, honest, and sensitive statements about exactly how one person feels and thinks about another.

Support

The tarpon, among the world's greatest sport fishes, will fight for hours longer against the hook and line when accompanied by others of its school than when alone. It is as if it couldn't give in with its peers watching, urging, goading it to fight a little longer. There is also a human need to give and receive support in groups. Our ancestors huddled together in their caves for security and division of labor. In the evolutionary scheme of things, the PTA, fraternity, and neighborhood club have inherited many of the social/protective functions of the bonds we originally formed as hunter/gatherers. Groups supply the nurturing elements of intimacy and psychological bonding—the cohesion that results from close proximity over time. A therapeutic group can develop into a surrogate family, without the rigid, authoritarian hierarchies of some natural families. Such an experience can even be sampled within the relative artificiality of your classroom. Although the physical environment, seating arrangement, competition, professional authority, and threat of grading are something less than ideal circumstances for promoting a sense of true cohesion, there is nevertheless a feeling of belongingness that develops among classmates. Students can draw support from one another, pool their emotional and cognitive energies to get through the hard times, and savor the enlightening experiences.

Structured Practice

Within a group, a person can not only receive feedback but also experience the support and encouragement necessary to practice new behaviors. Often individuals undergo stress and frustration in their daily lives because they lack needed skills. Shyness prevents them from initiating new relationships, or frustration keeps them hostile and defensive, or low self-esteem triggers procrastination; each of these limitations can be viewed as a skill deficit, and the group becomes a place to develop and refine useful life skills. A man who is passive with his wife, for instance, can practice assertive skills. Group members provide feedback and help him to monitor the development of those skills. Laboratory experiences such as these help group members to put insights to use and to rehearse new behaviors in a nonthreatening setting.

The group, as a learning laboratory, can also be used for reality testing. Fears, anxieties, and inhibitions can be examined and explored, permitting the member to test out the validity of those feelings. Commonly a person will hold feelings in to avoid "hurting" someone else. This concern can be tested in the group by checking out others' reactions and practicing giving both constructive and critical feedback to determine the recipient's reaction. Often the person will learn that being protective and withholding honesty are more "hurtful" than disclosing it and can then work toward a personal awareness of what "hurting" means.

BASIC ASSUMPTIONS ABOUT GROUPS

One human life is so complex in its origins, history, functioning, and conscious-ness as to defy complete understanding by all the social and physical scientists in the universe. Yet, when this solitary life is combined with a group of other lives, the network of ideas and interactions that could be generated is stagger-ing. A single action by an individual group member—rearranging his position on the chair, for example—could signify restlessness, agitation, back pain, hem-orrhoids, a desire for attention, postural difficulties, a need for increased blood flow, or an itch. If that same person were to communicate with another in the group, with his eyes or gestures, not to mention the possible variations of his voice, the effects would ripple like waves through the minds of all those present. Each person would seek a personal interpretation of the action and would respond to the stimulus both internally and externally. And it is the leader's task to sift through the confusing assortment of often conflicting stimuli, to attend to those that have relevance to the present situation and goals, to make sense of and give meaning to the behavior, to predict likely consequences, and, finally, to act therapeutically in the best interests of those who are present.

The group leader must not only have mastered basic counseling technology but must understand dynamics and assumptions as they are applied to group behavior. Initially, each client comes to the group with different expectations, interests, and goals. The most basic assumption about groups, therefore, is that there are often discrepancies among the participants' hopes and expectations and even between the leader's and the members'. Coalitions are formed on the basis of these common interests and backgrounds and often on the basis of per-ceived similarities in attitudes, abilities, or attractiveness. The leader may be viewed as the "outsider," as a function of his or her expert role, or possibly as the only "insider," since the counselor alone really knows what is going on dur-ing the beginning sessions.

Assuming a diversity of expectations helps the group leader to plan for and permit the realization of individual goals that are compatible with the flexible structure. Individual members are thus helped to clarify their reasons for attend-ing the group and encouraged to set specific goals that may be realistically attained during the time allotted.

LEADER:
> Before I discuss some ideas regarding what options are available for you in this group and how we can spend our time, let's hear from some of you as to why you decided to come.

ELKA:
> I didn't *decide* to come. My parents threatened to ground me for the semester unless I agreed to try this a few times. They think I'm too young to get married; I don't.

NANDO:
> I heard this was a good place to meet girls. I could always use some new ladies in my life.

BETH:
> I've got some problems at work. I don't know what to do. I was hoping to get some advice.

FRED:
> Too much dope. I get high too much. Every day. I want to stop. Maybe you guys can help me.

Another assumption about therapeutic groups to which most (but not all) practitioners would subscribe is that the leader is not a participant of the group but a trained expert. Efforts are thus devoted to keeping the focus on the members, avoiding self-indulgent excesses, and generally staying in the role of paid professional who does not deliberately use group time for self-serving purposes.

CASSANDRA:
> O wise one, you always sit here so omnipotent—like you know everything about anything. You are leading us, helping us. What are some of *your* problems? Why don't we help you?

LEADER:
> I do have lots of things I could work on in this group—my impatience, my overdriving ambition—and I know that you are all skilled enough to help me; but I don't feel comfortable using *your* time to work on *my* concerns. I'm being paid to help you. I can go to another group (and I do occasionally) where I get help. Thanks for your concern, Cassandra. But did I hear you resenting the control you feel I have? Is that something you would like to work on, since your lack of control has been an issue before?

For group work to be successful, or even to get off the ground, there must be an atmosphere of trust. Even more so than in individual sessions, the issue of confidentiality must be directly addressed so that it is clearly understood that all communication within the group is to be private and secure. Actually, there is no way confidentiality can ever be guaranteed or enforced in a group setting, for members are not legally bound to comply with any particular codes. Inadvertent breaches of trust can also occur, destroying the hard-won confidence. It is for these reasons that the leader openly, forcefully, and explicitly discusses the issue:

HECTOR:

Why should I ever spill my guts here? I don't know you people. How can I believe anyone is trustworthy if I don't know them?

LEADER:

Your point is a good one. There is a risk involved in being open, in this group or anywhere else. You should therefore pace yourself so that you disclose only what you feel ready to share. You will have to trust your own instincts on this. But remember, the degree to which you risk is related to how much you grow. Let's work on some situations that could test your confidential oath and discuss how they might be handled. What would you say, for instance, if your best friend asked what's going on in your group? OK, what are you permitted to talk about outside the group? And what are some of your fears about what would occur if someone in here did tell others what you said?

In counseling groups, perhaps even more than in individual sessions, client discomfort is associated with change. The very structure of a group environment, with its active audience, stimulates approval seeking, fear of failure, peer pressure, and other forces that do little to help the client feel at ease. This phenomenon isn't necessarily undesirable. A "healthy" amount of discomfort can motivate a person to get off dead center, to reduce dissonance, to make changes, and to restore equilibrium. As risk taking in a group accelerates, with members sharing their feelings, admitting inadequacies, and confronting themselves and one another, there are direct pressures from other members (which are usually held in check by the leader to protect individual rights) and subtle pressures from within to conform to the risky norm. Some begin to squirm as they watch others grow, leaving them behind. The more they hang back and remain passive, the more dissatisfied they become with their present ineffective functioning. The only way to reduce their discomfort is to leave the group (which sometimes happens if the leader doesn't carefully monitor readiness levels of each participant) or to make needed changes in themselves.

MONICA:

This is the eighth session and I know I haven't said much, but I'm just not all that good at talking in front of groups.

STEPHEN:

As long as you believe that crap, you don't have to do anything else. Just sit there and watch us sweat. I'm tired of you getting a free ride.

LEADER:

[Interrupting Monica before she can defend herself] Back off, Steve. Your point is well taken even if you put it so harshly. Monica, before you answer him, what's going on inside your head?

MONICA:

Just that maybe he's right. I wish I could get involved, but I'm too scared. And yet I hate coming here because I can't open up. I tried to stay home.

But I can't do that either. Then I'd really feel like a chicken. I'm so confused; I just don't know what to do.

LEADER:

How did you feel about what Steve said?

MONICA:

I think he—

LEADER:

Talk to him.

MONICA:

Ah. I don't know . . . OK. Steve, I think you're a bastard and you tried to hurt me. You didn't have to be so cruel about it. I heard what you said, but I didn't like the way you said it.

LEADER:

Now we're off and running.

Much of the growth in groups occurs through observation, identification, modeling, imitation, and other social-learning processes that are often not found in individual sessions. There are opportunities to watch the leader in action, presumably an expert in social-interactive skills, a model of the fully functioning person. The leader disperses wisdom or settles disputes with Solomon-like grace. The leader articulates metaphors and speeches worthy of a Shakespearean soliloquy. The leader orchestrates behavior, structures situations, organizes, takes charge. The leader radiates warmth and kindness and enthusiasm. And, all the while, the others watch carefully, nodding to themselves when they see something they like, consciously selecting behaviors for their own repertoire, captive to the power and force of the leader's personality.

A client also learns while watching peers struggle with their concerns. Every presented problem is internalized by the attentive audience, adapted to their particular lives. Clients learn from one another's successes and failures.

ORLANDO:

Last week, Gianina, when you were talking about how bored you were being a housewife, I was, at first, bored listening to you. I mean, what could I get out of your situation? My problem is that I'm too busy. I have too much work to do. Then I realized that, although our styles are different, we are both hiding from the same thing.

GIANINA:

I don't understand. Your life is far from boring. I stayed a housewife, until last week anyway, because I was afraid to venture out.

ORLANDO:

Exactly. And I keep myself so occupied so I don't have to deal with myself and confront how boring I feel I really am.

LEADER:

Were there others as well who identified with Gianina's concerns last week?

Groups provide many opportunities for realistic rehearsal of new behaviors. Much of what constitutes the permanent acquisition of new learning involves not only the observation of desired behaviors but also the opportunity to practice skills under supervision. Clients spend a good portion of their time applying what they have learned in the laboratory. They can experiment and refine interaction skills and social behaviors. They can take risks or confront others and, afterwards, receive constructive feedback. Before they venture out into the world to wrestle with a problem, they can first use other group members to help rehearse their performance.

LEADER:

OK, Jerry, who in the group most reminds you of your family members? Let's role-play the disaster you expect to occur when you get home tonight. Maybe we can even give you some ideas on how to handle it.

JERRY:

Well, Brenda for sure reminds me of my mother. No, Brenda—I mean you both are so calm and relaxed.

LEADER:

Don't apologize—just choose your characters.

JERRY:

OK. I guess Joe would be good to play my Dad. But act real gruff. Grunt a lot and don't look at me when you talk. That's right. Also fidget more. Perfect. Patty, you can be my older sister. But you have to act confident but aloof. And, Louis, you're crazy enough to be my older brother. I guess that's it. Unless someone wants to be my dog?

LEADER:

All right, now set the stage and program everyone the way they would normally act. Then you enter the scene and we'll see what happens. We will periodically stop the action, analyze what you did or didn't do, and give you some helpful suggestions. Perhaps we should even add a helper: Nancy will be your alter ego. Every time you are evasive or wishy-washy or back down, she will say aloud what you really want to say. Ready? Lights—camera—action.

The structure and ambience of therapeutic groups are well suited to working on interpersonal conflicts. The arrangement of chairs in a circle encourages direct communication among all as equals. If particular members make eye contact only with the leader while talking, that behavior is quickly extinguished. *Constructive* confrontations are stressed by encouraging the open and honest expression of feelings toward one another. Members are also helped to communicate and offer feedback sensitively and empathetically while they are taught to hear and interpret personal messages nondefensively.

CUES FOR INTERVENTION

Although a group leader's behavior involves mainly intuition, artistry, and feeling for the situation, there are some fairly specific instances in which therapeutic intervention is almost always necessary. In individual sessions the counselor relies heavily on "gut wisdom" but also knows that, when a client becomes self-deprecating or self-deceptive or drifts from reality, an intervention is called for. In group situations there is a virtual overload of stimuli to attend to. The most difficult task, therefore, is to describe not just how and when to intervene but with whom. A leader's behavior can be at best distracting or at worst destructive if ill timed or inappropriately directed. For these reasons, even the beginning student ought to become familiar with the minimally prescribed instances that signal therapeutic action.

Abusive Behavior

Without exception or qualification, in the event that it can be determined that the physical safety or emotional welfare of any participant is in danger, the leader must intervene. Much of the research on casualties in group work supports the idea that the leader should take responsibility for protecting client safety (Lieberman et al., 1973). This can be done only by carefully monitoring each member for cues of internal distress, as well as by keeping a close eye on group interactions to ensure that verbal abuse is minimized.

Usually, interactions that are hostile in their intent are quickly dissipated, or at least brought into the open to be dealt with in a relatively controlled manner. When a member is unaware of or insensitive to the negative effects generated by a comment or outburst, the leader also steps in to repair any damage. However, the vast majority of therapeutic efforts are directed toward heading off potential abuse *before* it occurs. With some experience, a leader can detect the signs of imminent explosive behavior and can therefore intervene before a fight or screaming match breaks out, in much the way that a skilled classroom teacher always knows when trouble is about to erupt.

Rambling and Digressions

For any number of reasons—to avoid meaningful dialogue, to resist treatment, to play games—or oftentimes simply because a client is verbally disorganized, the flow of conversation will stray from anything of therapeutic value. Perhaps someone will tell a long-winded story with no direct relevance. Or another might interrupt proceedings to prove some obscure point. Or there is a client (as inevitably there has been in every group we have ever known) who is just scatterbrained, "off the wall," or in a different hemisphere. His or her interjections can be maddening, interrupting a meaningful silence, badgering the leader with questions intended to win approval, or breaking into every interaction with the preface "That reminds me of the time. . . ."

Whether the group's ramblings are mildly inconvenient or downright pathological, the leader will usually establish some norm for appropriate input. Initially, interventions are used subtly to play down digressive comments and reinforce those that are on target. Sometimes the interventions must be more direct. For Cindy, a client who is particularly prone to digressions, the leader may finally cue feedback to indicate when comments aren't appropriate: "Jacob, was it helpful to hear what Cindy just said when she interrupted you? Oh, it wasn't? You wished she would wait until you were through?" and then "Cindy, what feedback did you just hear?"

Withdrawal and Passivity

Often the effects of verbal abuse, needless rambling, or other factors internal to the client will result in withdrawal in one or more members. Withdrawal is particularly difficult to deal with: the leader wants to safeguard the right to privacy yet does not want clients to slip into complete passivity. Furthermore, withdrawal is not obvious; it is recognized only by an absence of behavior. The leader must identify individual patterns for each client in order to read signs of withdrawal in averting one's eyes, scooting back one's chair, answering in monosyllables, or acting in some other uncharacteristic manner. The counselor may decide to draw the person into the group directly ("You're not saying much today. What's going on inside your head?"), consult with the person after the group in a private conference, or even wait and let other members bring up the issue.

Lethargy and Boredom

One function of the group leader is to spice up the learning experience to maintain participants' interest. After only a few sessions, a routine sets in that can become predictable or boring. The leader uses humor, spontaneous actions, dramatic gestures, and a playful spirit to keep things stimulating. Whenever yawning becomes prevalent, or monotonous voices, or behavior in which clients only appear to be going through the motions (which happens frequently), the leader intervenes.

> "It is up to each one of you to accept responsibility for your own growth in this group. Usually when you are confronted with a repetitive episode or when you feel lazy, you are content to daydream or doodle, biding your time until the ordeal is over. However, when you feel your mind drifting away in here, as many of you were doing just now, you are cheating yourself of a potentially valuable experience. It is too easy to write off the times you aren't intensely involved in what is happening. You are in this group because you wish to learn to be more focused in the present, to enjoy each moment to its fullest. Why not begin now? Throughout the rest of this session, and those thereafter, when you catch yourself feeling restless or bored, force yourself to focus on what is going on. There is *always* so much

to attend to, even if you find a particular discussion uninteresting. Watch the reactions of the others—how they are responding nonverbally to what they are hearing. Notice what I am doing or not doing and what my rationale might be. And closely scrutinize your own internal behavior. When you drift away, what are you hiding from? There is never a legitimate excuse for feeling bored in this group."

Semantic Errors

Depending on theoretical preferences and linguistic sensitivity, every counselor has a list of favorite semantic errors to pounce on. Language is the principal evidence we have of a client's thought patterns; how a person speaks aloud and expresses ideas, the choice and arrangement of words, accurately indicates how that person thinks and feels about his or her situation. Group leaders will intervene when clients distort reality, exaggerate, or use illogical communications. A facilitator versed in the client-centered approach may correct participants by asking them to change "I think" to "I feel." Rational-emotive counselors would interrupt members when they express themselves with "I must" or "I should," asking them instead to substitute more accurate verbalizations such as "I may" or "I could." And a follower of neurolinguistic programming techniques would correct variations that are incomplete in their surface structure. For example, "*They* made me do *it*" is converted from a statement having ambiguous referents to a complete communication: "Several of my elementary school teachers (they) made me play without making any kind of a mess (it)."

The leader of a group has the responsibility to understand, to relate, to facilitate, and to structure the interaction of the group members in a way that maximizes the therapeutic potential of the experience for all participants. This is a challenging and, at times, overwhelming task that demands the total energy and concentration of the group leader, who must be trained and skilled in individual and group-focused counseling skills.

SPECIALIZED SKILLS OF GROUP WORK

Working with groups requires the use of numerous techniques in addition to those used in individual counseling. Some practitioners are reluctant to lead counseling groups because of their anxiety over the responsibilities and techniques needed to function effectively. To some extent, inadequate preparation is the result of limited training in group leadership, and counselor educators have expressed concern over the teaching of group-counseling skills and abilities (Dye, 1980).

A summary of group skills presented by Corey (1990) (see Table 9-3) is based on the previous work of Dyer and Vriend (1975) and Nolan (1978). Many of these counselor behaviors are, of course, not unique to group leadership; they are part of the repertoire of any effective practitioner whether involved in individual, couples, family, or group sessions. Nevertheless, group leaders must be able to do everything individual counselors do, and more. Much more.

TABLE 9-3.   Summary of Group Skills

Skill	Description	Aims and Desired Outcomes
Facilitating	Opening up clear and direct communication within the group; helping members assume increasing responsibility for the group's direction.	To promote effective communication among members; to help members reach their own goals in the group.
Initiating	Promoting group participation and introducing new directions in the group.	To prevent needless group floundering; to increase the pace of group process.
Goal setting	Planning specific goals for the group process and helping participants define concrete and meaningful goals.	To give direction to the group's activities, to help members select and clarify their goals.
Evaluating	Appraising the ongoing group process and the individual and group dynamics.	To promote better self-awareness and understanding of group movement and direction.
Giving feedback	Expressing concrete and honest reactions based on observation of members' behaviors.	To offer an external view of how the person appears to others; to increase the client's self-awareness.
Suggesting	Offering advice and information, direction, and ideas for new behavior.	To help members develop alternative courses of thinking and action.
Protecting	Safeguarding members from unnecessary psychological risks in the group.	To warn members of possible risks in group participation; to reduce these risks.
Disclosing oneself	Revealing one's reactions to here-and-now events in the group.	To facilitate deeper levels of group interaction; to create trust; to model ways of revealing oneself to others.
Modeling	Demonstrating desired behavior through actions.	To provide examples of desirable behavior; to inspire members to fully develop their potential.
Linking	Connecting the work that members do to common themes in the group.	To promote member-to-member interactions; to encourage the development of cohesion.
Blocking	Intervening to stop counterproductive group behavior.	To protect members; to enhance the flow of group process.
Terminating	Preparing the group to close a session or end its existence.	To help members assimilate, integrate, and apply in-group learning to everyday life.

NOTE: The format of this chart is based on Edwin J. Nolan's article "Leadership interventions for promoting personal mastery," *Journal for Specialists in Group Work*, 1978, 3(3),132–138.

SOURCE: Corey, G. (1990). *Theory and practice of group counseling* (3rd ed.). Pacific Grove, CA: Brooks/Cole.

Donigian and Malnati (1987), for example, mention those critical incidents that are part of most therapeutic groups—situations that require skillful interventions—when members gang up to attack the leader, when there is mass denial or a mutual conspiracy among members to avoid real issues, when a member abruptly decides to leave the group, when a member withdraws, or when any of the other cues for intervention mentioned in the previous section occur. In addition, as Jacobs, Harvill, and Masson (1988) point out, group counselors need a thorough understanding of individual counseling methods and theory, a solid grounding in group dynamics and behavior, and good planning, organizational, and conflict-resolution skills.

It is for all these reasons that you will receive specialized training in group leadership as part of your counselor education. Ideally, you will have the opportunity to study the various approaches to group dynamics and leadership, to experience a therapeutic group as a client in order to work on personal issues, and, finally, to receive supervised experience as a coleader of a group. After you have completed this sequence of training, it is highly likely that you will find group leadership among the most invigorating, powerful, and satisfying professional experiences possible—not only for your clients but for yourself as well!

SUMMARY

Counseling in groups represents a powerful and economical strategy for counselors to deliver services in a variety of settings. Group work is especially effective because it more closely simulates social interactions and interpersonal communication patterns than does individual counseling. At the same time, group work is more demanding of the therapeutic counselor, who has a much more complex task in both structuring the effective development of the group and accepting the responsibility for the growth of multiple clients. Specialized training and supervision are essential so that counselors can learn to use group-focused skills effectively and include group work as a part of their professional activities.

SUGGESTED READINGS

Bera, R. C. (1990). *Group counseling: Concepts and procedures* (2nd ed.). Muncie, IN: Accelerated Development.

Corey, G. (1990). *Theory and practice of group counseling* (3rd ed.). Pacific Grove, CA: Brooks/Cole.

Dyer, W. W., & Vriend, J. (1980). *Group counseling for personal mastery*. New York: Sovereign.

Fuhriman, A., & Burlingame, G. M. (1990). Consistency of matter: A comparative analysis of individual and group process variables. *Counseling Psychologist,*
18(1), 6–63.

Gazda, G. M. (1989). *Group counseling: A developmental approach* (4th ed.). Boston:
Allyn & Bacon.

MacDevitt, J. W. (1987). Conceptualizing therapeutic components of group
counseling. *Journal for Specialists in Group Work, 12*(2), 76–84.

Yalom, I. (1985). *The theory and practice of group psychotherapy* (3rd ed.). New
York: Basic Books.

CHAPTER TEN

MARITAL, FAMILY, AND SEX COUNSELING

FAMILY COUNSELING THEORIES

POWER IN RELATIONSHIPS

SYMPTOMS AS SOLUTIONS

CASE EXAMPLE OF FAMILY
COUNSELING IN ACTION

INTERPRETING SYMPTOMS AS
METAPHORS

DIAGNOSTIC QUESTIONS

REFRAMING

DIRECTIVES
Forcing the Spontaneous
Opposition Through Compliance
Pretending
Slowing Down

ETHICAL ISSUES IN FAMILY
COUNSELING

SEX COUNSELING
Clinical Assessment Interview
Physical Exam and Medical
History
Exploration of Relationship
Sensate Focus Exercises
Specialized Techniques
Evaluation

SUMMARY

SUGGESTED READINGS

I t has been said that all counseling is, in fact, family counseling, since working with one person to change behavior cannot help affecting the feelings, attitudes, and behavior of others with whom the person lives. Whether the other family members are actually in attendance or not, they will most certainly be influenced by what happens in counseling sessions. It is for this reason that working with family members together is considered by many clinicians to be more humane, efficient, responsible, and realistic than individual counseling (Framo, 1981).

What was once an obscure specialty for radical social workers has recently become mainstream counseling for practitioners of all disciplines who seek to initiate changes through the involvement of those persons who wield a significant influence in the client's life. Since psychiatrists, psychologists, educators, counselors, and social workers have joined forces under the American Association for Marital and Family Therapy (AAMFT), an influential and relatively cohesive movement has developed.

Family counseling is significantly different from individual counseling because the practitioner must be more active, directive, and involved in the family's communication pattern. Rarely can the clinician afford the luxury of operating from single-theory allegiance, because strategies for working with a family tend to be extremely flexible and pragmatic (Jurek, Maier, Sandgren, Tall, & Searight, 1989). In addition to being knowledgeable about theory, research, and skills that are required for individual treatment modalities, the family counselor has expertise in several other areas.

For example, there are organizational structures and natural developmental processes that are part of all family systems. Each family is composed of a number of smaller coalitions and subsystems. Minuchin and Fishman (1981) label such groupings "holons"—those individual parts of the whole that make a couple, family, or community. Coalitions or holons are formed by spouses, parents, or siblings, each contributing to the ways in which the family functions. In viewing the family as an interdependent system of individuals governed by rules, Amatea and Fabrick (1981) have described several properties that are held in common. One pattern is circular: a cycle of repetitive, interrelated parts in which each family member responds to cues elicited by another (Figure 10-1 is an example). This structural analysis, originally proposed by Minuchin (1974), depicts the family unit as a delicately balanced, homeostatic mechanism that, similar to the body, resists and adapts to outside intrusions.

There are also developmental models that describe the natural evolution of families as they grow over time. The counselor needs to be familiar with the various developmental crises and tasks required of a family, such as those of adjusting to a newborn infant, launching a half-grown adolescent, or adapting to the "empty-nest syndrome."

In addition, the American family structure has diversified so much in recent years that the traditional model of two parents living with their children (father working, mother staying at home) is a decided minority (Goldenberg & Goldenberg, 1990). More often than not, any client you see will be a member of a nontraditional structure: a blended family of stepparents and children, a single-

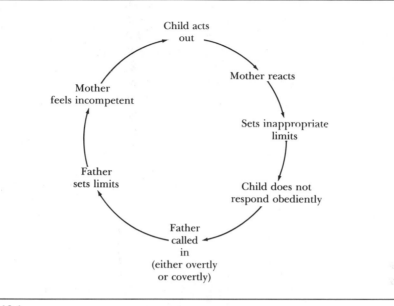

FIGURE 10-1.
Family interaction as a circular causal chain (Amatea & Fabrick, 1981, p. 226)

parent household, a dual-career family, a cohabiting heterosexual or homo-sexual couple.

The family counselor should consider family interactions and the impact theyhave on children's behavior. The research of Gregory Bateson and his associates on family interaction suggests that each family has unique patterns of functioning, some of which can predispose its members to confusion, and even schizophrenia (Bateson, Jackson, Haley, & Weakland, 1956). In their now-famous theory of the "double bind," Bateson and company described the "logical" process by which paradoxical messages are communicated simultaneously on different levels. In certain dysfunctional families, communications often take the bizarre form of "go away/come close" messages. A child may be overtly invited to be more intimate and loving with her parents while at the same time she is being subtly rejected for her affections: "Please leave us alone." In such a case, schizophrenia may be the *only* way of escape for a child.

FAMILY COUNSELING THEORIES

It should not be surprising to you that, like everything else in this field, there is a tremendous diversity in the ways in which family counselors operate. Similarly to the approaches we explored in the chapters on counseling theory, Fenell and Weinhold (1989) have organized the various counseling systems according to their basic perspectives. Thus some approaches examine underlying family structures or patterns of communication, others focus more on dysfunctional thinking or behavior, and still others concentrate on the individual

TABLE 10-1. A Comparison of Six Theoretical Viewpoints in Family Therapy

Dimension	Psychodynamic	Experiential/ Humanistic	Bowenian	Structural	Communication	Behavioral
1. Major time frame	Past; history of early experiences needs to be uncovered.	Present; here-and-now data from immediate experience observed.	Primarily the present, although attention also paid to one's family of origin.	Present and past; family's current structure carried over from earlier transactional patterns.	Present; current problems or symptoms maintained by ongoing, repetitive sequences between persons.	Present; focus on interpersonal environments that maintain and perpetuate current behavior patterns.
2. Role of unconscious processes	Unresolved conflicts from the past, largely out of the person's awareness, continue to attach themselves to current objects and situations.	Free choice and conscious self-determination more important than unconscious motivation.	Earlier concepts suggested unconscious conflicts, although now recast in interactive terms.	Unconscious motivation less important than repetition of learned habits and role assignments by which the family carries out its tasks.	Family rules, homeostatic balance, and feedback loops determine behavior, not unconscious processes.	Problematic behavior is learned and maintained by its consequences; unconscious processes rejected as too inferential and unquantifiable.
3. Insight versus action	Insight leads to understanding, conflict reduction, and, ultimately, intrapsychic and interpersonal change.	Self-awareness of one's immediate existence leads to choice, responsibility, and change.	Rational processes used to gain self-awareness into current relationships as well as intergenerational experiences.	Action precedes understanding; change in transactional patterns more important than insight in producing new behaviors.	Action oriented; behavior change and symptom reduction brought about through directives rather than interpretations.	Actions prescribed to modify specific behavior patterns.
4. Role of therapist	Neutral; makes interpretations of individual and family behavior patterns.	Active facilitator of potential for growth; provides family with new experiences.	Direct but nonconfrontational; detriangulated from family fusion.	Stage director; manipulates family structure in order to change dysfunctional sets.	Active; manipulative; problem-focused; prescriptive, paradoxical.	Directive; teacher, trainer, or model of desired behavior; contract negotiator.

Dimension	Psychodynamic	Experiential/Humanistic	Bowenian	Structural	Communication	Behavioral
5. Unit of study	Focus on individual; emphasis on how family members feel about and deal with one another.	Dyad; problems arise from interaction between two members (for example, husband and wife).	Entire family over several generations; may work with one dyad (or one partner) for a period of time.	Triads; coalitions, subsystems, boundaries, power.	Dyads and triads; problems and symptoms viewed as interpersonal communications between two or more family members.	Dyads; effect of one person's behavior on another; linear view of causality.
6. Major theoretical underpinnings	Psychoanalysis.	Existentialism; humanistic psychology; phenomenology.	Family systems theory.	Structural family theory; systems.	Communication theory; systems; behaviorism.	Behaviorism; social-learning theory.
7. Major theorists and/or practitioners	Ackerman, Framo, Boszormenyi-Nagy, Stierlin, Skynner, Bell	Whitaker, Kempler, Satir	Bowen	Minuchin	Jackson, Erickson, Haley, Madanes, Selvini-Palazzoli	Patterson, Stuart, Liberman, Jacobson, Margolin
8. Goals of treatment	Insight, psychosexual maturity, strengthening of ego functioning; reduction in interlocking pathologies; more satisfying object relations.	Growth, more fulfilling interaction patterns; clearer communication; expanded awareness; authenticity.	Maximization of self-differentiation for each family member.	Change in relationship context in order to restructure family organization and change dysfunctional transactional patterns.	Change in dysfunctional, redundant behavioral sequences ("games") between family members in order to eliminate presenting problem or symptom.	Change in behavioral consequences between persons leading to elimination of maladaptive or problematic behavior.

SOURCE: Goldenberg, L., & Goldenberg, H. (1991). *Family therapy: An overview* (3rd ed.). Pacific Grove, CA: Brooks/Cole.

issues that family members struggle with. In Table 10-1 Goldenberg and Goldenberg (1991) summarize the most prominent approaches to family counseling currently in practice.

A perusal of these various theories indicates not only their differences but also those factors that are somewhat universal:

1. Most family counselors rely on the same set of skills, such as "joining the family" or building rapport, assessing power hierarchies within the family system, restructuring coalitions among family members, reframing problems to make them more solvable, and engaging all members in resolving their difficulties (Fenell & Weinhold, 1989).

2. All family counselors think in terms of social systems. Rather than viewing problems in terms of linear causality—that Mother *causes* Child to act out—they are seen in terms of circular causality: chain reactions influence each family member, who in turn influences everyone else (Goldenberg & Goldenberg, 1990). For example, a mother becomes impatient because her daughter is slow getting dressed in the morning, making everyone late for work. The child feels pressured and resists the mother's efforts to control her. The father feels jealous because his wife is devoting so much attention to their child while ignoring him. He sabotages his wife's efforts to motivate the child. The mother feels angry at her husband for siding against her, withdrawing further. The child becomes even more obstinate, with more pressure applied by the increasingly exasperated mother. So who is causing the problem?

3. Family counselors, by and large, are more flexible, more active, and more structuring than practitioners of other treatment modalities. Because sessions can become so emotionally charged, things can rapidly get out of hand if the counselor allows family members to become abusive, violent, or out of control. In addition, family practitioners focus more on the present than on the past, tend to be more didactic in their style, and are concerned primarily with patterns of communication (Friedlander, Ellis, Raymond, Siegel & Milford, 1987).

Despite their similarities, each approach has distinctive features that permit the counselor to switch from one to the other according to the requirements of the situation. Stanton (1981) recommends that counselors begin structurally to diagnose, analyze, and test boundaries and rules, since this approach is more direct and comprehensible. They can move to strategic intervention once they have encountered resistance, defensiveness, or confusion. Then it may be effective to revert back to structural theory to pull together any loose ends. In this methodology, therefore, it is possible to *think* structurally and *work* strategically. By thinking structurally, the counselor is aware of various predictable patterns and styles that will commonly arise.

POWER IN RELATIONSHIPS

Relationships among family members can be symmetrical or complementary. In the former, according to Haley (1976), there is much competition; in the latter there is an emphasis on exchange as people maneuver for position and power.

A family counseling session in action, showing some of the alliances and coalitions as evidenced by the seating arrangement.

Minuchin introduces the notion of *boundaries* to describe how the various coalitions in family relationships tend to intersect. Sometimes, for example, the boundaries between parents and children are clearly defined, and at other times an alignment may develop between mother and son, with a disengaged boundary between them and the father. Matters become considerably more complicated as the counselor joins the family system, creates different boundaries by manipulating the various coalitions, and finally restructures the system so that more constructive lines of affiliation develop.

Power within the family must also be carefully understood and balanced. Each family has a regimented hierarchy, within which each person has a specified amount of control and responsibility. Counseling often takes the form of reestablishing a single hierarchical organization in which the boundaries are more clearly delineated so that the parents are in charge and the children have less power.

Madanes (1983) records the case of a depressed man whose symptom was treated by resolving the hierarchical incongruity in his marriage. The husband had previously been dominant in the relationship, but as the wife developed outside interests and a career as a therapist, his own life and business began to fail. The husband's depression became a source of power in the marriage because the wife, as a professional helper, could do nothing to bring relief. The counselor's interventions focused on restoring a more balanced power hierarchy by reorganizing the way the couple dealt with each other. No longer useful as a form of one-upmanship, the depression vanished.

Balance of power between spouses can be viewed as a metaphor for other communications in the marriage. Consider a case in which the husband has all the power—in career, in decision making, in finances. The wife develops symptoms of depression. Husband tries to help but fails repeatedly. Husband becomes restricted in his own life by catering to wife. Wife indirectly controls husband, and situation is reciprocal: husband tells wife what to do about her life, then complains because she doesn't comply. Wife complains that husband is insensitive and can't or won't solve the problem. Both use power and helplessness, metaphors for submissiveness and rebellion.

Following is another example of the power struggles within a family. The counselor initially plots the family organization, then identifies the problems of each member, and finally develops a series of interventions.

Family Structure
Mother is overinvolved with grandmother and daughter.
Grandmother and daughter have a friendly alliance.
Father and son have a weak and peripheral affiliation.
Father and mother are minimally involved.
Father and son are both isolated from power in family.
Daughter and son are actively engaged in conflict.
Complete circle (Figure 10-2) represents a closed boundary separating family
    from influences of outside world.

Structural map of a family organization

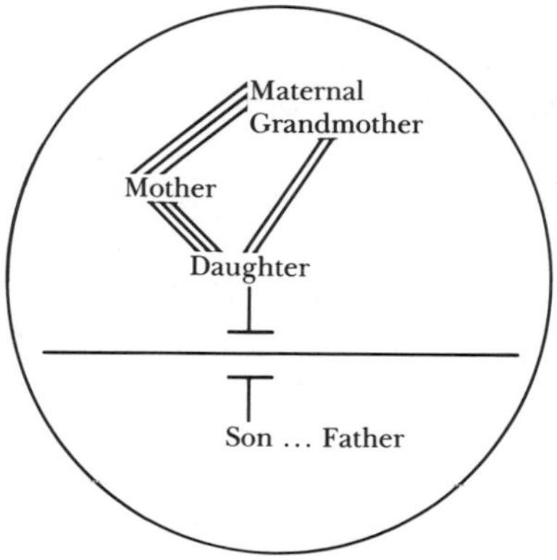

FIGURE 10-2.
Structural map of a family

Family Symptomology
Son is the identified client, who brought family to counseling because of
    fighting at school and home.
Father is passive, withdrawn, uncommunicative, and depressed.
Mother is domineering, controlling, manipulative, and anxious.

Father and mother have marital problems; only son's acting out keeps them together.

Grandmother is lonely, isolated, and dependent on mother.

Daughter spends more time with mother and grandmother than with age-mates; provokes her brother.

Initial Therapeutic Interventions

Solicit cooperation of mother, who is in control.

Rearrange coalitions with mother and father together against distracting influences of children and grandmother.

Invite father to take more power and control.

Strengthen bonds between mother and son, father and daughter, to equalize involvement.

Help grandmother to expand her social world.

Help son to stop rescuing parents.

Open boundary isolating family from outside world.

A child will often develop problems as a way to protect the parents from having to face their own difficulties (Madanes, 1984) . For example, the son in the family described above began to act out and became a common focus for the parents. In responding to the child's misbehavior, the parents were allowed to ignore their problem interaction pattern and the child felt powerful because he was keeping the family together. Although this intervention by the child kept the parents "together" in their interaction, it resulted in a serious family breakdown. As a counselor, you will often see families like this who present a "problem" child and view themselves as concerned parents who have no problems of their own.

SYMPTOMS AS SOLUTIONS

Family systems analysis provides a larger context within which to view the problems of the identified client. Rather than approaching treatment with the usual intention of promoting individual insight and then helping the client to make specific changes, the family counselor often looks at the behavior of the disruptive family member as helpful or constructive in some regard. The disruptive behavior continues because it is unconsciously supported and maintained by others within the family system.

Haley (1980) suggests that counselors, particularly when working with severely disturbed adolescents, view the child's disruptive behavior as stabilizing the family structure. The child's behavior protects the parents from each other, forcing them to find solace in sharing their frustrations over their inability to control the unruly behavior. *All* family members, therefore, must be seen together to clarify the power and hierarchy structures. The family counselor's role is to help the parents regain control over themselves and the adolescent.

Haley finds it helpful when working with disruptive children to assume the following: (1) the client's symptoms are serving a protective function; (2) the client has the capacity to assume responsibility for disruptive behavior (and is not a victim of external forces); (3) the power hierarchy of the family is confused, with the "little" people controlling the "bigger" people; (4) the *real* problem is the family communication pattern, not the young person; and (5) once power is restored to the parents and the child is no longer permitted self-indulgence and failure—once the confusions, inconsistencies, and conflicts in family communications are cleared up—then the child can act more normally and responsibly without destabilizing the other family members.

Therapist Salvador Minuchin is fond of using a simple procedure to restore the natural balance and power to a family with a rebellious adolescent. If the mother feels that she can no longer control her spirited child, and the boy, too, seems to be begging for limit-setting by his attention-seeking ploys, both family members may be asked to stand. Minuchin will then put them back to back, the son's head reaching his mother's shoulder, and thoughtfully consider the picture, finally asking "Who is taller and bigger?" After getting a confused response, he may ask them to arm wrestle, proving once again who is the stronger, bigger parent and who is the weaker child. He hopes to reestablish appropriate control and power by reminding the family members who is really in charge.

When the child's destructive acting-out behavior is diagnosed as the solution to another, more important problem within the family, then interventions can be directed toward helping the parents to resolve their conflicts. Once the child's "help" is no longer needed, the child can then revert to more appropriate behavior to deal with his or her own internal conflicts.

CASE EXAMPLE OF FAMILY COUNSELING IN ACTION

The diagnosis and analysis of the interdynamics within a family or even a couple's relationship are often extremely complex. A 45-year-old salesman and his 40-year-old lover enter counseling to attempt to resolve a long-standing and increasingly frustrating problem between them. Although George can quite easily become erect during sexual foreplay, he quickly loses penile rigidity once he attempts to initiate intercourse with Joanne. The questions that come immediately to the mind of the counselor operating strategically within a family diagnostic structure are: "How is this particular problem of erectile dysfunction helping this couple? What solutions to another problem is the symptom offering?"

Naturally, some data collection and exploration are in order. The counselor learns in due course that George had nursed his cancer-ridden wife for a period of 15 years, until her recent death, and suffers some residual guilt. Joanne, too, has had some life concerns. Her own romantic history is speckled by three failed marriages. Both Joanne and George are genuinely trying to create a loving, respecting relationship, and they care deeply for each other. Yet they are unable to proceed beyond their current impasse as long as their lovemaking is doomed to mutual frustration. Interestingly, however, George's "failure" occurs *only* with Joanne. In several attempts to test himself with prostitutes, he has found, to his relief, that he was easily able to consummate the sexual act.

What, then, do we know about this couple?

1. George's erectile problem is *not* organically caused, as evidenced by his awakening with morning erections and the occurrence of the problem only with Joanne.
2. George, as a salesman, has a high need for continual success to feel complete as a man. His area of greatest vulnerability is repeated failure at something—making a sale, for one thing, and, certainly, satisfying the woman he loves.
3. George still feels incredibly guilty about his failure to be a perfect nurse and husband to his dying wife. During the last three years of his wife's illness he had a few sexual relationships, but only for physical relief.
4. The most difficult thing for Joanne to handle is the idea that she may not be attractive or sexy enough for George. Her anger and frustration are building as she realizes that an unknown prostitute can elicit sustained sexual arousal in George and she, his intimate friend, cannot do the same.
5. In their adult lives neither George nor Joanne has ever been able to sustain an intimate romantic involvement. Joanne forces relationships by pushing things too quickly; George has a desperate fear of losing control in relationships in which he would feel vulnerable.

Now the counselor can begin to put pieces of the puzzle together. What would be the likely consequence of solving this problem? Answer: marriage.

Marriage is the one thing that both fear most. George still has unresolved guilt and feels the unconscious need to punish himself by not performing as he is capable. Joanne is desperately afraid that, once the relationship moves on to the next stage, it will certainly fall apart, as have all her other relationships. Yet, as long as they remain at this current stage—admittedly locked in a frustrating dance—they can at least stay together. Their fears are temporarily displaced by focusing on the sexual problem.

Most of the traditional sex-counseling techniques, of course, prove useless in eliminating a symptom that both partners unconsciously wish to continue. To remove much of the performance anxiety, the counselor tells them to do what they already can do—play in bed during foreplay—and not worry about intercourse. They comply, and the inexplicable occurs: George can no longer become erect at all.

"It's as if this were the smartest penis in the world," the counselor explains to the couple. "It is so smart that, in spite of our best efforts to resolve this problem, your penis persists in figuring out ways to continue its stubborn unwillingness to cooperate. The lack of complete sexual fulfillment is actually helping both of you in the *only* way that could ever save your relationship in the long run. You are forced to slow down the pace of your relationship. Since you can't relate sexually, you *have* to relate emotionally. You are spending hours together holding hands, hugging, talking. You are really developing intimacy before you can ruin the relationship by removing the sexual mystery.

"But that's not all. It is also permitting you, George, to pay for your guilt, or at least to work through your feelings. Yes, the problem provides you both with time to adjust to each other emotionally by restricting your sexual options."

George feels as if he has been saved! So he isn't a failure after all. Although he certainly doesn't believe that his penis has made decisions, he begins to recognize that he has, indeed, needed time to explore and develop a truly intimate relationship. He recognizes that subconsciously limiting his sexual activity is a way to force himself truly to know Joanne. Joanne, too, feels relieved. Maybe it isn't her fault after all. She does agree that she feels closer to George than she has to any other man in her life. The reason is that the absence of sex has allowed them to become more alluring to each other. They feel more nurturing and caring than they could have with a normal sex life because both have had so many other issues interfering with the development of intimacy along with active sex.

The counselor next instructs them to appreciate each other by talking about all they have gained from each other. Now they can finally relax and enjoy each other without worrying about their inadequacies. The counselor then sends the clients away from the session with a reminder: "This problem will be resolved when both of you are ready. Meanwhile, just enjoy each other and continue to work together to achieve complete intimacy."

With the pressure lifted, they are able to appreciate each other and their relationship in spite of the sexual dysfunction, which persists for a few more weeks. The following sessions deal with the issues of guilt, sense of failure, and intimacy, until they are able to experience sexual intimacy without fear. As of this writing, George and Joanne are happily married and able to appreciate each other sexually, emotionally, and intellectually.

INTERPRETING SYMPTOMS AS METAPHORS

Most communication has messages on two levels: digital and analogical. One part of communication is literal and content oriented, whereas another, deeper, communication expresses messages of a more subtle kind. For example, when a woman says to her spouse at the dinner table "You eat so fast I don't know how you can even taste or enjoy your food," she is, in fact, making a literal comment about her husband's table manners. However, in addition to this digital statement, she may also be communicating metaphorically about another aspect of their relationship that is rushed without enjoyment: their sex life.

Now, the counselor has the choice of interpreting the disguised meaning of the communication or responding on a likewise-symbolic level. Haley (1973), in writing about Milton Erickson's preferred strategy, relates that "whatever the patient says in metaphoric form, Erickson responds in kind. By parables, by interpersonal action, and by directives, he works within the metaphor to bring about change. He seems to feel that the depth and swiftness of that change can be prevented if the person suffers a translation of the communication" (p. 28). The couple in this example may be requested to go out and have a slow, drawn-out, leisurely meal. This message, and its subsequent action, permits the partners to practice their foreplay in an indirect, minimally threatening situation.

Since people communicate on these different levels, the family counselor must learn to recognize the ways in which children and adults express different issues through their behavior. Presenting complaints or identified symptoms are thus often interpreted as something quite different from their surface messages. This theoretical construct is common to many individual therapeutic approaches, such as psychoanalysis and Gestalt counseling. The only difference may be that the strategic family counselor is less interested in explaining or interpreting the metaphor and instead prefers to operate on the same level as the family members.

DIAGNOSTIC QUESTIONS

To aid in the diagnosis of family problems and to sort out the confusing connections among symptoms, metaphors, power hierarchies, and other relevant variables, there are some specific questions that will facilitate data collection:

What is the problem?
When does the problem occur?
Where does the problem occur?
Where are various family members when the problem occurs?
What is each member of the family doing when the problem occurs?
What are the effects on each family member?
What are the benefits to the client? (to other family members?)
Who in the family has had a similar problem?
Where is the power (money, decisions, time)?
Who is being protected?

The *genogram* is another useful tool for gathering information about family relationships and structures. It consists of a comprehensive map of all the members of a family over several generations, including their coalitions, conflicts, and connections. It thus provides a blueprint for the counselor in understanding the cross-generational themes that repeat themselves over time as well as the current interpersonal conflicts that are evident in the "structural map" (Figure 10-2) presented earlier.

For example, using symbols standardized by McGoldrick and Gerson (1985) in their book on family assessment, Erlanger (1990) plotted a four-generation genogram of Lucy, a 75-year-old client (see Figure 10-3). By studying this chart, it is evident that there are several issues that Lucy may wish to explore: her father's suicide, her son's alcoholism, her relationships with her aging husband and mother. All of this is clear before any efforts are made to include existing conflicts among family members.

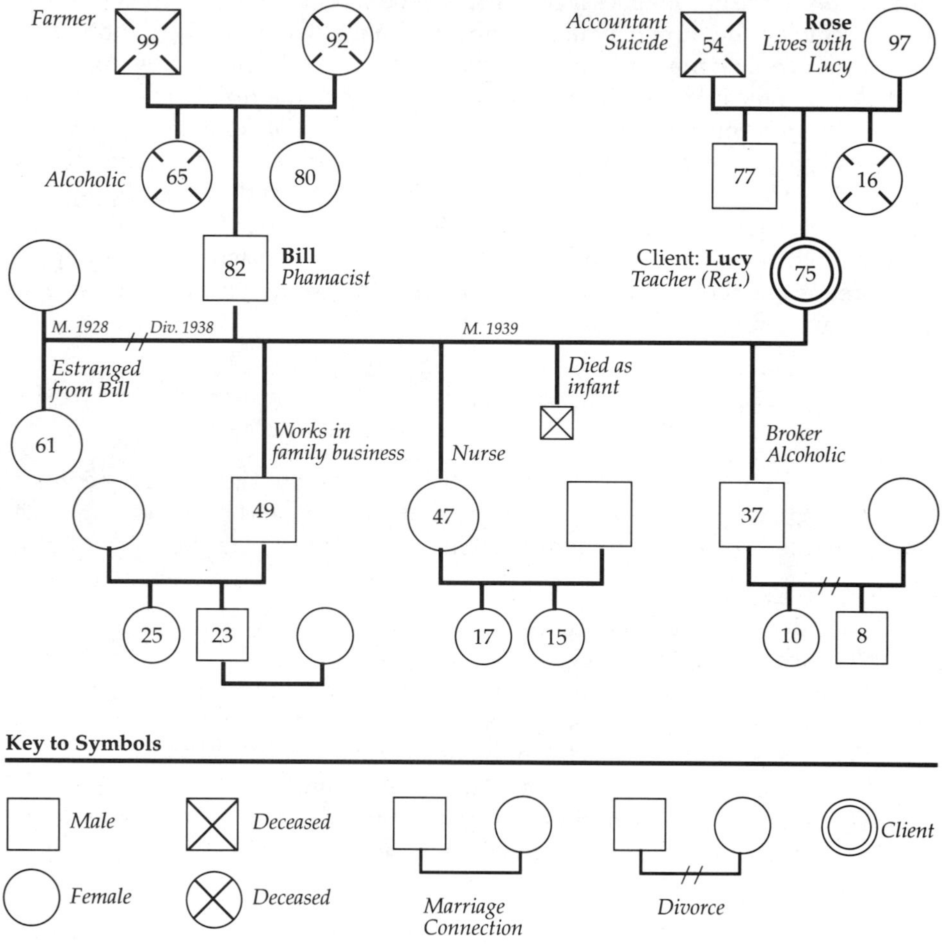

Key to Symbols

FIGURE 10-3.
A four-generation genogram (Erlanger, 1990)

REFRAMING

Two types of diagnosis are useful in family counseling. The first variety includes applying those labels that help the counselor to grasp the processes and problems involved. We have already mentioned diagnosing client position, family hierarchy, communication style, and symptoms as solutions and metaphors in this context. However, there is a second kind of diagnosis, the one communicated to the client. It is therefore the counselor's initial task to define or reframe the present problem to the client or clients in such a way that it may be resolved.

Clients come into counseling sessions with preconceived notions of what is wrong with them and why:

> "My marriage is on the rocks because my wife wants to go back to school and start a career rather than taking care of the family."
> "My boy is having trouble in school because his teachers are too strict and don't appreciate his uniqueness."
> "I've never been able to hold a job because everyone in my family has always been lazy."

In the process of reframing, the counselor redefines the presenting complaint for the family, using both ingenuity and creativity to think on concrete and metaphorical levels. In the resulting working diagnosis, the counselor identifies issues that can, in fact, be responsive to change, so that the family will be more willing to work on them. There isn't much that can be done to help a client who is complaining about another person's behavior, unless, of course, the other person will come in for counseling and willingly change what the accuser dislikes. In initiating counseling for clients with the complaints quoted above, the most important task would be to reframe the client's perceived difficulties. The husband who wants compliance from his wife would be helped to view the problem more as a lack of communication: he hasn't conveyed his desires in such a way that his wife could understand (and accept) them. The problem of the boy having trouble in school would be reframed to say that, although he is clearly a talented comic, he is performing for the wrong audience. The person without a job would be helped to redefine his problem as a lack of skills and/or motivation rather than a lack of employable genes.

The value of reframing is exemplified in the case of a 35-year-old client who arrived for his session, huffing and puffing, his face flushed, and his hand wrapped in a towel that was quickly turning red with blood. The flustered counselor, a tiny woman of 90 pounds, looked up at the 230-pound mechanic and responded "Oh, I see you had some trouble. What happened?"

Still standing in the foyer, the man smiled with a glazed, stunned look and answered "I locked my damn keys in the car and I got mad. And when I get mad I like to hit things. Anything. I can't help it. Boy, am I mad. Now, what's all this shit about you wanting to see me about my kid?"

The counselor went to her supervisor immediately following the session. She calmed down, at least enough to hear the more experienced clinician reframe the man's behavior: "What do you think about this guy? Blustering his way into a first session with his hand all bloody. *This* is funny. *This* is hysterical. This guy is no bully—this guy is a clown. Next time he comes in, treat him like a clown and see what happens. And, just in case you need me, I'll be close by."

During the next session the man responded with a burst of anger to the counselor's accurate confrontation about how he had been neglecting his son. He stamped the floor and rose with a menacing stare. The counselor, of course, was startled, but she regained her composure and looked at the humor in his behavior. She smiled, seemingly unaffected by his threatening behavior, thinking "This guy really is funny."

The man anxiously demanded some explanation of the counselor's calm appearance. He was used to having people feel afraid of him. She told him compassionately how silly he really looked stamping around like a child; then, as an afterthought, she moved back a little and waited.

Yes, he agreed, he probably did look funny, but he does get what he wants by intimidating other people. He eventually admitted, though, that he hated himself for behaving so badly and appreciated the counselor's seeing through the mask and allowing him to discuss his vulnerable feeling.

Although this was a risky strategy, it nevertheless demonstrated the power of reframing behavior, casting it in a different light. Not only is the client able to view his behavior as more manageable, but the counselor is also able to see the behavior in compassionate rather than threatening terms.

DIRECTIVES

The idea of deliberately telling clients what they should do goes against the grain of almost all counseling systems. Counselors are, after all, supposed to be neutral, objective, detached, and not prone to giving advice. A rationale for the violation of this golden rule is that such interventions are often successful. Furthermore, family counselors, by the very nature of their work, are more active, structuring, and directive than they would ever consider being when working with individual clients. Put all members of a family together in a room, particularly those who are so conflicted they had to ask for help, and the situation often turns chaotic. Unless the counselor is prepared to jump in and take the initiative, the family counseling session could make matters considerably worse.

A number of directive options are available to the family counselor. They may be designed to be either obeyed or disobeyed, depending on which is more likely to work. They can be simply and straightforwardly presented or explained in such a complicated and confusing way that the client will rebelliously do the opposite. The best directives are those that involve everyone in the family, are precisely described, provide sufficient motivation to encourage completion of the task, and are simple enough that they can be reasonably accomplished (Madanes, 1983).

In using directives, the counselor seeks to initiate changes in the family structure by getting people to act differently. The goal is to realign the hierarchy of power along more desirable paths—for instance, with the parents in charge rather than the children or grandparents, or with both spouses on an equal footing. The process of initiating all directives usually involves (1) redefining the problem in a less threatening form and describing it in a way that allows resolution, (2) motivating and preparing the client to follow (or not follow) the directive, and (3) presenting the directive clearly, simply, and realistically, ensuring that all participants understand what they are to do or not do.

According to Fisch, Weakland, and Segal (1982), all directives (and for that matter all therapeutic interventions) are designed to interrupt the current attempted solution to a family problem—that is, the symptoms of the identified client. Fisch et al. offer the following tactical maneuvers that require active counselor direction.

Forcing the Spontaneous

Many psychosomatic complaints, performance problems, and thought disturbances occur spontaneously, in spite of a client's attempts to control them. Trying too hard to fall asleep, reach orgasm, or stop a tic only makes things worse. It is not reasonable to ask the client to cease behavior that is not within conscious control. Instead, the client can be directed to continue the behavior at will. A person who can't sleep may be told to stay up or to get up after 15 minutes and work on an important but nonstimulating task. The client is then able to make the first step toward resolution of the problem: if she or he can exhibit some control of the uncontrollable problem by exercising some choices around its occurrence, then the problem seems less ominous and not as wayward as the client originally believed. A paradoxical directive of this type allows the counselor to be successful, and the client perceives himself or herself as making progress. The client who complies with the suggestion is exhibiting control, and the client who doesn't abide by the directive to fail is then cured of the problem. This type of directive is safe for both the counselor and the client because it provides ample opportunity for positive outcome.

Opposition Through Compliance

In the physical world, when we attempt without success to solve a problem by a certain action, we will try something else—usually the opposite action. If we try to open a door by pushing it, and it won't budge, we may try pulling it. If we attempt to loosen a screw by forcing it to the left, and it doesn't move, we will try turning it to the right. Yet, when an attempted strategy doesn't work in emotional family struggles, with participants locked into no-win battles, a person will often try the *same thing* harder. If a wife fights for her independence in the marriage by repeatedly resisting her husband's orders, and then discovers she is worse off, she will nevertheless struggle harder. If parents have attempted on numerous occasions to get their rebellious adolescent to comply to house rules and they have found that the youngster is only getting worse, the parents will demand even more compliant behavior.

This second category of directives takes the form of suggesting to those without power that the only way they will ever get any control is to back down. By deliberately taking a "weak position" and "giving in," they finally break the vicious, repetitive cycle. Thus, benevolent sabotage begins to defuse the conflict: "I'm sorry I burned your toast. I don't know what's getting into me." The powerless client is able to feel more dignity and control since she/he backs down by choice. The key to using compliant tactics effectively is to avoid sarcasm or overt game playing. The client must attempt a "one-down" instead of the "one-up" position that didn't work. Once the opposition ceases, the cycle is often broken, and the other family members no longer derive satisfaction from their positions. It's no fun to dominate if the other person won't fight back. And it's no fun to rebel if the others won't force compliance.

Pretending

A favorite ploy of Madanes in working with children is to direct the parents to encourage the symptom deliberately and to ask the child to *pretend* to have it. Much of the tension associated with the symptom is thereafter dissipated since everyone is "only pretending." Consider the case of a "28-year-old adolescent" who was still so dependent on his father that he carried around a paging device so that his father could reach him at any time, usually to scream at him for some mistake he had made in the family business. The young man was constantly late, missed appointments, and botched orders, and each time his father would furiously bawl him out. Neither man much enjoyed the pattern, but each felt powerless to stop it.

The counselor directed the son to bungle something deliberately, at least three times a day. He was to pretend to make mistakes so that his father could no longer determine when the young man was truly irresponsible and when he was only faking. The son improved after discovering that, since he could control when he made mistakes, and pretend to do so, he could certainly refrain from such errors whenever he chose.

A way to involve other family members is to encourage them to criticize the person's "performance." Another pattern is thus broken, since, instead of trying to deter the symptoms, they are now trying to help the person do them even better. With the introduction of directives to pretend, the metaphorical symptoms are no longer allowed to be part of reality. The problem diminishes because it is no longer taken seriously.

Slowing Down

Whenever anyone tries too hard to do something, the task becomes more difficult. The directive to slow down is often most effective during initial interviews, when clients are apprehensive about being asked to do something they won't be able to do. If the presenting problem is resolved too quickly, before the clients have had the opportunity to make new adjustments or discover other ways of relating to one another, it is possible that the family structure will break down.

During the first session with a woman complaining of a marriage that is falling apart, the counselor specifically directs her to stop trying to fix things: "Leave things just the way they are for now. This way your husband, too, will have the chance to get involved in solving the problem. I know he's saying that he won't come in for counseling. That is certainly the case as long as you keep nagging him, but let's see how things change once you slow down. The marriage isn't comfortable anyway, so by backing off you can hardly make things worse."

The therapeutic circumstances are now programmed for success no matter what the outcome. The client immediately feels released from her sole respon-sibility for fixing the marriage. She can loosen up and take a deep breath. She also focuses on herself rather than trying to change her husband. And, if things don't improve immediately, the client will be more patient and willing to keep working.

ETHICAL ISSUES IN FAMILY COUNSELING

If we have given you the impression that marital and family counseling is a powerful treatment method that can often effect "cures" in a matter of weeks, that is indeed true. However, it is because these modalities are so potent that they bring with them a number of moral dilemmas for the practitioner. A later chapter will focus on ethical and legal issues as they relate to the practice of counseling, but we nevertheless wish to briefly mention some of the conflicts you will face if you decide to do marital and family counseling. Some of the fol-lowing issues may already have occurred to you:

- If my primary function is to treat family problems, what about the *individual* goals of each member, which may conflict with those of the others?
- Is it ethical to be deceitful and manipulative (using paradoxical techniques, for example) if it is for the client's own good?
- How do I handle confidentiality issues if one family member confides a secret (that he or she is having an affair, for example) but instructs me not to tell anyone else?
- Since family conflicts frequently involve value issues related to fidelity, sexuality, promiscuity, divorce, child rearing, and life priorities, how can I possibly keep my own values in check regarding how I believe people should behave?
- Because family counselors are often very directive and dramatic in their interventions in order to break up dysfunctional patterns, aren't there greater risks for doing harm?

Last, but by no means least, is the area of family violence and the special ethical problems it raises. The abuse of children, spouses, and the elderly cre-ates problems not only for the victims and perpetrators but also for the helping professionals caught in the middle who are trying to stabilize explosive situa-tions (Green & Hansen, 1989). In their survey of ethical issues related to vio-lence, Gross and Robinson (1987) describe several cases that highlight the con-flicting loyalties counselors have (1) to state laws that mandate the reporting of abuse, (2) to the identified clients who are requesting help, and (3) to the vic-tims (or potential victims) of the dangerous action.

SEX COUNSELING

Sex counseling is the single most successful result of integrating many diverse theoretical structures into a unified technology of helping. With reported success rates of well into the 80–95% range for a variety of sexual dysfunctions, such as impotence, premature ejaculation, and orgasmic dysfunctions (in the absence of physical causes), sex counseling is one of the most well-developed therapeutic specialties. First, the treatment is successful because it attacks sexual problems using insight methods as well as structured homework. Second, the treatment is relatively short term (usually three to ten sessions). And, third, the nature of the counseling strategy requires the practitioner to be flexible and pragmatic enough to try a variety of interventions.

Helen Singer Kaplan (1974), in her classic book on the theory and techniques of sex therapy, readily admits that treating clients with sexual problems by insight methods alone is probably unethical, because the technology does exist to help people relatively quickly by more behavioral interventions. The sex counselor, therefore, not only uses much of the family counseling theory already discussed but also combines psychoanalytic and other insight theories with solid applications of behavior modification. Such techniques as relaxation training, sensate focus exercises, and cognitive restructuring are frequently used in counseling couples with sexual problems.

Sex counseling is a specialized application emphasizing behavioral treatment to reduce specific symptoms. It is often a part of marital and family counseling, begun once basic communication problems are resolved. For sex counseling to be effective, the couple's commitment to the relationship and willingness to experience the therapy are essential prerequisites. The basic treatment plan usually takes a six-step form: clinical assessment interview, physical exam and medical history, exploration of relationship, sensate focus exercises, specialized techniques, and evaluation.

Clinical Assessment Interview

With both partners present, or in separate intake interviews, the sex counselor does a detailed data-gathering interview to learn about family history, sexual attitudes in the childhood home, religious influences, early sex education, first sexual experiences, and current attitudes toward various sexual practices. The assessment includes consideration of previous sexual difficulties, as well as a detailed description of current problems and attempts to solve them.

Once a working relationship has been established, the counselor feels free to ask direct questions: "What do you think about during sex?" "When one of you wants to make love, how do you initiate?" "What would you like to do that you are not doing?"

Physical Exam and Medical History

It is extremely important with sexual difficulties (as well as with any other psychological problem having a possible organic origin) that any physical causes be ruled out before attempting psychological interventions. It would be important to know about any drugs that the clients are taking; certain medications for high blood pressure, for instance, will affect sexual responsiveness. Chronic alcoholism also presents special problems, as do diseases such as diabetes. Hormone levels can be assessed to detect estrogen or testosterone deficiencies in the blood. A thorough medical history and exam are also valuable to rule out certain physical processes that can affect sexual performance.

Exploration of Relationship

If organic causes are eliminated, the next place to look for the sources of sexual problems is in the relationship between the couple. Sexual behavior is one way in which partners communicate with each other. Time is generally spent (at least a few sessions) working to improve the communication between partners, helping them to build trust and commitment for the work that lies ahead. In the open, accepting therapeutic atmosphere, clients are helped to dispel their fears of failure, always a contributing factor to sexual problems. They are asked to share their likes, dislikes, and fantasies with each other, all the while becoming more sexually intimate in a nonthreatening, verbal manner.

Sensate Focus Exercises

The counselor will next introduce the behavioral sequence in the treatment, essentially a prescribed series of progressive exercises that the couples will do at home. Initially, all pressure is removed by specifically prohibiting the couple from any further attempts at intercourse. They are absolutely forbidden to try, thereby removing the threat of failure. The sensate focus exercises involve selfishly, yet sensitively and nondemandingly, giving and receiving nongenital pleasure through touching. Very gradually the couple add to their repertoire by (1) mutual backrubs for one week, (2) nongenital touching and mutual pleasuring in other areas of the body, (3) light genital stimulation without orgasm, (4) genital touching to orgasm, (5) intercourse without orgasm (or erection), and (6) intercourse to orgasm.

The couple are able to progress slowly through these steps, doing no more than they are comfortable doing. Success is virtually guaranteed if the couple will follow the structure and resist the temptation to jump ahead to fulfilling the sexual act.

Specialized Techniques

The sex counselor will use a variety of educational and therapeutic options to facilitate better communication, awareness, and sexual responsiveness. Films and books may be used for demonstration purposes. Vibrators are often recommended for inorgasmic women. There are also several specific procedures, such as the "squeeze technique," that are used for premature ejaculation. Certain sexual positions are often suggested for various problems, and focused fantasy exercises help combat distracting thoughts.

Evaluation

Throughout the duration of treatment, the counselor works with the couple to combat the usual resistances. The recognition that, when the symptoms go away, the couple will have to find another way to communicate is a problem that should be addressed early in the therapy. Once sexual functioning is restored, the counselor helps the spouses to integrate what they have learned and continue their marital growth and enrichment.

In addition to applying these sequential steps in the treatment of specific dysfunctions, sex counselors are also called upon to be of assistance to those suffering from sexually transmitted diseases such as AIDS and herpes, and to individuals troubled by chronic disease, aging, chemical dependency, sexual assault, abortion, and physical disabilities. In any and all of these situations, counselors not only must be highly trained in the technology of sex treatments, but they must also have thoroughly worked through their own inhibitions, discomforts, and values related to the subject (Weinstein & Rosen, 1988). Organizations such as the American Association of Sex Educators, Counselors, and Therapists (AASECT), and the Scientific Society for the Study of Sex (SSSS) and training centers such as the Institute for Sex Research (Kinsey Institute) and the Masters and Johnson Institute provide training experiences for those interested in specializing in these areas.

SUMMARY

In this chapter we have presented an overview of the basic theory and techniques of marital, family, and sex counseling. Most counselors are faced with many clients who experience adjustment problems in these areas. Professionals who work with children and adolescents in particular need knowledge and expertise in family counseling. The major focus of these techniques is to clarify the system of relationships occurring in marital and family interactions and to identify opportunities to interrupt dysfunctional patterns. In working with family systems, counselors attempt to help clients restructure relationships toward developmentally healthy goals and to reduce the impact of destructive systems of relationships. Counselors must skillfully blend specific marital, family, and sex techniques within the framework of individual and group counseling skills.

SUGGESTED READINGS

Goldenberg, H., & Goldenberg, I. (1990). *Counseling today's families*. Pacific Grove, CA: Brooks/Cole.

Green, S. L., & Hansen, J. C. (1989). Ethical dilemmas faced by family therapists. *Journal of Marital and Family Therapy, 15*(2), 149–158.

Huber, C., & Baruth, L. (1987). *Ethical, legal, and professional issues in the practice of marriage and family therapy.* Columbus, OH: Charles E. Merrill.

Leiblum, S. R., & Rosen, R. C. (1990). *Principles and practice of sex therapy* (2nd ed.). New York: Guilford Press.

Madanes, C. (1990). *Sex, love, and violence: Strategies for transformation.* New York: W. W. Norton.

Sherman, R., & Fredman, N. (1986). *Handbook of structured techniques in marriage and family therapy.* New York: Brunner/Mazel.

Whitaker, C. (1989). *Midnight musings of a family therapist.* New York: W. W. Norton.

CHAPTER ELEVEN

CAREER COUNSELING

THE FUNCTIONS OF WORK

ROLES OF COUNSELING
  Facilitating Self-Awareness
  Becoming Familiar with the
    World of Work
  Teaching Decision-Making Skills
  Teaching Employability Skills

THEORIES OF CAREER
  DEVELOPMENT
  Theodore Caplow's Theory
  Donald Super's Theory
  John Holland's Theory
  Robert Hoppock's Theory
  Anne Roe's Theory
  John Krumboltz's Theory
  Other Theories

CAREER EDUCATION
  Abilities
  Interests
  Values

CAREER DECISION MAKING

TRENDS AND ISSUES IN CAREER
  COUNSELING
  Changes in the Workplace
  Work and Leisure
  Use of Technology

SUMMARY

SUGGESTED READINGS

H istorically, career or vocational counseling has been the principal domain of counselors. It is through the process and techniques of vocational guidance that the counseling profession was introduced and implemented in numerous settings. In recent years, however, there has been a gradual yet perceptible shift in emphasis from vocational/career issues to personal/emotional issues (Dorn, 1986). Among the diverse reasons for this shift, several merit close examination, especially from the perspective of the novice in the field.

One reason, suggested by Whiteley (1980), involves the complexities of the transactions that are an integral part of career counseling. Many counselors prefer to focus on the interpersonal development of the individual, a process that is more manageable. Another reason for the seeming deemphasis on vocational counseling has to do with the contention that career preferences and choices are actually reflections of personality. This view supports an emphasis, then, on personal/emotional factors rather than vocational/career issues.

Another reason for the shift away from career counseling is the limitations of many of the theories and practices of this specialty. Theories of vocational choice tend to be microcosmic in their view of human experience; they are also somewhat outdated, reflecting a period of American culture in which a person training for a stable life career was the norm, manufacturing and industry were primary employers, and discrimination against women and minorities was accepted. Times have changed, and these theories may be much less useful now. Another aspect of this problem is the lack of clear empirical evidence on the effectiveness of career interventions and the limitations of career decision-making models (Fretz, 1981; O'Hare, 1987).

A final limitation involves the myth that "real" counseling is personal/emotional and that vocational/career counseling is somehow a second-class cousin that requires fewer skills and is more "routine." This attitude is not only false but dangerous. As we will see in this chapter, much of one's self-esteem and many of one's needs are met by career activities. To achieve a modicum of personal fulfillment, one must participate in effective life/career planning. Individuals who experience vocational chaos (such as unemployment, underemployment, and job dissatisfaction) report high stress, relationship difficulties, and low self-esteem. Perhaps some of you have experienced these situations and can recall the anxiety, fear, and loss of confidence. Economic dislocations and the impact of rapidly changing technology exacerbate the need for trained and effective career counselors. Few persons will not, at some point during their work life, require such counseling services.

THE FUNCTIONS OF WORK

"Rich man, poor man, beggar man, thief. Doctor, lawyer, Indian chief." From our first day at school, we first became eligible for that eternal question from well-meaning relatives—that question that still plagues (and will *always* plague) us: "What do you want to be when you grow up?" As if we had to grow up to *be* something . . . or as if we wanted to be something we are not . . . or as if we had to grow up. But even Peter Pan lost *that* fight.

Work is supposedly what we have prepared, educated, and trained our-selves to do. Long ago we shed our existence as hunter/gatherers whose only job was to find enough to eat. Now we are specialized. Everyone, and we mean *everyone*, is engaged in some purposeful, productive activity. Some receive financial remuneration for their efforts—they sell their time and talent. Others work for internal rewards, or receive other forms of compensation by way of a cooperative division of labor. But labor we all do. Even the children are work-ing—mastering new skills, taking in new knowledge. They may sometimes work in places called playgrounds, but we are not for a moment deceived that these little people are not laboring away at their age-related developmental tasks. They are working their bodies, testing their minds, and learning about cooperation, competition, and a million other things they will later find useful after they "grow up" and work in a "real" job.

Work is more than a source of income. For most people, vocation is very much tied into sense of identity, self-image, and sense of worth. Jobs are a mea-sure of status, a major object of devotion of one's time and energy. They are a testing ground for skills and information that have been accumulated over a lifetime. They are the source of many friendships.

People who are satisfied in their work are those who are probably most con-tent with their lives. Lonely, depressed, anxious, problem-ridden people—those who seek a counselor's help—are often those who are not content with their life's work, whether that role is one of homemaker, student, or corporate execu-tive. Career frustration, job stress, and discontent with one's decisions and cur-rent vocational development are thus major preoccupations for many people and therefore a significant part of a counselor's work.

ROLES OF COUNSELING

If work is what you *have* to do and play is what you *want* to do, then a major goal of counseling is to teach people never to work a day in their lives. Some people are able to adopt an attitude that helps them to enjoy their jobs, to have fun, and to feel fulfilled. When the alarm clock rings, they jump out of bed, eager to begin their day. Yet others, working in an exactly equivalent position, feel only dread, boredom, and disgust with what they do for a living. Take the case of the Pickens brothers described by Terkel (1972) in his book *Working*. Both boys have paper routes. They both get up at the same time and basically do the same things. Yet note how the difference in their attitudes about their jobs affects their perceptions. One boy plays; the other works.

CLIFF:

It's fun throwing papers. Sometimes you get it on the roof. But I never did that. You throw the paper off your bicycle and it lands someplace in the bushes. It'll hit part of the wall and it'll go booooongg! That's pretty fun, because I like to see it go booooongg!

TERRY:

... I don't see where people get all this bull about the kid who's gonna be President and being a newsboy made a President out of him. It taught him how to handle his money and this bull. You know what it did? It taught him how to hate the people in his route. And the printers. And dogs [Terkel, 1972, p. 16].

Counselors spend a lot of their time helping people: children who are searching for careers, adults who want to make job changes to think and feel differently about what they are doing. Attitude is all-important in any activity, and certainly in one that can become as routine as going to work. The ultimate goal of almost every person, and therefore every counselor who is giving assistance, is to wake up with energy and excitement, with enthusiasm and anticipation for the day's events that lie ahead.

Therapeutic counselors help people with career indecision on a number of fronts outlined by Fuqua and Hartman (1983). Developmental problems such as career immaturity are resolved by exploring the client's interests and career alternatives and applying decision-making strategies (Perosa & Perosa, 1987). Situational problems such as job stress are worked on within the context of a supportive, problem-solving relationship to develop alternative responses. And chronic problems such as psychological dysfunctions are resolved in longer-term counseling to initiate more extensive personality changes. In each case, counselors strive to develop more positive attitudes, as well as to accomplish the following objectives.

Facilitating Self-Awareness

The first step is to help clients discover what they really want and need—to become aware of what they value most. An exercise designed to clarify these issues might ask the person to rank-order the following work values according to personal preference:

____ long vacations	____ variety of tasks
____ flexible hours	____ minimum of pressure
____ power	____ friendly coworkers
____ responsibility	____ creative opportunities
____ big money	____ opportunity to be physically active
____ status	____ chance to help people
____ security	____ benevolent boss
____ independence	____ opportunities for advancement

The self-awareness or self-exploration process includes much more than clarifying one's values. Atkinson and Murrell (1988, pp. 375-376) describe three aspects of self-exploration:

1. *Concrete exploration* includes activities that allow the client to become more directly involved in career exploration activities. These activities might

include using computer-based career guidance systems such as SIGI or DIS-COVER to clarify values, needs, and interests; writing a detailed vocational history; and describing in writing pivotal experiences and/or life decisions.

2. *Reflective exploration* might include activities to clarify the personal importance of life decisions, events, and transitions and to evaluate personal needs, wants, desires, goals, interests, and dreams in terms of their relative importance. During this phase of self-evaluation it is useful to weigh the relative value of input from family, associates, friends, and other significant individuals regarding personal strengths, weaknesses, and skills.

3. *Actual exploration* might include activities such as resumé writing, videotaped practice interviews with feedback sessions, and informational interviews with individuals employed in possible career choices. The purpose of these activities is to increase self-awareness and to accurately assess strengths, weaknesses, aptitudes, skills, and lifestyle issues.

Becoming Familiar with the World of Work

Whatever structure is used—a Career Day, guest speaker, reading and research, experimentation, on-site visit to a workplace—the stated task is to help people become more aware not only of themselves but also of career options that are possible (Heitzman, Schmidt, & Hurley, 1986). A person might ask, "Given the parameters of a profession that allows me to work with people, use my verbal fluency, and structure my own time, what jobs are likely candidates?" Or, "Which careers would involve being outside, using my creative energies, and moving around a lot?"

There are more than 30,000 different occupations, each divided into one of nine categories, in the *Dictionary of Occupational Titles* (such as service, technical, processing, and clerical professions). Often entire families of careers can be explored, depending on a client's interest. A few may be examined in greater detail, eventually narrowing down the choices to realistic possibilities.

Because of the sheer numbers of available jobs and the complexity of matching aptitudes, interests, values, and required educational level to accurate career information, the use of microcomputer career information systems has become widespread. These systems allow users to access job information based on education, values, interests, and other user variables, greatly simplifying the task of becoming familiar with the world of work. Although these career information systems are useful, they cannot replace a trained counselor who can assist the client to understand, interpret, and apply the information (Sampson, Shahnasarian, & Reardon, 1987).

Teaching Decision-Making Skills

Since vocational development is an ongoing life process, it is hardly functional to focus only on finding a first job for a client. "All over the country, a generation of professionals is career hopping—switching occupations so promiscuously it's a wonder they don't collide with each other coming and going" (Gelman, 1984). People make decisions to try different careers for a number of reasons; for instance—early retirement, boredom, desire for growth, new opportunities, or new interests. In particular, many individuals at midlife are faced with the need to make career decisions; some do so for personal growth, whereas many others face forced career change because of structural factors in the workplace (Perosa & Perosa, 1987). Many companies have been taken over, with duplicate positions being eliminated. Budgetary issues have forced other firms into a reduction in workforce; some companies have eliminated entire departments in an attempt to sharpen their focus and reduce overhead. In each of these cases many high-performing individuals find themselves needing to make often-unanticipated career decisions.

People must learn to make quality decisions about when and how they should initiate career changes. As we get older, more established, and more secure, taking new risks becomes increasingly difficult, especially because career decision making impacts family dynamics (Lopez & Andrews, 1987; Kinnier, Brigman, & Noble, 1990).

The counselor can help by teaching people how to make intelligent decisions. The process often involves learning to collect and assess useful information, generating alternative courses of action and predicting their probable consequences, narrowing the field to a plan of action, taking risks, and dealing with the aftershocks of change. "The counselor performs a directive role in organizing the process, but also takes a nondirective position on the individual's actual choice and its outcome" (Hazler & Roberts, 1984, p. 409).

Teaching Employability Skills

There are other, even more practical, skills that can help people find and maintain satisfaction in their careers. Clients are helping to develop personal marketing strategies to sell themselves and their potential during interviews. They are also encouraged to work on overcoming inertia, resisting procrastination, relieving job-related stress, building an interpersonal support system, and avoiding feelings of frustration and failure (Brown & Kottler, 1979).

In other words, the goal of all career-counseling efforts ought to be to provide life skills for making and implementing decisions. How these decisions ought to be made and, in fact, how people even develop vocationally are topics of considerable debate.

THEORIES OF CAREER DEVELOPMENT

Just as there are a number of theories that attempt to explain learning processes, personality styles, cognitive development, abnormal behavior, social functioning, and models of motivation and change, so too are there varied approaches to vocational development with which counselors are required to familiarize themselves.

Career counseling often teaches decision-making and employability skills.

Pertinent questions come immediately to mind, many of them reviewed by Whiteley and Resnikoff (1978):

How do people make career choices?

Which facts are most influential in making career decisions?

What parts do genetics, the environment, and cognitive and emotional responses play in career development?

What are the characteristics of people most likely to be vocationally dissatisfied?

What roles ought counseling to play in the shaping of career development?

Ought counselors to be providing guidance or giving advice, teaching specific skills or facilitating awareness in these helping efforts?

How and why do people change occupational directions in midstream? Which theory best explains the reality of vocational development?

Clearly these questions need answering—if not for our own peace of mind, then to better enable us to help clients select fulfilling occupations and learn the skills for remaining satisfied and productive. As we review each of the major theories of career development, try to approach the subject with the same critical eye you applied to glean useful concepts from counseling models. Look for concepts that make sense and help explain this complex process of development. The theories of Caplow, Super, Holland, Hoppock, Roe, and Krumboltz will be briefly described. Note the value and applicability of their ideas to your own career choices and confusions.

Theodore Caplow's Theory

The first theory, and certainly the simplest, we will attend to is one based on the notion that career choices are the results of random events, accidents, errors of being at the right/wrong place at the right/wrong time. Although not exactly using an astrological model, the sociologist Caplow (1954) believed that birth order and the accidents of inheritance (parentage, race, nationality, and background) strongly influence one's chosen occupation.

When people are asked how they ended up in their current profession, their responses are often muddled. Answers such as these are not uncommon:

"I don't remember. I always wanted to be an electrician. My dad is one. And his father was too."

"My cousin got me this job, and it seemed kind of easy to stay with it."

"I didn't really intend to go into psychology, but there were no girls in business administration. So, at orientation, I walked out the door and psychology happened to be across the hall."

"I didn't have much choice. In our town there were only two options for a girl—waitressing and working in the mill."

"I was just walking down the street when I saw this sign that said 'Help Wanted.'"

Many of our life's decisions are affected by quirks of fate and the "roll of the die." However, if we were to subscribe to a theory of random movement, there wouldn't be much point in having counselors to provide guidance and encourage self-responsibility.

Donald Super's Theory

For Super (1957), a person's self-concept is all-important in determining vocational development, a process that he views as ongoing and orderly through successive stages. An occupation is the individual expression of one's interests and abilities at a particular time. As a person's preferences and skills evolve, so does his or her career, reflecting the changing self-concept.

Super introduced his theory in a series of ten propositions (1953) about the nature of developing career identities:

1. People differ in their abilities, interests, and personalities.
2. They are qualified, by virtue of these circumstances, for a number of occupations.

3. Each of these occupations requires a characteristic pattern of abilities, interests, and personality traits, with tolerances wide enough to allow both variety of occupations for each individual and variety of individuals in each occupation.

4. Vocational preferences, competencies, situations, and self-concepts change with time and experience, making choice and adjustment a continuous process.

5. This process may be summed up in a series of life stages, characterized as those of growth, exploration, establishment, maintenance, and decline, and these stages may in turn be subdivided into (a) fantasy, tentative, and realistic phases of the exploratory stage, and (b) the trial and stable phases of the establishment stage.

6. The nature of the career pattern (that is, the occupational level attained and the sequence, frequency, and duration of trial and stable jobs) is determined by the individual's parental socioeconomic level, mental ability, and personality characteristics, as well as by the opportunities to which he or she is exposed.

7. Development through the life stages can be guided partly by facilitating the process of maturation of abilities and interests and partly by aiding in reality testing and in the development of the self-concept.

8. The process of vocational development is essentially that of developing and implementing a self-concept; it is a compromise process in which the self-concept is a product of the interaction of inherited aptitudes, neural and endocrine makeup, opportunity to play various roles, and evaluation of the extent to which the results of role playing meet with approval of superiors and peers.

9. The process of compromise between individual and social factors, between self-concept and reality, is one of role playing, whether the role is played in fantasy, in the counseling interview, or in real-life activities such as school classes, clubs, part-time work, and entry jobs.

10. Work satisfaction and life satisfaction depend on the extent to which the individual finds adequate outlets for abilities, interests, personality traits, and values; they also depend upon establishment in a work situation and a satisfying way of life.

Super recognized that people differ in their personalities and unique strengths and therefore choose occupations that will permit them to use their competencies. The pattern of development begins during adolescence with the *exploratory stage,* in which a person uses fantasy, play, and role experimentation to help clarify the emerging self-concept, and moves tentatively onward in the early twenties to a first job. The *establishment stage,* through experimenting and trying out various options, helps the person to discover an occupation well suited to satisfy personal needs. The self-concept adjusts to fit the stabilized career choice. Stability may or may not last into the *maintenance stage;* during the 1950s, when Super was writing, there were far more opportunities and less mobility and economic pressure, and it was more the norm to continue evolving a single career. In today's times of high unemployment, greater flexibility, and changing situations, the maintenance phase may involve a return to earlier developmental tasks in the search for personal and professional satisfaction. The *decline stage* is characterized, naturally, by dealing with reduced energy and trying to maintain one's position until retirement.

Super sees counselors as aiding an individual's progressive development, facilitating maturation of ability, improving the self-concept, encouraging reality testing, expanding interest, and negotiating a compromise between fantasy and reality.

John Holland's Theory

Whereas Super focuses on self-concept, Holland (1973) believes that career choices are expressions of the total personality. Satisfaction thus depends on the compatibility of a person's work situation and personality style.

Holland rested his theory on four major assumptions:

1. Individuals can be categorized into six different personality types—realistic, investigative, artistic, social, enterprising, or conventional—depending on interests, preferences, and skills.
2. Environment can also be classified into the same six types and tends to be dominated by compatible personalities.
3. People search for environments in which their personality type can be comfortably expressed; artistic people search for artistic environments, whereas social people look for social environments. They wish to exercise their skills and abilities, express their attitudes and values, and participate in agreeable problems and roles.
4. The behavior of an individual is determined by the interaction between personality type and environmental characteristics. If personality type and work environment are known, the outcomes of vocational choice, achievement, and job changes can be predicted.

The six different personality types that Holland described predispose people to do well in certain careers that capitalize on their strengths. Certainly these personality types do not describe everyone, but they do provide a structure for understanding why some people do better than others in particular jobs. The following is a more detailed description of each type.

1. *Realistic:* This person is logical, objective, and forthright. Preference is given to dimensions such as physical prowess, aggression, and domination. A realistic type prefers activities in which to manipulate objects, tools, machines, and other tangible things. This person is likely to be emotionally stable but less sociable and inclined to select technical, agricultural, or trade occupations. He or she is practical and tends to have underdeveloped verbal and social skills but highly developed motor skills. The realistic person chooses careers such as laborer, farmer, carpenter, engineer, or machine operator. The realistic environment allows realistic people to perform preferred activities and be rewarded for technical abilities.

2. *Investigative:* By relying on intelligence and cognitive skills, this person-ality type is a problem solver. Socially aloof and introverted, the investigative individual prefers intellectual tasks that require academic proficiencies. He or she also tends to be analytical, critical, intellectual, methodical, precise, rational, and reserved. This person exhibits traits of creativity, independence, and self-confidence but is often not realistic or practical. Career choices for this type include scientist, scholar, research worker, and theoretician.

3. *Artistic:* This is a sensitive, impulsive, creative, emotional, independent, and nonconforming individual who values cultural activities and esthetic quali-ties. This person may develop competencies in art, drama, music, writing, and language and avoid structured situations. Not surprisingly, a creative type chooses careers such as actor, writer, musician, and artist.

4. *Social:* This person is highly skilled at dealing with other people. She or he is usually accepting, responsible, cheerful, nurturing, and caring. If you have noticed a similarity between this type and yourself or your classmates, it is because this category is most often descriptive of those who choose helping pro-fessions. Take note, however, because this type often evades intellectual or physical tasks, preferring to use strengths in interpersonal manipulations.

5. *Enterprising:* This person uses highly refined verbal skills for leadership and sales professions such as marketing, business, and politics. He or she is enthusiastic, energetic, dominating, persuasive, extroverted, and aggressive. Much concern is devoted to attaining status, power, and leadership roles. Some examples of enterprising vocations are business executives, salespeople, politi-cians, and promotional workers.

6. *Conventional:* This type of person prefers activities that are routine, struc-tured, and practical. A conventional type is self-controlled, orderly, inhibited, and efficient. Examples of conventional vocations include bankers, bookkeepers, office workers, and clerks.

To a large extent, Holland believes that there is a real relationship between personality and educational/vocational decision making. He further believes that interest inventories (such as the Strong-Campbell Interest Inventory) are really personality measures. Members of a vocational group have similar personalities, and each vocation tends to attract and retain people with similar personalities.

Because people in a vocational group have similar personalities, they respond to situations in like ways and therefore tend to create characteristic environments. Vocational satisfaction, stability, and achievement depend on the congruence between an individual's personality and the environment in which he or she works.

Robert Hoppock's Theory

Hoppock (1976) stressed the function of the job in satisfying personal needs, but his theory has attained wide popularity also because of his efforts to integrate ideas from a number of other theories. Vocational development begins with the first awareness that a job can help meet one's needs and continues as the person is better able to anticipate how potentially satisfying a particular career could be as compared with others. Once a person becomes aware of other jobs that could satisfy personal needs, then occupational choices are subject to change. The degree of job satisfaction can be determined by assessing the difference between what a person wants from a job (emotionally, financially, and so forth) and what she or he actually has attained.

Hoppock (1976) describes his composite theory in ten basic postulates:

1. Everyone has needs: basic physical needs and higher-order psychological needs such as self-esteem, respect, and self-actualization. People vary in the pattern of their need structures, and the individual reaction to needs influences occupational choice.

2. People tend to gravitate toward occupations that serve their perceived needs. A person who has a strong need for power and status will be influenced to seek occupations that have them. Few people are controlled by a single need; most have a variety of needs that act in concert to influence occupational choice.

3. It is not essential that a person have a clear intellectual awareness of needs for them to affect choices. Individuals with self-understanding and insight may understand the forces that influence them, and others may simply experience pleasure or satisfaction in certain occupational areas.

4. Life experiences help to develop a pattern of individual occupational preference and, as such, suggest a developmental perspective on vocational choice. Contact with occupations occurs both experientially and vicariously, supporting the need for both work or occupational experiences *and* occupational information, especially during the years of formative development.

5. Given the great diversity of occupational choices, it is necessary for the individual to develop effective decision-making skills based on solid self-awareness and a rich informational base. A trial-and-error process of occupational experimentation is usually not appropriate. The number of occupations and the extensive training many of them require preclude that approach.

6. Self-understanding is the basis on which occupational choice rests; thus it is a primary goal for career counseling.

7. Understanding the self is only half of the occupational choice process; one must also have accurate and thorough information about available occupations. A person cannot choose a career without the knowledge that it exists. Likewise, accurate information dispels stereotypes and myths about the activities involved in various types of work.

8. When a person's needs are met by a job, then he or she experiences job satisfaction. It is important to emphasize that money is not the only need satisfied by a job; other higher-order needs are just as crucial to satisfaction as basic security needs. For a worker to perform effectively and with the motivation to deliver quality, the ratio must be positive. Industrial and assembly workers are often good examples of this principle: although they may be well paid, many

do not have higher-order needs satisfied; as a result, their performance on the job is low, the quality is erratic, and absenteeism is a problem.

9. Individuals can delay need satisfaction if they perceive their job as having the potential to satisfy their needs in the future. Opportunities for advancement and career mobility are, therefore, important if a firm wishes to maximize satisfaction.

10. If the balance between needs and satisfaction is unfavorable, then a worker will change jobs if another position appears to offer the potential to meet needs more fully.

In using Hoppock's theory of occupational choice, the counselor's role is to (l) stimulate the client's self-awareness of interests and needs, including the clarification of values, (2) promote insight into that which gives life personal meaning, (3) provide accurate and complete occupational information, and (4) help match the client's perceived strengths and weaknesses with occupations likely to provide maximum need satisfaction. Hoppock's theory has a number of implications for counselors:

> The counselor should always remember that the needs of the client may differ from the needs of the counselor.
> The counselor should operate within the framework of the client's needs.
> The counselor should provide every possible opportunity for the client to identify and to express his or her own needs.
> The counselor should be alert to notice and to remember the needs that the client reveals.
> The counselor should help the client gather information about occupations that may meet his or her needs.
> The counselor should help the client to anticipate how well any contemplated occupation will meet the client's needs.
> The counselor should stay with the client through the process of placement in order to provide the further counseling that will be needed if the desired job is not available.
> The counselor should follow up with the client some months after placement in order to see how well the job is meeting the needs that the client thought it would meet [Hoppock, 1976].

Anne Roe's Theory

On the basis of her intensive investigations of scientists' early childhoods, Roe (1957) created a theory that emphasizes need satisfaction in career choices. Persons from child-centered, rejecting, or accepting homes are predisposed to compensate for (or duplicate) in their jobs experiences what they missed (or enjoyed) in their childhood homes.

Roe suggested that the emotional climate of the home is one of three types: (1) emotional concentration on the child, (2) avoidance of the child, or (3) acceptance of the child. Emotional concentration on the child has two extremes: overprotecting and overdemanding. Overprotecting parents limit exploration by the child and encourage dependency. Overdemanding parents set very high standards for the child and rigidly enforce conformity.

The avoidance type is divided into those ranging from rejecting to neglecting. A rejecting parent resents the child, expresses a cold and indifferent attitude, and works to keep the child from intruding into his or her life. A neglecting parent is less hostile toward the child but provides no affection or attention and only the bare minimum of physical care.

An accepting pattern is divided into casual acceptance and loving acceptance. Casually accepting parents are affectionate and loving but in a mild way and only if they are not otherwise occupied. They tend to be easygoing. Loving accepting parents provide much warmth, affection, praise, and attention. They encourage the child and help in an appropriate way.

These six subdivisions produce, according to Roe, two types of vocational behavior. The categories of loving, overprotective, and overdemanding tend to produce a major vocational orientation toward persons. The remaining categories—casual, neglecting, and rejecting—produce a major vocational orientation away from persons. The theory has generated considerable research, which has, overall failed to bear it out. However, Isaacson (1986) suggests that four limiting factors may account for that result:

1. An accurate evaluation would necessitate a long-term longitudinal study ranging from early childhood through maturity.
2. Many of Roe's statements are generalizations and are thus vague and ambiguous.
3. Parental behavior is inconsistent.
4. The home environment is only one influence on the child.

Roe's position has been criticized for its excessive focus on early determinants of vocational choice, yet Roe has been influential in helping counselors to understand the value of careers in satisfying a person's needs for belongingness, respect, self-esteem, independence, and self-actualization, in addition to Abraham Maslow's lower-level drives to provide economic security, safety, and fulfillment of physiological needs.

John Krumboltz's Theory

You may be more familiar with Krumboltz as a practitioner of behavioral counseling than as a theoretician of career development. Nevertheless, he has developed a social-learning theory that attempts to synthesize the factors that influence career decision making. First, Krumboltz acknowledges the impact of genetic endowment—how race, sex, physical characteristics, native intelligence, and abilities limit some choices and expand others. Not everyone can *choose* to be a professional basketball player, brain surgeon, or ballet dancer, regardless of motivation or interest.

Second, environmental factors play a part in career development. The economic climate, occupational opportunities available, labor laws, union rules, technological developments, family resources, educational systems, and other variables outside the individual's control influence occupational decision making.

Third, previous learning experiences (in behavioristic terminology, conditioned stimuli and reinforcers) shape the person's attitudes and interest toward
various professions. Some children are reinforced by their parents for reading,
others for their physical or mechanical powers.

A final factor to be considered, according to Krumboltz, is a person's "task
approach skills," which are his or her performance standards, work habits,
unique perceptions, and abilities to alter problem-solving strategies flexibly
according to the demands of the situation.

As examples, Krumboltz (1978) traces the career development of several
individuals, identifying how successive steps in the process are affected by
genetic, environmental, modeling, learning, and skill factors. The case of
"Barbara" (Figure 11-1) illustrates Krumboltz's various propositions in action.
He summarizes the responsibilities of a counselor in the career development
process as follows: "(a) to help the client learn a rational sequence of career decision-making skills, (b) to help the client arrange an appropriate sequence of
career-relevant exploration/learning experiences, and (c) to teach the client how
to evaluate the personal consequences of these learning experiences"
(Krumboltz, 1978, p. 127).

Other Theories

There are other theories, of course, besides those already mentioned. Eli
Ginzberg (1972), for example, described career development as a continual, life-
long process of decision making in which the person is trying to reconcile goals
and preparations with the reality of limited opportunity. Like Super and
Ginzberg, Tiedeman and O'Hara (1963) are developmentalists who suggest that
career development is a process of identifying with work through the interaction between personality and society. They suggest the importance of decision
making in the process of defining the relationship between personality and
career. They have, however, been more precise than most other theorists in plotting the changes people experience in their evolving sense of identity.

CAREER EDUCATION

Career education, career development, and vocational assistance are life-long
processes that often require supportive services at various developmental levels.
Career education can be defined as "a process that occurs over an extended
period to help the individual learn about work alternatives and make a career
choice leading to a satisfying, productive vocational life" (Hansen, Stevic, &
Warner, 1986).

Career education is an ongoing process that has crucial significance in elementary, secondary, and postsecondary schools. There are five basic components
of career education as defined by Hoyt, Evans, Mackin, and Mangum (1972):

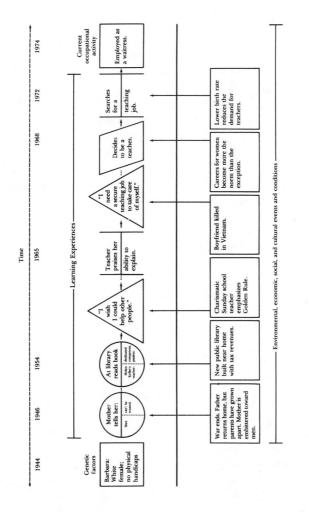

FIGURE 11—1.
Illustrative excerpt of factors affecting "Barbara's" occupation selection (Krumboltz, 1978, p. 115)

1. *There are career implications in every learning experience.* All school-related experiences have career implications that knowledgeable professionals can help students to understand. It is important that career education be accepted as an institutional responsibility rather than a function of the counseling and guidance staff.
2. *Skill training is necessary for entry into an occupation.* Educational experiences should have a work-related skill component attached to them. Counselors should be ready to work with clients and other professionals to structure appropriate skill-related activities.
3. *Cognitive and experiential ways must be provided for students to understand work-oriented values.* The counselor must help the student to gain self-understanding, knowledge of alternatives, awareness of values, and decision-making skills in both cognitive and experiential ways.
4. *Opportunities must be provided for observing work and work environments, and, ultimately, for work experience.* Individuals must have the opportunity to develop experiences and knowledge about work, occupations, and work environments. Counselors can work with students, employers, and educational institutions to create these opportunities.
5. *The interrelationships among home, family, community, and societal values should be identified.* The impact of these values on career decisions and preferences needs to be clarified.

Each of these general components, which are not necessarily sequential, requires the assistance of professional counselors who provide information as needed, consult with other involved personnel, and structure activities and experiences designed to facilitate career awareness, self-understanding, and occupational information. Counselors who work in career education and career guidance settings must also be prepared to implement and use the services and information available in a high-tech society. Hoyt (1985) points out several implications of new technology for career education and guidance:

1. Counselors must develop skills in computer-assisted management with regard to records and career assessment results, and they must attend to student confidentiality issues inherent in these systems.
2. Career guidance professionals must thoroughly understand the strengths and weaknesses of the various computerized career information and career guidance systems available to students.
3. Career education professionals must understand the need to integrate computerized career guidance and assessment systems as supplements to career education and career counseling (Kapes, Borman, & Frazler, 1989). It is essential that counselors structure technological systems to enhance rather than to direct student choice.
4. Videodisc and telecommunications systems must be identified and infused into the career education process.

Career education counselors must find ways to use available technology to improve student career assessment and to provide relevant information for career decision making. The use of computerized career guidance tools has the potential to improve career decision making and to increase career self-efficacy (Fukuyama, Probert, Neimeyer, Nevill, & Meetzler, 1988). Career development, as a lifelong learning experience, must be stressed, and the factors involved in career development need understanding by counselors and clients. Abilities, interests, and values are those factors.

Abilities

Individuals must have an understanding of their abilities in order to identify potential areas for job exploration and career development. Persons must recognize the need to develop basic academic skills and to maximize potential abilities to participate fully in the career development process. In an era of rapidly changing technology and job obsolescence, the task of identifying abilities will extend well into the adult years. It has been estimated that most adults will confront periods of unemployment in their lives (Herr & Watts, 1981). A thorough understanding of abilities, including needs for remediation, will be helpful to both students and adults as they participate in the career development process.

Interests

A knowledge of interests (and the personality tendencies they suggest) will be helpful to individuals as they attempt to match aptitudes with available occupations. Interests are often the key to occupational satisfaction; persons whose interests are not represented in their occupational choice can suffer much unrest and dissatisfaction. It is also important for the counselor to emphasize that abilities and interests are not always neatly related and that interest alone is not a sufficient condition for job satisfaction in positions requiring abilities that the client lacks.

Values

Values are an important factor affecting career development. Occupations that reflect values similar to those held by clients can lead to greater job satisfaction, especially with regard to motivation and job performance. The ill-defined or poorly defined values of many clients can interfere with effective decision making. Counselors must work with clients, helping them to clarify their values and relate them to abilities and interests. Clients who are aware of the relationship among values, interests, and aptitudes can be described as vocationally mature and more likely than others to experience job satisfaction and career advancement.

CAREER DECISION MAKING

In some ways, career development—and certainly career choices—can be viewed as a decision-making process. Clients who are unable to integrate knowledge about the self with occupational information will make little progress in career choice. Helping clients to develop refined decision-making skills is an essential dimension of occupational assistance.

Some clients will come to career counseling aware of the skills involved in decision making. For others, knowledge may be absent or fragmentary, requiring the counselor to assess the client's level of decision-making skills and provide appropriate information. Decision-making models contain several specific steps (Horan, 1979):

1. *Defining the problem.* The counselor helps the client define the problem, exploring various aspects and identifying a stated vocational issue. Specific counseling skills are used to elicit information, establish priorities, and crystallize salient issues. It is essential that sufficient time be spent on this step since it will set the tone for future steps. Problem identification may need to be done at several stages in the process.

2. *Finding and using information.* Once the vocationally related problem is identified, then the counselor assists the client to gather useful information. Sources might include testing, occupational, vocational, and educational information, and computer-assisted job search. The counselor must also help the client to use the information in an appropriate manner by interpreting tests, clarifying misunderstandings, and generating conclusions.

3. *Creating alternatives.* In this step the counselor and client combine forces to identify as many alternatives as possible. Those that are clearly inappropriate are excluded, and the remaining alternatives are examined in light of information on aptitudes, interests, values, and availability.

4. *Developing plans.* In this stage plans that may be either tentative or firm, depending on the client's needs, are developed. The planning stage should be detailed and sequenced and should have contingencies built into it. This is a crucial step in decision making because it translates the information into action-oriented steps.

5. *Implementing plans.* Implementing and following through on plans are primarily the responsibilities of the client, although the counselor should be available for consultation and support. Sometimes clients experience difficulty at this stage, and the counselor should intervene to determine if there are flaws in the plan or if personal counseling is needed.

6. *Evaluating plans.* Evaluation helps the client to determine the effectiveness of the decision-making process and to feed results into a new problem formulation. It is important to emphasize to clients that they are ultimately implementing a process as much as a specific decision. Vocational decision making is a life-long undertaking that requires continual refinement and development.

Career decision making is also influenced by such variables as state and trait anxiety (Hartman, Fuqua, & Blum, 1985; Fuqua, Blum, & Hartman, 1988), family influences (Lopez & Andrews, 1987; Kinnier, et al., 1990), and maladaptive beliefs and generalizations (Mitchell & Krumboltz, 1987). Counselors must be familiar with the decision-making process both generally and specifically as it is applied to career decision making so they can identify particular problems in decision-making style for clients who are experiencing difficulty. Career counseling, however, must focus not only on decision making but also on techniques to correct embedded or underlying difficulties beyond decision-making skills. For example, a family systems approach may be appropriate for individuals whose pattern of enmeshment interferes with career decision making; for others who exhibit irrational beliefs and attitudes, cognitive restructuring may be indicated (Nevo, 1987). Career counselors must be flexible and insightful as they diagnose the multiple variables affecting career decision making and be versatile in designing treatment approaches for specific problems.

The process of career education and vocational choice is highly complex. Counselors can help clients to perform this crucial life work in a systematic and objective fashion, providing information and assistance at critical points. The ultimate goal of career education is to assist individuals to optimize their resources and to make vocational choices that are likely to lead to job satisfaction and career development.

TRENDS AND ISSUES IN CAREER COUNSELING

The world of work is rapidly changing and evolving, requiring major adjustments on the part of the labor force and vocational counselors. There is little doubt that the fundamental nature of our society has changed from an industrial base to an information base. We are living in the information age, with the impact of technology felt in every sector of the world of work, simultaneously creating labor shortages (in the case of computer specialists) and surpluses (in the case of assembly and manufacturing workers). Given recent developments in microcomputers and the shift from industrial to service, professional, and technical work, there seem to be emerging two classes of workers: (1) skilled and specialized service, professional, and technical workers who form an elite and highly employable class and (2) an underclass of workers without employable skills (Cianni-Surridge, 1983). These forces are likely to create technical problems and labor shortages in addition to the human problems created by dislocations. Vocational counselors must be ready to respond to these issues. particularly those involving retraining and the use of technologically dense systems.

Changes in the Workplace

As the pace of change accelerates, many workers are likely to experience unemployment and job elimination. The National Alliance of Business in 1987 estimated that 75% of those who will be working in the year 2000 are currently in the labor force (cited in Hoyt, 1988). Career guidance professionals will have major responsibility for helping workers who become occupationally obsolete to cope with the stress of transition and dislocation and to develop marketable skills through retraining and retooling.

Additionally, career counselors must recognize that 83% of the new workers entering the labor market will be minorities, women, and immigrants. These groups are overrepresented in areas experiencing the least amount of growth and are less prepared educationally for the fastest growing segments of the labor market (Hoyt, 1988; Offermann & Gowing, 1990). These data illustrate the challenges for career counselors who must develop programs to improve the educational and employability levels of these new job seekers. Innovative procedures must be developed in response to the career development needs of women, minorities, and immigrants.

Work and Leisure

As productivity increases through the application of technology to work, efficiency is likely to increase, meaning that people will work less. In fact, productive work may become a relatively scarce resource. To compensate for decreased demands of work, individuals must increase their skills and abilities to use leisure in a manner that will be personally fulfilling.

Work and leisure must be seen not as antithetical but as psychologically related aspects of a career (Blocher & Siegal, 1981). Career counselors must recognize the importance of leisure as they assist clients to engage in life/career planning that will include creative and fulfilling ways in which to use their time. Leisure can be used effectively once the misperception of leisure as nonproductive is eliminated. Some of the productive uses of leisure might include alternative ways of seeking fulfillment, techniques for managing discretionary time, and resources for reducing stress and maximizing consciousness (Cianni-Surridge, 1983; McDowell, 1981). Leisure, then, must be seen by the vocational counselor as a companion concern to work.

Use of Technology

Technology is likely to affect career and vocational counseling more than any other specialty within the counseling and guidance field. As mentioned earlier, there has been an increase in the use of computer-based interactive career guidance systems (such as DISCOVER and SIGI), which allow users to integrate occupational and educational information with interests and values in order to improve career decision making. These systems are likely to continue to be used with refinements such as videodiscs that depict information more realistically. The availability of this technology requires that the career counselor be technologically literate and computer "smart" to assist clients effectively in career decision-making activities.

As microcomputers become more widely used, simulation is likely to emerge as an important career development strategy. Simulated work experiences will allow clients to gain concrete experience and to develop relevant career skills optimally in a "no-lose" environment. With computer networking, increasingly sophisticated software, and videodisc simulations, clients will be able to sample interactively an ever greater and more diverse range of jobs, actiities, and career guidance resources. These future technological developments will require a career counselor who has the skill and ability to use them in career education and vocational guidance.

SUMMARY

In this chapter we have provided an overview of the value and diversity of career counseling. The importance of this specialty will increase with the impact of technology on our society. The counselor's role in a high-tech society is to help individuals assimilate the effects of technology, thereby allowing them to develop to their fullest potential.

SUGGESTED READINGS

Crites, J. 0. (1981). *Career counseling*. New York: McGraw-Hill.

Healy, C. (1982). *Career development counseling through the life stages*. Boston: Allyn & Bacon.

Holland, J. L. (1985). *Making vocational choices: A theory of personalities and work environments* (2nd ed.). Englewood Cliffs, NJ: Prentice-Hall.

Isaacson, L. E. (1986). *Career information in counseling and career development* (4th ed.). Boston: Allyn & Bacon.

Michelozzi, B. N. (1980). *Coming alive from nine to five: The career search handbook*. Palo Alto, CA: Mayfield.

Osipow, S. H. (1983). *Theories of career development* (3rd ed.). Englewood Cliffs, NJ: Prentice-Hall.

Row, A. (1956). *Psychology of occupations*. New York: Wiley.

Super, D. E. (1957). *The psychology of careers*. New York: Harper & Row.

Terkel, S. (1979). *Working*. New York: Avon.

U.S. Department of Labor. *Dictionary of occupational titles* (latest ed.). Washington, DC: Author.

U.S. Department of Labor. *Occupational outlook handbook* (latest ed.). Washington, DC: Author.

Whiteley, J., & Resnikoff, A. (Eds.) (1978). *Career counseling*. Pacific Grove, CA: Brooks/Cole.

Zunker, V. G. (1990). *Career counseling: Applied concepts of life planning* (3rd ed.). Pacific Grove, CA: Brooks/Cole.

CHAPTER TWELVE

DRUG AND ALCOHOL COUNSELING

DRUG USE AND DRUG ABUSE

THE UNITED STATES
    AS A DRUG CULTURE

WHAT COUNSELORS SHOULD
    KNOW ABOUT DRUGS
    Marijuana
    Depressants
    Stimulants
    Narcotics
    Hallucinogens

EFFECTS OF DRUG ABUSE

ADOLESCENT DRUG USE

ABUSE IN SPECIAL POPULATIONS
    The Elderly
    The Disabled

PRINCIPLES FOR COUNSELING THE
    CHEMICALLY DEPENDENT
    Medical Model
    AA/NA Model
    Therapeutic Model

SUMMARY

SUGGESTED READINGS

DRUG USE AND DRUG ABUSE

Everyone without a drug habit, raise your hand. Now, let those who are smugly confident that they hold nothing in common with your basic drug addict (and so are holding their hands quite high) consider the following:

1. A drug can be *any* substance ingested into the body that produces an altered state of consciousness or change in body chemistry.
2. Andrew Weil (1972), a noted pharmacologist, has a theory that all humans have an innate drive to alter their consciousness. From spinning in circles as children to eating spicy foods as adults, the goal is to experience sensory overload.
3. Drug use not only is common among human beings but is found among other creatures. When animals in Africa are subjected to crowding, poaching, and other stressful conditions, they resort to intoxicants. Elephants will munch fermented fruit. Grasshoppers will literally get high (given their jumping prowess) after eating marijuana. Peruvian llamas are fond of cocoa leaves. Rats, when given choices between plain water and alcohol, prefer the booze, especially at bedtime.
4. The difference between drug use and drug abuse is a matter of degree (see Figure 12-1). Once a need for drugs has been established in order to maintain effective functioning, addiction and physiological dependence prevail. The most widely used (and probably abused) drugs are those that happen to be legal. Coffee, cigarettes, chocolate, and cola beverages all contain sufficient quantities of amphetamines to create full-fledged addictions.
5. Almost every person alive has some oral addiction, and the world is filled with regional choices. Whereas alcohol has permeated every known culture (except that of the Eskimo, who live in a climate too cold to grow anything), more exotic drugs are found in every region. Cocaine originated in the Andes of Peru and Bolivia, coffee and hashish in Southern Arabia, peyote in Mexico, opium in India and Mesopotamia, and, of course, tea in China.

It may now be evident that most people ingest drugs in some form, whether as food additive, beverage, medication, or intoxicant. Although the biological mechanism underlying drug use is not clearly established, one theory suggests that drugs have psychomotor stimulant properties that activate positive reinforcement mechanisms within the brain. This results in pleasurable sensations that are more powerful than those occurring naturally (Wise, 1988).

There are many factors that determine whether a person can safely and responsibly use drugs (such as an occasional cup of coffee or glass of beer) or will abuse addictive substances (heroin, for example) or become psychologically dependent (as is common with marijuana). Counselors are often required to work with these various forms of drug use and to make a determination with the client as to which behaviors are self-destructive and out of control.

The subject of drug use and abuse merits its own chapter in an introductory counseling text for a number of reasons. First, most people, and especially clients who tend to be externally controlled, regularly use drugs in some form. Often alcohol, marijuana, coffee, or tobacco is a troubled person's effort at self-

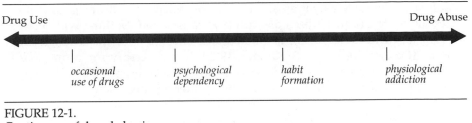

FIGURE 12-1.
Continuum of drug behavior

medication for distressing symptoms. The externally oriented drug abuser denies responsibility for problems, blames others for experienced misery, and feels that, since someone else has created the emotional pain, an externally available substance will fix things. The unfortunate part is that such a person is perfectly correct. Drugs *do* provide immediate relief. They dull pain and are great distracters. While using drugs at moderately abusive levels (whatever that means), people can still function through their day in a purple but painless haze. (See also Table 12-1 illustrating reasons for drug use and abuse.)

TABLE 12-1. Reasons for Drug Use and Drug Abuse

Why People Use Drugs	Why People Abuse Drugs
Euphoria	Biochemical predisposition
Availability	Physical addiction
Cultural exposure	Maintenance of intoxication
Pain suppressant	External control
Boredom	Habituation
Rebellion	Social reinforcement
Entertainment and curiosity	Poor self-image
Enhancement of reality	Addictive personality
Peer pressure	Escape
Stress reduction	Impulsivity
Social lubricant	Instant gratification
Self-medication	

The second reason for studying a specialty such as drug counseling is that traditional therapeutic interventions tend not to work. Insight into the reasons underlying self-destructive behavior in the form of drug and alcohol abuse is not sufficient to alter the behavior. Clients with drug and alcohol problems are so immune and resistant to change that sometimes very dramatic and creative interventions must be found.

Finally, clients have the same expectations for their counseling sessions as they have for their drugs: instant, magical relief. The addictive personality, found in many clients, belongs to an individual who is insecure, impatient, and impulsive, who refuses to postpone gratification, and who uses the treatment hour as he or she uses drugs in an attempt to provide a temporary lift in spirits (Burnett, 1979).

Many people engage in mood-altering behavior to create a sense of euphoria or well-being or to block out unpleasant events. It is important to recognize that drug taking is a behavior and follows patterns that can be understood and modified to the same extent as any other. The behavior will persist if it minimizes discomfort or maximizes pleasure and satisfaction. Nothing will decrease the hold of drugs unless there is an adequate substitute for the feelings drugs provide (Oakley, 1983; Cox & Klinger, 1988). It is necessary for counselors to assess and observe a client's behavior to determine whether the client is displaying symptoms of abuse and reliance on mood-altering substances.

THE UNITED STATES AS A DRUG CULTURE

People are constantly encouraged to purchase drugs in order to feel better and to buy products that help with weight loss. The implicit, if not explicit, message is that comfort and ease are of maximum importance. There is little glorification for the hard work or discipline involved in maintaining a healthy body. Advertising has clearly had some impact on drug use in our society (Cornacchia, Smith, & Bentel, 1978). Advertisements on television and in other media promise to make one feel happier, younger, sexier, more attractive, and less tense. They persuade people to buy over-the-counter drugs as a means of relief from suffering and to create a desirable personal image. Advertisements clearly imply not only that the use of these drugs will create wonderful results but also that the drugs are harmless.

The U.S. government has taken many steps to protect the consumer. In 1906 the Pure Food and Drug Act was passed to prohibit interstate commerce of adulterated or misbranded foods and drugs. The Harrison Act of 1914 required dealers and dispensers of narcotics to register annually with the Treasury Department's Bureau of Internal Revenue. The Narcotics Manufacturing Act passed in 1960 required all manufacturers of medical narcotic drugs to be licensed and made it illegal to manufacture or to attempt to manufacture narcotic drugs without a license. In addition, annual quotas were established for the purchase and manufacture of narcotic drugs. In 1965 Congress passed the Drug Abuse Control Amendment in order to provide better control over the manufacture and distribution of certain legal and illegal compounds.

The Controlled Substance Act of 1970 replaced or updated all previous laws concerned with both narcotics and dangerous drugs. Under this law the Food and Drug Administration (FDA) considers the state of current scientific knowledge of various drugs, the risk to public health, the psychosocial dependence liability, and the status of the substance regarding whether it is an immediate precursor of one already controlled under this title. This law established five schedules of drugs that must be continually updated. Class I drugs are the most highly regulated while Class V substances are available over the counter and are the least regulated.

Although legislators try to keep current in providing protection for the consumer, our society continues to approve and even encourage use of substances such as caffeine, tobacco, and alcohol. It is important to recognize that the acceptance of alcohol as an appropriate drug by all citizens over a certain arbitrary age encourages the development of a milieu in which drug use is considered normal.

Almost all drugs are available to adolescents, not only "on the street" but also on the school grounds. It is not uncommon to find adolescents sniffing glue,

The cocaine addict is among the most difficult clients that counselors are called upon to treat. Until he or she "hits bottom," the motivation to change is counteracted by the cravings for another high.

gasoline, or lighter fluid, using heroin, or taking barbiturates or amphetamines during school hours. Marijuana use is so prevalent among adolescents that it is often considered normal by school officials. There is also frequent use of PCP, an anesthetic employed in veterinary medicine that, when used in excess, produces a toxic psychosis often associated with violent and self-destructive behavior.

WHAT COUNSELORS SHOULD KNOW ABOUT DRUGS
Marijuana

Marijuana is one of several popular choices for most drug-using adolescents and young adults. Pharmacologically, marijuana (Cannabis sativa) is not a narcotic and does not produce physical dependence. (Although it is a hallucinogen, it is being discussed as a separate topic because of its prevalence in today's society.) Primarily among the middle class, the drug is used because limited doses produce mild euphoria and act as a pleasant relaxant. The abuse potential of marijuana is controversial. It is often argued that marijuana is a "healthy" drug; it does not suppress the appetite or lead to true addiction, although frequent use may result in psychological dependence. Some states and localities have decriminalized personal possession of marijuana, creating confusing messages for children who learn that pot is OK to use in some areas but not in others.

Yet many, many clients experience problems related to a *relatively* harmless drug (at least compared with narcotics, depressants, and amphetamines) such as marijuana. Whereas there may be no actual physiologically addictive potential, the side effects, such as withdrawal symptoms and increased tolerance, make marijuana easily habit forming. It is also relatively inexpensive and produces its exhilarating effects within minutes. The problems lie in the accompanying circumstances: daily users cannot seem to function without pot as a crutch. In this way marijuana can be seen as a "gateway" drug; it conditions individuals to view drug use as an acceptable way to deal with stress and personal discomfort, and they begin to associate "having fun" with drug use. It is common for some people to smoke their first joint before brushing their teeth in the morning and to continue smoking up to ten marijuana cigarettes as boosters throughout the day. Although all the evidence is not yet in regarding the long-term health effects of *Cannabis* use, it is clear that a sizable portion of the younger population does experience negative *psychological* effects such as lethargy, impaired judgment, and decreased internal control.

Depressants

If a relatively innocuous drug such as marijuana can create psychological problems for the user, then more powerful substances can lead to even greater difficulties. Drugs are usually classified according to the ways they affect the central nervous system. Depressants (see Table 12-2), of which alcohol is the most commonly used, slow down and sedate the nervous system. Although the depressant effect is often desired, by a physician prescribing barbiturates or by a user who is self-medicating for a calm, tranquilized state, the risk of overdose is great. Depressants are more easily addictive even than heroin and are widely abused as a "middle-class" drug in the form of sleeping pills and tranquilizers such as Valium and Xanex.

In addition to the dangers of addiction and potential for overdose, tranquilizers create problems for the counselor trying to work with clients who have come to depend on artificial means to reduce their anxieties. Such clients are often reluctant to learn new coping strategies when easy relief is just a swallow away. It is much more difficult to learn internal control of their emotions and ways to take charge of their life than it is to pop a few pills or down a few cocktails, particularly when the alternative is a very uncomfortable and painful withdrawal from the drug's grip.

TABLE 12-2. Commonly Used Depressants

Barbiturates	Major Tranquilizers	Minor Tranquilizers
(sleep medications)	(psychotic medications)	(sedative medications)
Amytal	Thorazine	Xanex
Seconal	Compazine	Valium
Tuinal	Taractan	Librium
Nembutal	Prolixin	Equanil

Stimulants

Stimulants (see Table 12-3) are a class of drugs that speed up the central nervous system, increasing heart rate, depressing appetite, stifling fatigue, and producing feelings of euphoria. Amphetamines are commonly prescribed as diet pills; mild forms of "speed," such as nicotine or caffeine, also suppress the appetite. "Uppers" are often abused by those who want extra energy or alertness, as well as by those who want a recreational high in social situations. Cocaine is probably the most common "social" stimulant used today and presents some very special treatment difficulties for the counselor.

TABLE 12-3. Commonly Used Stimulants

Amphetamines	Preludin	Ritalin	Cocaine
as stimulants	for weight reduction	for adults as antidepressant; for children to combat hyperactivity	for recreational use

Many practitioners require that a client use a therapeutic support system in addition to regular counseling sessions. Alcoholics Anonymous, Narcotics Anonymous, or any other good group experience is often used to help people to feel more accountable. We can recall only one case (out of perhaps two dozen) in which counseling alone was successful in helping a cocaine abuser. The treatment required only one session and took the following form:

> "I wish I could help you. I really do. You seem like a nice guy, and you have a lot going for you. But counseling just doesn't work too well with cocaine addicts. Actually, nothing works. I know I sound discouraging, but I'm trying to be honest: there is no known cure for your particular problem. My best advice is that you continue exactly what you're doing because ultimately that is what might save you. After you have spent all your money, used up all your credit, lost your job, your friends, your wife, your kids, and all your worldly possessions, perhaps then you can start over. You will have no other choice. Certainly you won't be able to beg, borrow, or steal more cocaine. I'm sorry, but there is nothing I can do to help you."

The gentleman left more than a little shaken. He called back a month later to report that he had, in fact, been so frightened that he had not touched cocaine since our one and only meeting.

Narcotics

Narcotics (see Table 12-4) are painkillers. They deaden everything—hunger, sex drive, appetite, physical complaints, depression, anxiety—and do so effectively enough that they can seduce a user into addiction very quickly. Within a week of daily use, a user will develop a tolerance, requiring higher dosages of the drug to get the same effect.

Counseling a person into and out of withdrawal is highly unlikely. More often, therapeutic sessions are used as adjuncts to medically supervised treatment programs that usually use other drugs as a bridge.

TABLE 12-4.   Commonly Used Narcotics

Morphine	Heroin	Codeine	Demerol
as a pain suppressant	for recreational use	as a cough suppressant	as a muscle relaxant

Hallucinogens

Hallucinogens (see Table 12-5), as a class of drugs, are used exclusively for their mind-altering properties and for recreational purposes. In all their varieties, psychedelic drugs alter perceptions, sensations, moods, and thought patterns. Some claim the drugs have educational value (those of the Timothy Leary school) or therapeutic value (those of the Carlos Castaneda school). According to Andrew Weil (1972), most of the dangers associated with psychedelic drugs occur when they are not used in ritualized ways. In those societies that have strict rules for who may use psychedelic drugs, under what specific conditions, and at what intervals, problems of drug abuse are rare. (Similarly, in our society those who restrict themselves to a nightcap or to a drink during the cocktail hour usually don't experience problems of alcohol abuse.)

TABLE 12-5.   Commonly Used Hallucinogens

Marijuana	LSD	PCP	Mescaline	Peyote	Psilocybin
(hemp plant)	(synthetic)	(synthetic)	(cactus)	(cactus)	(mushrooms)

EFFECTS OF DRUG ABUSE

Milby (1981) has listed many of the negative physical effects that result from drug abuse. These symptoms are in addition to the relationship casualties that usually occur as the abuser alienates friends, family members, and coworkers.

1. Death has to be at the top of the list. Reports of drug overdoses occur in the newspapers so routinely that they are no longer news. Suicide is cer-

tainly a distinct possibility for a person in an altered state of consciousness, and it is not unknown for people to die from convulsions while withdrawing from barbiturates.

2. Through neglect, disinterest, and distraction, the diet of a drug abuser often suffers. Many drugs tend to stifle the appetite; other drugs (narcotics, alcohol) lead the user toward malnourishment.

3. Disturbances of sleep are common results of introducing artificial stimulants or depressants into the bloodstream. Certainly anyone who has had a few cups of coffee before bedtime or who has fallen asleep while still feeling the effects of alcohol knows that the quality of sleep is impaired. The loss or disruption of sleep presents added dangers for the drug abuser, whose perceptions and reactions are already less than optimal.

4. Many other physical symptoms can develop as a result of long-term drug use. Naturally, after foreign substances are ingested, the body reacts. Some problems are the result of the ways in which the drugs are introduced into the body. For example, nasal damage results from repeated snorting of cocaine, lung damage has been reported in marijuana smokers, and skin disorders occur in those who inject heroin. A variety of musculoskeletal, respiratory, gastrointestinal, and central-nervous-system disorders are also possible—even likely—after long-term drug or alcohol abuse (Nace, 1987).

ADOLESCENT DRUG USE

Many counselors interpret the drug abuser's behavior within the context of family dynamics. Haber (1983) summarizes much of the theory and research on this point of view and suggests many ways in which the client expresses anger, dependence, aggression, and independence through drug problems. The family is stabilized in its distraction by and attention toward the abuser's behavior. The family has its scapegoat. And the abuser has feelings of control. Everyone continues helplessly along, unable to break the destructive patterns that bind the family members together.

Although noting the alarming number of adolescents involved in drug and alcohol use and abuse, we must also recognize that the age of onset is decreasing. It is almost a puberty rite to have experimented with drugs by early adolescence. Chassin, Mann, and Sher (1988) state that a substantial majority (80–93%) of adolescents have reported at least some experimentation with alcohol and that a significant minority drink at high levels; 13% in one representative study drank at least once per week, typically consuming five or more drinks. Schlaadt and Shannon (1982) state that "in 1965, the average age of a child's first encounter with alcohol was 13.6 years; in 1975, the age dropped to 12.9" (p. 128). Shedler and Block (1990) report that 68% of a representative sample of adolescents had tried marijuana, 39% used it at least once per month or more, and 21% reported weekly use. Additionally, 37% reported trying cocaine, 25% had tried hallucinogens, and 10% reported other drug use (p. 615).

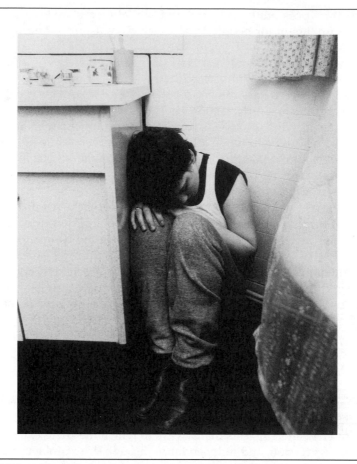

A young girl "medicates herself" for depression by staying high as often as she can.

The significance of such early use of drugs relates to the development of crucial social and personal skills in adolescence. This is a difficult time, and drugs are an available way to ease pain and discomfort. Unfortunately, they also increase antisocial behavior, block completion of normal developmental tasks, and sometimes lead to the development of a deviant lifestyle. Shedler and Block (1990) found in their study that "the picture of frequent user that emerges is one of a troubled adolescent, an adolescent who is interpersonally alienated, emotionally withdrawn, and manifestly unhappy, and who expresses his or her maladjustment through undercontrolled, overtly antisocial behavior" (p. 617).

Several studies report that, the earlier drug use starts, the longer it persists and the more intense it becomes (Oakley, 1983). Research shows, for example, that, the sooner a youngster begins experimenting with alcohol, the greater his or her chances of becoming an alcoholic (Alibrandi, 1978). Biddle, Bank, and Marlin (1980) found that parents exert more influence through normative standards and peers exert more influence through behavior modeling. They also found that parental influence declines in the midteen years and rises again as the adolescent finishes high school. North and Orange (1980), on the other hand, strongly suggest that peer pressure is more influential and see adolescent drinking as stemming from a desire to conform. Zucker and Gomberg (1986) found that parent/child relationships in prealcoholic families were characterized by inadequate parenting, lack of contact with parents, and a lack of normal adult role models. Shedler and Block (1990) report that the mothers of frequent adolescent drug users are cold, unresponsive, hostile, and nonspontaneous and tend to offer their children little encouragement. When there is a disparity between parental and peer pressure, there will clearly be dissonance for the adolescent. The resolution of this dissonance will depend on the resources, both internal and external, available to the adolescent in making decisions about drug use.

The frequency and intensity of adolescent drug use are of concern to the counselor. Early identification, treatment, and support are crucial to reducing the negative effects of drug and alcohol use in the next generation. Adolescent drug users present a troubled profile to counselors. They are unable to invest in or derive pleasure from personal relationships, work, or school or to direct energy to future goals. Consequently, they feel troubled and alienated and withdraw even more; this pattern, when combined with impaired impulse control, makes continued drug use likely (Shedler & Block, 1990). Working with adolescents on drug abuse and alcohol use is sensitive and complex. In addition to individual treatment, it is important to include family treatment, because abusive behavior of this variety often has its roots in family dysfunction (West, Hosie, & Zarski, 1987). Murphy (1984) recommends that family-counseling efforts focus on reducing current levels of denial, shame, resentment, guilt, anger, and insecurity.

ABUSE IN SPECIAL POPULATIONS

The major similarity among most special-population groups with regard to drug and alcohol abuse is the willingness of society to overlook or accept the behavior. This tendency results in part from sympathy and denial. Since the lives of special populations are often viewed as lower in quality, it is reasonable to view any form of pleasure as acceptable. Recognizing the serious problems of special populations means having to work with them to improve the quality of life; denial of problems reduces the responsibility to work toward change. The attitude of society and even of immediate family members is an important factor in treatment because it means that there will often be little support for behavior change. Two special populations that you are especially likely to encounter as a counselor are the elderly and the handicapped. (Chapter 13 will address further issues regarding these minorities and others.)

The Elderly

Drug abuse by the elderly may be intentional but often is not; most of the time it results from using prescribed medications. Older patients frequently visit several different doctors, each of whom prescribes a variety of medications. The elderly therefore form the largest group of consumers of legal drugs (Task Force on Prescription Drugs, 1968). Furthermore, the elderly have a decreased ability to metabolize medications and are more susceptible to their actions, interactions, and side effects (Pascarelli, 1981).

Although both prescription and nonprescription drugs are abused by the elderly, alcohol presents by far the most serious drug problem for this population. About one-third of elderly alcoholics have developed an alcohol problem later in life, usually as a reaction to stress. The remaining two-thirds of elderly alcoholics appear to be long-standing alcohol abusers who drank heavily into old age. Since both types of elderly alcoholics tend to drink in response to stress, favorable responses to treatment, especially in the company of contemporaries, have been reported (Pascarelli, 1981).

In the elderly, a number of characteristics have been identified that tend to trigger drug and alcohol abuse. Depression and its effects increase substantially with aging. Persons over 65 years of age account for 25% of all suicides. The health habits of elderly abusers are often poor; they do not eat regularly or properly, and their sleep is frequently disturbed. They tend to rely on medication for a sense of well-being. Behaviorally, they tend to stay at home, feel lonely and abandoned, and focus on the past; they have little interest in activities, remaining isolated and uninvolved. Drinking helps to pass the time.

Developmentally, elderly abusers are needy, lonely adults who are angry and feel a sense of despair about their lives and selves. They are depressed and often feel powerless and unwanted, a state of mind that is temporarily blunted by drugs and alcohol. They sense—rightly at times—an attitude of indifference toward them because they are old and worthless. Professionals and laypeople tend not to place a priority on counseling services for this population because they are old and set in their ways and are going to die soon anyway. As a result, much professional care of the elderly abuser focuses on management and custodial issues. Little emphasis is placed on identification, treatment, and rehabilitation.

The Disabled

Approximately 36 million people in the United States are physically or mentally disabled, a population particularly vulnerable to alcoholism, drug abuse, and related problems. Although the magnitude of the problem has not been clearly established, estimates range as high as 60% for patients with spinal-cord injury (Anderson, 1981). The National Institute of Alcohol Abuse and Alcoholism estimates a similarly high rate of alcohol problems for the disabled.

There are several explanations for the high risk of alcohol and drug abuse in the disabled population:

1. There is easy access to prescription medication, especially for pain and severe spasms. Physicians often prescribe drugs because of their own feelings of pity and guilt and a notion that this is the least they can do, given the tragedy of the situation.
2. The drug-abuse path is taken as a result of the frustration and anxiety of being disabled and being thrust into a nonproductive and dependent role.
3. The disabled are an oppressed minority in our society; therefore the lure of a substance that produces highs and numbness is an attractive alternative. According to initial findings of a study of the Center for Independent Living (CIL), 25% of the clients were abusing substances that caused social, mental, or physical dysfunction.
4. Abuse is often the result of medical intervention and the rehabilitation process. Of the disabled at CIL, 41% received drugs prescribed unnecessarily and often took them in combination with alcohol (Hepner, Kershbaum, & Landes, 1980).

A major problem in treating drug abuse and alcoholism in disabled populations relates to diagnosis. Counselors are often unaware of the problem, and treatment is often delayed until the symptoms become chronic (Vash, 1981). A growing advocacy movement has focused attention on the multidisabled alcoholic and encouraged programmatic responses at the community level. Although awareness of the problems of this population is improving, there is still a need for increased attention to the treatment of the disabled drug and alcohol user. Many people are unacquainted with the symptoms of alcoholism and drug abuse and unfamiliar with the treatability of the problems, and some administrators and clinicians are reluctant to become involved (Lowenthal & Anderson, 1980).

Alcohol and polydrug use is widespread among the disabled due to lack of access to prevention and treatment services, architectural barriers, lack of training and sensitivity to the specific problems and needs of the disabled, and attitudinal barriers that negate the desired effect of these services by reinforcing the client's poor self-image. Substance abuse is an easy way to avoid the difficult and painful work necessary to develop social skills and overcome social isolation (Hepner et al., 1980).

To varying degrees, the blind, deaf, paralyzed, and orthopedically impaired communities have reacted similarly in that they discourage the identification and treatment of alcohol or drug problems. They live in close association with one another and share a common identity and fear of being labeled by what a few deviant members might do. They already have shared the burden of the stigma of their disability. People who are constantly reminded of their disability rather than their ability find the addition of an alcohol or drug-abuse problem an unwanted burden. Treatment for this population is therefore difficult and dependent upon early identification, support, and reduction of the threat of stigma.

PRINCIPLES FOR COUNSELING
THE CHEMICALLY DEPENDENT
Medical Model

Pietrofesa, Hoffman, and Splete (1984) summarize the various treatment models that are used in alcohol and drug counseling. In the medical model favored by many hospital, mental health, and clinic settings, substance abuse and alcoholism are classified as diseases similar to diabetes or cancer. It is presumed that the patient has some genetic predisposition to chemical abuse that may be exacerbated by family conflicts or other life pressures. The abuser is helped through a detoxification program that may include forced abstinence, intensive psychotherapy, family support groups, and, possibly, medications to help with withdrawal symptoms. Antabuse, for example, is a prescribed drug that helps alcoholics stay sober by causing nausea at the first taste of an alcoholic beverage. Because the medical-model approach absolves the client of responsibility for his or her condition, the counselor works intensively on issues related to self-control and compliance to the prescribed program.

The medical-model operates on both an inpatient and outpatient basis. There is some evidence that, for the vast majority of individuals, outpatient treatment is equal in effectiveness to inpatient treatment at a fraction of the personal and monetary cost (Miller & Hester, 1986). Most programs will include the following elements (Beutler & Clarkin, 1990; Nace, 1987):

1. Detoxification.
2. Orientation to a treatment-structured regime, including substance abstinence.
3. Aversion therapy and behavioral self-control training to initiate change in drinking behavior.
4. Social-skills training.
5. Strong peer pressure/support.
6. Strong educational program.
7. Individual and group counseling.
8. Family counseling.
9. Follow-up by the treatment team.
10. AA/NA.

AA/NA Model

The Alcoholics Anonymous/Narcotics Anonymous (AA/NA) model is somewhat compatible with the medical approach in that the abuser is labeled as helplessly addicted forever unless complete withdrawal is initiated. Through powerful peer support groups the client is helped to make radical lifestyle changes, to abstain from all drugs and alcohol, and to admit that as an addict the only salvation is through rigorous adherence to the AA or NA program. As long as the abuser attends regular meetings (often several per week) and follows the pre-scribed steps, continued recovery is possible.

One problem associated with AA and NA programs is the emphasis placed on external control—often a conflict with the values of therapeutic counseling. Participants may learn to substitute one form of dependency for another: whereas they may no longer abuse drugs or alcohol, they nevertheless must go to meetings in order to maintain the cure. It is for this reason that individual counseling can be even more helpful in conjunction with AA and NA pro-grams, giving focus to issues of autonomy, independence, and self-control.

Therapeutic Model

In the therapeutic model the various approaches to counseling are applied to the specific problems of substance abuse. Whereas there isn't much evidence to support the effectiveness of traditional therapies with alcohol and drug prob-lems, there are practitioners who nevertheless attempt such strategies with mixed results. According to the various theories, the counselor may work on delving into repressed conflicts underlying the drug symptoms or perhaps con-centrate on issues related to self-control. Any of the theoretical models present-ed in Chapters 5 and 6 could conceivably be applied to substance-abuse pro-grams. However, regardless of the therapeutic model, several suggestions have been made for working with alcohol/drug abusers:

1. Recovery from drug or alcohol addictions is unlikely without some sup-port system as an adjunct to counseling (Armor, Polick, & Stambul, 1978).

2. Group counseling modalities are often helpful in providing support, positive modeling, motivation, intimacy, and constructive confrontation for substance abusers (Fuhrmann & Washington, 1984).

3. Family counseling strategies help the counselor to recruit more power and support, to collect more information about the problem, and to resolve con-flicts that are sabotaging recovery (Murphy, 1984).

4. The counselor should explore the motivation to use alcohol by examin-ing the availability of nonchemical incentives. Cox and Klinger (1988) observe that "people are motivated to bring about affective changes through the use of alcohol to the extent that they do not have satisfying positive incentives to pur-sue and enjoy and to the extent that their lives are burdened by negative incen-tives that they are not making satisfactory progress toward removing" (p. 178).

5. Alcohol and drug abuse is often a form of self-medication in which the client attempts to cope with debilitating depression or anxiety. Attempts should be made to identify and treat the underlying pain that is being anesthetized.

6. Physical exercise programs that involve daily structured commitments are often helpful in creating more positive addictions. Activities such as biking, running, swimming, and aerobics have been found to reduce tension, increase productivity, improve confidence, and provide an alternative to drugs (Sachs & Buffone, 1984).

7. The counselor should watch for manipulation, deceit, and lying, which are not uncommon among those who are used to saying anything to get what they want. Developing trust is a major issue in the counseling.

8. Rules and limits are often needed to structure acceptable and inappropriate behavior within the sessions. For example, the counselor may refuse to work with the client unless she or he can agree to maintain sobriety for at least eight hours prior to any session.

9. Because drug and alcohol abuse is often associated with low self-esteem, considerable work should be spent helping the client to improve confidence and self-worth (Capuzzi & Lecoq, 1983).

10. Varieties of adventure and risk taking other than the drug-induced kind should be substituted (Capuzzi & Lecoq, 1983). As the person finds more fulfillment in a career, course of study, hobby, intimate relationship, social network, travel experience, or any other passionate project, the need to use drugs for excitement or boredom decreases.

SUMMARY

Drug and alcohol abuse presents some special challenges for the counselor because (1) the problems are so widespread; (2) the effects of the drugs are intrinsically rewarding and resistant to extinction; (3) there may be pressure from peers to continue the abuse; (4) the abuser tends to be externally controlled and thus unresponsive to efforts toward self-control; (5) abusers tend toward irresponsibility—they may miss or break appointments—and so may be uncooperative clients; (6) physiological addictive effects complicate change efforts made on a psychological level; (7) abusers are ambivalent in their motivation, since the drugs *do* work, in spite of side effects, to temporarily reduce symptoms of boredom, anxiety, or depression; (8) there is some evidence that genetic factors may predispose some people to abuse in spite of their best intentions; and (9) drug and alcohol abusers have learned, as a matter of survival, to be manipulative, deceitful con artists—qualities not generally considered optimal for a productive therapeutic encounter.

Because of these many factors contributing to an abuser's situation, the counselor should develop a multifaceted treatment program to combat resistance on physiological, psychological, family, and cultural levels. Traditional insight-oriented counseling interventions are largely useless without additional therapeutic measures. Even with the best resources available, prognoses for chronic drug and alcohol abusers are guarded.

In general, when working with any kind of alcohol/drug abuser, the counselor would be well advised to use every possible resource available in the client's world and in the repertoire of therapeutic options. Particular attention should be paid to factors such as family influences, peer pressures, underlying internal conflicts, and tendencies toward escapism and immediate gratification of needs. It is normally necessary for the counselor to spend more time than usual on trust dimensions of the therapeutic relationship and to define clearly what constitutes responsible behavior, both within and outside the counseling sessions.

SUGGESTED READINGS

American Psychological Association (1988). *Models of addiction.* Special issue of the *Journal of Abnormal Psychology.* Washington, DC: Author.

Gelenberg, A. J., Bassuk, E. L, & Schoonover, S. C. (Eds.) (1991). *The practitioner's guide to psychoactive drugs.* New York: Plenum.

Lewis, J. A., Dana, R. Q., & Blevins, G. A. (1988). *Substance abuse counseling: An individualized approach.* Pacific Grove, CA: Brooks/Cole.

Nace, E. P. (1987). *The treatment of alcoholism.* New York: Brunner/Mazel.

Oakley, R. (1983). *Drugs, society, and human behavior.* St. Louis: C. V. Mosby.

Seymour, R. B., & Smith, D. E. (1987). *Drugfree.* New York: Sawh Lazin Books.

CHAPTER THIRTEEN

COUNSELING SPECIAL POPULATIONS

INFLUENCE OF BIASES

BELIEFS AND ATTITUDES

PREFERRED CLIENT TYPES

COUNSELING WOMEN

COUNSELING ETHNIC
   MINORITIES

COUNSELING THE AGED

COUNSELING LESBIAN
   WOMEN AND GAY MEN

Gay Identity Development
Other Issues for Gay/
   Lesbian Clients
The Counselor and AIDS

COUNSELING CLIENTS WITH
   DISABILITIES

SUMMARY

SUGGESTED READINGS

W orking with special populations requires the skills needed for all therapeutic counseling, plus knowledge about and sensitivity to the needs of
particular groups. The same counseling skills are used with women and
with men; the same theories of change apply to the physically handicapped as to the athlete. Depression or anxiety does not feel qualitatively different to a Chicano, African American, or Caucasian. Group dynamics operate in
similar ways in groups of children, middle-aged adults, and older adults. Gay
men and lesbian women feel loneliness, frustration, or anger just as do hetero-
sexuals. The delinquent, disabled, or drug-addicted clients all respond to empathy, confrontation, and other therapeutic strategies, depending on the counselor's finesse and sensitivity.

Culturally sensitive counselors have been identified as having several qualities:

1. They embrace the concept of cultural pluralism and are extremely committed to learning all they can about racial/ethnic groups different from their
own (Ibrahim & Arredondo, 1990).

2. They are aware of how their own ethnicity and cultural backgrounds
influence their practice.

3. They realize the extent to which they are not only enriched but also limited by their own ethnic and cultural heritage, a circumstance that can be reme-
died only through greater openness to new experiences (Corey, Corey, &
Callanan, 1988).

4. They have developed a perspective in which each person is seen as a
unique individual with values that have been influenced by the cultural context
of the environment in which he or she was raised (Pedersen, 1985).

5. They are extremely flexible and eclectic in the ways they work with people, depending on where the client comes from and what he or she needs (Sue,
1981).

6. They recognize the influence of cultural background on a client's concepts of "power," "growth," "time," "solution," and other terms that are part of
counseling vernacular (Pedersen, 1990). "Privacy," for example, is viewed differently by Westerners, who value space and thick doors, than by those from
the overcrowded Middle East or Orient, who can find solitude only when they
stop talking and retreat inside their own heads (Kottler, 1990).

7. They are free of prejudices and biases that tend to stereotype people and
that alienate them by communicating an ignorant or patronizing attitude
(Axelson, 1985).

INFLUENCE OF BIASES

Finesse *does* make a difference. Working successfully with special populations
requires special knowledge and special applications of therapeutic skills. It is
necessary to understand the language, customs, and culture of a variety of ethnic groups. In addition, an awareness of your own biases and how they affect

your perceptions and behavior is important. Even if you do not believe that you perceive the deaf, the elderly, the minorities, the disadvantaged, or the disabled as different from other people, *they* often perceive others as unaware of and unresponsive to their needs. So, although your desire to treat all people as equals is laudable, it might cause you to appear insensitive. Members of special populations know they have some unique issues, and a counselor who fails to acknowledge them will likely be perceived as ineffective.

Biases and prejudices work both ways. As a counselor, you must be prepared to examine how your beliefs might interfere with counseling. Counselors reflect the beliefs of the larger American social structure and validate "theories that determine general perceptions of women, minorities, and poor people" (Cayleff, 1986, p. 345). But that is only half the problem. Clients also have prejudices, which can affect their reactions to the counselor and interfere with the development of a therapeutic relationship. A client may perceive you as too young, too straight, or too inexperienced, for example, and those perceptions may alter how the client responds to you.

Biases and prejudices are caused by a lack of tolerance for individual differences. People who deviate too far from accepted standards are socially restricted or locked into mental institutions or prisons. Many people feel uncomfortable or threatened by people who have different views, skin color, dress codes, sexual orientation, or patterns of social interaction. Some fears are caused by lack of exposure. Some result from the awareness that "bad" things can happen to all of us; the discomfort people experience at seeing a disabled or mentally ill person is often related to our own fears. Rigidity of thinking, fear of the unknown, avoidance of risks, and many other self-defeating behaviors likewise contribute to an individual's inflexibility.

There is also a danger that teachers and counselors who work with large numbers of students or clients will class them in groups rather than seeing them as individuals. Their generalizations are likely to be misconceptions.

All persons who are members of any group do not possess all the same characteristics, but an uninformed point of view can lead us to judge a whole group by a few individuals members. Thus biases are formed. We urge students and practitioners to assess their own thoughts, feelings, and behaviors and identify those biases that might interfere with effective communication with people who are members of a different group. To change a belief system you have operated with for many years requires learning new information, acquiring new behaviors, and establishing new ways of thinking. But the desire to change is the first step.

It is not uncommon for people to believe or even to say that although they are prejudiced against a certain group of people, they never let that prejudice interfere with their work. It is unlikely that anyone who has strong biases and/or prejudices is completely able to conceal those feelings from others. In counseling, for example. diagnostic biases abound. (Snowden & Cheung, 1990). There are many examples that demonstrate the greater frequency of certain diagnoses among specific groups (Jones & Gray, 1986). Diagnosticians are often seen to have a bias against lower-class patients. A diagnosis of severe psychosis is more likely to be bestowed on a lower-class patient than on a middle-class patient, given similar manifestations of pathological symptoms.

Counselors, regardless of their sex, rated female clients with deviate career goals as being more in need of counseling than those with conforming career goals (Thomas & Stewart, 1971). This finding raises an important issue: bias is not necessarily directed toward someone who is different from us—the opposite sex, in this case—but can also be directed toward people who are like us. The societal expectations, norms, and socialization processes operate systematically to define appropriate roles for women, African Americans, senior citizens, and disabled persons. Prejudices and biases can be and are formed against any conceivable definable group of people: veterans, WASPS, Ku Klux Klansmen, homosexuals, hunters, blue-collar workers, executives, long-haired hippies, middle-class suburban housewives, and Cadillac owners are all groups of people for whom certain stereotypes have been established in our society. There are, of course, many more.

BELIEFS AND ATTITUDES

A person's beliefs and attitudes are founded in four human activities: thinking, feeling, behaving, and interacting. Firmly anchored attitudes are resistant to change; even repeated contradictions of stereotypes fail to alter attitudes because the contradictions are treated as exceptions (Bem, 1970). Festinger (1957) suggests in his theory of cognitive dissonance that, if individuals engage in behavior that is inconsistent with their beliefs, they will be sufficiently motivated to resolve the conflict by changing their beliefs to coincide with their behavior. That is, we were compelled by peer pressure, legal mandates, or professional requirements to behave in a less biased way toward a particular population, we would, in order to restore a state of equilibrium, alter our beliefs to be congruent with the new behavior. Following public compliance, private opinion will change (Festinger, 1964; Bandura, Blanchare, & Ritter, 1969). If behavior change does produce a change in attitudes, then the legal mandate against racial or sexual biases in hiring practices may indeed have an impact on attitudes.

Another theory of behavior change is the self-perception theory, which views behavior as the observable manifestation of inner states. How one acts is an indication of inner feelings. According to this theoretical position, it is possible, by observing a person's overt behavior in specific situations, to infer what the person's beliefs are about that situation. Likewise, changing our biased behavior in counseling can effect a change in our biased beliefs (Bandura, 1971).

The point of view proposed by Ellis (1962) is that changing one's beliefs and attitudes will result in a change of behavior. According to rational-emotive theory, it is the way one thinks about experiences that governs behavior, rather than the other way around. Still other theories see the process as circular in nature, with each part influencing the next. It is probably difficult to determine whether biased and prejudiced behavior is a result of attitudes or beliefs or whether the behavior itself causes the attitudes and beliefs. Maybe you as a beginning counselor ought to examine what the process is like for you: are your behaviors the result of what you think and believe, or do you see your beliefs as stemming from your behavior? Understanding how this process works may help you to determine which method you can use to attack your own biases. It is important, of course, that you not generalize from yourself in working with clients and assume that they will be influenced exactly as you are. You will have to help them ascertain their own best methods for attacking any biases that they may want to change.

PREFERRED CLIENT TYPES

In a classic study of professional biases, psychiatrists, social workers, and clinical psychologists were surveyed to find out their preferred client types. What emerged was the YAVIS profile (Schofield, 1964). The YAVIS client is young, attractive, verbal, intelligent, and successful. All groups of clinicians in the survey preferred female clients between the ages of 20 and 40. Social workers and psychiatrists preferred married females. whereas psychologists did not differentiate. Psychologists and psychiatrists had rigid levels of acceptable education and preferred high school graduates with some college experience—but not "too much" education. For example, graduate-school experience was considered to create a difficult client. Nonpreferred clients included the very young (under 15) and those over 50, widowed or divorced clients, uneducated people, and those in agriculture, fishery, forestry, and semiskilled or unskilled types of jobs. Although the evidence indicates that counselors and other professionals have definite preferences, the YAVIS population represents but a small proportion of the types of clients that most of you will work with in counseling settings. Part of the reason for preferring particular clients is that those clients make us, as professionals, feel more successful about our work. Clients who improve quickly allow counselors to feel more powerful and competent.

It is important in counseling to use your distinctiveness and individuality to help others without imposing your morality or beliefs on them. The following is a list of suggestions originally designed for counselors who work with minority populations (Ho & Shipley, 1974); it can be adapted for counseling with a client group of any target population:

1. Do not deny cultural or physical differences. Your client is aware and will be made uncomfortable by your denial.
2. Feelings of warmth and genuineness transcend all ethnic, religious, cultural, and physical barriers.
3. Treat each client as an individual rather than as a member of a group.
4. Avoid projection, but use your own life experiences effectively to help others.
5. Share your own personal involvement and discoveries in ways that will benefit your client without imposing your views.

COUNSELING WOMEN

The majority of counseling clients are women. Although gender has long been an important issue in counseling, its influence will likely be even greater in the future (Scher & Good, 1990). Women represent a special population that is often the victim of bias in diagnosis and treatment for mental health problems. There is limited literature that "provides careful analyses of how gender as a multidimensional construct is related to psychological problems faced by women and men" (Cook, 1990, p. 371).

With a few notable exceptions (Melanie Klein, Anna Freud), men created most of the foundational theories of this field, some showing biases regarding the roles women should play. Certainly Freud's portrayal of the "weaker sex" as dependent, hysterical, inferior people established a precedent. Most of the theories that followed continued to reinforce conventional stereotypes of women as sex objects who need counseling for their boredom.

Hare-Mustin (1983) reviews several psychological problems that have a high incidence in women but that have been neglected by counselors. Because women are often limited to stereotypical roles in the family, they may experience frustration associated with blocked goals and routine lifestyles.

Marriage and parenthood can be sources of satisfaction for women, but they are also likely to be sources of extreme distress (Russo, 1990). Their husbands may complain about how hard they are working to make money, yet, when they are recruited as temporary baby-sitters while the mother takes a "breather," they often develop a new respect for the strain of managing a household. Even when women work the same number of hours outside the home as their husbands, an inequitable division of labor in household chores is common, especially when there are children at home.

Parenthood increases the symptoms of psychological distress for women whether or not they work outside the home (Thoits, 1986), and almost 70% of employed women do have children at home (McBride, 1988). A great number of female clients report feeling misunderstood, unappreciated, and underutilized because of their responsibilities in the home.

Women are more likely than men to be diagnosed with major depression (Mowbray & Benedek, 1988), and, when they are depressed, they stay depressed longer (Weissman & Klerman, 1977). The books of Sylvia Plath, Doris Lessing, Alice Walker, and other writers document the depressive episodes all too familiar to women who feel powerless, ignored, abused, and neglected in their lives.

Kaplan (1983) claims that one reason why more women than men are labeled and treated as mentally ill is that the current diagnostic system is founded on inherently masculine-biased assumptions. The American Psychiatric Association's DSM-III-R overemphasizes disorders that are caricatures of traditional female roles—that is, diagnoses that describe women who are overconforming in their efforts to satisfy sex-role stereotypes. Thus, favorite labels include terms like "hysterical," "passive-dependent," and "anorexia," which all describe the symptoms of a woman trying too hard to be subordinate, emotional, dependent, and skinny. Although critics (Williams & Spitzer, 1983; Kass, Spitzer, & Williams, 1983) argue that there is no empirical evidence to support the validity of Kaplan's claims, counselors nevertheless ought to be aware of the danger of creating additional problems for female clients by labeling overconforming behavior as pathological.

Most women interviewed by Sanford and Donovan (1985) reported having a negative body image. Women strive to fulfill some ideal concept of how they should look and in the process often develop distorted images of their body and poor self-concepts. Eating disorders are a particularly dramatic example of the attempts of women to live up to the ideal standards of body image created by our culture. All models are tall and thin. While striving for this narrow conception of beauty as slimness, some women lose control of their original goal to become thinner and perceive losing weight as a contest. One prevalent problem is anorexia nervosa, or drastic weight loss to the point of starvation. This disorder almost always has its onset in adolescent girls who are overdependent, perfectionistic, and self-critical. Bulimia, or compulsive food gorging, is another way women destroy their bodies through abusive eating habits, often the consequence of rejection and a poor self-concept. Until recent efforts by Salvador Minuchin (Minuchin, Rosman, & Baker, 1978) and others to treat eating disorders in a family counseling context, the prognosis for these female-oriented problems was not positive. Now counselors are experiencing successful outcomes by intervening on a structural level within the family unit.

Women also experience problems with their reproductive functions. There are stresses associated with pregnancy (or its avoidance) and breastfeeding. The menstrual cycle may present special difficulties, as when mood swings precede the onset of the monthly period. New research on women who have severe reactions or PMS (premenstrual syndrome) has brought attention to these bodily changes (Turkington, 1984).

Schlossberg and Kent (1979) present a model for working with women and their special problems that includes an emphasis on developmental transitions. The counselor's role, after becoming aware of transitional crises such as the birth of a child, is to educate the client about universal problems and then to make needed adjustments. A developmental model is often difficult to put into practice, particularly since the traditional theories of Erikson, Freud, Kohlberg, and others are so sex biased. Schlossberg (1984) has attempted to downplay the traditional roles of women as caretakers in an effort to equalize the developmental life cycle for both sexes.

Doherty (1978) also raises serious questions about the validity of our counseling interventions with women on the grounds that the personality theories from which they derive are authored by men and focused primarily on male concerns. Concepts such as "penis envy" and "oedipal complex" and stereotypical portrayals of women as emotional and nurturing make it more difficult for them to attain the autonomy and independence so prized by most psychological theories. McBride (1990) suggests that the multiple roles of women who juggle parenting, work outside the home, and the care of elderly parents should be considered in treatment models for women.

The importance of women's mental health issues is underscored by their recent inclusion on the research agenda of the National Institutes of Mental Health (Russo, 1990). Women in American society are frequent victims of poverty and violence. There is a well-documented positive correlation between poverty and psychiatric disorders (Belle, 1990). Women who live in poverty conditions are unable to gain access to such support systems as child care, health care, and counseling, so they are more likely to develop serious problems before they receive help. Although women are frequent victims of violence, they are reluctant to reveal their experiences or seek help, in part because victims tend to be viewed as losers (Koss, 1990). The family is not a safeguard against violence for women, because a majority of violent incidents directed toward women involves family members.

Current lifestyle issues such as juggling roles, coping with poverty, and responding to violence, combined with developing an identity and positive self-concept in the shadow of theories that discount many aspects of the female experience, demonstrate the importance of acquiring knowledge and insight to counsel women. In particular, female counselors must be careful not to assume that being female correlates with understanding the problems and concerns of all women.

COUNSELING ETHNIC MINORITIES

Most counselors work in settings where they are called upon to engage in encounters with clients whose backgrounds differ from their own (Christensen, 1989). Thus it is important to know how to interact with clients in a way that will help you develop an understanding of each individual so his or her behaviors, thoughts, and emotions can be interpreted in the appropriate context.

Hall and Maloney (1983) ascribe much of the failure and ineffectiveness of mental health programs to the lack of recognition given to the needs of minority groups. In their review of the literature pertaining to treatment of minority populations, they concluded the following:

1. Minority clients are diagnosed as having more severe disturbances and pathological conditions than white persons—a not surprising finding, considering that most tests of mental illness are culturally biased and most diagnosticians are not members of minority groups.

2. Minority clients will tend to use mental health services only in cases of emergency or severe psychopathology, again skewing the perceptions of clinicians, who may be used to working with normal or neurotic whites but very disturbed minorities. It is a cultural norm, for instance, among South American populations to handle most psychological problems through the resources of the family and church, relying on counselors or therapists only in extreme cases.

3. Minority clients more often drop out of treatment prematurely, usually within the first six sessions (Sue, 1977). Whether this tendency is a function of poor motivation or a difference in how they are treated is not clear.

4. In inpatient settings, evidence does indicate that African American clients are treated differently from whites, more often receiving stronger medication, seclusion, restraints, and other punitive "therapies" and less often receiving recreational or occupational therapy (Flaherty & Meagher, 1980).

5. Minority group attitudes toward psychological disturbances are markedly different from those of whites, more often stressing the roles of organic factors. Hispanics have more faith in the power of prayer than in psychotherapy for healing what they believe are inherited illnesses (Edgerton & Karno, 1971). The expectations of minority clients are thus not conducive to success, since so often the faith and hope that are so important are not operating at high levels.

6. Many people feel more comfortable and prefer working with others whom they perceive as similar (particularly with regard to race or ethnic background). Yet there are relatively few trained minority counselors who are available to serve this need.

7. With minority clients, and particularly with those of the lower class, it is important that counselors adapt their strategies and interventions to cultural differences. Eye contact and attention patterns can be interpreted variously as resistance, passivity, or aggression, depending on the client's culture (Hall, 1976).

8. Counseling can be viewed as a form of social control, because its goals are most often to help deviants better adjust to the cultural norms of the majority. For the minority client this sort of adjustment presents special problems, since more conflict can result from the clash between subcultural values and those of the majority.

Hall and Maloney (1983) suggest that it would be effective to minimize conflicts that result from a clash of values by reducing dominance factors. When two culturally different viewpoints are in conflict, counselors need to recognize that both are right within their own cultural context (Pedersen, 1990).

Sue (1983) recommends recognizing our cultural biases as only the first of several steps to ensure effective treatment of minority clients. Counselors must also be highly motivated to educate themselves about other cultural groups. Finally, counselors must develop cross-cultural intervention skills to work with each client as an individual. By endlessly focusing on the differences among various ethnic groups, we can fall into the trap of neglecting the uniqueness of each member of the group. A person's ethnic identity is only one of several contextual variables to help us understand and work with him or her as a client. "Knowing that Americans tend to be open, competitive, verbally direct, independent minded, or whatever, provides very few clues to the conduct of therapy with clients" (Sue, 1983, p. 589). Similarly, understanding the cultural heritage of clients is a necessary but insufficient condition for attaining true empathic contact.

There is a serious need not only for increased awareness of racial and ethnic minority groups but also for educational programs to prepare counselors to work with these groups (Casas, Ponterotto, & Gutierrez, 1986). Pedersen (1988) describes the role of multicultural awareness:

> Multicultural awareness provides a safe and accurate approach to differences across groups in a multicultural population. Multicultural awareness is safe because it provides a third alternative to judgments of right or wrong between two culturally different persons in conflict. Multicultural awareness is accurate because it interprets behaviors in the context of the culturally different client's intended meaning. Culture is not a vague or exotic label attached to faraway persons and places, but a personal orientation to each decision, behavior, and action in our lives [p. vii].

He further states that the three stages of multicultural development are awareness, knowledge, and skills. Thus, as students of counseling, you must begin or continue to develop awareness of your own attitudes, acquire knowledge about the different culture, and develop skills for interacting with persons from that culture (Pedersen, 1988). These steps are equally important for all students and practicing counselors, regardless of race or ethnic origin. Oler (1989) points out that both African American and white clinicians can improve their treatment plans with increased understanding of black psychological and behavioral functioning. Belonging to the same race does not mean that you know or understand all the experiences of other members of that race.

Snowden and Cheung (1990), in reporting marked ethnic-related differences in psychiatric hospitalization, suggested that differences in culture between diagnostician and patient may account for misdiagnosis because behavior is not understood in its cultural context. According to them, "Blacks and Native Americans are considerably more likely than Whites to be hospitalized; Blacks are more likely than Whites to be admitted as schizophrenic and less likely to be diagnosed as having an affective disorder; Asian Americans/Pacific Islanders are less likely than Whites to be admitted, but remain for a lengthier stay, at least in state and county mental hospitals" (p. 347).

In addition to the need for awareness and understanding, counselors must also develop specific skills for working effectively with clients with different backgrounds. Although the literature on this topic is becoming extensive, there is unfortunately no consensus of the actual behavioral criteria that represent expertise in multicultural counseling (Johnson, 1987). Sue and Zane (1987) even suggest that the repeated recommendations to be sensitive and to know the culture of the client have not been helpful because counselors need to know about interventions that work with individual clients. This task is difficult because there are many special populations, each with their own characteristics. As a student you may consider designing a step-by-step approach that involves first learning about human behavior and basic counseling skills and then challenging yourself to develop awareness of the broader culture. Later in your studies you can read about and integrate some of the specific approaches presented in the professional journals.

COUNSELING THE AGED

At the turn of the 21st century, when most of us will be at our peaks of professional productivity, a disproportionate part of the North American population will be considered elderly citizens. In just one century the single specialty within the helping professions that is most likely to flourish, if not explode, will be counseling older adults. The number of people over 65 has increased sevenfold: from 1 in 30 Americans in 1900 to an expected 1 in 5 Americans by 2020 (Eisdorfer, 1983). The children of the baby boom will, by the year 2000, be grandparents. Life expectancies will continue to lengthen, stretching normal lifespans well into the 80s and perhaps 90s. Age 65 will be considered a part of the productive rather than the retirement years. Older citizens will dominate the consumer markets as they will control a significant part of industry, families, and lifestyle. And with these changing roles, opportunities, and expectations will come new problems of adaptation for the aged—and important responsibilities for therapeutic counselors to aid adjustment and resolution of conflicts.

Although there are more similarities than differences in counseling old and young people, it is important to realize that the assessment process is more complex with the mature client. Not only are there more life experiences to take into account, but the diagnosis may be affected by underlying medical or physiological problems (Waters & Goodman, 1990).

These special diagnostic problems are more than compensated for by the tremendous satisfaction that geriatric counselors experience in their work. Hausman (1991) believes that the primary attraction to working with older adults is that we so need wise elders in our lives. She noted that most specialists in this field report having enjoyed especially close relationships with a grandparent. They enjoy working with this population despite the many challenges— being called "Dearie," arguing about your fees, stirring up all kinds of countertransference feelings, and dealing with people who resent your interrupting their long stories they have told many times before.

Some models of aging view older people as helpless, disabled, and burdensome to society. There are special facilities where the aged may be cleaned, clothed, and fed until they die. Institutional environments of this type are generally depressing places where people wander about, forgetting who or where they are. The more agile can play cards, turn the channels on the television, or even shuffle along for walks outside the home.

Alternative conceptions of aging proposed by Eisdorfer (1983) view older persons as senior adults with a wealth of valuable experiences and skills accumulated over a lifetime. Elders used to be considered the wise men and women of the community to whom the young would come for advice and assistance; now they are the elderly—the shuffleboard and Geritol generation. Old age is a time of physical changes—hair thinning and turning white, skin losing its moisture and smoothness, the body actually shrinking in size, muscles becoming flabby and losing their strength. Joints become progressively stiff, bones are fragile, the heart is less efficient, and the arteries that circulate blood work like a slow train. Digestion is slowed, reaction times are diminished, and lungs work at less than peak efficiency and bring less oxygen to provide energy. All the senses lose their precision, and the older person, receiving less information from vision, hearing, taste, touch, and smell, is thus more isolated, irritable, and moody.

Yet in spite of these symptoms of physical deterioration, their effects are often slight and the stereotype of the elderly person as slow moving and fragile, with dulled and distorted perceptions, is hardly accurate. In a review of experimental findings of biochemical and physiological changes in the elderly, Hussian (1981) concludes that slowed intellectual, perceptual, and mental behavior, particularly in those who are free of debilitating diseases, need not necessarily restrict functioning levels in major life areas. He suggests that, although a clinician may wish to alter assessment techniques, length of sessions, or the therapeutic process, highly specialized approaches are not required when working with elderly clients. The aged retain the capacity for self-awareness and insight. They respond to reinforcement. They may be a bit more cautious in their mental and physical movements, but they still think, feel, and act and wish to do so more effectively.

Traditionally, at least at the time Erik Erikson was formulating his theory of psychosocial development, later maturity was a time for resolution of the crisis of despair and for introspective integration of one's life. The elderly were supposed to be giving meaning to their life's work and preparing themselves to accept the inevitability of death. At age 81, himself engaged in this final life stage, Erikson revised many of his thoughts about old age to place much more emphasis on the creative, productive elements supposedly restricted to earlier stages (Hall, 1983). Through their roles in grandparenting, volunteer work, and involvement in intimate relationships, older people can retain the playfulness, joy, and wonder that were so much a part of childhood.

B. F. Skinner, another influential thinker of this century, also wrote about his own struggle to maintain his desired levels of effectiveness and to avoid growing old as a thinker even though his body stubbornly persisted in its progressive decline (Skinner, 1983).

The principal developmental task of the older adult, then, is to maintain maximum levels of productivity and mental activity in the face of physical deterioration. "Old age is like fatigue, except that its effects cannot be corrected by relaxing or taking a vacation" (Skinner, 1983, p. 241). The older adult must learn to accept his or her incapacities and to find alternative ways to accomplish the same goals and to meet the same needs. Death, certain and inevitable, is a difficult issue for the older person as it looms ahead, closer and closer. Some people become crippled by their fears; others welcome their final deliverance. Yet, when old persons are given the opportunity to talk through their fears, most are able to resolve the developmental task, accept what they cannot change, and go on about the business of living fully in what little time remains. When discomfort arises in confronting the topic of death—with relatives, friends, nurses, doc-

An unretired senior working at the office. For some active and productive people, youth is more a state of mind than chronological age.

tors, or counselors—it is important to distinguish who exactly is uncomfortable, the older adult or the helper (Wass & Myers, 1982).

Dying is the last developmental task for everyone. Whether it comes unexpectedly, with or without pain, during sleep or sex, death is patiently waiting. Woody Allen (1976) freely admits "It's not that I'm afraid to die. I just don't want to be there when it happens" (p. 106). If there is a "process" of dying, even beyond Elizabeth Kübler-Ross's stages of denial, rage, bargaining, depression, and acceptance, (assuming death is patient enough to wait for the complete cycle), then certainly counselors could help make the experience easier. In *Island*, his novel of a utopian society, Aldous Huxley (1962) imagines the distinct role of a death counselor, one who helps the dying in their final transition, the last exit from life:

> "So now you can let go, my darling." He stroked her grey hair. "Now you can let go. Let go," he insisted. "Let go of this poor old body. You don't need it any more. Let it fall away from you. Leave it lying here like a pile of worn-out clothes" [p. 268].

Whether to aid in the client's fight against death until the last breath or to help a client accept its inevitability and let go peacefully, the counselor can help to make the process easier.

Only 3% of the clientele who are currently served by community mental health centers and private clinics are over 65, and 70% of clinicians report that they are not treating a single elderly client (Nissenson, 1984). Do the older adults not come because they feel they are incapable of changing or because administrators and clinicians believe that their problems are incurable, irreversible, and not amenable to treatment? Even Freud suggested that counseling is useless with people over 50.

Tolliver (1983) reports that three-fourths of older persons would prefer to be working rather than retired. With enforced mandatory retirement it is even more crucial for older people to feel productive after they leave their formal jobs. They must feel that they are occupied "doing something that is within their capacity, that gives them satisfaction, and that is needed by and useful to other people" (Swensen, 1983, p. 331).

Throughout history the aged have always served the important function of passing on wisdom from one generation to the next. Whether in the role of teacher, guru, medicine man, or grandparent, the elders have taught their accumulated knowledge, experience, and skills to youth so that they too might survive life's tests. The aged are responsible, through storytelling and sharing of life experiences, for maintaining family and ethnic traditions. It is through listening to accounts of their own mistakes, failures, and weaknesses that, they hope, their protégés will learn to avoid similar traps.

According to Levinson (1978), the mentor role also involves several other tasks:

1. To act as an inspired leader, a model for the young to emulate.
2. To enrich the intellectual and emotional development of the young.
3. To use whatever influence is available to aid the advancement of youth.
4. To communicate the values and customs of the previous generation.
5. To provide guidance, advice, and moral support in times of expressed need.
6. To help the young believe in themselves and in their dreams.

It is in part this mentoring role that allows the elderly to remain productive and feel that their existence is still meaningful.

Publications about adult development and aging are plentiful (Birren, Cunningham, & Yamamoto, 1983). So as counseling students you will be able to read and learn much about the issues involved in counseling the elderly. Even if this is not an area of special interest, you will find it necessary to acquire some background knowledge and skills because the number of older people who will be needing and seeking services will continue to grow. It is also important to see aging as a natural part of the developmental cycle that should not be ignored when you counsel adult clients.

COUNSELING LESBIAN WOMEN AND GAY MEN

Until recently, professional counselors have historically paid scant attention to the counseling and development needs of gay people. To a large extent there has been a historical pattern of discrimination and repression directed toward lesbian women and gay men. Negative social attitudes and a pattern of stigmatization institutionalized in laws, religion, and the mental health system have kept gay people an invisible or hidden minority (Fassinger, 1991; Dworkin &

Gutierrez, 1989). Homosexuality was viewed by psychiatry as a mental illness until 1973, and it wasn't until the publication of DSM-III-R (1987) that all references to homosexuality were declassified (Dworkin & Gutierrez, 1989). Thus the counseling and development needs of gay men and lesbian women have not historically been addressed, and the majority of graduate counselor-training programs have neglected lesbian and gay issues (Buhrke & Douce, 1991; Iasenza, 1989). A study of published articles in counseling journals between 1978 and 1989 found only 42 of 6661 articles addressing gay and lesbian issues (Buhrke & Douce, 1991). It is clear that there exists a paucity of information in counselor-training and in the professional journals on these topics, although it is encouraging to note that special issues on gay/lesbian counseling concerns have been published by the *Journal of Counseling and Development* (1989) and *The Counseling Psychologist* (1991).

The Human Rights Committee of the American Association for Counseling and Development (AACD) in a 1987 position paper affirmed the responsibility of counselors to facilitate the development of potential in *all* clients. To achieve this goal, each member of AACD was charged to:

> (a) engage in ongoing examination of his/her own attitudes, feelings, stereotypic views, perceptions, and behavior that might have prejudicial or limiting impact on women, ethnic minorities, elderly persons, gay/lesbian persons, and persons with handicapping conditions; (b) contribute to an increased sensitivity on the part of other individuals, groups, or institutions to the barriers to opportunity imposed by discrimination; (c) advocate equal rights for all individuals through concerted personal, professional, and political activity [p. 1].

Thus counselors in training must challenge stereotyped attitudes regarding sexual orientation and actively gather information about gay/lesbian lifestyles, identity development, interpersonal issues, and other issues so that effective and appropriate counseling and development services can be provided to the estimated 22 million gay men and lesbian women living in the United States (Fassenger, 1991).

Gay Identity Development

The issue of identity development and the acquisition of a positive lesbian or gay identity, which can be defined as "acceptance of and satisfaction with one's sexual orientation," is an important one for psychological adjustment (Miranda & Storms, 1989, p. 91). The developmental tasks associated with a positive gay identity are self-labeling and self-disclosure (Fassinger, 1991; Miranda & Storms, 1989). Self-labeling refers to integrating sexual feelings and sexual identity, whereas self-disclosure or "coming out" refers to confronting negative social and self-attitudes regarding one's gay identity.

Fassinger (1991, p. 167) has described a six-stage model of gay identity development:

1. *Identity confusion*, characterized by feelings of turmoil, in which one questions previously held assumptions about one's sexual orientation.

2. *Identity comparison,* characterized by feelings of alienation, in which one accepts the possibility of being gay and becomes isolated from nongay others.
3. *Identity tolerance,* characterized by feelings of ambivalence, in which one seeks out other gays but maintains separate public and private images.
4. *Identity acceptance,* characterized by selective disclosure, in which one begins the legitimization (publicly as well as privately) of one's sexual orientation.
5. *Identity pride,* characterized by anger, pride, and activism, in which one becomes immersed in the gay subculture and rejects nongay people, institutions, and values.
6. *Identity synthesis,* characterized by clarity and acceptance, in which one moves beyond a dichotomized world view to an incorporation of one's sexual orientation as one aspect of a more integrated identity.

Shannon and Woods (1991) affirm the central importance of establishing a positive gay identity. They suggest that counselors address a number of critical areas to assess level of development for gay men:

> (a) early relationships with parents (especially the father), siblings, and other significant caretakers; (b) ways in which tenderness/affection was or was not expressed in the family; (c) how conflict was handled within the family; (d) at what age he knew he was "different" from other boys and his understanding of this difference; (e) his first awareness of sexual/affectual feelings for other males; (f) a careful description of his process of "coming out"; (g) a history of significant romantic relationships (i.e., dating, boyfriends, and lover relationships); (h) a thorough sexual history, including a frank discussion of sexual fantasies and sexual preferences; and (i) gender-role conformity/nonconformity and the impact this had/has on the individual's process of coming out [p. 198].

A challenge for counselors is to be aware of the identity issues faced by lesbian women and gay men and to facilitate a positive resolution of these issues.

Other Issues For Gay/Lesbian Clients

Shannon and Woods (1991) describe a number of other counseling issues for gay men that may also have relevance for counseling lesbian women (their list also includes the topic of AIDS, which will be discussed separately in the next section):

Coming Out. As mentioned earlier, coming out or confronting negative social attitudes about sexual orientation is an important dimension to the development of a positive gay identity and is related to psychological adjustment.

Occupational/Career Issues. Discrimination in the work/career arena is a reality for many gay people, and counselors must be sensitive to the special life/career-planning issues for gay men and lesbian women. Counselors must be aware of occupations or professions that are more tolerant of sexual orientation, be sensitive to the dual-career issues of lesbian and gay couples, and be knowledgeable about the special resources available to gays.

Racial Ethnic, and Regional Issues. Gay men and lesbian women have historically experienced discrimination and violence as a result of living in a homophobic and heterosexual society. When social-class and racial issues are added, gay individuals may experience double- or triple-minority status with increasing attendant discrimination. Geography and regional differences also impact the gay subculture and may affect the available resources and networking opportunities for gay people. Counselors must be knowledgeable about these issues and be prepared to offer support and encouragement to gay clients experiencing multiple layers of discrimination.

Isolation. An openly gay lifestyle in a heterosexist society can result in a feeling of isolation and a fear of discrimination and rejection. Counselors must recognize the dangers of an isolated lifestyle and encourage gay people to develop a full and wide pattern of interaction with both gay and nongay individuals.

Couple Issues. It is necessary for gay individuals to affirm the validity of their lifestyles and their commitment to their primary partner. In addition to the special issues that confront gay/lesbian couples, there are the typical types of conflicts and stresses inherent in all intimate relationships. Counselors must be cognizant of the special challenges and strengths of the gay/lesbian couple as well as the more traditional problems of all couples.

Antigay Violence. Hate crimes against gays and lesbians have been prevalent throughout history. They range from verbal insults and slurs to acts of violence, including murder. This reality extracts a toll on the gay person's self-esteem and can lead to depression and feelings of hopelessness, shame, and guilt. Counselors must provide support to the victims of antigay abuse and work with them to counteract the negative effects on their self-esteem. Counselors can also help their clients to direct their feelings into positive, activist channels to counter antigay violence.

The Counselor and AIDS

The AIDS virus was first identified in 1981, although it has subsequently been traced back as far as the late 1960s. Initially it was seen as a threat only to specific population subgroups. However, the virus has spread, and the United States is presently in the "third wave" of the disease (Gordon & Shontz, 1990). The "first wave" primarily affected homosexual men, the "second wave" expanded the risk to intravenous drug users, and now the "third wave" finds the virus expanding into the heterosexual population. The importance of the AIDS epidemic was emphasized in 1983, when the U.S. Public Health Service declared AIDS its number-one priority and in 1988 sent an educational brochure to every household in the United States. Given the seriousness of the disease, its continuing spread, and the unique issues surrounding it, counselors must be prepared and knowledgeable about AIDS counseling.

AIDS presents an unusual and complex issue for counselors. Although it is a physical disease and as such requires medical management and treatment, the transmission of the virus is largely a volitional activity subject to psychosocial factors and influences (Cochran & Mays, 1989). The presence of the AIDS virus in humans is identified by a test for the HIV virus (human immunodeficiency virus); when individuals test HIV positive, it is an indication that they have the AIDS virus. The role of the counselor in working with AIDS issues has two major focal areas: (1) providing services to HIV-positive individuals and (2) providing education to non-HIV-positive individuals regarding practices designed to prevent AIDS.

This role of health educator is a new and complex one for counselors, yet it is essential because AIDS is an incurable but largely preventable disease (Gordon & Shontz, 1990). The mechanism for prevention is education. Counselors must be prepared to discuss sexual practices frankly and to provide information to assist in prevention efforts. AIDS education programs must increase awareness of the risks associated with the disease, promote an understanding of the principles of "safe sex," and encourage the necessary behavioral controls to confront denial and increase the probability of implementing AIDS prevention behaviors (Castronovo, 1990; Cochran & Mays, 1989; Gordon & Shontz, 1990) .

Related issues that have a critical impact on gay clients and demand sensitivity and accurate information from counselors involve monogamy and fidelity, decisions regarding whether to take an HIV test, and mechanisms for coping with a positive test result for self or friends. Counselors should also be aware of the possibility of posttraumatic stress disorder, especially in gay men or lesbian women who have experienced multiple losses because of AIDS (Martin, 1989).

Counselors also must work with HIV-positive individuals and those who fear they may be HIV-positive. Allers and Katrin (1988) propose a five-phase model for working with AIDS clients:

1. *Overcoming the initial fear of AIDS.* Fear is the first reaction of clients who know they are carrying the HIV virus; they must deal with the stigma and the uncertainty over the onset and course of the disease. Counselors must provide support, acceptance, and education regarding the process of the disease and the resources required for coping.
2. *Redefining relationships.* A second phase involves redefining relationships with family of origin, primary partner, and friends.
3. *Modifying lifestyle.* The third phase involves decisions about sexual practices, employment, old patterns of behavior, and leisure activities.
4. *Reevaluating life's meaning.* This phase requires the individual to develop a perspective on the self, the disease, and the remaining period of life. In particular, clients must learn to continue living, to set and pursue long-term goals, and to not diminish their existence.
5. *Adjusting to physical and social limitations.* The last phase involves developing coping strategies and identifying resources to assist in adjusting when physical and social limitations surface.

Individual, group, couples, and family counseling approaches are beneficial in helping clients work through each of these phases. Supportive group therapy, in particular, has been found to be an effective adjunct to individual counseling to reduce the emotional impact of AIDS-related problems (McKusick, 1988).

The AIDS epidemic poses a difficult and complex challenge to therapeutic counselors because of the need to develop new approaches and techniques, to provide leadership in primary prevention efforts, and, perhaps most important, to confront personal vulnerability and discomfort about a tragic and dangerous disease.

COUNSELING CLIENTS WITH DISABILITIES

Disabled persons generally become involved in counseling through rehabilitation services provided to assess the needs of the client and establish a program of physical and emotional restoration. Career exploration and establishment of training goals are a major focus of rehabilitation efforts. It is important, however, to recognize that handicapped persons may have emotional problems not necessarily related to their abilities or disabilities.

People with disabilities are often able to participate fully in life as a result of social, political, and technological developments (Greenwood, 1987). Today we are challenged to think of disabled or handicapped people as "differently abled" to remove their stigma. In fact, Warnath (1989) takes the opposite perspective and believes that we are all "temporarily abled" persons. He suggests that the conditions in one's life are variable and likely to change over time. Such a perspective can be discouraging in that it emphasizes lack of control over our individual fate or it can be reassuring in that it assumes that we can adapt to whatever happens.

Counselors need to be knowledgeable about and sensitive to the issues faced by disabled clients. Greenwood (1987) offers a list of things counselors can do to help their disabled clients:

Monitor your own belief systems and language to reflect awareness and sensitivity.
Act in an advocacy role whenever possible.
Include clients with disabilities in integrated group programs.
Approach people with disabilities from a competency perspective.

Family members of disabled individuals may experience guilt, anger, resentment, and insecurity because they do not know how to handle problems. These symptoms may be manifested by siblings as well as by spouses and parents. Because the disabled family member requires extra assistance and attention, other family members may not be comfortable asking to have their needs met. The counselor can help the family develop ways to manage time, money, and emotional resources so that everyone can receive appropriate attention and support.

Disabled children, in particular, can cause stresses in the family for the parents and the other children. Seligman (1983) points out that, because disabled children need excessive caretaking, other family members must bear the responsibility and burden, often neglecting themselves and one another in the process. But it is certainly not always the case that the presence of a disabled child adversely affects the family. Often the experience encourages brothers and sisters to develop a sensitivity and caring that they will maintain their whole lives. However, it is important to realize that the "identified client"—the disabled child—may not be the only one with problems.

This reminder is but a specific application of the principle that holds true for all presenting problems that occur in a family: when one person develops symptoms, they inevitably disrupt the daily lives of everyone else. Particularly when the disabled individual is making a poor psychological adjustment, the added strain and stress place the other children at risk to develop problems. In addition to feeling guilt and resentment, they may also act out as a way to win attention according to family norms that emphasize being taken care of. For all these reasons, it is often advisable to work with the disabled in the context of their families.

SUMMARY

We have selected a few special-population groups to profile, but many others that were not discussed are equally important. The complexity of the problems and special considerations for each group is evidenced by the amount of literature detailing the characteristics and methods of treatment. The challenges facing you as a counselor include learning about special populations, developing skills to counsel individuals and families, and understanding your own biases and how they impact your thoughts and behavior with clients.

As a counselor you will work with women, minorities, the aged, and disabled and ill clients. All of them will possess some "group" characteristics, but they will also be unique. Basic counseling skills and theories will be useful in developing treatment plans and initiating the counseling relationship, but your ultimate success depends on your being knowledgeable and sensitive to your clients. Background, heritage, and culture are more of an issue when working with special populations because of the significant impact these factors have had on the development of their personalities and lifestyles. We believe it is a privilege of the counseling profession that we are permitted entry into the rich complexity of all human life.

SUGGESTED READINGS

Kain, C. (Ed.) (1989). *No longer immune: A counselor's guide to AIDS*. Alexandria, VA: American Association for Counseling and Development.

Kus, R. J. (Ed.) (1990). *Keys to caring: Assisting your gay and lesbian clients*. Boston: Alyson.

Laidlow, T. A., & Malmo, C. (1990). *Healing voices: Feminist approaches to therapy with women.* San Francisco: Jossey-Bass.

Pedersen, P., Draguns, J. G., Lonner, W. J., & Trimble, J. E. (1989). *Counseling across cultures.* Honolulu: University of Hawaii Press.

Ramierez, M. (1991). *Psychotherapy and counseling with minorities: A cognitive approach to individual and cultural differences.* New York: Pergamon Press.

Sue, D. W., & Sue, D. (1990). *Counseling the culturally different* (2nd ed.). New York: Wiley.

Waters, E. B., & Goodman, J. (1990). *Empowering older adults.* San Francisco: Jossey-Bass.

PART FOUR

PROFESSIONAL
PRACTICE

CHAPTER FOURTEEN

RESEARCH AND PRACTICE

THE MARRIAGE BETWEEN
    RESEARCH AND PRACTICE
RESEARCH FOR THE COUNSELOR
RESEARCH ON THERAPEUTIC
    ATTRIBUTES
    Reliability and Validity in
      Counseling
    Outcome Effects in Counseling

THE GENERIC SKILLS OF
    COUNSELING
SIGNIFICANCE OF ATTENDING
    SKILLS
SKILLS THAT FACILITATE CLIENT
    CHANGE
SUMMARY
SUGGESTED READINGS

W e have presented many different counseling theories and approaches as well as discussed how they may be applied to diverse populations and settings. Each counselor must determine which interventions to use and evaluate their suitability for various clients and types of presenting complaints. This complex task requires an understanding of the counseling process, a mastery of basic therapeutic skills, and a functional knowledge of research methodologies.

Research and the practice of counseling have typically been seen as two divisions of the same profession. Practitioners and scientists are generally viewed as approaching a common problem from different directions—the clinician actually works with clients and learns from them, whereas the scientist has little contact with direct service but studies human behavior. Brown (1988) suggests that practice and research need not be at odds with each other; each serves to make the other activity more meaningful.

THE MARRIAGE BETWEEN RESEARCH AND PRACTICE

In this chapter we discuss a unique approach to research for the therapeutic counselor, one that integrates the methodologies of science with the skills of clinical practice. As Eldridge (1982) and Strupp (1989) have noted, the roles of the counselor and researcher can fit together effectively, making it possible for the practitioner to become literate in both areas.

The process of counseling involves not only *doing* but *assessing* the impact of various behaviors on client change. We wish to know precisely the effects of any given theory, attitude, or action so that we may reliably duplicate the intervention in the future. We want to know which counseling skills are most likely to produce desirable results. And we would like to standardize certain therapeutic rituals in order to predict consistently how the client will respond to almost any action we might take. We know, for example, after years of investigation, that the skill of reflecting feelings has certain predictable outcomes: (1) the focus of the session stays with present-oriented affect, (2) communication continues with the client taking the lead, (3) the client feels that his or her messages are understood and processed, (4) emotional catharsis is encouraged, (5) conditions of trust and respect are generated, and (6) exploration is facilitated (Rogers & Truax, 1967; Truax & Carkhuff, 1967). This counseling skill is therefore valuable when it is desirable to reach these particular goals.

There are many things that influence what a counselor does in a session with a client. Certainly many of the previously presented theories on the practitioner's personal philosophy and style of practice play a significant role. The counselor's personality or mood on any given day and the client's concerns and goals might also influence the choice of interventions. Nevertheless, there is also a core of fairly specific skills that most counselors use on a regular basis, and a fairly solid research base exists to support their effectiveness.

This chapter not only will introduce you to a group of pivotal skills that describe what counselors do during much of their time but also will illustrate the part research plays in our field to identify discrete behaviors, to test their effectiveness in a variety of situations, to help make decisions about which interventions to use with various clients, concerns, and settings, and generally to help the clinician to function as a practical scientist. You will, therefore, become familiar with the terminology and methodology of the research process and its relationship to the process of therapeutic counseling. Both activities follow a consistent pattern:

1. Awareness of a problem in need of a solution.
2. Systematic study of the context and background of the problem.
3. Summary of what is known about the problem and what has been tried before to solve it.
4. Functional definition of the problem in such a way that it may be solved.
5. Generalization from the study of particular instances to a similar class of events.
6. Prediction of outcome and selection of actions with their probability of success.
7. Testing of hypotheses in a plan of action.
8. Evaluation of results.
9. Inferences drawn and generalizations made to other situations.

Both the researcher and the counselor are systematic in their efforts to understand the world—how it works and how changes can be most effectively implemented. Consider, for example, the scientific method outlined above as it is applied to a particular case in counseling.

1. *Awareness of problem:* A young woman sought professional help because of anxiety, an inability to sleep, and panic attacks that left her feeling dizzy and wobbly.

2. *Relevant background:* The woman was employed as a medical assistant and worked in the same office as her husband and father, who are both physicians. Prior to the onset of her symptoms she had been a person in remarkable control of her body, her mind, her life. She was generally happy but discussed some career dissatisfaction. Exploration of her past revealed that she felt much resentment toward her parents for showing favoritism to a younger, rebellious sister and for forcing her into a medical career she never liked.

3. *Prior attempts at resolution:* Antianxiety medication, psychoanalytic therapy, and a variety of neurological tests produced no further insight into the problem and no alleviation of the symptoms.

4. *Functional definition:* Her symptoms were defined by the counselor as her body's attempt to break through her overcontrolled exterior and let her know she was not living her own life. Further, the symptoms gave her an excuse to quit her job, put distance between herself and her parents, and at the same time create more intimacy with her husband without the added work strain. The problem was defined as career-induced anxiety that was exaggerated by irrational thinking processes, repressed feelings, and a tendency toward overcontrol.

5. *Generalizations:* A series of counseling skills, including restatement of content, reflection of feeling, advanced-level accurate empathy, interpretations,

open-ended questioning, probing, self-disclosure, and confrontations were used to explore the connections between her specific symptoms and her life history. It was discovered that it had always been difficult for her to ask for help or initiate life changes; generally some dramatic event precipitated action in such a way that she didn't have to make decisions. Insights into her relationships with family members were also generated, and she was helped to explore her feelings.

6. *Predictions:* It was predicted that, if she would quit her job, reduce the unnecessary pressures in her life, begin an exercise regime, confront her parents with denied feelings, and work toward being her own person within the nurturing environment of the counseling relationship, her symptoms would significantly diminish.

7. *Hypothesis testing:* The prediction was tested as a hypothesis by implementing the plan of action within the context of the supportive counseling relationship.

8. *Evaluation:* Within days after she quit her job, the woman's symptoms reduced in frequency and intensity. However, as weeks progressed and the woman was forced to deal with issues of feeling boredom, structuring her time, and confronting her family members, the anxiety returned. As successive parts of the treatment program continued and she dealt more constructively with her need for control, the anxious and panicky feelings as well as psychosomatic complaints eventually diminished. A 90-day followup visit indicated that although her symptoms occasionally returned, she was able to deal successfully with them by applying rehearsed cognitive self-talk strategies.

9. *Inferences:* The client was able to generalize the work she did on these few aspects of her life to other components. She learned to relinquish complete control in other relationships and situations and to live a more spontaneous and flexible existence. The counselor was able to draw inferences from this case to other therapeutic situations. His own theory of counseling was sufficiently refined to include the new wisdom gleaned from this experience. It is thus likely that future therapeutic efforts will be even more effective as the practitioner incorporates the lessons of this case into his counseling approach.

This case study illustrates the research process in action as the counselor systematically identifies and defines the underlying complaints, intervenes, and assesses the impact of treatment. As you become more comfortable with the language and strategies involved in interpreting research literature as well as conducting meaningful evaluation projects, it will become easier to apply the skills of helping in a more intentional and consistent manner.

RESEARCH FOR THE COUNSELOR

There are three aspects of research that are important for students of therapeutic counseling to learn. First is the terminology and language of the field, by which communication is possible with other professionals. Many of the terms we use in everyday practice, such as "hypothesis," "variable," and "variance," are an integral part of the research process. Second is knowledge of the classic studies of the field and their implications for clinical work (see Table 14-1). Third is the means to conduct one's own systematic studies of topics that have personal interest.

TABLE 14-1. A Sampling of Classic Research in Therapeutic Counseling

Date	Author(s)	Title	Contribution
1920	Watson and Rayner	"Conditioned Emotional Reactions"	Demonstrated that emotional reactions to stimuli can be conditioned or learned
1938	Skinner	*The Behavior of Organisms*	Demonstrated the principles of instrumental conditioning
1950	Dollard and Miller	*Personality and Psychotherapy*	Applied learning theory to the psychotherapy process
1950	Fiedler	"A Comparison of Therapeutic Relationships in Psychoanalytic, Nondirective, an Adlerian Therapy"	Suggested that personal variables other than the therapist's theoretical orientation determine the effectiveness of the therapeutic relationship
1952	Eysenck	"The Effects of Psychotherapy: An Evaluation"	Suggested that persons receiving psychotherapy did not improve more than persons not receiving psychotherapy
1954	Super	"Career Patterns as a Basis for Vocational Counseling"	Demonstrated the relationship between self-concept and occupational choice
1954	Whitehorn and Betz	"A Study of Psychotherapeutic Relationships between Physicians and Schizophrenic Patients"	Suggested that patient improvement was tied to the personality of the physician
1956	Bateson, Jackson, Haley, and Weakland	"Toward a Theory of Schizophrenia"	Brought emphatic attention to the influence of family on psychological conditions
1957	Rogers	"The Necessary and Sufficient Conditions of Therapeutic Personality Change"	Clarified the core conditions necessary to facilitate therapeutic change
1958	Wolpe	*Psychotherapy by Reciprocal Inhibition*	Developed desensitization as a therapeutic technique
1963	Truax	"Effective Ingredients in Psychotherapy: An Approach to Unraveling the Patient–Therapist Interaction"	Suggested that therapist-offered conditions would result in either improvement or deterioration in patients
1966	Holland	*The Psychology of Vocational Choice*	Presented the hexagonal model to describe the relationship between personality and occupational interests
1968	Strong	"Counseling: An Interpersonal Influence Process"	Suggested that counselors effect change through a social rather than a therapeutic process

(continued)

TABLE 14-1.   *(continued)*

Date	Author(s)	Title	Contribution
1969	Bandura	*Principles of Behavior Modification*	Clarified the effects and empirical base of behavior modification
1969	Carkhuff	*Helping and Human Relations*	Summarized research on "core" conditions of counseling and developed rating scales to measure counselor effectiveness
1971	Bergin	"The Evaluation of Therapeutic Outcomes"	Suggested that psychotherapy is not much more effective than absence of treatment
1971	Ivey	*Microcounseling: Innovations in Interviewing Training*	Presented a trainings system for interviewers based on microanalysis of skills and feedback
1974	Meichenbaum	*Cognitive Behavior Modification*	Presented a research base to support the use of cognitive intervention in behavior modification
1977	Smith and Glass	"Meta-Analysis of Psychotherapy Outcome Studies"	Used meta-analysis techniques to describe the effectiveness of psychotherapy

   Most counseling students (and many practitioners) approach discussions of research with great trepidation, much ambivalence, and a healthy degree of skepticism. But the value of developing research expertise is undeniable, as Remer (1981) enumerates:

1. As consumers of research, counselors must be capable of critical analysis of the various methodologies, statistical procedures, arguments, and conclusions of their professional literature.
2. Knowledge of research helps counselors to put new findings to work in clinical practice.
3. It is more expedient to interpret summaries and syntheses of the research literature than to wade through all the studies in a particular area. Research skills save time and energy.
4. Research permits the practitioner to generate new knowledge and share the results of creative enterprises, experimentation, or systematic study with others who are encountering similar difficulties.
5. Exposure to research trains the counselor to think analytically, intentionally, and systematically about problems.
6. Most important of all, according to Remer, research serves an important function in building new models of behavior. It helps counselors to sort out and organize the great mass of information to which they are exposed.

7. Counselors have an ethical responsibility to know the effects and limitations of the methods they use.

You will be expected, before graduation, to have a good working knowledge of basic research skills in addition to your counseling skills. Barkley (1982) suggests that the student should be able, at the very minimum, to pose good research questions, to use clear definitions of terms, to understand sources of confusion and ambiguity and how they may be controlled, to be aware of problems associated with observation and measurement, to understand the value of documentation in the literature, and, above all, to be knowledgeable about the process of research and be motivated to learn more about it throughout his or her professional life.

Research has traditionally been thought of as basic science that relies on the controls required for scientific discovery or solutions to questions posed by theory. Recent researchers, especially in education and the social sciences, have broadened the scope of research to include applied scientific methodology. In applied research, the researcher/practitioner attempts to understand a problem so it can be resolved (Forsyth & Strong, 1986). The rigor of applied research has been questioned, especially by proponents of experimental research, who maintain that the findings of applied research cannot be generalized and cannot add to existing knowledge bases . As students it is important for you to understand that systematic documentation is required in applied research. Just like basic research, applied research relies on "objective, empirical methods rather than logical claims or subjective feelings. Both involve striving for consensus among members of the discipline concerning acceptable, unacceptable, and to-be-evaluated explanations of empirical observations" (Forsyth & Strong, 1986, p. 114).

As Table 14-2 shows, there are different types of research designs that can be used to accomplish the various goals of researchers. When you engage in research, you should select the methodology that fits with the purpose of your research. Regardless of the methodology, research should always be specific and clear. It is best to determine the exact purpose of the research project by posing a research question. A question causes you to focus on exactly what it is you want to know. For example, you might wonder if a certain treatment works with adolescent clients. So you would formulate a question as follows:

Will group counseling help adolescents improve their social skills?

This initial question provides only an outline of what your project will actually become. The next step is to clearly define each of the important terms. In this example, adolescents must be defined. So you might specify adolescents aged 15–17. You could also narrow the subjects further by limiting the gender to all males or all females, or you could include both. Social skills would need to be defined specifically for this study. They could include any number of specific demonstrable behaviors such as, talking to teachers, joining an extracurricular activity, or helping parents with chores at home. Finally—and perhaps most important to the success of the research study—is the necessity to define what improvement means and how it will be measured. So you can see that the research question becomes the vehicle for only beginning to define the purpose and method of the research.

TABLE 14-2.   A Taxonomy of Research Methodologies in Counseling

Type	Goals	Methods	Limitations	Clinical Examples
Historical	Develop perspective on future based on analysis of past; especially concerned with trends, causes, and effects	Collection and criticism of source materials; examination of evidence and investigation of chronological events	Reliability, objectivity; complete data not available for analysis	A meta-analysis of counseling outcome studies to determine the effect of therapeutic interventions
Descriptive	Describe relationships among variables in the present; intensively investigate a case or program over a period of time; collect data within a conceptual framework	Surveys, case studies, comparative studies, longitudinal studies, developmental studies	Prone to experimental biases; expensive and labor intensive; liable to sampling errors	An analysis of stage theory as it applies to adult developmental tasks
Experimental	Hold some variables constant and manipulate others to predict results in controlled conditions	Laboratory studies, hypothesis tests, well-controlled experimental designs	Group rather than individual focus, difficulty in control, reductionist orientation, possible lack of external validity, oversimplification of interactions among phenomena	An analysis of the effect of counselor-offered facilitative conditions on depth of self-disclosure in initial interviews
Evaluative	Gather information to make judgments on the merit or performance of various programs or procedures, to improve decisions about competing programs or treatments	Experimental method, case study, cost-benefit analysis, impact analysis	Objectivity, availability of relevant data, resistance by sponsoring organization	The effect of group counseling on the self-concept and school behavior of low-achieving adolescents

The next step is to formulate the hypothesis to be tested in the research process. A hypothesis is essentially a prediction about one relationship that can be measured. A good hypothesis will specify the following elements:

1. The population for the study.

2. The independent variable or the variable that will be manipulated by the researcher. The independent variable is also referred to as the treatment variable.
3. The dependent variable or the variable that can be observed and measured. The dependent variable is often referred to as the outcome variable.

> *Examples:*
> If counseling students pass a course in research, they will be able to read and understand research-based articles.
> If heart-attack patients in rehabilitation treatment participate in group counseling, they will improve faster.

These two hypotheses make a prediction about one relationship that can be measured with a specified population. The treatment variables are stated as "a course in research" and "group counseling." The outcomes to be measured are specified as "ability to read and understand research articles" (could be measured by a test at the end of the research course) and "rate of improvement" (could be measured by standard physical health tests and compared to a control group that did not participate in group counseling).

If the goal is to describe specific characteristics of a population (such as the social skills of adolescents, student perceptions of the usefulness of a course in research methodology, or the outcomes of group counseling on heart-attack patients in rehabilitation), then a descriptive research study should be designed without a treatment variable. When the goal of the research is to determine the effectiveness of a treatment or to compare two treatments, then an experimental design with one or more treatment variables is required to successfully complete the study.

The area of research that usually causes the most concern for students is statistics. Because statistics involves math, formulas, and a special reasoning process, many students believe they cannot understand statistics. Statistics can be thought of as a tool to aid in the interpretation of results. For each type of research there are statistical procedures that clarify the outcome of research. Descriptive statistical procedures summarize data for clearer understanding and describe a sample population. Experimental statistical procedures allow researchers to generalize results from a sample to a population.

RESEARCH ON THERAPEUTIC ATTRIBUTES

The purpose of research is to answer questions, satisfy curiosity, and expand the existing knowledge base. In the counseling field, education in research is designed to create counselors who bring "an 'analytical mind' to their professional practice and would actively participate in, if not actually initiate, clinical research in the context of their applied work. They would be empirical in their practice and accountable for their interventions. . ." (Lichtenberg, 1986, p. 366). The task of converting a somewhat mysterious enterprise (counseling) into a comprehensible model of helping, with discrete, sequential, and behaviorally specific components, has been an enormous one for the counseling student and the practitioner. Because of historical analyses, case studies, and developmental, experimental, applied, and descriptive research, we have been able to accurately define and teach the core skills that most clinicians use in work with clients.

One aspect of the therapeutic encounter that has been extensively researched is the role of the counselor's interpersonal influence on client change (Heppner & Dixon, 1981). Strong (1968) originally conceptualized those dimensions of influence, those attributes of power, that make counselors effective. After two decades of systematically exploring his compelling hypothesis—that there are specific variables in a counselor's presence that affect the client's perceptions and capacity for change—three main characteristics emerged: perceived expertness, perceived attractiveness, and perceived trustworthiness.

Perceived expertness was found to be an influential factor: stature, titles, diplomas, credentials, and status all have their impact (Strong & Dixon, 1971; Siegel & Sell, 1978; Atkinson & Carskadden, 1975; Strong & Schmidt, 1970). Yet here we see an aspect of research that the student might as well get used to: often there are later studies that fail to replicate the original results. In this case seven other investigators, among them Claiborn and Schmidt (1977), did not find that perceived expertness was especially crucial.

The second dimension of perceived attractiveness was also considered important. Counselors who are better looking were considered to be more intelligent, friendly, and helpful (Cash, Begley, McCown, & Weise, 1975; Carter, 1978; Fretz, Corn, Tuemmler, & Bellet, 1979). But there are measures of attractiveness other than physical characteristics. Nonverbal behaviors such as smiling and responsive attending favorably influence the client's opinion (LaCrosse, 1975; Claiborn, 1979), as do certain types of self-disclosure (Merluzzi, Banikiotes, & Missbach, 1978; Hoffman-Graff, 1977).

Finally, interpersonal influence is, in part, affected by the counselor's perceived trustworthiness, especially as it is communicated nonverbally (Kaul & Schmidt, 1971; Claiborn, 1979).

Whereas it is likely that current and future research efforts will continue to alter Strong's conceptual model of interpersonal influence, this example gives us a realistic glimpse of how investigators approach the problem of identifying those counselor attributes, behaviors, and skills that make the most difference. Observations are made about the nature of reality (in this case, therapeutic counseling). The effects of specific components of a complex process are isolated, defined, and tested. Finally, results are replicated and applied to related situations. Often there are as many new questions generated as there are answers supplied.

Reliability and Validity in Counseling

Validity and reliability, although technical concepts, are a major part of our everyday lives. It is impossible to watch TV for more than 30 minutes without using these concepts several times. Any commercial challenges our ability to discern the validity of amazing claims made for a variety of products. Will mouthwash X really improve (1) my love life, (2) my professional career, or (3) my social status? These claims are made daily, and the stakes are enormous. If advertisers can persuade the public that their claims are valid, tremendous success in the marketplace can follow. And so we have all been duped!

Determining reliability is the other half of the consumer challenge: can the product not only deliver on its claims but do so for longer than 17 seconds? Think of the frustration surrounding a product that breaks, disintegrates, or refuses to move on the second use.

Manufacturing and service personnel, if they expect to compete and develop a clientele, must pay particular attention to both the validity and reliability of their products and services, working diligently to achieve a high standard for both. The same issue confronts therapeutic counselors and their clients.

Developing skills, techniques, and procedures that are valid and tend to influence clients to experience constructive change is a primary concern of counselors. The discussion of validity is thorny. Everyone claims validity for his or her favored approach—and to some extent each is right. Everything *is* valid. All techniques, approaches, and styles (even the most bizarre) work—with *some* clients at *some* times. The debate over whether or not something works can often be better replaced with an exploration of when it works. Kagan (1973) has stated it succinctly: "The most important issue for our field is not if counseling works but rather what methods work consistently" (p. 234).

We can define reliability as the consistency of valid treatment effects with a wide range of client types. In other words, do your basic counseling/human relations skills influence most clients with whom you have professional contact to experience constructive change? Consistency of effects is the trademark of the intentional counselor. Achieving reliability in counseling is a function of several factors: selection of valid and appropriate techniques, careful training, and integration of one's personal style into a systematic counseling approach. In a sense, being intentional and reducing the impact of chance effects maximize the potential for delivering valid and reliable counseling services. Such is the essence of professionalism and integrity.

Achieving reliability in counseling—that is, reducing the impact of chance on counseling relationships—is often related to the counselor's being consistent. Intentionality refers to the development of a cognitive flexibility integrated into an open and dynamic world view. An intentional person will clarify choices, focus priorities, and implement goals and action. In a sense, an intentional person is an opposite to those who come for assistance or counseling. Often these persons will lack direction in their lives, evidencing an immobility in feeling, acting, and doing that results in their inability to see choices.

Our goal, naturally, is to help clients create more options and to do so with methods of demonstrated reliability and validity. This task is more difficult than it seems, for many counselors can feel successful without really being able to prove they have made an impact. This problem has, not surprisingly, received some attention in the literature and is often an unspoken client concern. Personally, we have a responsibility to answer the question for ourselves and to be convinced in our own minds that this thing called counseling actually works—and works consistently.

Outcome Effects in Counseling

Implicit in a discussion of outcome effects in counseling is a challenge to the validity of the process itself. How do we know it works? Counseling can be described as a process that is designed to influence clients toward constructive change. If the process is a valid one—that is, if it does what it claims to do—then we should see evidence of constructive change in clients following counseling, especially as compared with clients not receiving counseling services.

A number of studies (although fewer than one might suspect) have been conducted to explore this question. Eysenck (1952) started a controversy by his conclusions, based on a study of 8000 clients in therapy, that the clients did not improve significantly more than those who received no treatment. As may be expected, these findings generated considerable response. Carkhuff (1969) argued that such challenges to the profession failed to take into account two very basic factors: the effectiveness of the helper and the general availability of nonprofessional helping.

As we have seen earlier, the personal skills of the counselor to a large extent determine the directionality of the helping process: counselors who function at low levels on basic helping skills can exert a deteriorative impact on clients; counselors who function at high levels can exert a constructive impact (Carkhuff, 1969). These observations, then, provide one explanation of the puzzling lack of differences in treatment effects. It is possible that, within the treatment groups, some of the clients (those who had effective counselors) experienced constructive change, whereas other clients (those who had ineffective counselors) experienced deteriorative change. Thus, when we average the treatment effects for the group receiving counseling, we find that the constructive changes can be counterbalanced by the deteriorative changes, with the result that no *average* differences appeared between clients in the treatment groups and those in the control group. However, individuals may have actually experienced significant positive change. These results suggest that the validity of the counseling process is related to the effectiveness of the counselor, who can influence clients in positive or negative directions.

A second factor involved in the lack of difference between treatment and control groups may have to do with the general potential availability of helping relationships. Clients assigned to a treatment group have a counselor and are less likely to seek nonprofessional helping experiences. Clients assigned to control groups will not have counseling and are therefore much more likely to seek nonprofessional help from persons in their environments. If this help is facilitative and action oriented, then it is possible that these persons will also experience constructive change in more informal settings. So it may be that we have constructive client changes occurring in both treatment and control groups because, first, helping is directional (for better or for worse) and, second, facilitative helping relationships are not the exclusive province of trained counselors and therapists.

Whereas the research by Eysenck (1952), Levitt (1957), Rachman (1971), and others has subsequently been criticized and disputed by other investigators (Bergin, 1971; Smith & Glass, 1977), an interesting and very fruitful dialogue began in which counselors were being asked to demonstrate—to *prove*—that their efforts do indeed make a lasting difference in people's lives.

In summarizing the researchers (Truax & Carkhuff, 1967; Bergin, 1971; Strupp & Hadley, 1977; Smith & Glass, 1977; Smith, Glass, & Miller, 1980; Wolpe, 1982) who have been carefully and systematically documenting the known outcome effects of counseling, Osipow, Walsh, and Tosi (1984) draw the following conclusions:

1. Counseling does have a consistently positive outcome effect.
2. All treatment approaches appear to be effective, and there is little evidence that one theory is significantly more effective than another.
3. Some treatment approaches and personality styles seem to be more effective with certain kinds of problems and clients.
4. Counseling tends to work best with specific anxieties, fears, or phobias.
5. Counseling is less effective at changing personality traits or improving achievement.
6. Perceived similarity between counselor and client in background, status, and education was a contributing factor to successful outcomes.
7. The longer counseling relationship doesn't necessarily produce better results.
8. Individual and group counseling are equally effective.
9. There is no evidence to indicate that the changes made in counseling will necessarily be permanent.

There are many procedural errors and methodological shortcomings in counseling-outcome research that weaken the validity of the results and make accountability difficult (Lambert, Christensen, & DeJulio, 1984). Counselors often complain that they don't have the time or training to conduct well-controlled, meaningful studies. Shertzer and Stone (1980) mention other problems, such as adequately defining and measuring change, developing suitable control groups to compare with those receiving actual treatment, creating accurate assessment instruments, and even conceptualizing which counseling outcomes are actually desirable. No one is exactly certain if counseling ought to help people become better adjusted or more independent, more rational or more emotionally expressive, more risky or more cautious, or if the definition of success ought to depend on the client.

Although we are intuitively certain that counseling works, we can be only reasonably optimistic on the basis of empirical evidence. Our humility is probably constructive in helping us continually to question whether a specific intervention is actually helpful or merely appears to be effective through our biased perceptions.

THE GENERIC SKILLS OF COUNSELING

There are a number of counseling skills that can be considered generic; that is, they provide a technical base for the counseling process that can be used in a variety of theoretical approaches. In a broad sense, these skills can be seen as essential ingredients of the counseling process, as components that are necessary but not sufficient for effective therapeutic counseling.

Before discussing specific steps and skills involved in the helping process, let's review the goals of helping. The overall goal of therapeutic counseling is the development of new behavior that is more adaptive, self-enhancing, and personally fulfilling. Self-exploration is the first goal of helping, and subsequent steps follow a pattern that employs the skills of attending, responding, initiating, and communication, eventually leading to constructive action.

The process of exploration, understanding, and action is continuously recycled in the helping process. Action provokes feedback, which provides a stimulus for further self-exploration, which in turn facilitates increased and more accurate self-understanding. Real understanding is often the result of learning that follows action. Finally, action is further modified in accordance with a more accurate understanding of self.

Until now, we have focused on how counselors think. We will now introduce what counselors *do* in their sessions—the specific interventions that are often used to facilitate client self-exploration, self-understanding, and desired changes in behavior, feelings, and thoughts.

Significance of Attending Skills

Perhaps the basis for all therapeutic interventions is the physical and psychological attending to persons in need of help (Ivey & Authier, 1978; Claiborn, 1979; Carkhuff & Anthony, 1979). It is through posture, body position, head nods, facial expressions, eye contact, gestures, and verbal encouragements that the counselor communicates intense interest in everything a client says and feels. And it is through such active attending that the counselor can also observe the nonverbal cues evident in the client's behavior. A quivering lip, clenched hand, or furrowed brow provides evidence that is helpful in understanding what the client is experiencing.

Effective listening, the core of attending skills, involves the following elements:

1. *Have a reason for listening.* Know what to listen for and how it will be important to the client's exploration, understanding, and action.
2. *Be nonjudgmental.* To listen effectively, you must suspend temporarily the things you say to yourself. Let the client's message sink in without making decisions about it.
3. *Resist distractions.* Resist both internal and external distractions so that your attention and listening focus will not be disturbed.
4. *Wait to respond.* Give yourself time to respond fully and deeply to the

client's statements, avoiding hasty and possibly superficial responses.

5. *Reflect content.* Reflecting back to the client what you hear him or her saying both communicates understanding and provides an opportunity to check out the accuracy of your perceptions.

6. *Look for themes.* Be selective with all the stimuli presented, and attend to only the content that is relevant and meaningful. Identifying themes will help you to understand where the client is "coming from" and how the client perceives his or her relationship to the world.

Skills That Facilitate Client Change

Listening Skills. There are several response options that tend to promote verbal expression and convey interest:

1. Passive listening—the use of verbal encouragement and nonverbal attending to acknowledge messages communicated by the client.
   Examples:
   "I see."
   "Uh huh."
   "Go on."
   "Yes."

2. Parroting—repetition of the client's words to indicate interest, demonstrate accuracy of listening, or stall for time until a more elegant response can be formulated.
   Example:
   CLIENT: Boy, am I upset!
   COUNSELOR: You're really upset!

3. Paraphrasing—restatement of a message's content to clarify or to focus the client's attention.
   Example:
   CLIENT: My life feels useless. My job is a dead end. I don't have any friends. And my parents are always on my case.
   COUNSELOR: You are isolated, trapped, badgered, and don't see a way out.

4. Clarification—confirmation of a message's accuracy or encouragement of further elaboration of an idea.
   Example:
   COUNSELOR: Are you saying that this issue of feeling vulnerable and getting hurt when you trust others has been a life-long theme?

5. Reflection of feeling—focus on affect to promote catharsis and self-expression.
   Example:
   CLIENT: I don't know. Maybe this marriage isn't worth holding together any longer. We've already tried just about every option.
   COUNSELOR: You feel so frustrated and overwhelmed trying to resolve your conflicts without help from your wife. It's as if she had already given up on your relationship and now you are feeling hopeless and helpless.

6. Summation—the linking of several ideas together in a condensed way to promote insight, cut off rambling, identify significant themes, or draw closure.
   Example:
   COUNSELOR: So far you have talked a lot about the ways you keep people at a distance. You tend to hang back whenever you feel a potential for a friendship, and those who approach you are quickly discouraged by your reluctance. You have also mentioned that you might have learned your aloofness from your parents, who never seemed to have much time for you.

Exploration Skills. There are also counselor behaviors that are helpful in drawing out client concerns, facilitating insight, and exploring thoughts and feelings. Most client-centered counselors use these skills as the staple of their therapeutic efforts:

1. Probe—questioning in an open-ended manner to gather relevant data or to encourage self-examination.
   Example:
   "What are the things you've tried to do throughout your life when you have faced similar struggles?"
2. Immediacy—attempting to bring the focus to the present, to comment on the style of interaction in the session, or to give feedback.
   Example:
   "Right this very moment you are deferring to me in just the same way you back down from your boss."
3. Self-disclosure—sharing personal anecdotes from your life to build trust, model personal effectiveness, or capitalize on identification processes.
   Example:
   "I can recall the time in my life, at about your age, when I would see someone I liked. I finally swallowed hard and started taking risks. Although I felt rejected a lot, eventually I started meeting new people."
4. Interpretation—promoting insight by pointing out the underlying meaning of a behavior or pattern.
   Example:
   "So to compensate for the lack of attention you got from your father, you have constantly searched out relationships with men who are nurturing and dependent."
5. Confrontation—diplomatically identifying discrepancies among (a) what a client has said in the past and is saying now, (b) what a client says versus what she or he does, and (c) what a client describes about herself or himself and what you actually observe.
   Example:
   "Whereas you have repeatedly called yourself shy, withdrawn, boring, and a loser, I notice that in our sessions you are usually quite animated, outgoing, and assertive in getting what you want."

Action Skills. Behavioral counselors rely on several action responses to move the client beyond self-understanding to constructive life changes:

1. Information giving—providing concise, accurate, and factual information to dispel myths, pique client interest, or create structure.
   Example:
   "One of the reasons why you may be having difficulty initiating sex with your girlfriend is that you are not beginning a series of pleasurable activities called 'foreplay' that slowly lead to lovemaking. Instead, you just rip off your clothes and jump into bed."
2. Advice giving—offering interventions designed to provide practical suggestions or motivate the client to action.
   Example:
   "Perhaps the next time you go out on a job interview you might want to give more attention to your appearance and the impression you give."
3. Goal setting—structuring a direction, planning for the future, providing a basis for measuring progress, and obtaining the client's commitment to make needed changes.
   Example:
   "You are saying, then, that in the next week you would like to concentrate on being more open with your friends and that, on at least three occasions, you will tell people something that they don't already know about you."
4. Reinforcement—giving support and encouragement to increase the likelihood that desirable behaviors will continue.
   Example:
   "The more risks you take, the more courageous and confident you feel. After the great week you have had, I can hardly believe you are the same person."
5. Directives—giving instructions designed to change the structural patterns of interaction or communication by specific means.
   Example:
   "Since you aren't having much success by urging your husband to come in for counseling, I think it would be best if you tried a different approach and let him know you'd prefer he didn't come in."

SUMMARY

In this chapter we have discussed the importance of research skills for the therapeutic counselor and the relationship between the counseling and research processes. The acquisition of knowledge about research methodology may increase the integration of research and practice by therapeutic counselors. Although practitioners may not be able to cite references that support their therapeutic interventions, most of them have been educated about processes that are well researched and documented in the professional literature

(Heppner & Anderson, 1985). Research is responsible for defining the current skill and knowledge base of the counseling profession. Counselors must continue to systematically identify useful techniques and test their effectiveness with clients. They should critically and empirically evaluate their use of skills and techniques from the perspective of developing effective action programs for the clients they serve. The research process provides the tools for developing, describing, and reporting new ideas and skills for working with clients. It also allows us to assess the impact of what we do and make adjustments as needed with particular clients and therapeutic situations.

SUGGESTED READINGS

Carkhuff, R. R. (1987). *The art of helping* (6th ed.). Amherst, MA: Human Resources Development Press.

Cormier, W. H., & Cormier, L. S. (1991). *Interviewing strategies for helpers* (3rd ed.). Pacific Grove, CA: Brooks/Cole.

Egan, G. (1990). *The skilled helper* (4th ed.). Pacific Grove, CA: Brooks/Cole.

Evans, D. R., Hearn, M. T., Uhlemann, M. R., & Ivey, A. E. (1989). *Essential interviewing: A programmed approach to effective communication* (3rd ed.). Pacific Grove, CA: Brooks/Cole.

Garfield, S., & Bergin, A. (Eds.) (1986). *Handbook of psychotherapy and behavior change: An empirical analysis* (3rd ed.). New York: Wiley.

Wiersma, W. (1986). *Research methods in education: An introduction* (4th ed.). Boston: Allyn & Bacon.

CHAPTER FIFTEEN
ETHICAL AND LEGAL ISSUES

PROFESSIONAL CODES

OUR DIVIDED LOYALTIES

AREAS OF ETHICAL DIFFICULTY
    Seduction
    Misjudgment
    Deception
    Confidentiality
    Recent Trends

MAKING ETHICAL DECISIONS

LEGAL ISSUES IN COUNSELING

SUMMARY

SUGGESTED READINGS

Y ou have been working with a young client for three months. He was, at first, wary, reticent, and cautious. It has taken patience and careful use of your trust- and relationship-building skills to break through the resistance. Finally he is beginning to talk and share something of his life with you in the counseling sessions. Yet, each time you begin to make progress, he draws back into his shell with a defensive remark: "You shrink types are all the same. You get your kicks out of prying into other people's lives." You repeatedly reassure him, reminding him of the sanctity and privacy of your office and the confidentiality of your relationship. He has tested your integrity a number of times and has attempted to probe your attitudes and values. You have responded by keeping the focus on him. You have thus spent a disproportionate amount of counseling time reaffirming your trustworthiness.

Finally your persistence and patience pay off. After much hesitation and several false starts, he slowly discloses his secret, meanwhile closely monitoring your reactions to him. He is satisfied as to your neutrality and acceptance of him (which you are consciously controlling) and so continues to describe his problem. This 16-year-old boy has quite a successful career selling various drugs—downers, speed, cocaine, pot, and sometimes heroin—to other kids in the junior and senior high school. He has no intention of quitting. In fact, he loves the work. He explains that finally he has power, respect, and friends. He likes the excitement and the risks. He enjoys having his "clients" dependent on him. And he can't complain about the money. No, he certainly has no intention of quitting this lucrative "career." But he does feel a little guilty, and he wants you to help him soothe his conscience. He reminds you that, if you can't help him, he can always find someone who will. He notices your hesitancy and so, laughingly, throws your own words back in your face: "Remember, everything you say in here is privileged communication, and nothing disclosed will ever leave this room." You have but a moment to respond, to decide upon one of several possible courses of action:

1. Since the most sacred principle of counseling is to protect the confidentiality of the client, as well as to act in his best interests, you would have no choice but to honor your commitments. It is, after all, not your purpose to tell people how to live their lives or to judge them.

2. The protection of public welfare (in this case, the young victims of drug abuse) takes precedence over a vow of confidentiality to a single client, especially one who is so irresponsible and unconscionable in his acts. It would be for the greater good of the community, and perhaps, ultimately, for the client's own welfare, to notify the appropriate authorities of his illegal acts so that corrective action may be taken.

3. The young man should be persuaded to stop his predatory behavior and told that, otherwise, you will be forced to notify his parents and the school authorities of his crimes.

4. The boy is obviously disturbed and not responsible for his actions. The counseling relationship ought to continue as it has been developing. It is to

be hoped that he will alter his behavior as he gains insight into his self-destructive acts and learns more socially acceptable ways of earning money and social approval.

There are, naturally, a myriad of other alternatives open to the counselor, according to therapeutic goals, state laws, institutional policies, and even personal feelings toward the particular client. The most difficult aspect of making ethical decisions such as this is that there are rarely single, perfect solutions.

PROFESSIONAL CODES

There are professional codes of ethics published by a number of organizations that work with therapeutic counselors, such as the American Association for Counseling and Development, the Association for Specialists in Group Work, the American Association for Marriage and Family Therapy, the American Psychological Association, the National Academy of Certified Clinical Mental Health Counselors, and the American Association for Sex Educators, Counselors, and Therapists (see Appendixes A–C). However, these guidelines are often difficult to apply to individual cases, are sometimes contradictory, and are difficult for the professional organization to enforce (Talbutt, 1981). For this reason, ethical rules cannot just be memorized; rather, ethical behavior must be learned and decision-making skills developed to be internally consistent and yet compatible with acceptable societal and professional standards.

Ethics can be particularly frustrating to discuss in relation to the counseling profession. The nature of our field—its young history, conflicting theoretical base, and emphasis on the ambiguous and abstract content of the human mind—makes it difficult to define sanctioned professional behavior, much less enforce such professional standards. There are sometimes conflicts of opinion among practicing counselors about what constitutes acceptable standards of behavior. Each practitioner uses different labels and terms to describe the processes and has different goals and techniques. Depending on the state or country in which they reside, the institutions in which they work, their training, type of degree, and client needs, they can differ widely in what may be described as "ethical conduct." You would get no such impression from studying the ethical codes of our profession, wherein each point is neatly organized, numbered, and coded and set down in dignified, precise language. Many experienced practitioners have spent their whole careers attempting to set forth these standards of acceptable conduct.

There *is* a distinction between the ethical decision making of the beginner and that of the experienced practitioner. Whereas the seasoned expert has logged years of therapeutic hours, the beginning counselor is starting out in a haze of confusion. It is difficult enough to track client statements, analyze underlying meanings, plan intervention strategies, and respond effectively without having additionally to contemplate open-ended moral issues and ethical conflicts. It is for this reason that we urge you to read and study your professional ethical codes and follow them to the letter. It is only with vast experience and intensive study that a scholar or practitioner can expect to improvise individual moral decisions based on solid empirical and philosophical grounds. And even those with such wisdom may believe, or publicly announce, something different from what they actually do within the privacy of their offices. The problem is further compounded by the often conflicting demands from a number of sources.

OUR DIVIDED LOYALTIES

Who, exactly, does a counselor work for? We learn in school that it is our clients. As professional helpers we are to be their advocates, to hold their trust and confidence and protect their rights. However, sometimes our loyalties are divided between two or more constituents. If the client is a child, we are answerable to the parents for our actions, often a source of conflict when the parties disagree about the best course of action. If we were to comply with parental wishes and keep them informed of our work, inevitably we would lose the trust of the child. If we are uncooperative with the parents, they may sabotage the child's efforts or remove the child from counseling. To complicate matters further, counselors must answer to their school, agency, or institution for their actions. Counselors are also subject to the personal preferences of supervisors and the norms of the colleagues with whom they work. Then there are state and federal laws that regulate behavior, sometimes against the welfare of clients and the best interests of institutions. As has been previously mentioned, there are also professional codes of various organizations. And through them all come the urgent whispers of our own inner voices.

Within ourselves are many competing loyalties. The fact that ultimately we answer to ourselves for our actions, and not to a judge, the government, or our boss, would seem to simplify the matter. Yet it is further confounded by our responsibility to various parts of our own history (for instance, a client we once failed, on whose account we promised ourselves to act differently thereafter) or to the shapers of our values and formulators of our conscience (parents, grandparents, mentors, teachers, and friends).

It is not unusual for a particular agency to dictate to the counselor a rule such as "Any drug use by clients of this agency must be reported to the authorities." Fine. Your first client walks in and casually reports that she smokes marijuana on weekends. You are obligated by contract to report this offense. But, if you do, you will surely be betraying the client. Obviously you can't consult your supervisor, who is sworn to uphold the agency's regulations. You desperately want to keep your job and may not believe the offense is serious. The professional dilemma is clear: do you follow your conscience, or do you abide by the policies you agreed to uphold when you took the job? Some rules are foolish and may be judged as immoral. There comes a time when each person must choose a course of action and live with the consequences.

AREAS OF ETHICAL DIFFICULTY

Ethics could quite legitimately be discussed under the topic of "fear." The subject is not usually given much thought until the prospect arises that something could go wrong. Ethics is the analysis of good versus bad choices, moral versus immoral motives, helpful versus harmful action. The ethical implications of a problem are considered the last step of therapeutic decision making. Ethical consequences of behavior are usually examined only after a narrowly avoided mishap or the threat of a problem. Ethical discussions are often postmortem autopsies, analyses of what should have been done and/or will be done next time.

It is more useful to consider ethical issues, their implications, and possible resolutions *before* they occur, during a time when personal and professional needs and beliefs can be rationally thought out and decisions made about behavior. Predicting and identifying the conflicts that are likely to develop in the practice of counseling allow examination of implications, exploration of personal values, and an opportunity to evaluate several preferred responses. This preparation can demystify the process and diminish much of the fear and apprehension that will arise during a crisis.

Right now, what is the ethical conflict you fear most? What situation might occur within a session that would create for you a moral nightmare of confusion and frustration? To help stimulate self-exploration, we present a realistic review of some common problems that frequently present themselves in the first year of practice.

Seduction

Do you fear being seduced by a client?

F. Scott Fitzgerald's *Tender Is the Night,* a classic in American literature, popularized the theme of the inevitable magnetism between a vulnerable, idolizing young client and her omnipotent therapist, each attracted to the other during the intimacy of a therapeutic encounter. Only within the last few years have many clients had the courage to publicize their experiences of seduction with former and current helping professionals. Before you act indignant and rush to swear that it could *never* happen to you, first consider the dynamics that operate in a counseling situation: (1) a client who feels helpless, vulnerable, and confused, (2) with few satisfying relationships in his or her life, (3) who feels undying gratitude to the counselor who has provided crucial help at a desperate time, (4) to whom she or he has disclosed the most intimate details of her or his life, (5) whom he or she worships as a professional who at once appears so omnipotent, warm, affectionate, and understanding, and (6) whose attraction is magnified by the inequality in power and control of the relationship. Add to this potent mix the variables of countertransference, involvement, respect, and affection that the counselor will come to feel for some clients, and you have a potentially explosive situation.

   This explanation is not meant to excuse or pardon unprofessional conduct that is a dangerous, abusive, and exploitive breach of trust, but rather to encourage a healthy amount of legitimate apprehension about such situations. It is not altogether impossible for a counselor to find that a grateful hug has turned unexpectedly amorous. Often, in such intense situations, emotions don't respond to a half-prepared conscience. A counselor must be constantly aware of the detrimental results that are likely to follow sexually intimate entanglement with clients. The negative consequences will often cancel the previous therapeutic effects and send the client into a tailspin of mistrust for professionals who use their power to their own advantage. It may be helpful to rehearse and role-play sexual encounters, including responses that can be made to initiations from clients. For example, "I have a confession to make. The *only* reason I keep coming to counseling is that I am so attracted to you. You have helped me *so* much. I owe it all to you. You are so different from other people I have known. How do you feel about me?"

   What is your response?

A. "Ah. Our time is about up. Maybe we can continue next time."
B. "How would it be helpful to know my feelings?"
C. "You're feeling attracted to me because I've been helpful and supportive to you, and you're hoping that I am attracted to you."
D. "It is not appropriate for you to think about me personally. We have a professional relationship, and it is necessary that we keep our relationship nonpersonal in order to work together effectively."
E. "Since your personal feelings seem to be getting in the way of our professional relationship, perhaps we should discuss the possibility of your working with another counselor."
F. "Your place or mine?"

   No matter how you look at the situation, with levity or seriousness, this incident may test the resolve of the most experienced counselor. As with all other ethical behaviors, it is insufficient merely to memorize a moral commandment: "Thou shalt not be sexually involved with thy client." You must thoroughly and genuinely believe it as a guiding principle—an internal, personal belief that certain behaviors are crucial to maintaining professional standards. The fear of being caught is *not* enough to prevent a problem. The counselor must understand the responsibilities, moral obligations, and consequences that come with the territory.

   Time after time research has demonstrated that sexual/romantic entanglements between client and counselor are almost always harmful, no matter what the circumstances or how they are justified (Taylor & Wagner, 1976; Feldman-Summers & Jones, 1984; Pope, Keith-Spiegel, & Tabachnick, 1986; Coleman & Schaefer, 1986; Rutter, 1989; Pope & Vasquez, 1991). This is true even if the personal relationship begins after the professional one has been formally terminated, because there are always lingering dependency and attachment issues (Sell, Gottlieb, & Schoenfeld, 1986; Schafer, 1990a).

Although sexual entanglements are the most dangerous and destructive kind of dual relationship between a counselor and client, there are other ways that people can be harmed. A number of professional organizations (American Association for Counseling and Development, American Psychological Association, American Association of Marriage and Family Therapists) as well as several writers (Pope & Vasquez, 1991; Herlihy & Corey, 1992) have been debating the potential liabilities of other client/counselor relationships, such as the following cases: (1) when a business relationship also exists between the counselor and client, (2) when the client is also a student of the counselor's, (3) when a student in an experiential course dealing with personal issues is also required to be a client, (4) when bartering for a fee takes place, (5) when a supervisor also becomes a trainee's counselor, and (6) when the counselor becomes friends with a client.

When you are a professional counselor, you are bestowed a special trust. You are not only in a position to help people, but you can hurt people as well, especially if the boundaries become muddled between what is professional and what is personal. As we will remind you again and again, when in doubt, consult with a supervisor.

Misjudgment

Are you fearful of making a terrible mistake that might hurt a client and unsure whether you would take responsibility for the consequences?

Making mistakes is inevitable in therapeutic counseling. Some of the time we are working without a clear, detailed map of the desired direction for the counseling process. Clients often don't know themselves what is troubling them, and they frequently mask their true feelings as a defense. Sometimes the deception is even deliberate, part of an elaborate game-playing scheme intended to test the counselor's ability to see through the cover-up.

The counselor's judgment is further subject to error by the relatively low reliability and validity inherent in counseling techniques. Practitioners disagree as often as they agree on the diagnosis of a client; even when they do agree on the diagnosis, they may still choose different treatment plans. Consecutive consultations with different therapeutic helpers might well yield quite different diagnostic assessments. Suppose a client presents symptoms of irritability, listlessness, low energy, failed performance at work, lack of sex drive, and loss of appetite; these symptoms may be diagnosed in a number of ways, ranging from anorexia nervosa to depression to an acute stress reaction. Errors are possible not only in the conclusions drawn about a case but also in the ways chosen for working with the client.

The issue in this discussion is not whether or not mistakes and misjudgments will occur (many of which *will* hurt clients) but what can be done about them. What is gained by apologizing to the victim ("I'm awfully sorry. But, ah, remember when I said that it would be best to confront? Well, ah, I've thought about it and think that might not be the best alternative.")? What would be the likelihood of keeping a job if you rigorously reported every mistake to the supervisor ("Boss, I messed up again. This time, when I should have been supportive, I started confronting. I'm afraid the client won't be coming back.")? The important part of such ethical conflicts is, first, learning from mistakes to prevent repeating the same errors and, second, minimizing or reversing any negative effects on the client, possibly by seeking counsel from a peer or supervisor or perhaps by admitting to the client the problem and solutions.

It is easy to hide transgressions. No one else will ever know what goes on within the privacy of the office. Clients usually don't challenge a process so mysterious that almost anything can be viewed as potentially therapeutic from at least one theoretical point of view. It becomes all the more essential, then, to develop and internally monitor professional behavior from an ethical perspective. The individual counselor's awareness of and commitment to ethical principles will, in the final analysis, determine the ethical content of interviews.

Deception

Would you ever deliberately lie to or deceive a client, even if it were for his or her own good?

Counselors stand for truth, honesty, sincerity, and genuineness. But influence is also an important counseling skill. Is it justifiable to manipulate a client into experimenting with a new behavior? Is it ethical to disguise a trap waiting for the unsuspecting client? Is it even appropriate to water down the truth with clients? Although students may respond with a resounding chorus of "NO," most experienced counselors will reluctantly admit that therapeutic deception may be necessary when it is intended for the benefit of the client.

When a client straightforwardly asks a direct question (for instance, a subnormal client asks "Do you think I'm intelligent?"), we are confronted with the inevitable choice of whether or not to tell the truth. The client might not yet be ready for the truth or, alternatively, might respond poorly to protective lies. The counselor must make a choice representative of his or her ethical standards and live with the consequences of the choice. While you are making your own decisions as to your preferred response, consider a case that occurred with one of the authors.

> The client is a young woman, inhibited, rigid, fearful, and shy. She is petrified of anything remotely spontaneous, since the outcome is not 100% predictable. She is also terrified of anything that might require her verbal performance, for failure (which she very loosely defines) would certainly crush her already fragile ego.
>
> The counselor quickly (and probably accurately) decides that the vicious cycle of self-defeating beliefs ("I can't do it because I'm—") can be broken only by encouraging her, just once, to try acting differently from the way she has in the past. If she would pretend, even within the safety of the session, to be somewhat playful and spontaneous, she could not continue to use the excuse "I can't do it," since she would have revealed an exception to her self-defeating behavior.
>
> Role playing would obviously be the technique of choice to encourage the

client's creativity and spontaneity, but she is vehement in her refusal to try it. The counselor agrees to back off, and discussion continues in other directions until an opportunity arises: the client, in talking about her mother's endless complaining and cackling, starts to change her voice in imitation of her mother, thus initiating spontaneous role playing. The counselor need only change roles and start imitating the client, knowing that it will provoke her continued performance as her mother. After having previously promised *not* to pressure her into role playing, the counselor now has an easy chance to trick her into trying it, obviously for her own therapeutic growth. Is the counselor ethically justified in proceeding, when he has said he will not, because the outcomes are so potentially desirable?

In this case the counselor chose to stop the action, disclose aloud the temptation to be manipulative, and then deal with the reactions. The client felt so grateful for the maintenance of trust that she was then able to experiment slowly, not at the same dramatic level as would have been possible in the incident of spontaneous role playing, but well enough to make progress. For every example in which honesty produces the best results, there are also cases in which other, less direct actions might also be defensible.

Confidentiality

Are you worried that you may inadvertently or deliberately violate your client's confidence?

Struggles with maintaining confidentiality are among the most common ethical dilemmas that counselors face. Not a week will go by when you won't be tested in some way—parents wanting to know what their child said to you, another professional calling you for information about a previous case, a current client you are seeing who has AIDS and is sexually active, another client who threatens suicide and may carry out that threat, or even a colleague or a spouse who casually asks you about a client you are seeing. Yet, as challenging as these dilemmas seem to you, you can make things easier for yourself by thoughtfully preparing responses to the situations that trouble you the most (Stadler, 1990; Pope & Vasquez, 1991).

In a situation such as the one presented at the beginning of this chapter, a counselor may quite deliberately decide to break a previous promise because the client is committing a crime. Ethical dilemmas do arise because of a conflict between what is best for the client and what is best for other people. In a landmark court case, now referred to as the Tarasoff decision, a counselor failed to warn a murder victim of potential danger from his client and was held responsible and ordered to pay damages to the victim's parents. Although the judgment was eventually overturned, the case has brought much attention to the limitations of confidentiality.

Berger (1982) concludes that, in addition to our ethical obligations to uphold a promise of confidentiality, we also have an ethical and legal responsibility to breach the vow (1) when the client is a danger to himself or others, (2) when the client is engaged in criminal actions, (3) when the counselor is so ordered by the court, and (4) when it is in the best interests of a child who is a victim of abuse. Unfortunately, the courts do not offer to counselors the same protection they do to others whose communications are privileged, such as lawyers, physicians, clergy, and spouses. We must, therefore, painfully decide when our previous vow to maintain secrecy with clients should be overruled by an even more pressing moral imperative to protect human life.

Inadvertent slips that reveal confidential information are quite another matter. There is no justifiable excuse. That is not to say that we are not constantly tempted to share information with friends, spouses, or colleagues. But we must endure the isolation of not being able to talk about our work in any revealing detail because clients deserve to have their information protected by professional, ethical behavior.

Recent Trends

Because ethical and value issues in counseling are reflective of contemporary culture, the standards for professional practice continue to evolve. Several recent surveys of practitioners in the field (Hayman & Covert, 1986; Robinson & Gross, 1989), as well as state licensing boards (Herlihy, Healy, Cook, & Hudson, 1987) and ethics committees (American Psychological Association, 1988), identified the most common current violations of ethical behavior as well as those dilemmas that are likely to be most salient in the future. The following situations are ones that you should be especially vigilant to monitor closely.

Duty to Warn. You will be asked to assess the potential dangerousness of your clients, to determine if they have the potential to harm themselves or others. This potential can include the threat of physical violence, or it could conceivably apply to the dilemma of working with a client who has AIDS (Knapp & VandeCreek, 1990). If you believe there is imminent danger, you will be required to take action, which could involve warning potential victims, initiating commitment proceedings, or even calling the police (Herlihy & Sheeley, 1988). All of those choices, of course, violate your vow of confidentiality, so your assessments must be accurate.

Reporting Child Abuse. The law is clear: if you suspect that emotional or physical harm is being inflicted on a child, you must report it to the authorities within 24 hours. The ethical dilemma, however, is not whether to report suspected abuse but *when* to report it. In some instances it may be in the child's best interests not to report an incident until after safeguards can be instituted to protect the child from retaliation. In other cases it may be helpful to at least make preliminary explorations as to whether the accusations are, in fact, true. More than half the cases of reported child abuse are false claims made by parents involved in custody disputes (Schafer, 1990b).

Computer Usage. As more and more client information is stored on computers in schools and agencies, it is becoming increasingly difficult to restrict unauthorized access and guarantee the confidentiality of records (Talbutt, 1988). Remember that prying eyes may find it easy to see what you put into a client's files unless your records are locked away in a drawer to which you have the only key.

Relationships with Former Clients. Although ethical codes are quite clear about the inappropriateness of becoming romantically involved with a client, or even conducting a friendship with a client at the same time he or she is in treatment (dual relationship), there is a recent trend to also restrict relationships with former clients (Sell et al., 1986). This issue is complicated by confusion as to when counseling actually ends: after the last scheduled session? when the client stops thinking of you as a professional (which could take a lifetime)? It is also important to keep in mind that it is not acceptable to end a therapeutic relationship expressly for the purposes of beginning a personal one.

MAKING ETHICAL DECISIONS

Counselors will be confronted on a regular basis with the necessity of making ethical decisions. When an ethical issue emerges, the counselor will have to make a virtually instantaneous decision; little opportunity will exist for careful analysis and thoughtful reflection. Thus the first recommendation in making ethical decisions is to anticipate. It is essential to develop a reasonably clear ethical style based on analysis and reflection to guide decision making and a capacity for making sound moral decisions that are compatible with the consensual standards created by the profession and consistent with your own personal and professional identity (Woody, 1990). Van Hoose and Kottler (1985) present a model for making ethical decisions (Figure 15-1). It exemplifies a systematic approach in which the counselor considers the consequences of each action as it affects personal, client, and societal demands.

In addition to the introspective analysis that leads one to select a defensible moral choice, the decision-making process should also take into account the guidelines established by professional organizations and the legal system. Most of these sources mandate the following actions:

1. *Don't attempt any therapeutic intervention without sufficient knowledge, skills, training, and supervision.* You should never attempt helping actions that are outside the bounds of your qualifications and competence. Workshops, certification programs, postgraduate training, internships, and intensive supervision are the means by which you can legitimately augment your therapeutic skills and continue to grow as a professional. Make referrals to specialists and other helping professionals when appropriate.

2. *You should be free of all biases and prejudices that might interfere with the capacity for objectivity, neutrality, and positive regard in the therapeutic relationship.*

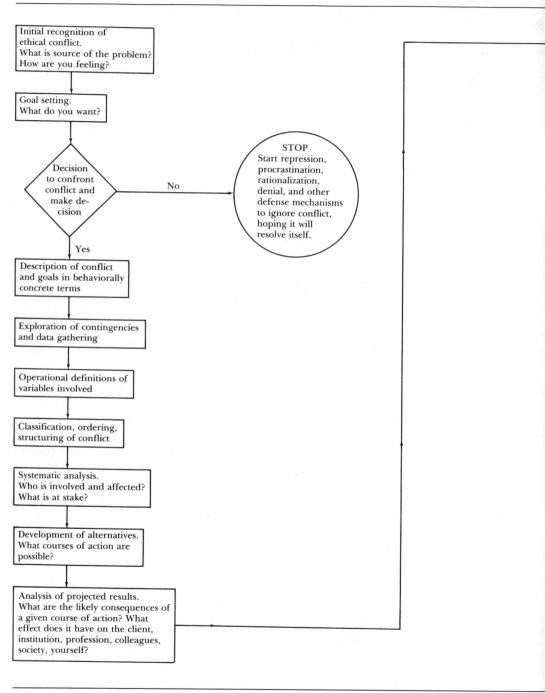

FIGURE 15-1.
Flowchart for making ethical decisions (Van Hoose & Kottler, 1985, pp. 42–43)

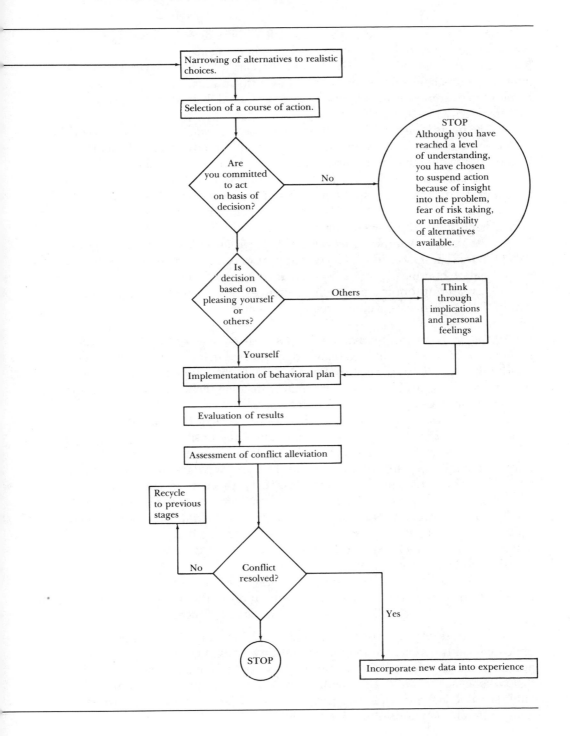

This includes sexual and racial biases, as well as those directed toward any ethnic or religious group, special population, or belief system.

3. *Sexual involvement with clients is strictly prohibited.* Under no circumstances should you as counselor ever engage in erotic contact, act seductively, or respond to overtures made by those who have offered their trust in your professional integrity.

4. *The rights of all participants in research projects should be carefully protected.* All experimental procedures that could conceivably produce side effects must be thoroughly described and *informed* consent obtained from all subjects.

5. *You are responsible for protecting the privacy and confidentiality of all sessions.* Except in those circumstances wherein human life is in danger, you must preserve the sanctity of the therapeutic encounter. Information regarding a case may be released only with proper client authorization or under legal compulsion.

6. *The focus of counseling is on helping the client to reach self-determined goals.* Except in those instances in which goals appear to be destructive, self-defeating, or in violation of principles of reality, you are committed to working toward the client's greater autonomy and independence. You should therefore avoid manipulating clients; as well as creating dependencies or meeting your own needs in the session.

7. *You are committed to continuing professional training and growth after completing your formal education.* The knowledge and research in our field change so rapidly that practitioners must continually update their expertise. For this reason, many professional organizations and certification/licensing boards require annual continuing-education credits of members.

8. *You have an obligation to confront colleagues engaged in unethical, illegal, or incompetent practices.* As a professional you have a responsibility to your profession, your community, and the safety of those who seek counseling services. Your duty is to challenge directly the behavior of those who are transcending the bounds of generally accepted principles. If the problem is not sufficiently resolved, you are then required to report such behavior to appropriate authorities.

9. *You are committed to maintaining high standards of integrity, honesty, and moral fiber.* Therapeutic counselors accept their responsibility as professional helpers, recognize their powerful influence, and work toward functioning as effective models for their clients.

10. *As a counselor you act for the general welfare of clients and society.* You attempt to prevent discrimination, to help the needy and disadvantaged, to promote social justice, and to help all persons become more fully functioning.

As a counselor you must be sensitive to the cultural, ethnic, religious, and philosophical differences among people of diverse backgrounds, all of whom operate by rules, values, and customs that may not be familiar to you. Recognize that, whenever you are dealing with moral issues (and counseling is most certainly a value-laden discipline), there are many different paths to "truth" and many different standards of what is "right."

LEGAL ISSUES IN COUNSELING

In addition to the ethical codes of our profession, counselors must also be familiar with the ways their work intersects with the legal system (see Woody, 1988; Huey & Remley, 1989; Hopkins & Anderson, 1990; Bennett, Bryant, VandenBos, & Greenwood, 1990; Bednar, Bednar, Lambert, & Waite, 1991 as resources). You will be expected to apply legal principles and make difficult decisions that may conflict with your own values, the ethical principles of your profession, or the policies of your institution in situations like the following:

- when a client's civil rights are violated, such as in cases involving sex, age, or racial discrimination.
- when clients are involved in custody battles or divorce action.
- when clients are seeking eligibility for disability or unemployment compensation.
- when you believe a client is a danger to him- or herself or to others.
- when you suspect that child abuse has taken place.
- when a client you are seeing is engaged in planning or carrying out criminal acts.
- if you are subjected to malpractice litigation because of claims that you caused harm or injury to a client or acted negligently.

As if these examples are not frightening enough, Woody, Hansen, and Rossberg (1989) list several other situations in which counselors may find themselves embroiled in legal disputes: (1) there is a charge of sexual misconduct, (2) there is a breach of confidentiality, (3) a client has committed suicide, (4) there is violation of civil rights, (5) there are accusations of libel or slander, (6) there has been a failure to diagnose properly, (7) there is a breach of contract, (8) client abandonment is alleged, (9) the counselor has exerted undue influence, and (10) there has been an accident on the premises.

Our intention is not to alarm you to the point where you select a safer occupation, but rather to convince you of the importance that legal and ethical training will have in your work. By familiarizing yourself thoroughly with the legal statutes of your state and the ethical codes of your profession, and by learning to apply them in real-life situations, you will protect your clients from harm and also protect yourself from needless vulnerability. In addition, you will guarantee your clients' rights in several circumstances:

• *The right to informed consent.* The client is entitled to receive accurate and clear information regarding the therapeutic process, expected roles, risks and benefits of treatment, costs and contractual arrangements, right to access his or her files, implications of diagnostic labeling, alternative treatment options available, and qualifications and training of the counselor.

- *The right to privacy.* This involves helping the client to understand the meaning of confidentiality and privileged communication, as well as the circumstances under which they may be breached. It also means keeping records secure and protecting the content of counseling sessions.
- *The right to protection against harm.* This means following the major dictum of all helping professions: do no harm! But it involves more than not hurting a client through negligence; it also means protecting the client against him- or herself. There are certain circumstances—notably when clients are suicidal or otherwise self-destructive—that require intervention to avoid a disaster.
- *The right to competent treatment.* The client is entitled to a counselor who is well trained in the profession and in any specialties that are practiced (for example, substance-abuse counseling, family therapy, hypnosis, and so on). In legal language this means that you will abide by the usual and customary standards of care that are agreed upon by members of the profession. You can familiarize yourself with these "standards of care" by carefully reading the ethical codes in Appendixes A–C and consulting a knowledgeable supervisor when you have some questions.

It is the perceived violation of this last client right that most often embroils counselors in the legal system, usually in the form of a malpractice suit. When a client's rights are compromised, or, more specifically, when the counselor's actions may be deemed as negligent, malpractice may be claimed. Such a charge must meet several criteria: (1) a professional relationship existed between the client and counselor, (2) a demonstrable standard of care was breached, (3) the client suffered harm, and (4) the counselor's behavior was the probable cause of the client's injury (Bennett et al., 1990).

Let's apply these factors to a particular case:

A client comes to you complaining of anxiety and poor self-esteem. He has trouble sleeping at night and feels agitated. You attempt to treat him with weekly counseling, but his condition worsens to the point where he requires hospitalization. During routine tests at admission, it is discovered that his symptoms are not psychologically based but were, in fact, caused by an underlying neurological disease. Does this situation constitute negligence on your part and justify a malpractice suit against you?

A. No. You were *not* the cause of his injury—the neurological disease was.
B. No. Because you are not a physician, you are not qualified or expected to diagnose neurological problems.
C. Yes. You violated the standard of customary care. Through your negligence in not referring the client for a medical consultation, he suffered undue pain and hardship.

This last choice is correct. It illustrates the kinds of professional challenges you will face and the fact that you must safeguard your client's welfare by getting adequate consultation and supervision when you even suspect the possibility of problems outside your specialty.

As frightening as these situations may be for you to consider (and as tragic as they may be for some clients), the risks can be significantly decreased by following several guidelines:

1. Study the ethical codes, state laws, and standards of care for your profession *very* carefully. Review some of the "casebooks" that are available (American Psychological Association, 1988; Herlihy & Golden, 1990) to help you to reason through professional decision making.
2. Make sure that you carry liability insurance to protect yourself from malpractice claims (as a student you are eligible for coverage at very reasonable rates).
3. As a beginner in the field, do not attempt *any* treatments without adequate supervision by *qualified* experts.
4. Document carefully your case records, demonstrating your thorough exploration of client history, your recommendations and treatment interventions, and client responses. Be especially prudent in checking out suicidal/homicidal ideation, history, and intent.
5. Consult frequently with medical personnel, and make appropriate referrals when there is a possibility of some underlying organic problem.
6. Take steps to improve your level of competence by pursuing continuing education and advanced training.
7. Alert yourself to signs of fatigue and burnout that may lead you to miss important information or make needless mistakes.

Remember, as a beginner to this field you are not expected to know everything and be able to do everything perfectly. Making mistakes is part of your growth and crucial to your learning. You are, however, responsible for making certain that you find the best possible training and supervision so that you can become the most proficient and responsible professional possible.

SUMMARY

The first step in making ethically sound decisions is to anticipate some possible dilemmas and to think through alternatives and preferred responses in an objective and analytical manner. These personal resolutions must be congruent with professional standards, state and federal laws, and institutional policies in order to be useful.

A systematic approach will yield ethical decisions that are personally meaningful, have a specific rationale for behavior, and are objectively defensible. It will also enable the counselor to respond to challenges, legal or personal, with a sense of integrity and a clear rationale for any behavior. The counselor should maintain an open, questioning attitude toward ethical decision making, recognizing the need to challenge and question decisions, values, and attitudes.

Ethical decision making is not a state we achieve but an ongoing process of learning, growth, and maturation. Ethical decision making means that we take responsibility for functioning at our highest possible level of moral behavior, both to serve our clients better and to avoid legal entanglements. Periodic reflection and a full examination of ethically challenging situations are essential factors in this process. It is often helpful to consult with colleagues and supervisors. Yet, in this profession, confusion has its healthy side; it helps us to avoid rigidity and forces us to personalize the meaning of our behavior.

SUGGESTED READINGS

Corey, G., Corey, M. S., & Callanan, P. (1988). *Issues and ethics in the helping professions* (3rd ed.). Pacific Grove, CA: Brooks/Cole.

Herlihy, B., & Golden, L. B. (1990). *Ethical standards casebook* (4th ed.). Alexandria, VA: American Association for Counseling and Development.

Hopkins, B. R., & Anderson, B. S. (1990). *The counselor and the law* (3rd ed.). Alexandria, VA: American Association for Counseling and Development.

Huey, W. C., & Remley, T. P. (Eds.) (1989). *Ethical and legal issues in school counseling.* Alexandria, VA: American Association for Counseling and Development.

London, P. (1986). *The modes and morals of psychotherapy* (2nd ed.). New York: Holt, Rinehart & Winston.

Pope, K. S., & Vasquez, M. J. T. (1991). *Ethics in psychotherapy and counseling.* San Francisco: Jossey-Bass.

Thompson, A. (1990). *A guide to ethical practice in psychotherapy.* New York: Wiley.

Van Hoose, W. H., & Kottler, J. A. (1985). *Ethical and legal issues in counseling and psychotherapy* (2nd ed.). San Francisco: Jossey-Bass.

Woody, R. H. (1988). *Protecting your mental health practice: How to minimize legal and financial risk.* San Francisco: Jossey-Bass.

CHAPTER SIXTEEN
TOWARD CLOSURE

ADVICE FOR THE PASSIONATELY
   COMMITTED COUNSELING
   STUDENT
Be Self-Directed
Read
Find a Mentor
Volunteer to Do Research
Ask Questions
Challenge Your Teachers
Challenge Yourself

Experience Counseling as a
   Client
Personalize Everything
Become Active in Professional
   Organizations
Develop a Flexible Specialty
Resist Burnout
Confront Your Fears of Failure
VARIATIONS ON A THEME
SUGGESTED READINGS

ADVICE FOR THE PASSIONATELY COMMITTED COUNSELING STUDENT

This chapter is for those dedicated individuals who, after completing their introductory course in counseling, have decided to devote their lives to helping other people. Your commitment to the counseling profession is not to be taken lightly; nor can you realistically expect to treat your career as a mere job in which you just put in your time. Counselors are passionately committed to helping their clients to become more productive, fully functioning beings. The counseling student, too, must be intensely motivated to pursue a path of life-long learning. It is only through your own hunger to understand, your thirst to know, your craving to find truth, and your skill in communicating your ideas that you become able to influence people in constructive ways.

In the spirit of enthusiasm for the mission of counselors, we offer the following advice to students.

Be Self-Directed

The best way to become passionate about learning is to follow your own natural curiosity to make sense of the world. So much of counseling deals with abstractions and complex queries that defy understanding. Your teachers, supervisors, and authors will only begin to tantalize you with answers to the questions that plague you the most. How does counseling work? Why does counseling work? Your assigned readings, lectures, and class discussions are but stimuli for you to begin resolving many of these difficult issues. It is through personal reflection, self-directed study, and leisurely wandering through the library that you can really begin to educate yourself.

Read

We would encourage you, in your self-directed study, systematically to research the works that have had the most impact in the counseling profession. Make a list of classic books in the field, and read them. Solicit nominations from teachers and peers. Notice in the literature those titles that are most frequently cited. Most of all, find a few reliable persons whose opinions you respect (such as a mentor) and read *everything* they recommend. Don't restrict yourself to just the books in counseling, but become familiar with the literature in related fields such as psychology, social work, psychiatry, education, sociology, and philosophy.

Find a Mentor

In all chosen professions—the arts, sciences, law, medicine, business—and especially in a people-oriented career like counseling, it is important to have a model to emulate. A mentor, usually a teacher, senior colleague, or other benevolent friend/coach, helps the neophyte to learn the ropes during the period of apprenticeship. A mentor does more, much more, than give homespun advice or recommend books; she or he becomes an advocate. It is through this relationship that the beginning counselor receives support, encouragement, constructive feedback, and a guiding hand.

Select a mentor whom you admire, who has skills and knowledge you respect and wish to acquire for yourself, and who has a genuine, nonpossessive interest in you. Find someone you can trust and confide in, yet one who does not feel that such a commitment is a burden. A mentor can be a source not only of nurturance and wisdom during the formative years of professional development but also of invaluable assistance in securing a job.

Volunteer to Do Research

Getting actively involved in a research project is helpful in a number of obvious ways. It allows you to apply learning to the solution of real-life problems and personalizes the usefulness of the scientific method. Upon publication a writing credit can be a marketable commodity for gaining entrance to a doctoral program or a competitive job. Doing research also permits interaction with professors and colleagues on a level that would not be possible in the classroom. Finally, research gives you practical experience in exploring the issues, problems, and methodology of the profession. It is an opportunity to advance the growth of counseling and your own knowledge.

Ask Questions

When you don't know the answer to a question, *ASK*.

Many of the questions students ask in class are posed less to learn new ideas than to win brownie points, demonstrate what they already know, or express opinions in diplomatic ways—for example, "Aren't you saying that students are afraid to take risks by displaying their ignorance?"

Unfortunately, yes, that's what we're saying. In our experience, it is rare that a student really feels comfortable enough to ask the questions that she or he would most like to have answered. As we flash back to our graduate-school days, we recall that there were scores of things we didn't understand, but we felt too timid to admit our uncertainty—as if, by questioning the professors, we might reveal to others that we were not so bright and didn't really belong in class. It was only much later, when we were playing "I'll show you mine (ignorance) if you show me yours," that we discovered our universal passivity.

We therefore encourage you to take risks in class and ask about those things you don't understand. How, after all, can you expect your future clients to open up if *you* feel such reluctance? Right at this moment, make a list of the questions you never got around to asking. Good news! There are still many opportunities left in future classes.

Challenge Your Teachers

Challenging those ideas presented in class with which you disagree is even riskier than questioning—but potentially more fun too. This style of learning is critical to the development of your own ideas, especially with those teachers who don't react defensively.

There are many concepts central to the core of therapeutic counseling that some beginning students accept with great difficulty. For example, the notion of avoiding absolutes, shoulds, and other moralistic "rights" and "wrongs" cannot be internalized except through active dialogue with others who have reflected on the implications and tested the principles. It is through interesting debates and challenging new ideas that these principles can be understood and personalized.

Challenge Yourself

The most difficult task of a student is to maintain an openness to new ideas while simultaneously retaining a critical perspective. When ideas, concepts, and theories are presented that at first seem threatening, rather than immediately leaping to defend yourself against other classmates or professors, *first* challenge yourself to explore the merits of the point of view. Ask yourself why you are responding so emotionally to the subject. What would it mean for you if you had to change your ideas to conform to this added information?

A related danger is that of too enthusiastically embracing a particular point of view, sowing the seeds of terminal rigidity and closing out the possibility of other ideas. Initially it *is* helpful to be suspicious and tentative. After exploring a theory that seems attractive and useful, do not fall into the destructive trap of confusing it with ultimate truth.

Experience Counseling as a Client

In the process of challenging oneself, there is no vehicle more appropriate than experiencing counseling as a client. Many programs encourage participation in a form of counseling prior to graduation. For anyone who hopes to *do* counseling, it is important to know intimately the fears, joys, and apprehensions that clients experience.

Participating in counseling as a client allows you to work through inhibitions, distracting conflicts, and unresolved problems that may interfere with the ability to remain objective, focused, and therapeutic. It also helps you to believe fervently in the power of the process when you have experienced firsthand its beneficial effects.

We urge you to seek out both individual and group-counseling experiences for another reason. Clearly, while a counseling student is engaged in a therapeutic relationship, there is always a part of him or her that is closely observing the process, noting the interventions that work best and knowing, really *knowing*, how the process works. If we truly believe that counseling is for everyone, then it is most certainly for us. All of us.

Personalize Everything

Counseling is a joy to study because all the abstract ideas, theoretical constructs, research hypotheses, clinical interpretations, class lectures, and textbook discourses can be personalized and applied to our own lives. All of a sudden the behavior of those around us no longer appears the same. We seem more critical yet more forgiving.

The novels we read, movies we see, and conversations we participate in become wonderful opportunities to think, act, and feel differently. Learning has more meaning to us if we can make it more relevant. And that, primarily, is the student's job—to take the nucleus of an idea from one's teacher, mentor, counselor, or colleague and apply it in such a way that it becomes personally useful.

Become Active in Professional Organizations

The American Association for Counseling and Development, the American Association for Marriage and Family Therapy, and the American Psychological Association are a few of the groups that advance the profession of therapeutic counseling. Through their lobbying activities, public relations and consumer education programs, and professional development courses, these organizations help support practitioners. They also develop written ethical codes, work toward certification and training standards, provide referral services, sponsor national and regional conventions, fund research projects, publish professional journals, run job-search programs, and provide social activities for their members.

There are many opportunities for students to get actively involved in the organizations by attending conventions, contributing articles to journals, serving on committees, presenting papers and workshops, and working on special projects of interest. Participating in state, regional, and national conventions is especially interesting because of the opportunities to make life-long friendships with colleagues around the world. Conventions are also ideal places to receive specialized training and find jobs, since many employers are present to interview for positions. Finally, organizational activities help one to identify with counseling as a profession.

Develop a Flexible Specialty

As we have already said, the advanced degree in counseling does not guarantee employment in a specific career. Graduates may have to market themselves in such a way that they will fit a particular position, or even tailor-make a job to fit their own unique skills, training, and interest.

Practically everyone knows what the psychologist, psychiatrist, or social worker can and cannot do. Counseling practitioners, however, now function in many diverse settings. Five students in the same program, with the same course work, may eventually find employment in five different settings: school counseling, industrial relations, consumer education, rehabilitation counseling, and mental health center counseling. The counseling degree, then, reflects education for the generalist who, through specialized training and interests, develops a unique professional identity.

We therefore suggest to the beginning student the following course of action to find eventual employment in a desired area:

1. Talk to counselors in the field about what they do and how they feel about their jobs.
2. Find excuses to talk to prospective employers to determine what they are looking for in candidates.
3. Discover a few particular types of client populations (disabled, gifted), age groups (preschoolers, older adults), settings (hospitals, schools), and counseling skills (consultation, group interventions) in which you can gain specialized experience.
4. Use elective courses, workshop experiences, and your internship sites to become expert in a few flexible specialties.
5. Volunteer your time at local community agencies to accumulate additional professional experiences.

Resist Burnout

In recent years there has developed a considerable body of literature describing the burnout phenomenon, especially as it relates to counselors, psychologists, social workers, teachers, and other human services personnel. In a review of the literature, Maher (1983) describes the symptoms of burnout as fatigue, irritation, reduced work performance, apathy, boredom, and negative attitudes. The condition is caused, in part, by such factors as an excessive workload, monotony, a lack of control, and isolation.

The only antidotes for burnout are renewed enthusiasm or a job change. Those counselors who are most committed to their jobs and to the profession may be less likely to experience the effects of burnout and disillusionment. They also tend to be practitioners who, despite having high standards of excellence for their work, are accepting of their limitations. They are able to let go of those aspects of their jobs that they can't control and focus instead on what is within their power to change.

Confront Your Fears of Failure

Both authors recall sitting in our first counseling class, looking around the room, and feeling utterly despondent because everyone else seemed so much brighter and more talented than we were. Doubts assailed us: "Am I smart enough to get through this program?" "Do I have what it takes to be a counselor?" "What will my professors think when they find out how weird I really am?"

These doubts, and many others like them, not only are a normal part of most students' inner thoughts, but they continue to plague practitioners in the field. Counselors often worry about failure. What if they inadvertently harm a client? What if they are confronted with a situation in which they don't know what to do? What if they are caught making a mistake? Yet these doubts become unmanageable only when they are avoided and denied; it is by confronting our fears that we are able to work through them (Kottler & Blau, 1989).

We therefore urge you to find a support group of peers in which you can confide your doubts and fears, disclose your fantasies of being an impostor, and talk about your imperfections and misunderstandings. We can confidently reassure you that, although it is difficult to recruit confidants who are compatible in any walk of life, you are definitely not alone in your apprehensions. Even after several decades of practicing and teaching counseling, we still continue to confront our own fears of failure.

The implications for the beginning counselor are clear. It is necessary to work diligently to develop a sense of professional commitment to clients, colleagues, the profession, and, ultimately, ourselves as professional counselors. This sense of commitment will result in renewal and provide the energy base necessary to perform creatively and enthusiastically. The time to begin developing that sense of commitment is now.

VARIATIONS ON A THEME

Naturally, we wish to leave you with the appropriate balance of healthy confusion and eager enthusiasm to grow, to learn more, to find your own truth, and to continue in a profession that helps others to clarify their directions. Farber (1983) has concluded from interviews with practitioners that one consequence of doing counseling is an increase in the counselor's own self-awareness, self-assurance, and psychological sensitivity. This phenomenon is, perhaps, the best reason of all for feeling passionate about and committed to the role.

In the 16th century a Samurai warrior and master of Kendo ("he who wields the sword") wrote a manual of instruction for those who wished to learn his strategy. Musashi's *A Book of Five Rings* (1982) has since become a bible for Japanese businessmen. We believe that his wisdom also speaks to prospective counselors—to those who wish to learn "the Way of Water," to become calm, unbiased, with a settled spirit, and to those who follow "the Way of Fire," who research and train diligently. Musashi prescribes the following advice for those who want to follow his way:

1. Do not think dishonestly.
2. The Way is in training.
3. Become acquainted with every art.
4. Know the Ways of all professions.
5. Distinguish between gain and loss in worldly matters.
6. Develop intuitive judgment and understanding for everything.

7. Perceive those things which cannot be seen.
8. Pay attention to trifles.
9. Do nothing which is of no use.

The greatest obstacle to any significant discovery is the illusion of knowledge. Boorstein (1983) explains that it was not ignorance that precipitated our descent into the Dark Ages of history, but rather those imaginative bold strokes that temporarily pacified fears and served hopes for simple solutions. True knowledge always advances slowly, with contradictions, conflicts, and controversy. And it is precisely these furiously passionate debates among discrepant views that produce an approximation of truth. With each course you take, with each book you read, with each workshop you attend, with each supervision session you complete, and with each client you see, greater wisdom and competence will evolve *if* (1) you learn from mistakes, (2) you passionately search for greater mastery in personal and professional skills, and (3) you retain sufficient humility to continue asking questions that have no simple answers.

In a supervision conference, one counselor lamented her frustrations and confusions about a particular case in which she felt lost, inept, and discouraged. "How, after all," she pleaded, "can I work with this client when I have no idea what is going on?"

The supervisor, Dr. Williams, softly responded in a voice that rose above the chatter of advice directed to the counselor.

"Don't worry when you don't know what you're doing," he said. "Worry when you think you do."

SUGGESTED READINGS

Corey, G., & Corey, M. S. (1991). *Helping the helper*. Pacific Grove, CA: Brooks/Cole.

Ellenbogen, G. C. (Ed.) (1989). *The primal whimper*. New York: Guilford Press.

Farber, B. (1983). *Stress and burnout in the human service professions*. New York: Pergamon Press.

Kottler, J. A., & Blau, D. (1989). *The imperfect therapist: Learning from failure in therapy*. San Francisco: Jossey-Bass.

Ram Das, & Gorman, P. (1985). *How can I help? Stories and reflections on service*. New York: Knopf.

Yalom, I. (1989). *Love's executioner and other tales of psychotherapy*. New York: Basic Books.

REFERENCES

Adler, A. (1929). *The practice and theory of individual psychology* (2nd ed.) (P. Radin, Trans.). New York: Humanities Press.

Adler, A. (1958). *What life should mean to you.* New York: Putnam.

Alexander, F. G., & Selesnick, S. T. (1966). *The history of psychiatry.* New York: Mentor.

Alibrandi, T. (1978). *Young alcoholics.* Minneapolis: CompCare Publications.

Allen, W. (1976). *Without feathers.* New York: Warner.

Allers, C. T., & Katrin, S. E. (1988). AIDS counseling: A psychosocial model. *Journal of Mental Health Counseling, 10,* 235–244.

Amatea, E., & Fabrick, F. (1981). Family systems counseling: A positive alternative to traditional counseling. *Elementary School Guidance and Counseling, 15,* 223–236.

American Association for Counseling and Development. (1988). *Ethical standards.* Alexandria, VA: Author.

American Psychiatric Association. (1987). *Diagnostic and statistical manual of mental disorders* (third ed., rev.). Washington, DC: Author.

American Psychological Association. (1987). *Casebook on ethical principles of psychologists.* Washington, DC: Author.

American Psychological Association. (1989). *Ethical principles of psychologists* (rev. ed). Washington, DC: Author.

American Psychological Association, Ethics Committee. (1988). Trends in ethics cases, common pitfalls, and published resources. *American Psychologist, 43* (7), 564–572.

Anastasi, A. (1988). *Psychological testing* (6th ed.). New York: Macmillan.

Anderson, P. (1981, November). Substance abuse and the disabled. *Paraplegia News,* p. 8.

Anderson, W. P., & Heppner, P. P. (1986). Counselor applications of research findings to practice: Learning to stay current. *Journal of Counseling and Development, 65,* 152–155.

Argyris, C. (1974). *Theory in practice: Increasing professional effectiveness.* San Francisco: Jossey-Bass.

Armor, D. J., Polick, M. J., & Stambul, H. B. (1978). *Alcoholism and treatment.* New York: Wiley.

Association for Specialists in Group Work. (1982). Ethical guidelines for group leaders. *Journal for Specialists in Group Work, 7* (3), 174–181.

Atkinson, D. R., & Carskadden, G. (1975). A prestigious introduction, psychological jargon, and perceived counselor credibility. *Journal of Counseling Psychology, 22,* 180–186.

Atkinson, G., Jr., & Murrell, P.H. (1988). Kolb's experiential learning theory: A meta-model for career exploration. *Journal of Counseling and Development, 66,* 374–377.

Avila, D. L., Combs, A. W., & Purkey, W. W. (Eds.) (1977). *The helping relationship source-book* (2nd ed.). Boston: Allyn & Bacon.

Axelson, J. A. (1985). *Counseling and development in a multicultural society.* Pacific Grove, CA: Brooks/Cole.

Baird, J. E., Jr., & Weinberg, S. B. (1981). *Group communication* (2nd ed.). Dubuque, IA: William C. Brown.

Bandler, R., & Grinder, J. (1975). *The structure of magic* (Vol. I). Palo Alto, CA: Science and Behavior Books.

Bandler, R., & Grinder, J. (1979). *Frogs into princes.* Moab, UT: Real People Press.

Bandura, A. (1969). *Principles of behavior modification.* New York: Holt, Rinehart & Winston.

Bandura, A. (1971). Psychotherapy based upon modeling principles. In A. E. Bergin & S. L. Garfield (Eds.), *Handbook of psychotherapy and behavior change* (pp. 653–708). New York: Wiley.

Bandura, A. (1977). *Social learning theory.* Englewood Clifts, NJ: Prentice-Hall.

Bandura, A., Blanchare, E. B., & Ritter, R. (1969). The relative efficacy of desensitization and modeling approaches for inducing behavioral, affective, and attitudinal changes. *Journal of Personality and Social Psychology, 13,* 173–199.

Barkley, W. M. (1982). Introducing research to graduate students in the helping professions. *Counselor Education and Supervision, 21* (4), 327–331.

Bateson, G. (1972). *Steps to an ecology of the mind.* New York: Ballantine.

Bateson, G. (1979). *Mind and nature.* New York: Bantam Books.

Bateson, G., Jackson, D. D., Haley, J., & Weakland, J. (1956). Toward a theory of schizophrenia. *Behavioral Science, I,* 251–264.

Bauer, G. P., & Kobos, J. C. (1984). Short-term psychodynamic psychotherapy: Reflections on the past and current practice. *Psychotherapy: Theory, Research, and Practice, 21* (2), 153–170.

Beck, A. T. (1976). *Cognitive therapy and the emotional disorders.* New York: International Universities Press.

Bednar, R. L., Bednar, S. C., Lambert, M. J., & Waite, D. R. (1991). *Psychotherapy with high-risk clients: Legal and professional standards.* Pacific Grove, CA: Brooks/Cole.

Beers, C. (1945). *A mind that found itself.* New York: Doubleday.

Belkin, G. (1981). *Practical counseling in the schools* (2nd ed.). Dubuque, IA: William C. Brown.

Belkin, G. (1987). *Contemporary psychotherapies* (2nd ed.). Pacific Grove, CA: Brooks/Cole.

Belle, D. (1990). Poverty and women's mental health. *American Psychologist, 45* (3), 385–389.

Bem, D. J. (1970). *Beliefs, attitudes, and human affairs.* Pacific Grove, CA: Brooks/Cole.

Bennett, B. E., Bryant, B. K., VandenBos, G. R., & Greenwood, A. (1990). *Professional liability and risk management.* Washington, DC: American Psychological Association.

Bennett, M. J. (1984). Brief psychotherapy and adult development. *Psychotherapy: Theory, Research, and Practice, 21* (2), 171–177.

Berger, M. (1982). Ethics and the therapeutic relationship. In M. Rosenbaum (Ed.), *Ethics and values in psychotherapy,* (pp. 67–95). New York: Free Press.

Bergin, A. E. (1971). The evaluation of therapeutic outcomes. In A. E. Bergin & S. L. Garfield (Eds.), *Handbook of psychotherapy and behavior change.* New York: Wiley.

Bergin, A. E., & Garfield, S. L. (Eds.) (1978). *Handbook of psychotherapy and behavior change* (2nd ed.). New York: Wiley.

Berne, E. (1961). *Transactional analysis in psychotherapy*. New York: Grove Press.

Berne, E. (1964). *Games people play*. New York: Grove Press.

Berne, E. (1972). *What do you say after you say hello?* New York: Grove Press.

Beutler, L. E. (1983). *Eclectic psychotherapy: A systematic approach*. New York: Pergamon Press.

Beutler, L. E. (1989). Differential treatment selection: The role of diagnosis in psychotherapy. *Psychotherapy, 26*, 271–281.

Beutler, L. E., & Clarkin, J. F. (1990). *Systematic treatment selection: Toward targeted therapeutic interventions*. New York: Brunner/Mazel.

Biddle, B. J., Bank, B. J., & Marlin, M. M. (1980, March). Social determinants of adolescent drinking: What they think, what they do and what I think and do. *Journal Studies on Alcohol, 41* (3), 215–241.

Biggs, D., & Keller, K. (1982). A cognitive approach to using tests in counseling. *Personnel and Guidance Journal, 60*, 528–532.

Birren, J. E., Cunningham, W. R., & Yamamoto, K. (1983). Psychology of adult development and aging. *Annual Review of Psychology, 34*, 543–575.

Blocher, D. H. (1966). *Developmental counseling*. New York: Ronald Press.

Blocher, D. H., & Siegal, R. (1981). Toward a cognitive developmental theory of leisure and work. *Counseling Psychologist, 9* (3), 33–44.

Boorstein, D. (1983). *The discoverers*. New York: Random House.

Bordin, E. S. (1968). *Psychological counseling*. New York: Appleton-Century-Crofts.

Boy, A. V. (1989). Psychodiagnosis: A person-centered perspective. *Person-Centered Review, 4* (2), 132–151.

Boy, A. V., & Pine, G. J. (1982) . The effectiveness of a counseling theory. *Michigan Personnel and Guidance Journal, 4*, 39–42.

Boy, A. V., & Pine, G. J. (1983). Counseling: Fundamentals of theoretical renewal. *Counseling and Values, 27*, 248–255.

Boy, A. V., & Pine, G. J. (1990). *A person-centered foundation for counseling and psychotherapy*. Springfield, IL: Charles C Thomas.

Brammer, L. M., & Shostrum, E. L. (1982). *Therapeutic psychology: Fundamentals of counseling and psychotherapy*. Englewood Cliffs, NJ: Prentice-Hall.

Brilhart, J., & Jochem, L. (1964). Effects of different patterns on outcomes of problem-solving discussions. *Journal of Applied Psychology, 48*, 175–179.

Brooks, D. K., & Gerstein, L. H. (1990). Counselor credentialing and interpersonal collaboration. *Journal of Counseling and Development, 68*, 477–484.

Brown, M. T. (1988). The mental health counselor and research: And never the twain shall meet? *Journal of Mental Health Counseling, 10* (1), 9–15.

Brown, R. W. (1978). Choosing and evaluating group techniques: A systematic framework. *Journal for Specialists in Group Work, 3*, 146–153.

Brown, R. W., & Kottler, J. A. (1979). Increasing client employability through skill development. *Journal of Employment Counseling, 16*, 164–171.

Budman, S. H., & Gurman, H. S. (1988). *Theory and practice of brief therapy*. New York: Guilford Press.

Bugental, J. F. T. (1991). Outcomes of an existential-humanistic psychotherapy. *Humanistic Psychologist, 19*, 2–9.

Buhrke, R. A., & Douce, L. A. (1991). Training issues for counseling psychologists in working with lesbian women and gay men. *Counseling Psychologist, 19*, 216–234 .

Burke, J. F. (1989). *Contemporary approaches to psychotherapy and counseling*. Pacific Grove, CA: Brooks/Cole.

Burks, H. M., Jr., & Stefflre, B. (1979). *Theories of counseling* (3rd ed.). McGraw-Hill.

Burnett, M. (1979). Understanding and overcoming addictions. In S. Eisenberg & L. E. Patterson (Eds.). *Helping clients with special concerns* (pp. 343–362). Chicago: Rand McNally.

Buros, O. (Ed.). (1978). *Mental measurements yearbook* (8th ed.). Lincoln: University of Nebraska Press.

Butler, R. N., & Lewis, M. I. (1973). *Aging and mental health.* St. Louis: C.V. Mosby.

Caplow, T. (1954). *The sociology of work.* Minneapolis: University of Minnesota Press.

Capuzzi, D., & Lecoq, L. L. (1983, December). Social and personal determinants of adolescent use and abuse of alcohol and marijuana. *Personnel and Guidance Journal,* pp. 199–205.

Carkhuff, R. R. (1969). *Helping and human relations* (Vols. 1–2). New York: Holt, Rinehart & Winston.

Carkhuff, R. R. (1971). Training as a preferred mode of treatment. *Journal of Counseling Psychology, 18,* 123–131.

Calkhuff, R. R., & Anthony, W. A. (1979). *The skills of helping: An introduction to counseling.* Amherst, MA: Human Resources Development Press.

Carkhuff, R. R., & Berenson, B. G. (1967). *Beyond counseling and therapy.* New York: Holt, Rinehart & Winston.

Carkhuff, R. R., & Berenson, B. G. (1977). *Beyond counseling and therapy* (2nd ed.). New York: Holt, Rinehart & Winston.

Carter, J. A. (1978). Impressions of counselors as a function of counselor physical attractiveness. *Journal of Counseling Psychology, 25,* 28–34.

Casas, J. M., Ponterotto, J. G., & Gutierrez, J. M. (1986). An ethical indictment of counseling research and training: The cross-cultural perspective. *Journal of Counseling and Development, 64,* 347–349.

Cash, T. F., Begley, P. J., McCown, D. A., & Weise, B. C. (1975). When counselors are heard but not seen: Initial impact of physical attractiveness. *Journal of Counseling Psychology, 22,* 273–279.

Castaneda, C. (1971). *A separate reality.* New York: Pocket Books.

Castronovo, N. R. (1990). Acquired immune deficiency syndrome education on the college campus: The mandate and the challenge. *Journal of Counseling and Development, 68,* 578–580.

Cayleff, S. E. (1986). Ethical issues in counseling gender, race, and culturally distinct groups. *Journal of Counseling and Development, 64* (5), 345–347.

Chassin, L., Mann, L. M., & Sher, K. J. (1988). Self-awareness theory, family history of alcoholism, and adolescent alcohol involvement. *Journal of Abnormal Psychology, 97,* 206–217.

Cherniss, C,. (1980). *Staff burnout: Job stress in the human services.* Beverly Hills, CA: Sage.

Choate, O., & Epstein, N. (1982, May 9). Workers in the future retool: Nothing to lose but your jobs. *Washington Post.*

Christensen, C. P. (1989). Cross-cultural awareness development: A conceptual model. *Counselor Education and Supervision, 28,* 270–287.

Cianni-Surridge, M. (1983). Technology and work: Future issues for career guidance . *Personnel and Guidance Journal, 61,* 413–416.

Claiborn, C. D. (1979). Counselor verbal intervention, non-verbal behavior, and social power. *Journal of Counseling Psychology, 26,* 378–383.

Claiborn, C. D., & Schmidt, L. D. (1977). Effects of presession information on the perception of the counselor in the interview. *Journal of Counseling Psychology, 24,* 259–263.

Cochran, S. D., & Mays, V. M. (1989). Women and AIDS-related concerns: Roles for psychologists in helping the worried well. *American Psychologist, 44,* 529–535.

Cohen, R. J., Montague, P., Nathanson, L. S., & Swerdlik, M. (1988). *Psychological testing: An introduction to tests and measurements*. Mountain View, CA: Mayfield.

Coleman, E., & Schaefer, S. (1986). Boundaries of sex and intimacy between client and counselor. *Journal of Counseling and Development, 64* (5), 341–344.

Coleman, S. (1979, July). People who read people. *Psychology Today,* pp. 66–78.

Combs, A. W., Avila, D. L., & Purkey, W. W. (1971). *Helping relationships: Basic concepts for the helping professions*. Boston: Allyn & Bacon.

Conoley, J.C., & Kramer, J. J. (Eds.) (1989). *The tenth mental measurements yearbook*. Lincoln: University of Nebraska Press.

Conroy, P. (1982). *The lords of discipline*. New York: Bantam Books.

Cook, E. P. (1990). Gender and psychological distress. *Journal of Counseling and Development, 68* (4), 371–375.

Corazzini, J. G., & Anderson, S. M. (1980). An apprentice model for training group leaders: Revitalizing group treatment. *Journal for Specialists in Group Work, 5,* 29–35.

Corey, G. (1990). *Theory and practice of group counseling* (3rd ed.). Pacific Grove, CA: Brooks/Cole.

Corey, G. (1991). *Theory and practice of counseling and psychotherapy* (4th ed.) Pacific Grove, CA: Brooks/Cole.

Corey, G., & Corey, M. S. (1990). *I never knew I had a choice* (4th ed.). Pacific Grove, CA: Brooks/Cole.

Corey, G., & Corey, M. S. (1991). *Groups: Process and practice* (4th ed.). Pacific Grove, CA: Brooks/Cole.

Corey, G., Corey, M. S., & Callanan, P. (1988). *Issues and ethics in the helping professions* (3rd ed.). Pacific Grove, CA: Brooks/Cole.

Corey, M. S., & Corey, G. (1989). *Becoming a helper*. Pacific Grove, CA: Brooks/Cole.

Cormier, W. H., & Cormier, L. S. (1991). *Interviewing strategies for helpers* (3rd ed.). Pacific Grove, CA: Brooks/Cole.

Cornacchia, H. J., Smith, D. E., & Bentel, D. J. (1978). *Drugs in the classroom*. St. Louis: C. V. Mosby.

Cox, W. M., & Klinger, E. (1988). A motivational model of alcohol involvement. *Journal of Abnormal Psychology, 97,* 168–180.

Cronbach, L. J. (1975). Five decades of public controversy over mental testing. *American Psychologist, 30,* 1–14.

Cronbach, L. J. (1984). *Essentials of psychological testing* (4th ed.). New York: Harper & Row.

Dasberg, H. & Winoker, M. (1984). Teaching and learning short-term dynamic psychcotherapy: Parallel processes. *Psychotherapy: Theory, Research, and Practice, 21* (2), 184–188.

Davanloo, H. (1978). *Basic principles and techniques in short-term dynamic psychotherapy*. New York: Spectrum.

Derlega, V. J., Hendrick, S. S., Winstead, B. A., & Berg, J. H. (1991). *Psychotherapy as a personal relationship*. New York: Guilford.

Dimond, R. E., Havens, R. A., & Jones, A. C. (1978). A conceptual framework for the practice of prescriptive eclecticism in psychotherapy. *American Psychologist, 33,* 239–248.

Dinkmeyer, D. C., Dinkmeyer, D. C., Jr., & Sperry, L. (1987). *Adlerian counseling and psychotherapy* (2nd ed.). Muncie, IN: Accelerated Development.

Doherty, M. A. (1978). Sexual bias in personality theory. In L. Harmon, J. M. Birk, L. E. Fitzgerald, & M. F. Talmey (Eds.), *Counseling women* (pp. 94–105). Pacific Grove, CA: Brooks/Cole.

Dollard, J., & Miller, N. (1950). *Personality and psychotherapy*. New York: McGraw-Hill.

Donigian, J., & Malnati, R. (1987). *Critical incidents in group therapy.* Pacific Grove, CA: Brooks/Cole.

Dorn, F. J. (1986). Needed: competent, confident, and committed career counselors. *Journal of Counseling and Development, 65,* 216–217.

Douglas, C. (1990). *Counseling same-sex couples.* New York: W. W. Norton.

Downing, H. D., & Paradise, L. V. (1989). Using the DSM-III-R in counseling. *Journal of Counseling and Development, 68,* 226–227.

Drane,. J. F. (1982). Ethics and psychotherapy: A philosophical perspective. In M. Rosenbaum (Ed.), *Ethics and values in psychotherapy* (pp. 15–50). New York: Free Press.

Dreikurs, R. (1950). *Fundamentals of Adlerian psychology.* Chicago: Alfred Adler Institute.

Driscoll, R. H. (1984). *Pragmatic psychotherapy.* New York: Van Nostrand Reinhold.

Dworkin, S. H., & Gutierrez, F. (1989). Introduction to the special issue. Counselors be aware: Clients come in every size, shape, color, and sexual orientation. *Journal of Counseling and Development, 68,* 6–8.

Dye, A. (1980). Thoughts on training. *Journal for Specialists in Group Work, 5,* 5–7.

Dyer, W. W., & Vriend, J. (1974). Vital components in conducting the initial interview. *Educational Technology, 14,* 24–32.

Dyer, W. W., & Vriend, J. (1975). *Counseling techniques that work.* Alexandria, VA: American Association for Counseling and Development.

Dyer, W. W., & Vriend, J. (1980). *Group counseling for personal mastery.* New York: Sovereign.

Eber, M., & O'Brien, J. M. (1982). Psychotherapy in the movies. *Psychotherapy: Theory, Research, and Practice, 19*(1), 116–120.

Edgerton, R. B., & Karno, M. (1971). Mexican-American bilingualism and the perception of mental illness. *Archives of General Psychiatry, 24,* 286–290.

Edwards, R. B. (1982). Mental health as rational autonomy. In R. B. Edwards (Ed.), *Psychiatry and ethics* (pp. 68–78). Buffalo: Prometheus Books.

Egan, G. (1975). *Exercises in helping skills.* Pacific Grove, CA: Brooks/Cole.

Egan, G. (1990). *The skilled helper* (4th ed.). Pacific Grove, CA: Brooks/Cole.

Eisdorfer, C. (1983). Conceptual models of aging. *American Psychologist, 38,* 197–202.

Eldridge, W. D. (1982). A perspective on the similarities among selected concepts of traditional scientific research and clinical counseling. *Journal of Clinical Psychology, 38*(2), 452–460.

Ellis, A. (1962). *Reason and emotion in psychotherapy.* New York: Lyle Stuart.

Ellis, A. (1973). *Humanistic psychotherapy.* New York: Julian Press.

Ellis, A. (1977a). The basic clinical theory of rational-emotive therapy. In A. Ellis & R. Grieger (Eds.), *Handbook of rational emotive-therapy.* New York: Springer.

Ellis, A. (1977b). Rational-emotive therapy: Research data that supports the clinical and personality hypothesis of RET and other modes of cognitive behavior therapy. *Journal of Counseling Psychology, 7,* 5–42.

Ellis, A. (1988, September). Albert Ellis on the essence of RET. *Psychology Today,* pp. 56–58.

Ellis, A., & Dryden, W. (1987). *The practice of rational-emotive therapy.* Secaucus, NJ: Lyle Stuart.

Ellis, A., & Grieger, R. (Eds.) (1986). *Handbook of rational-emotive therapy.* New York: Springer.

Ellis, A., & Harper, R. (1975). *A new guide to rational living.* Hollywood: Wilshire Books.

Ellis, A., & Whiteley, J. M. (Eds.) (1979). *Theoretical and empirical foundations of rational-emotive therapy.* Pacific Grove, CA: Brooks/Cole.

Erikson, E. (1950). *Childhood and society*. New York: W. W. Norton.

Erlanger, M. A. (1990). Using the genogram with the older client. *Journal of Mental Health Counseling, 12* (3), 321–331.

Eysenck, H. (1952). The effects of psychotherapy: An evaluation. *Journal of Consulting Psychology, 16,* 319–324.

Farber, B. A. (1983). The effects of psychotherapeutic practice upon psychotherapists. *Psychotherapy: Theory, Research, and Practice, 20* (2), 174–182.

Fassinger, R. E. (1991). The hidden minority: Issues and challenges in working with lesbian women and gay men. *Counseling Psychologist, 19,* 157–176.

Feldman-Summers, S., & Jones, G. (1984). Psychological impacts of sexual contact between therapists or other health care practitioners and their clients. *Journal of Consulting and Clinical Psychology, 52,* 1054–1061.

Fenell, D. L., & Weinhold, B. K. (1989). *Counseling families*. Denver: Love.

Festinger, L. (1957). *A theory of cognitive dissonance*. Stanford, CA: Stanford University Press.

Festinger, L. (1964). Behavioral support for opinion change. *Public Opinion Quarterly, 28,* 404–417.

Fiedler, F. E. (1950). A comparison of therapeutic relationships in psychoanalytic, nondirective, and Adlerian therapy. *Journal of Consulting Psychology, 14,* 436–445.

Fisch, R., Weakland, J. H., & Segal, L. (1982). *The tactics of change*. San Francisco: Jossey-Bass.

Fish, J. (1973). *Placebo therapy*. San Francisco: Jossey-Bass.

Fish, W. C. (1981). The intrinsic connection between ethics and psychotherapy. *Counseling and Values, 25,* 269–278.

Flaherty, J. A., & Meagher, R. (1980). Measuring racial bias on inpatient treatment. *American Journal of Psychiatry, 137,* 679–682.

Forsyth, D. R., & Stanley, R. S. (1986). The scientific study of counseling and psychotherapy. *American Psychologist, 41* (2), 113–119.

Framo, J. L. (1981). Family theory and therapy. *Elementary School Guidance and Counseling, 15,* 205–213.

Frank, J. D. (1973). *Persuasion and healing*. Baltimore: Johns Hopkins University Press.

Frank, P. (1949). *Modern science and its philosophy*. Cambridge, MA: Harvard University Press.

Frankl, V. (1962). *Man's search for meaning*. Boston: Beacon Press.

Frankl, V. (1978). *The unheard cry for meaning*. New York: Simon & Schuster.

Fraser, J. S. (1982). Structural and strategic family therapy: A basis for marriage, or grounds for divorce. *Journal of Marital and Family Therapy, 8* (2), 13–22.

French, T. M. (1933). Interrelations between psychoanalysis and the experimental work of Pavlov. *American Journal of Psychiatry, 89,* 1165–1203.

Fretz, B. R. (1981). Evaluating the effectiveness of career intervention. *Journal of Counseling Psychology, 28,* 77–90.

Fretz, B. R., Corn, R., Tuemmler, J. M., & Bellet, W. (1979). Counselor nonverbal behaviors and client evaluations. *Journal of Counseling Psychology, 26,* 304–311.

Fretz, B. R., & Mills, D. H. (1980). *Licensing and certification of psychologists and counselors*. San Francisco: Jossey-Bass.

Freud, S. (1924). *A general introduction to psychoanalysis*. New York: Washington Square Press.

Freud, S. (1954). *The origins of psycho analysis*. New York: Basic Books.

Freudenberger, H. J. (1974). Staff burnout. *Journal of Social Issues, 30,* 159–165.

Freudenberger, H. J. (1983). Hazards of psychotherapeutic practice. *Psychotherapy in Private Practice, 1*, 83–89.

Friedlander, M. L., Ellis, M. V., Raymond, L., Siegel, S. M., & Milford, D. (1987). Convergence and divergence in the process of interviewing families. *Psychotherapy, 24* (3), 570–583.

Fromm-Reichmann, F. (1952). Some aspects of psychoanalysis and schizophrenics. In F. C. Redlich & E. R. Brody (Eds.), *Psychotherapy with schizophrenics.* New York: International Universities Press.

Fuhrmann, B. S., & Washington, C. S. (1984). Substance abuse: An overview. *Journal for Specialists in Group Work, 9* (1), 2–6.

Fukuyama, M. A., Probert, B. S., Neimeyer, G. J., Nevill, D. D., & Metzler, A. E. (1988). Effects of Discover on career self-efficacy and decision making of undergraduates. *Career Development Quarterly, 37*, 56–62.

Fuqua, D. R., Blum, C. R., & Hartman, B. W. (1988). Empirical support for the differential diagnosis of career indecision. *Career Development Quarterly, 36*, 364–373.

Fuqua, D. R., & Hartman, B. W. (1983). Differential diagnosis and treatment of career indecision. *Personnel and Guidance Journal, 62*, 27–30.

Galvin, M., & Ivey, A. E. (1981). Researching one's own interviewing style: Does your theory of choice match your actual practice? *Personnel and Guidance Journal, 59*, 536–541.

Garfield, S. L., & Bergin, A. E. (Eds.) (1986). *Handbook of psychotherapy and behavior change* (3rd ed.). New York: Wiley.

Geis, H. J. (1973). Effectively leading a group in the present moment. *Educational Technology, 13* (1), 76–88.

Gelman, D. (1984, May 28). The switch is on. *Newsweek*, pp. 93–95.

Gendlin, E. T. (1973). *Experiential psychotherapy.* In R. Corsini (Ed.), *Current psychotherapies.* Itasca, IL: F. E. Peacock.

Gentner, D. S. (1991). A brief strategic model for mental health counseling. *Journal of Mental Health Counseling, 13*, 58–68.

Gill, S. J., & Barry, R. A. (1982). Group-focused counseling: Classifying the essential skills. *Personnel and Guidance Journal, 60*, 302–305.

Ginzberg, E. (1972). Toward a theory of occupational choice: A restatement. *Vocational Guidance Quarterly, 20*, 169–176.

Glantz, K., & Pearce, J. K. (1989). *Exiles from eden: Psychotherapy from an evolutionary perspective.* New York: W. W. Norton.

Glasser, W. (1965). *Reality therapy.* New York: Harper & Row.

Glasser, W. (1976). *Positive addiction.* New York: Harper & Row.

Goldberg, C. (1977). *Therapeutic partnership: Ethical concerns in psychotherapy.* New York: Springer.

Goldenberg, H., & Goldenberg, I. (1990). *Counseling today's families.* Pacific Grove, CA: Brooks/Cole.

Goldenberg, I., & Goldenberg, H. (1991). *Family therapy: An overview* (3rd ed.). Pacific Grove, CA: Brooks/Cole.

Goldfried, M. R. (Ed.) (1982). *Converging themes in psychotherapy.* New York: Springer.

Goldman, L. (1972). Tests and counseling: The marriage that failed. *Measurement and Evaluation in Guidance, 4*, 213–220.

Goldstein, A. P. (1972). Drug education worthy of the name. *Impact, 1* (4), 18–24.

Goldstein, A. P. (1980). Relationship-enhancement methods. In F. H. Kanfer & A. P. Goldstein (Eds.), *Helping people change.* New York: Pergamon Press.

Gordon, J., & Shontz, F. C. (1990). Living with the AIDS virus: A representative case. *Journal of Counseling and Development, 68*, 287–292.

Gordon, T. G. (1970). *Parent effectiveness training.* New York: Peter Wyden.

Gordon, T. G. (1974). *Teacher effectiveness training.* New York: Peter Wyden.

Gottman, J. M., & Leiblum, S. R. (1974). *How to do psychotherapy and how to evaluate it.* New York: Holt, Rinehart & Winston.

Green, S. L., & Hansen, J. C. (1989). Ethical dilemmas faced by family therapists. *Journal of Marital and Family Therapy, 15* (2), 149–158.

Greenberg, L. S., & Pinsof, W. M. (Eds.) (1986). *The therapeutic process: A research handbook.* New York: Guilford Press.

Greenspan, S. I., & Wieder, S. (1984). Dimensions and levels of the therapeutic process. *Psychotherapy: Theory, Research, and Practice, 21* (1), 5–23.

Greenwood, R. (1987). Expanding community participation by people with disabilities: Implications for counselors. *Journal of Counseling and Development, 66,* 185–187.

Gregory, S., & Lee, S. (1986). A psychoeducational assessment of racial and ethnic minority groups: Professional implications. *Journal of Counseling and Development, 64,* 635–637.

Groden, G., & Cautela, J. R. (1981). Behavior therapy: A survey of procedures for counselors. *Personnel and Guidance Journal, 60,* 175–180.

Gross, D. R., & Robinson, S. E. (1987). Ethics, violence, and counseling: Hear no evil, see no evil, speak no evil? *Journal of Counseling and Development, 65* (7), 340–344.

Groth-Marnat, G. (1990). *Handbook of psychological assessment* (2nd ed.). New York: Wiley.

Gurman, A. S., & Razin, M. (Eds.) (1977). *Effective psychotherapy: A handbook of research.* New York: Pergamon Press.

Haber, R. A. (1983). The family dance around drug abuse. *Personnel and Guidance Journal, 61,* 428–431.

Haley, J. (1969). The art of being a failure as a therapist. *American Journal of Orthopsychiatry, 39* (1), 691–695.

Haley, J. (Ed.) (1971). *Changing families.* New York: Grune & Stratton.

Haley, J. (1973). *Uncommon therapy.* New York: W. W. Norton.

Haley, J. (1976). *Problem solving therapy.* New York: Harper & Row.

Haley, J. (1980). How to be a marriage therapist without knowing practically anything. *Journal of Marital and Family Counseling, 6* (4), 385–392.

Haley, J. (1984). *Ordeal therapy: Unusual ways to change behavior.* San Francisco: Jossey-Bass.

Haley, J. (1989). *The first therapy session.* San Francisco: Jossey-Bass.

Hall, C. (1954). *A primer of Freudian psychology.* New York: New American Library.

Hall, E. (1983, June). A conversation with Erik Erikson. *Psychology Today,* pp. 22–30.

Hall, E. T. (1976). *Beyond culture.* New York: Anchor.

Hall, G. C. N., & Maloney, H. N. (1983). Cultural control in psychotherapy with minority clients. *Psychotherapy: Theory, Research, and Practice, 20* (2), 131–142.

Hammond, R. I. (1981). *Almost all you wanted to know about alcoholism but didn't know to ask* (rev. ed.). Lansing: Michigan Clearinghouse for Substance Abuse Information.

Haney, W. (1981). Validity, vaudeville, and values: A short history of social concerns over standardized testing. *American Psychologist, 36,* 1021–1034.

Hansen, J. C., Stevic, R. R., & Warner, R. W., Jr. (1986) *Counseling: Theory and process* (4th ed.). Boston: Allyn & Bacon.

Hare-Mustin, R. (1983). An appraisal of the relationship between women and psychotherapy. *American Psychologist, 38,* 593–601.

Harris, T. A. (1969). *I'm OK, you're OK.* New York: Avon.

Hartman, B. W., Fuqua, D. R., & Blum, C. R. (1985). A path analytic model of career indecision. *Vocational Guidance Quarterly, 33,* 231–246.

Harvill, R., Masson, R. L., & Jacobs, E. (1983). Systematic group leader training: A skills development approach. *Journal for Specialists in Group Work, 8,* 226–232.

Hausman, C. P. (1991, January/February). Treating the elderly client. *Family Therapy Networker,* pp. 21–24.

Hayman, P. M., & Covert, J. A. (1986). Ethical dilemmas in college counseling centers. *Journal of Counseling and Development, 64* (5), 318–320.

Hazler, R. J., & Roberts, G. (1984). Decision making in vocational theory: Evolution and implications. *Personnel and Guidance Journal, 62,* 408–410.

Heitzman, D., Schmidt, A. K., & Hurley, F. W. (1986). Career encounters: Career decision making through on-site visits. *Journal of Counseling and Development, 66,* 209–210.

Held, B. S. (1984). Toward a strategic eclecticism. *Psychotherapy: Theory, Research, and Practice, 21* (2), 232–241 .

Hepner, R., Kershbaum, H ., & Landes, D. (1980). Counseling substance abusers with additional disabilities: The Center for Independent Living. *Alcohol Health and Research World, 5* (2), 11–15.

Heppner, P. P., & Dixon, D. N. (1981). A review of the interpersonal influence process in counseling. *Personnel and Guidance Journal, 59,* 542–550.

Heppner, P. P., & Anderson, W. P. (1985). On the perceived non-utility of research in counseling. *Journal of Counseling and Development, 63,* 545–547.

Herlihy, B., & Corey, G. (1992). *Dual relationships in counseling.* Alexandria, VA: American Association for Counseling and Development.

Herlihy, B., Healy, M., Cook, E. P., & Hudson, P. (1987). Ethical practices of licensed professional counselors: A survey of state licensing boards. *Counselor Education and Supervision, 27,* 69–76.

Herlihy, B., & Sheeley, V. L. (1988). Counselor liability and the duty to warn: Selected cases, statutory trends, and implications for practice. *Counselor Education and Supervision, 27* (3), 203–215.

Hermans, H. J., Fiddelaers, R., de Groot, R., & Nauta, J. F. (1990). Self-confrontation as a method for assessment and intervention in counseling. *Journal of Counseling and Development, 69,* 156–162.

Herr, E., & Watts, A. (1981). The implications of youth employment for career education and for counseling. *Journal of Career Education, 7,* 184–202.

Herron, W. G., & Rouslin, S. (1984). *Issues in psychotherapy.* Washington, DC: Oryn.

Hills, C. E. (1990). Is individual therapy process really different from group therapy process? The jury is still out. *Counseling Psychologist, 18* (1), 126–130.

Hindman, M., & Widem, P. (1980). The multidisabled: Emerging responses. *Alcohol Health and Research World, 5* (2), 11–15.

Ho, M. K., & Shipley, A. (1974). The culturally different counselor. *Elementary School Guidance and Counseling, 8,* 286–289.

Hoffman-Graff, M. A. (1977). Interviewer use of positive and negative self-disclosure and interviewer-subject sex pairing. *Journal Counseling Psychology, 24,* 184–190.

Holland, J. (1966). *The psychology of vocational choice.* Waltham, MA: Blaisdell.

Holland, J. (1972). *Self-directed search: Professional manual.* Palo Alto, CA: Consulting Psychologists Press.

Holland, J. (1973). *Making vocational choices: A theory of careers.* Englewood Cliffs, NJ: Prentice-Hall.

Holub, E. A., & Lee, S. S. (1990). Therapists' use of nonerotic physical contact: Ethical concerns. *Professional Psychology, 21* (2), 115–117.

Hood, A. B., & Johnson, R. W. (1991). *Assessment in counseling: A guide to the use of psychological assessment procedures.* Alexandria, VA: American Association for Counseling and Development.

Hopkins, B. R., & Anderson, B. S. (1990). *The counselor and the law* (3rd ed.). Alexandria, VA: American Association for Counseling and Development.

Hoppock, R. (1976). *Occupational information* (4th ed.). New York: McGraw-Hill.

Horan, J. (1979). *Counseling for effective decision making.* North Scituate, MA: Duxbury Press.

Horney, K. (1939). *New ways in psychoanalysis.* New York: W. W. Norton.

Horney, K. (1950). *Neurosis and human growth.* New York: W. W. Norton.

Hosford, R. E. (1969). Behavioral counseling: A contemporary overview. *Counseling Psychologist, 1,* 1–33.

Hoyt, K. B. (1985). Career guidance, educational reform, and career education. *Vocational Guidance Quarterly, 34,* 6–14.

Hoyt, K. B. (1988). The changing workforce: A review of projections—1986 to 2000. *Career Development Quarterly, 37,* 31–39.

Hoyt, K., Evans, R., Mackin, E., & Mangum, G. (1972). *Career education: What it is and how to do it.* Salt Lake City: Olympus.

Huey, W. C., & Remley, T. P. (Eds.) (1989). *Ethical and legal issues in school counseling.* Alexandria, VA: American Association for Counseling and Development.

Hussian, R. A. (1981). *Geriatric psychology: A behavioral perspective.* New York: Van Nostrand Reinhold.

Huxley, A. (1962). *Island.* New York: Harper & Row.

Iasenza, S. (1989). Some challenges of integrating sexual orientations into counselor training and research. *Journal of Counseling and Development, 68,* 73–76 .

Ibrahim, F. A., & Arredondo, P. (1990). Ethical issues in multicultural counseling. In B. Herlihy & L. B. Golden (Eds.), *Ethical standards casebook.* Alexandria, VA: American Association for Counseling and Development.

Issacson, L. E. (1986). *Career information in counseling and career development* (4th ed.). Boston: Allyn & Bacon.

Ivey, A. (1971). *Microcounseling: Innovations in interviewing training.* Springfield, IL: Charles C Thomas.

Ivey, A. (1987). *Intentional interviewing and counseling* (2nd ed.). Pacific Grove, CA: Brooks/Cole.

Ivey, A. (1991). *Development strategies for helpers.* Pacific Grove, CA: Brooks/Cole.

Ivey, A., & Authier, J. (1978). *Micro-counseling* (2nd ed.). Springfield, IL: Charles C Thomas.

Ivey, A., & Simek-Downing, L. (1987). *Counseling and psychotherapy* (2nd ed.). Needham Hts., MA: Allyn & Bacon.

Jacobs, E. E., Harvill, R. L., & Masson, R. L. (1988). *Group counseling: Strategies and skills.* Pacific Grove, CA: Brooks/Cole.

James, M., & Jongeward, D. (1971). *Born to win. Transactional analysis with gestalt experiments.* Reading, MA: Addison-Wesley.

James, W. (1907). *Pragmatism.* New York: New American Library.

Johnson, S. D. (1987). Knowing that versus knowing how: Toward achieving expertise through multicultural training for counseling. *Counseling Psychologist, 15* (2), 320–331.

Jones, B. E., & Gray, B. A. (1986). Problems in diagnosing schizophrenia and affective disorders among blacks. *Hospital and Community Psychiatry, 37,* 61–65 .

Jones, W. T., Sontag, F., Becker, M. O., & Fogelin, R. J. (1969). *Approaches to ethics.* New York: McGraw-Hill.

Jurek, A. W., Maier, M. E., Sandgren, A. K., Tall, K. M., & Searight, H. R. (1989). Challenging the uniformity myth in family therapy: Toward prescriptive intervention. *Family Therapy, 16* (3), 271–281.

Kagan, N. (1973). Can technology help us toward reliability in influencing human interaction? In J. Vriend & W. Dyer (Eds.), *Counseling effectively in groups.* Englewood Cliffs, NJ: Educational Technology Publications.

Kaiser, H. (1965). *Effective psychotherapy: The contribution of Hellmuth Kaiser,* L. Fierman (Ed.). New York: Free Press.

Kanfer, F. H., & Goldstein, A. P. (1991). *Helping people change* (4th ed.). New York: Pergamon Press.

Kanfer, F. H., & Phillips, J. S. (1970). *Learning foundations of behavior therapy.* New York: Wiley.

Kapes, J. T., Borman, C. A., & Frazier, N. (1989). An evaluation of the SIGI and DISCOVER microcomputer-based career guidance systems. *Measurement and Evaluation in Counseling and Development, 22,* 126–136.

Kaplan, H. S. (1974). *The new sex therapy.* New York: Brunner/Mazel.

Kaplan, M. (1983). A woman's view of DSM-III. *American Psychologist, 38* (7), 786–792.

Kass, F., Spitzer, R. L., & Williams, J. B. W. (1983). An empirical study of the issue of sex bias in the diagnostic criteria of DSM-III—Axis II personality disorders. *American Psychologist, 38,* 799–801.

Katkin, E. S., & Goldband, S. (1980). Biofeedback. In F. H. Kanfer and A. P. Goldstein (Eds.), *Helping people change* (pp. 537–578). New York: Pergamon Press.

Kaul, T. J., & Schmidt, L. D. (1971). Dimensions of interviewer trustworthiness. *Journal of Counseling Psychology, 18,* 542–548.

Keith-Spiegel, P. (1977, August). Violation of ethical principles due to ignorance or poor professional judgment versus willful disregard. *Professional Psychology,* pp. 288–296.

Kelly, K. R. (1991). Theoretical integration is the future for mental health counseling. *Journal of Mental Health Counseling, 13,* 106–111.

Kempler, W. (1973). *Gestalt therapy.* In R. Corsini (Ed.), *Current psychotherapies.* Itasca, IL: F.E. Peacock.

Kimmel, D. C. (1988). Ageism, psychology, and public policy. *American Psychologist, 43* (3), 175–188.

Kinnier, R. T., Brigman, S. L., & Noble, F. C. (1990). Career indecision and family enmeshment. *Journal of Counseling and Development, 68,* 309–312.

Knapp, S., & VandeCreek, L. (1990). Application of the duty to protect HIV-positive patients. *Professional Psychology, 21* (3), 161–166.

Koffka, K. (1935). *Principles of Gestalt psychology.* New York: Harcourt Brace & World.

Kohlberg, L. (1969). *Stages in the development of moral thought and action.* New York: Holt, Rinehart & Winston.

Köhler, W. (1929). *Gestalt psychology.* New York: Liveright.

Konner, M. (1982). *The tangled wing: Biological constraints on the human spirit.* New York: Harper & Row.

Koss, M. P. (1990). The women's mental health research agenda: Violence against women. *American Psychologist, 45,* 374–380.

Kottler, J. A. (1983). *Pragmatic group leadership.* Pacific Grove, CA: Brooks/Cole.

Kottler, J. A. (1986). *On being a therapist.* San Francisco: Jossey-Bass.

Kottler, J. A. (1990a). On the dangers of traditional diagnoses. *Humanistic Psychologist, 18*(4).

Kottler, J. A. (1990b). *Private moments, secret selves: Enriching our time alone.* Los Angeles: Jeremy Tarcher.

Kottler, J. A. (1991). *The compleat therapist*. San Francisco: Jossey-Bass.

Kottler, J. A. (1992). *Self-guided exploration for beginning counseling students*. Pacific Grove, CA: Brooks/Cole.

Kottler, J. A., & Blau, D. (1989). *The imperfect therapist: Learning from failures in therapeutic practice*. San Francisco: Jossey-Bass.

Kovacs, A. L. (1982). Survival in the 1980s on the theory and practice of brief psychotherapy. *Psychotherapy: Theory, Research, and Practice, 19* (2), 142–159.

Kroll, J. (1988). *The challenge of the borderline patient*. New York: W. W. Norton.

Krumboltz, J. D. (1965). Behavioral counseling: Rationale and research. *Personnel and Guidance Journal, 44*, 373–387.

Krumboltz, J. D. (Ed.) (1966). *Revolution in counseling: Implications of behavioral science*. Boston: Houghton Mifflin.

Krumboltz, J. D. (1978). A social learning theory of career selection. In J. M. Whiteley & A. Resnikoff (Eds.), *Career counseling*. Pacific Grove, CA: Brooks/Cole.

Kubie, L. S. (1934). Relation of the conditioned reflex to psychoanalytic technique. *Archives of Neurology and Psychiatry, 32*, 1137–1142.

LaCrosse, M. B. (1975). Nonverbal behavior and perceived counselor attractiveness and persuasiveness. *Journal of Counseling Psychology, 22*, 563–566.

Lambert, M. J., Christensen, E. R., & DeJulio, S. S. (1984). *The assessment of psychotherapy outcome*. New York: Wiley.

Lambert, M. J., Shapiro, D. A., & Bergin, A. E. (1986). The effectiveness of psychotherapy. In J. Garfield & A. E. Bergin (Eds.), *Handbook of psychotherapy and behavior change* (3rd ed.). New York: Wiley.

Lazarus, A. A. (1981). *The practice of multi-modal therapy*. New York: McGraw-Hill.

Levinson, D. J. (1978). *The seasons of a man's life*. New York: Ballantine.

Levitt, E. E. (1957). The results of psychotherapy with children: An evaluation. *Journal of Consulting Psychology, 21*, 189–196.

Lichtenberg, J. W. (1986). Counseling research: Irrelevant or ignored? *Journal of Counseling and Development, 64*, 365–366.

Lieberman, M., Yalom, I., & Miles, M. (1973). *Encounter groups: First facts*. New York: Basic Books.

Loevinger, J. (1976). *Ego development*. San Francisco: Jossey-Bass.

Lopez, F. G., & Andrews, S. (1987). Career indecision: A family systems perspective. *Journal of Counseling and Development, 65*, 304–307.

Lowenthal, A., & Anderson, P. (1980). Network development: Linking the disabled community to alcoholism and drug abuse programs. *Alcohol Health and Research World, 5* (2), 16–19.

Lundin, R. W. (1989). *Alfred Adler's basic concepts and implications*. Muncie, IN: Accelerated Development.

Madanes, C. (1983). *Strategic family therapy*. San Francisco: Jossey-Bass.

Madanes, C. (1984). *Beyond the one-way mirror*. San Francisco: Jossey-Bass.

Madanes, C. (1990). *Sex, love, and violence*. New York: W. W. Norton.

Maher, E. L. (1983). Burnout and commitment: A theoretical alternative. *Personnel and Guidance Journal, 61*, 390–393.

Mahoney, M. J. (1974). *Cognition and behavior modification*. Cambridge, MA: Ballinger.

Mahrer, A. R. (1987). These are the components of any theory of psychotherapy. *Journal of Integrative and Eclectic Psychotherapy, 6* (1), 28–31.

Mahrer, A. R. (1989). *The integration of psychotherapies*. New York: Human Sciences Press.

Malan, D. (1963). *A study of brief psychotherapy*. New York: Plenum.

Markowitz, L. M. (1991, January/February). Homosexuality: Are we still in the dark? *Family Therapy Networker*, pp. 27–35.

Marks, S. R. (1977). Multiple roles and role strain: Some notes on human energy, time, and commitment. *American Sociological Review, 42*, 921–936.

Marmor, J., & Woods, S. M. (Eds.) (1980). *The interface between psychodynamic and behavioral therapists.* New York: Plenum.

Martin, D. J. (1989). Human immunodeficiency virus infection and the gay community: Counseling and clinical issues. *Journal of Counseling and Development, 68*, 67–72.

Maslow, A. (1954). *Motivation and personality.* New York: Harper & Row.

Maultsby, M. C. (1975). *Help yourself to happiness.* New York: Institute for Rational-Emotive Therapy.

Maultsby, R. C. (1984). *Rational behavior therapy.* Englewood Cliffs, NJ: Prentice-Hall.

May, R. (1958). *Existence.* New York: Simon & Schuster.

May, R. (1967). *The art of counseling.* Nashville: Abingdon Press.

May, R. (1981). *Freedom and destiny.* New York: W. W. Norton.

May, R. (1983). *The discovery of being.* New York: W. W. Norton.

McBride, A. B. (1988). Women's mental health research agenda: Multiple roles. *Women's Mental Health Occasional Paper Series.* Rockville, MD: National Institutes of Mental Health.

McBride, A. B. (1990). Mental health effects of women's multiple roles. *American Psychologist, 45* (3), 381–384.

McDowell, D. F. (1981). Leisure: Consciousness, well-being, and counseling. *Counseling Psychologist, 9* (3), 3–31.

McGoldrick, M., & Gerson, R. (1985). *Genograms in family assessment.* New York: W. W. Norton.

McKusick, L. (1988). The impact of AIDS on practitioner and client: Notes for the therapeutic relationship. *American Psychologist, 43*, 935–940.

Meador, B. D., & Rogers, C. R. (1973). *Client centered therapy.* In R. Corsini (Ed.), *Current psychotherapies.* Itasca, IL: F. E. Peacock.

Meadow, A., Parnes, S., & Reese, J. (1959). Influence of brainstorming instructions and problem sequence on creative problem solving. *Journal of Applied Psychology, 43*, 413–436.

Mehrabian, A. (1970). *Tactics of social influence.* Englewood Cliffs, NJ: Prentice-Hall.

Mehrens, W. P., & Lehmann, J. J. (1985). Interpreting test scores to clients: What score should one use? *Journal of Counseling and Development, 63*, 317–320.

Meichenbaum, D. H. (1974). *Cognitive behavior modification.* Morristown, NJ: General Learning Press.

Meichenbaum, D. H. (1977). *Cognitive-behavior modification: An integrative approach.* New York: Plenum.

Merluzzi, T. V., Banikiotes, P. G., & Missbach, J. W. (1978). Perceptions of counselor sex, experience, and disclosure level. *Journal of Counseling Psychology, 25*, 479–482.

Milby, J. B. (1981). *Addictive behavior and its treatment.* New York: Springer.

Miller, G. M. (1982). Deriving meaning from standardized tests: Interpreting results to clients. *Measurement and Evaluation in Guidance, 15*, 87–94.

Miller, R. B. (1983). A call to armchairs. *Psychotherapy: Theory, Research, and Practice, 20* (2), 208–219.

Miller, W. R., & Hester, R. K. (1986). Inpatient alcoholism treatment: Who benefits? *American Psychologist, 41*, 794–805.

Millon, T. (1988). Personologic psychotherapy: Ten commandments for a posteclectic approach to integrative treatment. *Psychotherapy, 25* (2), 209–219.

Minuchin, S. (1974). *Families and family therapy*. Cambridge, MA: Harvard University Press.

Minuchin, S., & Fishman, H. C. (1981). *Family therapy techniques*. Cambridge, MA: Harvard University Press.

Minuchin, S., Rosman, B., & Baker, L. (1978). *Psychosomatic families: Anorexia nervosa in context*. Cambridge, MA: Harvard University Press.

Miranda, J., & Storms, M. (1989). Psychological adjustment of lesbians and gay men. *Journal of Counseling and Development, 68*, 41–45.

Mitchell, L. K., & Krumboltz, J. D. (1987). The effects of cognitive restructuring and decision-making training on career indecision. *Journal of Counseling and Development, 66*, 171–174.

Moustakas, C. (1986). Being in, being for, and being with. *Humanistic Psychologist, 14* (2), 100–104.

Mowbray, C. T., & Benedek, E. P. (1988). Women's mental health research agenda: Services and treatment of mental disorders in women. *Women's Mental Health Occasional Paper Series*. Rockville, MD: National Institutes of Mental Health.

Murphy, J. P. (1984). Substance abuse and the family. *Journal for Specialists in Group Work, 9* (2) 106–112.

Musashi, M. (1982). *A book of five rings*. Woodstock, NY: Overlook Press.

Nace, E. P. (1987). *The treatment of alcoholism*. New York: Brunner/Mazel.

Napier, R. W., & Gershenfeld, M. K. (1985). *Groups: Theory and experience* (3rd ed.). Boston: Houghton Mifflin.

Nelson-Jones, R. (1990). *Human relations: A skills approach*. Pacific Grove, CA: Brooks/Cole.

Neugarten, B. (1968). *Middle age and aging*. Chicago: University of Chicago Press.

Nevo, O. (1987). Irrational expectations in career counseling and their confronting arguments. *Career Development Quarterly, 35*, 239–250.

Newman, B., & Newman, P. (1991). *Development through life* (5th ed.). Pacific Grove, CA: Brooks/Cole.

Nissenson, M. (1984, January). Therapy after sixty. *Psychology Today*, pp. 22–26.

Nolan, E. J. (1978). Leadership interventions for promoting personal mastery. *Journal for Specialists in Group Work, 3* (3), 132–138.

Norcross, J. C. (1986). Preface. In J. C. Norcross (Ed.), *Handbook of eclectic psychotherapy*. New York: Brunner/Mazel.

Norcross, J. C., Prochaska, J. O., & Gallagher, K. M. (1989). Clinical psychologists in the 1980s. *Clinical Psychologist, 42* (2).

North, R., & Orange, R., Jr. (1980). *Teenage drinking: The #1 drug threat to young people today*. New York: Collier Books.

Oakley, R. (1983). *Drugs, society and human behavior*. St. Louis: C.V. Mosby.

Offermann, L. R., & Gowing, M. K. (1990). Organizations of the future. *American Psychologist, 45* (2), 95–108.

O'Hanlon, W. H., & Weiner-Davis, M. (1989). *In search of solutions*. New York: W. W. Norton.

O'Hare, M. M. (1987). Career decision-making models: Espoused theory versus theory-in-use. *Journal of Counseling and Development. 65*, 301–303.

Ohlsen, M. M., Horne, A. M., and Lawe, C. F. (1988). *Group counseling* (3rd ed.). New York: Holt, Rinehart & Winston.

Okun, B. F. & Rappaport, L. J. (1980). *Working with families*. Pacific Grove, CA: Brooks/Cole.

Oler, C. H. (1989). Black clients' racial identity. *Psychotherapy, 26* (2), 233–241.

Osberg, T. M. (1988). Self-report reconsidered: A further look at its advantages as an assessment technique. *Journal of Counseling and Development, 68*, 111–113.

Osipow, S. H. (1983). *Theories of career development* (3rd ed.). New York: Appleton-Century-Crofts.

Osipow, S. H., Walsh, W. B., & Tosi, D. J. (1984). *A survey of counseling methods.* Homewood, IL: Dorsey Press.

Othmer, E., & Othmer, S. C. (1989). *The clinical interview: Using DSM-III-R.* Washington, DC: American Psychiatric Press.

Palmer, J. O. (1980). *A primer of eclectic psychotherapy.* Pacific Grove, CA: Brooks/Cole.

Paritzky, R. S., & Magoon, T. M. (1982). Goal attainment scaling models for assessing group counseling. *Personnel and Guidance Journal, 60,* 381–384.

Parloff, M. (1956). Some factors affecting the quality of therapeutic relationships. *Journal of Abnormal and Social Psychology, 52,* 5–10.

Parsons, F. (1909). *Choosing a vocation.* Boston: Houghton Mifflin.

Pascarelli, E. F. (1981). Drug abuse and the elderly. In J. H. Lowinson & P. Ruiz (Eds.), *Substance abuse: Clinical problems and perspectives.* Baltimore: Williams & Wilkins.

Patterson, C. H. (1972). Ethical standards for groups. *Counseling Psychologist, 3,* 93–101.

Patterson, C. H. (1986). *Theories of counseling and psychotherapy* (4th ed.). New York: Harper & Row.

Patterson, L. E., & Eisenberg, S. (1983). *The counseling process.* Boston: Houghton Mifflin.

Pedersen, P. (Ed.) (1985). *Handbook of cross-cultural counseling and therapy.* Westport, CT: Greenwood Press.

Pedersen, P. (1988). *A handbook for developing multicultural awareness.* Alexandria, VA: American Association for Counseling and Development.

Pedersen, P. (1990). The constructs of complexity and balance in multicultural counseling theory and practice. *Journal of Counseling and Development, 68,* 550–554.

Perls, F. (1969a). *Gestalt therapy verbatim.* Lafayette, CA: Real People Press.

Perls, F. (1969b). *In and out of the garbage pail.* Lafayette, CA: Real People Press.

Perosa, S. L., & Perosa, L. M. (1987). Strategies for counseling midcareer changers: A conceptual framework. *Journal of Counseling and Development, 65,* 558–561.

Pfeiffer, J. W., & Jones, J. E. (1973-1977). *A handbook of structured experiences for human relations training* (Vols. 1–11). Iowa City: University Publications.

Phillips, B. N. (1982). Regulations and control in psychology. *American Psychologist, 37* (8), 919–926.

Piaget, J. (1926). *The language and thought of the child.* New York: Harcourt Brace Jovanovich.

Pietrofesa, J., Hoffman, A., & Splete, H. (1984). *Counseling: An introduction.* Boston: Houghton Mifflin.

Pietrofesa, J. J., Pietrofesa, C. J., & Pietrofesa, J. D. (1990). The mental health counselor and "duty to warn." *Journal of Mental Health Counseling, 12* (2), 129–137.

Pines, A., & Maslach, C. (1978). Characteristics of staff burnout in mental health settings. *Hospital and Community Psychiatry, 29,* 223–237.

Pope, K. S., Keith-Spiegel, P., & Tabachnick, B. G. (1986). Sexual attraction to clients. *American Psychologist, 41* (2), 147–158.

Pope, K. S., & Vasquez, M. J. (1991). *Ethics in psychotherapy and counseling.* San Francisco: Jossey-Bass.

Prochaska, J. O. (1984). *Systems of psychotherapy: A transtheoretical approach* (2nd ed.). Pacific Grove, CA: Brooks/Cole.

Prochaska, J. O., & DiClemente, C. C. (1984). *The transtheoretical approach: Crossing the traditional boundaries of therapy.* Homewood, IL: Dow Jones-Irwin.

Rachman, S. (1971). *The effects of psychotherapy.* London: Pergamon Press.

Remer, R. (1981). The counselor and research: An introduction. *Personnel and Guidance Journal, 59,* 567–571.

Rice, L. N., & Greenberg, L. S. (1984). The new research paradigm. In L. N. Rice & L. S. Greenberg (Eds.), *Patterns of change.* New York: Guilford Press.

Robertiello, R. C. (1978). The occupational disease of psychotherapists. *Journal of Contemporary Psychotherapy, 123–129.*

Robinson, S. E., & Gross, D. R. (1989). Applied ethics and the mental health counselor. *Journal of Mental Health Counseling, 11* (3), 289–299.

Roe, A. (1957). Early determinants of vocational choice. *Journal of Counseling Psychology, 4,* 212–217.

Rogers, C. R. (1942). *Counseling and psychotherapy.* Boston: Houghton Mifflin.

Rogers, C. R. (1951). *Client-centered therapy.* Boston: Houghton Mifflin.

Rogers, C. R. (1957). The necessary and sufficient conditions of therapeutic personality change. *Journal of Consulting Psychology, 21,* 93–103.

Rogers, C. R. (1958). Characteristics of a helping relationship. *Personnel and Guidance Journal, 37,* 6–16.

Rogers, C. R. (1959). A theory of therapy, personality, and interpersonal relationships as developed in the client-centered framework. In S. Koch (Ed.), *Psychology: A study of a science:* Vol. 3. *Formulations of the person and the social content.* New York: McGraw-Hill.

Rogers, C. R. (1961). *On becoming a person.* Boston: Houghton Mifflin.

Rogers, C. R. (1969). *Freedom to learn.* Columbus, OH: Charles E. Merrill.

Rogers, C. R. (1970). *On encounter groups.* New York: Harper & Row.

Rogers, C. R. (1980). *A way of being.* Boston: Houghton Mifflin.

Rogers, C. R., & Truax, C. B. (1967). The therapeutic conditions antecedent to change: A theoretical view. In C. R. Rogers (Ed.), *The therapeutic relationship and its impact.* Madison: University of Wisconsin Press.

Rosenzweig, S. (1936). Some implicit common factors in diverse methods in psychotherapy. *American Journal of Orthopsychiatry, 6,* 412–415.

Russo, N. F. (1990). Overview: Forging research priorities for women's mental health. *American Psychologist, 45* (3), 368–373.

Rutter, P. (1989). *Sex in the forbidden zone.* Los Angeles: Jeremy Tarcher.

Sachs, M. L., & Buffone, C. W. (Eds.) (1984). *Running as therapy.* Lincoln: University of Nebraska Press.

Sampson, J. P., Jr. (1983). Computer-assisted testing and assessment: Current status and implications for the future. *Measurement and Evaluation in Guidance, 15,* 293–299.

Sampson, J. P., Jr., Shahnasarian, M., & Reardon, R. C. (1987). Computer-assisted career guidance: A national perspective on the use of DISCOVER and SIGI. *Journal of Counseling and Development, 65,* 416–419.

Sanford, L. T., & Donovan, M. E. (1985). *Women and self-esteem.* New York: Penguin Books.

Sartre, J.-P. (1957). *Existentialism and human emotions.* New York: The Wisdom Library.

Satir, V. (1972). *Peoplemaking.* Palo Alto, CA: Science and Behavior Books.

Schafer, C. (1990a, March 1). Ethics, dual relationships come under scrutiny. *Guidepost,* pp. 2–3.

Schafer, C. (1990b, August 19). Reporting child abuse: Dilemmas and grey areas explored. *Guidepost,* p. 1.

Schaie, K. W. (1988). Ageism in psychological research. *American Psychologist, 43* (3), 179–188.

Scher, M., & Good, G. E. (1990). Gender and counseling in the twenty-first century: What does the future hold? *Journal of Counseling and Development, 68* (4), 388–391.

Schlaadt, R. G., & Shannon, P. T. (1982). *Drugs of choice.* Englewood Cliffs, NJ: Prentice-Hall.

Schlossberg, N. K. (1984). *Counseling adults in transition.* New York: Springer.

Schlossberg, N. K., & Kent, L. (1979). Effective helping in women. In S. Eisenberg & L. E. Patterson (Eds.), *Helping clients with special concerns* (pp. 263–286). Chicago: Rand McNally.

Schlossberg, N. K., & Pietrofesa, J. (1973). Perspectives on counseling bias: Implications for counselor education. *Counseling Psychologist, 4,* 44–54.

Schofield, W. (1964). *Psychotherapy: The purchase of friendship.* Englewood Cliffs, NJ: Prentice-Hall.

Schultz, D. P. (1960). *A history of modern psychology.* New York: Academic Press.

Seligman, L. (1990). *Selecting effective treatments.* San Francisco: Jossey-Bass.

Seligman, M. (1983). Sources of psychological disturbance among siblings of handicapped children. *Personnel and Guidance Journal 61,* 529–531.

Sell, J. M., Gottlieb, M. C., & Schoenfeld, L. (1986). Ethical consideration of social/romantic relationships with present and former clients. *Professional Psychology, 17* (6), 504–508.

Sexton, T. L., & Whiston, S. C. (1991). A review of the empirical basis for counseling: Implications for practice and training. *Counselor Education & Supervision, 30,* 330–354.

Shannon, J. W., & Woods, W. J. (1991). Affirmative psychotherapy for gay men. *Counseling Psychologist, 19,* 197–215.

Shedler, J., & Block, J. (1990). Adolescent drug use and psychological health: A longitudinal inquiry. *American Psychologist, 45,* 612–630.

Shertzer, B., & Linden, J. (1979). *Fundamentals of individual appraisal. Assessment techniques for counselors.* Boston: Houghton Mifflin.

Shertzer, B., & Stone, S. (1980). *Fundamentals of counseling.* Boston: Houghton Mifflin.

Siegel, J. C., & Sell, J. M. (1978). Effects of objective evidence of expertness and nonverbal behavior on client perceived expertness. *Journal of Counseling Psychology, 25,* 188–192.

Sifneos, P. (1967). Two different kinds of psychotherapy of short duration. *American Journal of Psychiatry, 123,* 1069–1073.

Simon, G. M. (1991). Theoretical eclecticism: A goal we are obligated to pursue. *Journal of Mental Health Counseling, 13,* 112–118.

Singer, P. (1981). *The expanding circle: Ethics and sociobiology.* New York: New American Library.

Skinner, B. F. (1938). *The behavior of organisms: An experimental analysis.* New York: Appleton-Century-Crofts.

Skinner, B. F. (1953). *Science and human behavior.* New York: Macmillan.

Skinner, B. F. (1983). Intellectual self-management in old age. *American Psychologist, 38,* 239–244.

Smith, D. S. (1982). Trends in counseling and psychotherapy. *American Psychologist, 37,* 802–809.

Smith, M. C., & Glass, G. V. (1977). Meta-analysis of psychotherapy outcome studies. *American Psychologist, 32,* 752–761.

Smith, M. C., Glass, G. V., & Miller, T. J. (1980). *The benefits of psychotherapy.* Baltimore: Johns Hopkins University Press.

Snowden, L. R., & Cheung, F. K. (1990). Use of inpatient mental health services by members of ethnic minority groups. *American Psychologist, 45* (3), 347–355.

Snyderman, M., & Rothman, S. (1987). Survey of expert opinion on intelligence and aptitude testing. *American Psychologist, 42,* 137–144.

Spicuzza, F. J., & Devoe, M. W. (1982). Burnout in the helping professions: Mutual aid groups as self-help. *Personnel and Guidance Journal, 61,* 95–99.

Spitzer, R. L., Skodol, A. E., Gibbon, M., & Williams, J. (1981). *DSM-III case book.* Washington, DC: American Psychiatric Association.

Stadler, H. A. (1990). Confidentiality. In B. Herlihy & L. B. Golden (Eds.), *Ethical standards casebook* (4th ed.). Alexandria, VA: American Association for Counseling and Development.

Stanton, M. D. (1981). One integrated structural/strategic approach to family therapy. *Journal of Marital and Family Therapy, 427–439.*

Stein, H. (1982). *Ethics (and other liabilities).* New York: St. Martin's Press.

Strong, S. R. (1968). Counseling: An interpersonal influence process. *Journal of Counseling Psychology, 15, 215–224.*

Strong, S. R., & Claiborn, C. D. (1982). *Change through interaction.* New York: Wiley-Interscience.

Strong, S. R., & Dixon, D. N. (1971). Expertness, attractiveness, and influence in counseling. *Journal of Counseling Psychology, 18, 562–570.*

Strong, S. R., & Schmidt, L. D. (1970). Expertness influence in counseling. *Journal of Counseling Psychology, 17, 81–87.*

Strupp, H. (1973). On the basic ingredients of psychotherapy. *Journal of Consulting and Clinical Psychology, 41* (1), 1–8.

Strupp, H. (1989). Can the practitioner learn from the researcher? *American Psychologist, 44* (4), 717–724.

Strupp, H. H., & Binder, J. L. (1984). *Psychotherapy in a new key.* New York: Basic Books.

Strupp, H. H., & Hadley, W. S. (1977). A tripartite model of mental health and therapeutic outcome. *American Psychologist, 32, 187–197.*

Stuart, R. B. (1970). *Trick or treatment: How and when psychotherapy fails.* Champaign, IL.: Research Press.

Sue, D. W. (1981). *Counseling the culturally different.* New York: Wiley.

Sue, S. (1977). Community health services to minority groups: Some optimism, some pessimism. *American Psychologist, 32, 616–624.*

Sue, S. (1983). Ethnic minority issues in psychology. *American Psychologist, 38, 583–592.*

Sue, S., & Zane, N. (1987). The role of culture and cultural techniques in psychotherapy: A critique and reformulation. *American Psychologist, 42* (1), 37–45.

Super, D. E. (1953). A theory of vocational development. *American Psychologist, 8, 185–190.*

Super, D. E. (1954). Career patterns as a basis for vocational counseling. *Journal of Counseling Psychology, 1, 12–19.*

Super, D. E. (1957). *The psychology of careers.* New York: Harper & Row.

Sweeney, T. J. (1989). *Adlerian counseling: A practical approach for a new decade* (3rd ed.). Muncie, IN: Accelerated Development.

Swensen, C. H. (1983). A respectable old age. *American Psychologist, 38, 327–334.*

Talbutt, L. C. (1981). Ethical standards: Assets and limitations. *Personnel and Guidance Journal, 60, 110–112.*

Talbutt, L. C. (1983). Recent court decisions: A quiz for APGA members. *Personnel and Guidance Journal, 61* (6), 355–357.

Talbutt, L. C. (1988). Ethics and computer usage: Hidden answers for school counselors. *The School Counselor, 35* (3), 199–203.

Task Force on Prescription Drugs. (1968). *The drug users.* Washington, DC: U. S. Government Printing Office.

Taylor, B., & Wagner, M. (1976). Sex between therapist and clients: A review and analysis. *Professional Psychology, 7, 593–601.*

Temerlin, M. K. (1968). Suggestion effects in psychiatric diagnosis. *Journal of Nervous and Mental Disease, 147, 349–353.*

Terkel, S. (1972). *Working.* New York: Avon.

Thoits, P. A. (1986). Multiple identities: Examining gender and marital status differences in distress. *American Sociological Review, 51,* 259–272.

Thomas, A. H., & Stewart, N. R. (1971). Counselor response to female clients wlth deviate and conforming career goals. *Journal of Counseling Psychology, 18,* 352–357.

Thomas, L. (1979). *The medusa and the snail.* New York: Viking.

Thompson, C. (1950). *Psychoanalysis: Evolution and development.* New York: Grove Press.

Thoresen, C. E. (1969). The counselor as an applied behavioral scientist. *Personnel and Guidance Journal, 47,* 841–848.

Thoresen, C. E., & Mahoney, M. J. (1974). *Behavioral self-control.* New York: Holt, Rinehart & Winston.

Thorne, F. C. (1950). *The principles of personal counseling.* Brandon, VT: Clinical Psychology Publishing.

Thorne, F. C. (1967). *Integrative psychology.* Brandon, VT: Clinical Psychology Publishing.

Tiedeman, D. V., & O'Hara, R. P. (1963). *Career development: Choice and adjustment.* New York: College Entrance Examination Board.

Tinsley, H. E., & Bradley, R. W. (1986). Test interpretation. *Journal of Counseling and Development, 64,* 462–466.

Toffler, A. (1970). *Future shock.* New York: Bantam Books.

Tolliver, L. M. (1983). Social and mental health needs of the aged. *American Psychologist, 38,* 316–318.

Tramel, D. (1981). A lesson from the physicists. *Personnel and Guidance Journal, 59,* 425–429.

Troll, L. (1975). *Early and middle adulthood.* Pacific Grove, CA: Brooks/Cole.

Trotzer, J. P. (1979). Developmental tasks in group counseling: The basis for structure. *Journal for Specialists in Group Work, 4,* 177–185.

Trotzer, J. P. (1989). *The counselor and the group* (2nd ed.). Pacific Grove, CA: Brooks/Cole.

Truax, C. B. (1963). Effective ingredients in psychotherapy: An approach to unraveling the patient–therapist interaction. *Journal of Counseling Psychology, 10,* 256–263.

Truax, C. B., & Carkhuff, R. R. (1965). The experimental manipulation of therapeutic conditions. *Journal of Consulting Psychology, 29,* 119–124.

Truax, C. B., & Carkhuff, R. R. (1967). *Toward effective counseling and psychotherapy.* Chicago: Aldine.

Turkington, C. (1984, January). Ideology affects approach taken to alleviate PMS. *APA Monitor,* pp. 28–29.

Tyler, L. (1970). Thoughts about theory. In W. H. Van Hoose & J. J. Pietrofesa (Eds.), *Counseling and guidance in the twentieth century* (pp. 298–305). Boston: Houghton Mifflin.

Tyler, L. E. (1984). What tests don't measure. *Journal of Counseling and Development, 63,* 48–50.

Umbarger, C. C. (1983). *Structural family therapy.* New York: Grune & Stratton.

Van Hesteren, F., & Ivey, A. E. (1990). Counseling and development: Toward a new identity for a profession in transition. *Journal of Counseling and Development, 68,* 524–528.

Van Hoose, W. H., & Kottler, J. A. (1985). *Ethical and legal issues in counseling and psychotherapy* (2nd ed.). San Francisco: Jossey-Bass.

Vash, C. (1981). *The psychology of disability.* New York: Springer.

Vriend, J., & Kottler, J. A. (1980). Initial interview checklist increases counselor effectiveness. *Canadian Counsellor, 14* (3), 153–155.

Vroman, C. S., & Bloom, J. W. (1991, March 14). A summary of counselor credentialing legislature. *Guidepost,* pp. 17–22.

Wachtel, P. (1977). *Psychoanalysis and behavior therapy: Toward an integration.* New York: Basic Books.

Wachtel, P. (1987). *Action and insight*. New York: Guilford Press.

Wagner, E. E. (1987). A review of the 1985 standards for educational and psychological testing: User responsibility and social justice. *Journal of Counseling and Development. 66*, 202–203.

Wallace, M. E. (1982). A common base for psychotherapy and family therapy. *Psychotherapy: Theory, Research, and Practice, 19*, 297–306.

Walsh, W. B., & Betz, N. E. (1985). *Tests and assessment*. Englewood Cliffs, NJ: Prentice-Hall.

Warnath, C. F. (1989). We are all TAPS (temporarily able persons). *Journal of Counseling and Development, 67*, 518–519.

Wass, H ., & Myers, J. E. (1982). Psychosocial aspects of death among the elderly: A review of the literature. *Personnel and Guidance Journal, 61*, 131–137.

Waters, E. B., & Goodman, J. (1990). *Empowering older adults*. San Francisco: Jossey-Bass.

Watkins, C. E., Lopez, F. G., Campbell, V. L., & Himmell, C. D. (1986). Contemporary counseling psychology: Results of a national survey. *Journal of Counseling Psychology, 33*, 301–309.

Watson, J. B., & Rayner, R. (1920). Conditioned emotional reactions. *Journal of Experimental Psychology, 3*, 1–14.

Watzlawick, P., Weakland, J. H., & Fisch, R. (1974). *Change: Principles of problem formation and problem resolution*. New York: Norton.

Weil, A. (1972). *The natural mind*. Boston: Houghton Mifflin.

Weinstein, E., & Rosen, E. (1988). *Sexuality counseling. Issues and implications*. Pacific Grove, CA: Brooks/Cole.

Weissman, M., & Klerman, G. (1977). Sex differences in epidemiology of depression. *Archives of General Psychiatry, 34*, 98–111.

Weltner, J. (1988, May/June). Different strokes: A pragmatist's guide to intervention. *The Family Therapy Networker*, pp. 53–57.

West, J. D., Hosie, T. W., & Zarski, J. J. (1987). Family dynamics and substance abuse: A preliminary study. *Journal of Counseling and Development, 65*, 487–490 .

Westerman, M. A. (1989). A naturalized view of the role played by insight in psychotherapy. *Journal of Integrative and Eclectic Psychotherapy, 8* (3), 197–221 .

White, L. C. (1980). Competences counselor educators value. *Personnel and Guidance Journal, 59*, 31–36.

White, T. H. (1939). *The once and future king*. New York: Berkley Books.

Whitehorn, J., & Betz, B. (1954). A study of psychotherapeutic relationships between physicians and schizophrenic patients. *American Journal of Psychiatry, 3*, 321–331.

Whiteley, J. M. (1980a). Counseling psychology in the year 2000 A.D. *Counseling Psychologist, 8*, 2–16.

Whiteley, J. M. (1980b). *History of counseling psychology*. Washington, DC: AACD Press.

Whiteley, J. M., & Fretz, B. R. (1980). *The present and future of counseling psychology*. Washington, DC: AACD Press.

Whiteley, J. M., & Resnikoff, A. (1978). *Career counseling*. Pacific Grove, CA: Brooks/Cole.

Wiener, E. A., & Stewart, B. J. (1984). *Assessing individuals*. Boston: Little, Brown.

Wilcoxon, S. A. (1989). Contemporary developments in marital and family therapy. *Family Therapy, 16* (1), 87–95.

Williams, J. B. W., & Spitzer, R. L. (1983). The issue of sex bias in DSM-III. *American Psychologist*, 793–798.

Williamson, E. G. (1939). *How to counsel students: A manual for clinical counselors*. New York: McGraw-Hill.

Williamson, E. G. (1950). *Counseling adolescents*. New York: McGraw-Hill.

Williamson, E. G., & Biggs, D. A. (1979). Trait-factor theory and individual differences. In H. M. Burks & B. Stefflre, *Theories of counseling* (3rd ed.). New York: McGraw-Hill.

Wilson, E. O. (1978). *On human nature.* New York: Bantam Books.

Wise, R. A. (1988). The neurobiology of craving: Implications for the understanding and treatment of addiction. *Journal of Abnormal Psychology, 97,* 118–132.

Wolberg, L. R. (1967). *The technique of psychotherapy.* New York: Grune & Stratton.

Wolpe, J. (1958). *Psychotherapy by reciprocal inhibition.* Stanford, CA: Stanford University Press.

Wolpe, J. (1969). *The practice of behavior therapy.* Elmsford, NY: Pergamon Press.

Wolpe, J. (1982). *The practice of behavior therapy* (2nd ed.). Elmsford, NY: Pergamon Press.

Woody, J. D. (1990). Resolving ethical concerns in clinical practice: Toward a pragmatic model. *Journal of Marital and Family Therapy, 16* (2), 133–150.

Woody, R. H. (1984). *The law and the practice of human services.* San Francisco: Jossey-Bass.

Woody, R. H. (1988). *Protecting your mental health practice: How to minimize legal and financial risk.* San Francisco: Jossey-Bass.

Woody, R. H., Hansen, J. C., & Rossberg, R. H. (1989). *Counseling psychology: Strategies and services.* Pacific Grove, CA: Brooks/Cole.

Yalom, I. (1980). *Existential psychotherapy.* New York: Basic Books.

Yalom, I. (1985). *The theory and practice of group psychotherapy* (3rd ed.). New York: Basic Books.

Yalom, I. (1989). *Love's executioner and other tales of psychotherapy.* New York: Basic Books.

Zeig, J. K. (1986). The evolution of psychotherapy—Fundamental issues. In J. K. Zeig (Ed.), *The evolution of psychotherapy.* New York: Brunner/Mazel.

Zucker, R. A., & Gomberg, E. S. L. (1986). Etiology of alcoholism reconsidered: The case for a biopsychosocial process. *American Psychologist, 41,* 783–793.

ETHICAL STANDARDS, AMERICAN ASSOCIATION FOR COUNSELING AND DEVELOPMENT

PREAMBLE

The Association is an educational, scientific, and professional organization whose members are dedicated to the enhancement of the worth, dignity, potential, and uniqueness of each individual and thus to the service of society.

The Association recognizes that the role definitions and work settings of its members include a wide variety of academic disciplines, levels of academic preparation, and agency services. This diversity reflects the breadth of the Association's interest and influence. It also poses challenging complexities in efforts to set standards for the performance of members, desired requisite preparation or practice, and supporting social, legal, and ethical controls.

The specification of ethical standards enables the Association to clarify to present and future members and to those served by members the nature of ethical responsibilities held in common by its members.

The existence of such standards serves to stimulate greater concern by members for their own professional functioning and for the conduct of fellow professionals such as counselors, guidance and student personnel workers, and others in the helping professions. As the ethical code of the Association, this document establishes principles that define the ethical behavior of Association members. Additional ethical guidelines developed by the Association's Divisions for their speciality areas may further define a member's ethical behavior.

Section A: General

1. The member influences the development of the profession by continuous efforts to improve professional practices, teaching, services, and research. Professional growth is continuous throughout the member's career and is exemplified by the development of a philosophy that explains why and how a member functions in the helping relationship. Members must gather data on their effectiveness and be guided by the findings. Members recognize the need for continuing education to ensure competent service.

2. The member has a responsibility both to the individual who is served and to the institution within which the service is performed to maintain high standards of professional conduct. The member strives to maintain the highest levels of professional services offered to the individuals to be served. The member also strives to assist the agency, organization, or institution in providing the highest caliber of professional services. The acceptance of employment in an institution implies that the member is in agreement with the general policies and principles of the institution. Therefore the professional activities of the member are also in accord with the objectives of the institution. If, despite concerted efforts, the member cannot reach agreement with the employer as to acceptable standards of conduct that allow for changes in institutional policy conducive to the positive growth and development of clients, then terminating the affiliation should be seriously considered.

3. Ethical behavior among professional associates, both members and nonmembers, must be expected at all times. When information is possessed that raises doubt as to the ethical behavior of professional colleagues, whether Association members or not, the member must take action to attempt to rectify such a condition. Such action shall use the institution's channels first and then use procedures established by the Association.

4. The member neither claims nor implies professional qualifications exceeding those possessed and is responsible for correcting any misrepresentations of these qualifications by others.

5. In establishing fees for professional counseling services, members must consider the financial status of clients and locality. In the event that the established fee structure is inappropriate for a client. assistance must be provided in finding comparable services of acceptable cost.

6. When members provide information to the public or to subordinates, peers, or supervisors, they have a responsibility to ensure that the content is general, unidentified client information that is accurate, unbiased, and consists of objective, factual data.

7. Members recognize their boundaries of competence and provide only those services and use only those techniques for which they are qualified by training or experience. Members should only accept those positions for which they are professionally qualified.

8. In the counseling relationship, the counselor is aware of the intimacy of the relationship and maintains respect for the client and avoids engaging in activities that seek to meet the counselor's personal needs at the expense of that client.

9. Members do not condone or engage in sexual harassment which is defined as deliberate or repeated comments, gestures, or physical contacts of a sexual nature.

10. The member avoids bringing personal issues into the counseling relationship, especially if the potential for harm is present. Through awareness of the negative impact of both racial and sexual stereotyping and discrimination, the counselor guards the individual rights and personal dignity of the client in the counseling relationship.

11. Products or services provided by the member by means of classroom instruction, public lectures, demonstrations, written articles, radio or television programs, or other types of media must meet the criteria cited in these Standards.

Section B:
Counseling Relationship

This section refers to practices and procedures of individual and/or group counseling relationships.

The member must recognize the need for client freedom of choice. Under those circumstances where this is not possible, the member must apprise clients of restrictions that may limit their freedom of choice.

1. The member's primary obligation is to respect the integrity and promote the welfare of the client(s), whether the client(s) is (are) assisted individually or in a group relationship. In a group setting, the member is also responsible for taking reasonable precautions to protect individuals from physical and/or psychological trauma resulting from interaction within the group.

2. Members make provisions for maintaining confidentiality in the storage and disposal of records and follow an established record retention and disposition policy. The counseling relationship and information resulting therefrom must kept confidential, consistent with the obligations of the member as a professional person. In a group counseling setting, the counselor must set a norm of confidentiality regarding all group participants' disclosures.

3. If an individual is already in a counseling relationship with another professional person, the member does not enter into a counseling relationship without first contacting and receiving approval of that other professional. If the member discovers that the client is in another counseling relationship after the counseling relationship begins, the member must gain the consent of the other professional or terminate the relationship unless the client elects to terminate the other relationship.

4. When the client's condition indicates that there is clear and imminent danger to the client or others, the member must take reasonable personal action or inform responsible authorities. Consultation with other professionals must be used where possible. The assumption of responsibility for the client's(s') behavior must be taken only after careful deliberation. The client must be involved in resumption of responsibility as quickly as possible.

5. Records of the counseling relationship, including interview notes, test data, correspondence tape recordings, electronic data storage, and other documents are to be considered professional information for use in counseling and they should not be considered a part of the records of the institution or agency in which the counselor is employed unless specified by state statute or regulation. Revelation to others of counseling material must occur only upon the expressed consent of the client.

6. In view of the extensive data storage and processing capacities of the computer, the member must ensure that data maintained on a computer is: (a)

limited to information that is appropriate and necessary for the services
being provided; (b) destroyed after it
is determined that the information is
no longer of any value in providing
services; and (c) restricted in terms of
access to appropriate staff members
involved in the provision of service
by using the best computer security
methods available.

7. Use of data derived from a counseling relationship for purposes of
counselor training or research shall
be confined to content that can be
disguised to ensure full protection of
the identity of the subject client.

8. The member must inform the client
of the purposes, goals, techniques,
rules of procedures and limitations
that may affect the relationship at or
before the time that the counseling
relationship is entered. When working with minors or persons who are
unable to give consent, the member
protects these clients' best interests.

9. In view of common misconceptions
related to the perceived inherent
validity of computer generated data
and narrative reports, the member
must ensure that the client is provided with information as part of the
counseling relationship that adequately explains the limitations of
computer technology.

10. The member must screen prospective
group participants, especially when
the emphasis is on self-understanding and growth through self-disclosure. The member must maintain an
awareness of the group participants'
compatibility throughout the life of
the group.

11. The member may choose to consult
with any other professionally competent person about a client. In choosing a consultant, the member must
avoid placing the consultant in a conflict of interest situation that would
preclude the consultant's being a

proper party to the member's efforts
to help the client.

12. If the member determines an inability
to be of professional assistance to the
client, the member must either avoid
initiating the counseling relationship
or immediately terminate that relationship. In either event, the member
must suggest appropriate alternatives.
(The member must be knowledgeable
about referral resources so that a satisfactory referral can be initiated.) In the
event the client declines the suggested
referral, the member is not obligated
to continue the relationship.

13. When the member has other relationships, particularly of an administrative, supervisory, and/or evaluative
nature with an individual seeking
counseling services, the member must
not serve as the counselor but should
refer the individual to another professional. Only in instances where such
an alternative is unavailable and
where the individual's situation war-
rants counseling intervention should
the member enter into and/or maintain a counseling relationship. Dual
relationships with clients that might
impair the members objectivity and
professional judgement (e.g., as close
friends or relatives) must be avoided
and/or the counseling relationship
terminated through referral to another competent professional.

14. The member will avoid any type of
sexual intimacies with clients. Sexual
relationships with clients are unethical.

15. All experimental methods of treatment must be clearly indicated to
prospective recipients, and safety
precautions are to be adhered to by
the member.

16. When computer applications are
used as a component of counseling
services, the member must ensure
that: (a) the client is intellectually,
emotionally, and physically capable
of using the computer application;

(b) the computer application is appropriate for the needs of the client; (c) the client understands the purpose and operation of the computer application; and (d) a follow-up of client use of a computer application is provided to both correct possible problems (misconceptions or inappropriate use) and assess subsequent needs.

17. When the member is engaged in short-term group treatment/training programs (e.g., marathons and other encounter-type or growth groups), the member ensures that there is professional assistance available during and following the group experience.

18. Should the member be engaged in a work setting that calls for any variation from the above statements, the member is obligated to consult with other professionals whenever possible to consider justifiable alternatives.

19. The member must ensure that members of various ethnic, racial, religious, disability, and socioeconomic groups have equal access to computer applications used to support counseling services and that the content of available computer applications does not discriminate against the groups described above.

20. When computer applications are developed by the member for use by the general public as self-help stand-alone computer software, the member must ensure that: (a) self-help computer applications are designed from the beginning to function in a stand-alone manner, as opposed to modifying software that was originally designed to require support from a counselor; (b) self-help computer applications will include within the program statements regarding intended user outcomes. suggestions for using the software, a description of the conditions under which self-help computer applications might

not be appropriate, and a description of when and how counseling services might be beneficial; and (c) the manual for such applications will include the qualifications of the developer, the development process, validation data, and operating procedures.

Section C:
Measurement and Evaluation

The primary purpose of educational and psychological testing is to provide descriptive measures that are objective and interpretable in either comparable or absolute terms. The member must recognize the need to interpret the statements that follow as applying to the whole range of appraisal techniques including test and nontest data. Test results constitute only one of a variety of pertinent sources of information for personnel, guidance, and counseling decisions.

1. The member must provide specific orientation or information to the examinee(s) prior to and following the test administration so that the results of testing may be placed in proper perspective with other relevant factors. In so doing, the member must recognize the effects of socioeconomic, ethnic, and cultural factors on test scores. It is the member's professional responsibility to use additional unvalidated information carefully in modifying interpretation of the test results.

2. In selecting tests for use in a given situation with a particular client, the member must consider carefully the specific validity, reliability, and appropriateness of the test(s). General validity, reliability, and related issues may be questioned legally as well as ethically when tests are used for vocational and educational selection, placement, or counseling.

3. When making any statements to the

public about tests and testing, the member must give accurate information and avoid false claims or misconceptions. Special efforts are often required to avoid unwarranted connotations of such terms as IQ and grade equivalent scores.

4. Different tests demand different levels of competence for administration, scoring, and interpretation. Members must recognize the limits of their competence and perform only those functions for which they are prepared. In particular, members using computer-based test interpretations must be trained in the construct being measured and the specific instrument being used prior to using this type of computer application.

5. In situations where a computer is used for test administration and scoring, the member is responsible for ensuring that administration and scoring programs function properly to provide clients with accurate test results.

6. Tests must be administered under the same conditions that were established in their standardization. When tests are not administered under standard conditions or when unusual behavior or irregularities occur during the testing session, those conditions must be noted and the results designated as invalid or of questionable validity. Unsupervised or inadequately supervised test-taking, such as the use of tests through the mails, is considered unethical. On the other hand, the use of instruments that are so designed or standardized to be self-administered and self-scored, such as interest inventories, is to be encouraged.

7. The meaningfulness of test results used in personnel, guidance, and counseling functions generally depends on the examinee's unfamiliarity with the specific items on the test. Any prior coaching or dissemina-

tion of the test materials can invalidate test results. Therefore, test security is one of the professional obligations of the member. Conditions that produce most favorable test results must be made known to the examinee.

8. The purpose of testing and the explicit use of the results must be made known to the examinee prior to testing. The counselor must ensure that instrument limitations are not exceeded and that periodic review and/or retesting are made to prevent client stereotyping.

9. The examinee's welfare and explicit prior understanding must be the criteria for determining the recipients of the test results. The member must see that specific interpretation accompanies any release of individual or group test data. The interpretation of test data must be related to the examinee's particular concerns.

10. Members responsible for making decisions based on test results have an understanding of educational and psychological measurement, validation criteria, and test research.

11. The member must be cautious when interpreting the results of research instruments possessing insufficient technical data. The specific purposes for the use of such instruments must be stated explicitly to examinees.

12. The member must proceed with caution when attempting to evaluate and interpret the performance of minority group members or other persons who are not represented in the norm group on which the instrument was standardized.

13. When computer-based test interpretations are developed by the member to support the assessment process, the member must ensure that the validity of such interpretations is established prior to the commercial distribution of such a computer application.

14. The member recognizes that test results may become obsolete. The member will avoid and prevent the misuse of obsolete test results.

15. The member must guard against the appropriation, reproduction, or modification of published tests or parts thereof without acknowledgement and permission from the previous publisher.

Section D:
Research and Publication

1. Guidelines on research with human subjects shall be adhered to, such as:
   a. Ethical Principles in the Conduct of Research with Human Participants, Washington, D.C.: American Psychological Association, Inc., 1982.
   b. Code of Federal Regulation, Title 45, Subtitle A, Part 46, as currently issued.
   c. *Ethical Principles of Psychologists,* American Psychological Association, Principle #9: Research with Human Participants.
   d. Family Educational Rights and Privacy Act ("the Buckley Amendment").
   e. Current federal regulations and various state rights privacy acts.

2. In planning any research activity dealing with human subjects, the member must be aware of and responsive to all pertinent ethical principles and ensure that the research problem, design, and execution are in full compliance with them.

3. Responsibility for ethical research practice lies with the principal researcher, while others involved in the research activities share ethical obligation and full responsibility for their own actions.

4. In research with human subjects, researchers are responsible for the subjects' welfare throughout the experiment, and they must take all reasonable precautions to avoid causing injurious psychological, physical, or social effects on their subjects.

5. All research subjects must be informed of the purpose of the study except when withholding information or providing misinformation to them is essential to the investigation. In such research the member must be responsible for corrective action as soon as possible following completion of the research.

6. Participation in research must be voluntary. Involuntary participation is appropriate only when it can be demonstrated that participation will have no harmful effects on subjects and is essential to the investigation.

7. When reporting research results, explicit mention must be made of all variables and conditions known to the investigator that might affect the outcome of the investigation or the interpretation of the data.

8. The member must be responsible for conducting and reporting investigations in a manner that minimizes the possibility that results will be misleading.

9. The member has an obligation to make available sufficient original research data to qualified others who may wish to replicate the study.

10. When supplying data, aiding in the research of another person, reporting research results, or making original data available, due care must be taken to disguise the identity of the subjects in the absence of specific authorization from such subjects to do otherwise.

11. When conducting and reporting research, the member must be familiar with and give recognition to previous work on the topic, as well as to observe all copyright laws and follow the principles of giving full credit to all to whom credit is due.

12. The member must give due credit through joint authorship, acknowledgement, footnote statements, or other appropriate means to those who have contributed significantly to the research and/or publication, in accordance with such contributions.

13. The member must communicate to other members the results of any research judged to be of professional or scientific value. Results reflecting unfavorably on institutions, programs, services, or vested interests must not be withheld for such reasons.

14. If members agree to cooperate with another individual in research and/or publication, they incur an obligation to cooperate as promised in terms of punctuality of performance and with full regard to the completeness and accuracy of the information required.

15. Ethical practice requires that authors not submit the same manuscript or one essentially similar in content for simultaneous publication consideration by two or more journals. In addition, manuscripts published in whole or in substantial part in another journal or published work should not be submitted for publication without acknowledgement and permission from the previous publication.

Section E: Consulting

Consultation refers to a voluntary relationship between a professional helper and help-needing individual, group, or social unit in which the consultant is providing help to the client(s) in defining and solving a work-related problem or potential problem with a client or client system.

1. The member acting as consultant must have a high degree of self-awareness of his/her own values, knowledge, skills, limitations, and needs in entering a helping relationship that involves human and/or organizational change and that the focus of the relationship be on the issues to be resolved and not on the person(s) presenting the problem.

2. There must be understanding and agreement between member and client for the problem definition, change of goals, and prediction of consequences of interventions selected.

3. The member must be reasonably certain that she/he or the organization represented has the necessary competencies and resources for giving the kind of help that is needed now or may be needed later and that appropriate referral resources are available to the consultant.

4. The consulting relationship must be one in which client adaptability and growth toward self-direction are encouraged and cultivated. The member must maintain this role consistently and not become a decision maker for the client or create a future dependency on the consultant.

5. When announcing consultant availability for services, the member conscientiously adheres to the Association's Ethical Standards.

6. The member must refuse a private fee or other remuneration for consultation with persons who are entitled to these services through the member's employing institution or agency. The policies of a particular agency may make explicit provisions for private practice with agency clients by members of its staff. In such instances, the clients must be apprised of other options open to them should they seek private counseling services.

Section F: Private Practice

1. The member should assist the profession by facilitating the availability of counseling services in private as well as public settings.

2. In advertising services as a private practitioner the member must advertise the services in a manner that accurately informs the public of professional services, expertise, and techniques of counseling available. A member who assumes an executive leadership role in the organization shall not permit his/her name to be used in professional notices during periods when he/she is not actively engaged in the private practice of counseling.

3. The member may list the following: highest relevant degree, type and level of certification and/or license, address, telephone number, office hours, type and/or description of services, and other relevant information. Such information must not contain false, inaccurate, misleading, partial, out-of-context, or deceptive material or statements.

4. Members do not present their affiliation with any organization in such a way that would imply inaccurate sponsorship or certification by that organization.

5. Members may join in partnership/corporation with other members and/or other professionals provided that each member of the partnership or corporation makes clear the separate specialties by name in compliance with the regulations of the locality.

6. A member has an obligation to withdraw from a counseling relationship if it is believed that employment will result in violation of the Ethical Standards. If the mental or physical condition of the member renders it difficult to carry out an effective professional relationship or if the member is discharged by the client because the counseling relationship is no longer productive for the client, then the member is obligated to terminate the counseling relationship.

7. A member must adhere to the regulations for private practice of the locality where the services are offered.

8. It is unethical to use one's institutional affiliation to recruit clients for one's private practice.

Section G:
Personnel Administration

It is recognized that most members are employed in public or quasi-public institutions. The functioning of a member within an institution must contribute to the goals of the institution and vice versa if either is to accomplish their respective goals or objectives. It is therefore essential that the member and the institution function in ways to: (a) make the institution's goals explicit and public; (b) make the member's contribution to institution's goals specific; and (c) foster mutual accountability for goal achievement.

To accomplish these objectives, it is recognized that the member and the employer must share responsibilities in the formulation and implementation of personnel policies.

1. Members must define and describe the parameters and levels of their professional competency.

2. Members must establish interpersonal relations and working agreements with supervisors and subordinates regarding counseling or clinical relationships, confidentiality, distinction between public and private material, maintenance and dissemination of recorded information, work load, and accountability. Working agreements in each instance must be specified and made known to those concerned.

3. Members must alert their employers to conditions that may be potentially disruptive or damaging.

4. Members must inform employers of conditions that may limit their effectiveness.

5. Members must submit regularly to professional review and evaluation.

6. Members must be responsible for in-

service development of self and/or staff.

7. Members must inform their staff of goals and programs.

8. Members must provide personnel practices that guarantee and enhance the rights and welfare of each recipient of their service.

9. Members must select competent persons and assign responsibilities compatible with their skills and experiences.

10. The member, at the onset of a counseling relationship, will inform the client of the member's intended use of supervisors regarding the disclosure of information concerning this case. The member will clearly inform the client of the limits of confidentiality in the relationship.

11. Members, as either employers or employees, do not engage in or condone practices that are inhumane, illegal, or unjustifiable (such as considerations based on sex, handicap, age, race) in hiring, promotion, or training.

Section H: Preparation Standards

Members who are responsible for training others must be guided by the preparation standards of the Association and relevant Division(s). The member who functions in the capacity of trainer assumes unique ethical responsibilities that frequently go beyond that of the member who does not function in a training capacity. These ethical responsibilities are outlined as follows:

1. Members must orient students to program expectations, basic skills development, and employment prospects prior to admission to the program.

2. Members in charge of learning experience must establish programs that integrate academic study and supervised practice.

3. Members must establish a program directed toward developing students'

skills, knowledge, and self-understanding, stated whenever possible in competency or performance terms.

4. Members must identify the levels of competencies of their students in compliance with relevant Division standards. These competencies must accommodate the paraprofessional as well as the professional.

5. Members, through continual student evaluation and appraisal, must be aware of the personal limitations of the learner that might impede future performance. The instructor must not only assist the learner in securing remedial assistance but also screen from the program those individuals who are unable to provide competent services.

6. Members must provide a program that includes training in research commensurate with levels of role functioning. Paraprofessional and technician-level personnel must be trained as consumers of research. In addition, personnel must learn how to evaluate their own and their program's effectiveness. Graduate training, especially at the doctoral level, would include preparation for original research by the member.

7. Members must make students aware of the ethical responsibilities and standards of the profession.

8. Preparatory programs must encourage students to value the ideals of service to individuals and to society. In this regard, direct financial remuneration or lack thereof must not influence the quality of service rendered. Monetary considerations must not be allowed to overshadow professional and humanitarian needs.

9. Members responsible for educational programs must be skilled as teachers and practitioners.

10. Members must present thoroughly varied theoretical positions so that students may make comparisons and have the opportunity to select a position.

11. Members must develop clear policies within their educational institutions regarding field placement and the roles of the student and the instructor in such placement.

12. Members must ensure that forms of learning focusing on self-understanding or growth are voluntary, or if required as part of the educational program, are made known to prospective students prior to entering the program. When the educational program offers a growth experience with an emphasis on self-disclosure or other relatively intimate or personal involvement, the member must have no administrative, supervisory, or evaluating authority regarding the participant.

13. The member will at all times provide students with clear and equally acceptable alternatives for self-understanding or growth experiences. The member will assure students that they have a right to accept these alternatives without prejudice or penalty.

14. Members must conduct an educational program in keeping with the current relevant guidelines of the Association.

ETHICAL PRINCIPLES OF PSYCHOLOGISTS, AMERICAN PSYCHOLOGICAL ASSOCIATION

PREAMBLE

Psychologists respect the dignity and worth of the individual and strive for the preservation and protection of fundamental human rights. They are committed to increasing knowledge of human behavior and of people's understanding of themselves and others and to the utilization of such knowledge for the promotion of human welfare. While pursuing these objectives, they make every effort to protect the welfare of those who seek their services and of the research participants that may be the object of study. They use their skills only for purposes consistent with these values and do not knowingly permit their misuse by others. While demanding for themselves freedom of inquiry and communication, psychologists accept the responsibility this freedom requires: competence, objectivity in the application of skills, and concern for the best interests of clients, colleagues, students, research participants, and society. In the pursuit of these ideals, psychologists subscribe to principles in the following areas: 1. Responsibility, 2. Competence, 3. Moral and Legal Standards, 4. Public Statements, 5. Confidentiality, 6. Welfare of the Consumer, 7. Professional Relationships, 8. Assessment Techniques, 9. Research With Human Participants, and 10. Care and Use of Animals.

Ethical Principles of Psychologists, by the American Psychological Association. Copyright 1989 by the American Psychological Association. Reprinted by permission of the publisher.

This version of the *Ethical Principles of Psychologists* was adopted by the American Psychological Association's Board of Directors on June 2, 1989. On that date, the Board of Directors rescinded several sections of the Ethical Principles that had been adopted by the APA Council of Representatives on January 24, 1981. Inquiries concerning the substance or interpretation of the *Ethical Principles of Psychologists* should be addressed to the Administrative Director, Office of Ethics, American Psychological Association, 1200 Seventeenth Street, N.W., Washington, DC 20036.

These Ethical Principles apply to psychologists, to students of psychology, and to others who do work of a psychological nature under the supervision of a psychologist. They are intended for the guidance of nonmembers of the Association who are engaged in psychological research or practice.

Acceptance of membership in the American Psychological Association commits the member to adherence to these principles.

Psychologists cooperate with duly constituted committees of the American Psychological Association, in particular, the Committee on Scientific and Professional Ethics and Conduct, by responding to inquiries promptly and completely. Members also respond promptly and completely to inquiries from duly constituted state association ethics committees and professional standards review committees.

Principle 1: Responsibility

In providing services, psychologists maintain the highest standards of their profession. They accept responsibility for the consequences of their acts and make every effort to ensure that their services are used appropriately.

a. As scientists, psychologists accept responsibility for the selection of their research topics and the methods used in investigation, analysis, and reporting. They plan their research in ways to minimize the possibility that their findings will be misleading. They provide thorough discussion of the limitations of their data, especially where their work touches on social policy or might be construed to the detriment of persons in specific age, sex, ethnic, socioeconomic, or other social groups. In publishing reports of their work, they never suppress disconfirming data, and they acknowledge the existence of alternative hypotheses and explanations of their findings. Psychologists take credit only for work they have actually done.

b. Psychologists clarify in advance with all appropriate persons and agencies the expectations for sharing and utilizing research data. They avoid relationships that may limit their objectivity or create a conflict of interest. Interference with the milieu in which data are collected is kept to a minimum.

c. Psychologists have the responsibility to attempt to prevent distortion, misuse, or suppression of psychological findings by the institution or agency of which they are employees.

d. As members of governmental or other organizational bodies, psychologists remain accountable as individuals to the highest standards of their profession.

e. As teachers, psychologists recognize their primary obligation to help others acquire knowledge and skill. They maintain high standards of scholarship by presenting psychological information objectively, fully, and accurately.

f. As practitioners, psychologists know that they bear a heavy social responsibility because their recommendations and professional actions may alter the lives of others. They are alert to personal, social, organizational, financial, or political situations and pressures that might lead to misuse of their influence.

Principle 2: Competence

The maintenance of high standards of competence is a responsibility shared by all psychologists in the interest of the public and the profession as a whole. Psychologists recognize the boundaries of their competence and the limitations of their techniques. They only provide services and only use techniques for which they are qualified by training and experience. In those areas in which recognized standards do not yet exist, psychologists take whatever precautions are necessary to protect the welfare of their clients. They maintain knowledge of current scientific and professional information related to the services they render.

a. Psychologists accurately represent their competence, education, training, and experience. They claim as evidence of educational qualifications only those degrees obtained from institutions acceptable under the By-laws and Rules of Council of the American Psychological Association.

b. As teachers, psychologists perform their duties on the basis of careful preparation so that their instruction is accurate, current, and scholarly.

c. Psychologists recognize the need for continuing education and are open to new procedures and changes in expectations and values over time.

d. Psychologists recognize differences among people such as those that may be associated with age, sex, socioeconomic, and ethnic backgrounds. When necessary, they obtain training, experience, or counsel to assure competent service or research relating to such persons.

e. Psychologists responsible for decisions involving individuals or policies based on test results have an understanding of psychological or educational measurement, validation problems, and test research.

f. Psychologists recognize that personal problems and conflicts may interfere with professional effectiveness. Accordingly, they refrain from undertaking any activity in which their personal problems are likely to lead to inadequate performance or harm to a client, colleague, student, or research participant. If engaged in such activity when they become aware of their personal problems, they seek competent professional assistance to determine whether they should suspend, terminate, or limit the scope of their professional and/or scientific activities.

Principle 3: Moral and Legal Standards

Psychologists' moral and ethical standards of behavior are a personal matter to the same degree as they are for any other citizen, except as these may compromise the fulfillment of their professional responsibilities or reduce the public trust in psychology and psychologists.

Regarding their own behavior, psychologists are sensitive to prevailing community standards and to the possible impact that conformity to or deviation from these standards may have upon the quality of their performance as psychologists. Psychologists are also aware of the possible impact of their public behavior upon the ability of colleagues to perform their professional duties.

a. As teachers, psychologists are aware of the fact that their personal values may affect the selection and presentation of instructional materials. When dealing with topics that may give offense, they recognize and respect the diverse attitudes that students may have toward such materials.

b. As employees or employers, psychologists do not engage in or condone practices that are inhumane or that result in illegal or unjustifiable actions. Such practices include, but are not limited to, those based on considerations of race, handicap, age, gender, sexual preference, religion or national origin in hiring, promotion, or training.

c. In their professional roles, psychologists avoid any action that will violate or diminish the legal and civil rights of clients or of others who may be affected by their actions.

d. As practitioners and researchers, psychologists act in accord with Association standards and guidelines related to practice and to the conduct of research with human beings and animals. In the ordinary course of events, psychologists adhere to relevant governmental laws and institutional regulations. When federal, state, provincial, organizational, or institutional laws, regulations, or practices are in conflict with Association standards and guidelines, psychologists make known their commitment to Association standards and guidelines and, wherever possible, work toward a resolution of the conflict. Both practitioners and researchers are concerned with the development of such legal and quasi-legal regulations as best serve the public interest, and they work toward changing existing regulations that are not beneficial to the public interest.

Principle 4: Public Statements

Public statements, announcements of services, advertising and promotional activities of psychologists serve the purpose of helping the public make informed judgments and choices. Psychologists represent accurately and objectively their professional qualifications, affiliations, and functions, as well as those of the institutions or organizations with which they or the statements may be associated. In public statements providing psychological information or professional opinions or providing information about the availability of psychological products, publications, and services, psychologists base their statements on scientifically acceptable psychological findings and techniques with full recognition of the limits and uncertainties of such evidence.

a. When announcing or advertising professional services, psychologists may list the following information to describe the provider and services provided: name, highest relevant academic degree earned from a regionally accredited institution, date, type, and level of certification or licensure, diplomate status, APA membership status, address, telephone number, office hours, a brief listing of the type of psychological services offered, an appropriate presentation of fee information, foreign languages spoken, and policy with regard to third-party payments. Additional relevant or important consumer information may be included if not prohibited by other sections of these Ethical Principles.

b. In announcing or advertising the availability of psychological products, publications, or services, psychologists do not present their affiliation with any organization in a manner that falsely implies sponsorship or certification by that organization. In particular and for example,

psychologists do not state APA membership or fellow status in a way to suggest that such status implies specialized professional competence or qualifications. Public statements include, but are not limited to, communication by means of periodical, book, list, directory, television, radio, or motion picture. They do not contain (i) a false, fraudulent, misleading, deceptive, or unfair statement; (ii) a misinterpretation of fact or a statement likely to mislead or deceive because in context it makes only a partial disclosure of relevant facts; (iii) a statement intended or likely to create false or unjustified expectations of favorable results.

c. Psychologists do not compensate or give anything of value to a representative of the press, radio, television, or other communication medium in anticipation of or in return for professional publicity in a news item. A paid advertisement must be identified as such, unless it is apparent from the context that it is a paid advertisement. If communicated to the public by use of radio or television, an advertisement is prerecorded and approved for broadcast by the psychologist, and a recording of the actual transmission is retained by the psychologist.

d. Announcements or advertisements of "personal growth groups," clinics, and agencies give a clear statement of purpose and a clear description of the experiences to be provided. The education, training, and experience of the staff members are appropriately specified.

e. Psychologists associated with the development or promotion of psychological devices, books, or other products offered for commercial sale make reasonable efforts to ensure that announcements and advertisements are presented in a professional, scientifically acceptable, and factually informative manner.

f. Psychologists do not participate for personal gain in commercial announcements or advertisements recommending to the public the purchase or use of proprietary or single-source products or services when that participation is based solely upon their identification as psychologists.

g. Psychologists present the science of psychology and offer their services, products, and publications fairly and accurately, avoiding misrepresentation through sensationalism, exaggeration, or superficiality. Psychologists are guided by the primary obligation to aid the public in developing informed judgments, opinions, and choices.

h. As teachers, psychologists ensure that statements in catalogs and course outlines are accurate and not misleading, particularly in terms of subject matter to be covered, bases for evaluating progress, and the nature of course experiences. Announcements, brochures, or advertisements describing workshops, seminars, or other educational programs accurately describe the audience for which the program is intended as well as eligibility requirements, educational objectives, and nature of the materials to be covered. These announcements also accurately represent the education, training, and experience of the psychologists presenting the programs and any fees involved.

i. Public announcements or advertisements soliciting research participants in which clinical services or other professional services are offered as an inducement make clear the nature of the services as well as the costs and other obligations to be accepted by participants in the research.

j. A psychologist accepts the obligation to correct others who represent the psychologist's professional qualifications, or associations with products or services, in a manner incompatible with these guidelines.

k. Individual diagnostic and therapeutic services are provided only in the context of a professional psychological relationship. When personal advice is given by means of public lectures or demonstrations, newspaper or magazine articles, radio or television programs, mail, or simi-

lar media, the psychologist utilizes the most current relevant data and exercises the highest level of professional judgment.

l. Products that are described or presented by means of public lectures or demonstrations, newspaper or magazine articles, radio or television programs, or similar media meet the same recognized standards as exist for products used in the context of a professional relationship.

Principle 5: Confidentiality

Psychologists have a primary obligation to respect the confidentiality of information obtained from persons in the course of their work as psychologists. They reveal such information to others only with the consent of the person or the person's legal representative, except in those unusual circumstances in which not to do so would result in clear danger to the person or to others. Where appropriate, psychologists inform their clients of the legal limits of confidentiality.

a. Information obtained in clinical or consulting relationships, or evaluative data concerning children, students, employees, and others, is discussed only for professional purposes and only with persons clearly concerned with the case. Written and oral reports present only data germane to the purposes of the evaluation, and every effort is made to avoid undue invasion of privacy.

b. Psychologists who present personal information obtained during the course of professional work in writings, lectures, or other public forums either obtain adequate prior consent to do so or adequately disguise all identifying information.

c. Psychologists make provisions for maintaining confidentiality in the storage and disposal of records.

d. When working with minors or other persons who are unable to give voluntary, informed consent, psychologists take special care to protect these persons' best interests.

Principle 6: Welfare of the Consumer

Psychologists respect the integrity and protect the welfare of the people and groups with whom they work. When conflicts of interest arise between clients and psychologists' employing institutions, psychologists clarify the nature and direction of their loyalties and responsibilities and keep all parties informed of their commitments. Psychologists fully inform consumers as to the purpose and nature of an evaluative, treatment, educational, or training procedure, and they freely acknowledge that clients, students, or participants in research have freedom of choice with regard to participation.

a. Psychologists are continually cognizant of their own needs and of their potentially influential position vis-à-vis persons such as clients, students, and subordinates. They avoid exploiting the trust and dependency of such persons. Psychologists make every effort to avoid dual relationships that could impair their professional judgment or increase the risk of exploitation. Examples of such dual relationships include, but are not limited to, research with and treatment of employees, students, supervisors, close friends, or relatives. Sexual intimacies with clients are unethical.

b. When a psychologist agrees to provide services to a client at the request of a third party, the psychologist assumes the responsibility of clarifying the nature of the relationships to all parties concerned.

c. Where the demands of an organization require psychologists to violate these Ethical Principles, psychologists clarify the nature of the conflict between the demands and these principles. They inform all parties of psychologists' ethical responsibilities and take appropriate action.

d. Psychologists make advance financial arrangements that safeguard the best interests of and are clearly understood by their clients. They contribute a portion of their services to work for which they receive little or no financial return.

e. Psychologists terminate a clinical or consulting relationship when it is reasonably clear that the consumer is not benefiting from it. They offer to help the consumer locate alternative sources of assistance.

Principle 7: Professional Relationships

Psychologists act with due regard for the needs, special competencies, and obligations of their colleagues in psychology and other professions. They respect the prerogatives and obligations of the institutions or organizations with which these other colleagues are associated.

a. Psychologists understand the areas of competence of related professions. They make full use of all the professional, technical, and administrative resources that serve the best interests of consumers. The absence of formal relationships with other professional workers does not relieve psychologists of the responsibility of securing for their clients the best possible professional service, nor does it relieve them of the obligation to exercise foresight, diligence, and tact in obtaining the complementary or alternative assistance needed by clients.

b. Psychologist know and take into account the traditions and practices of other professional groups with whom they work and cooperate fully with such groups. If a psychologist is contacted by a person who is already receiving similar services from another professional, the psychologist carefully considers that professional relationship and proceeds with caution and sensitivity to the therapeutic issues as well as the client's welfare. The psychologist discusses these issues with the client so as to minimize the risk of confusion and conflict.

c. Psychologists who employ or supervise other professionals or professionals in training accept the obligation to facilitate the further professional development of these individuals. They provide appropriate working conditions, timely evaluations, constructive consultation, and experience opportunities.

d. Psychologists do not exploit their professional relationships with clients, supervisors, students, employees, or research participants sexually or otherwise. Psychologists do not condone or engage in sexual harassment. Sexual harassment is defined as deliberate or repeated comments, gestures, or physical contacts of a sexual nature that are unwanted by the recipient.

e. In conducting research in institutions or organizations, psychologists secure appropriate authorization to conduct such research. They are aware of their obligations to future research workers and ensure that host institutions receive adequate information about the research and proper acknowledgment of their contributions.

f. Publication credit is assigned to those who have contributed to a publication in proportion to their professional contributions. Major contributions of a professional character made by several persons to a common project are recognized by joint authorship, with the individual who made the principal contribution listed first. Minor contributions of a professional character and extensive clerical or similar nonprofessional assistance may be acknowledged in footnotes or in an introductory statement. Acknowledgment through specific citations is made for unpublished as well as published material that has directly influenced the research or writing. Psychologists who compile and edit material of others for publication publish the material in the name of the originating group, if appropriate, with their own name appearing as chairperson or editor. All contributors are to be acknowledged and named.

g. When psychologists know of an ethical violation by another psychologist, and it seems appropriate, they informally attempt to resolve the issue by bringing the

behavior to the attention of the psychologist. If the misconduct is of a minor nature and/or appears to be due to lack of sensitivity, knowledge, or experience, such an informal solution is usually appropriate. Such informal corrective efforts are made with sensitivity to any rights to confidentiality involved. If the violation does not seem amenable to an informal solution, or is of a more serious nature, psychologists bring it to the attention of the appropriate local, state, and/or national committee on professional ethics and conduct.

Principle 8: Assessment Techniques

In the development, publication, and utilization of psychological assessment techniques, psychologists make every effort to promote the welfare and best interests of the client. They guard against the misuse of assessment results. They respect the client's right to know the results, the interpretations made, and the bases for their conclusions and recommendations. Psychologists make every effort to maintain the security of tests and other assessment techniques within limits of legal mandates. They strive to ensure the appropriate use of assessment techniques by others.

a. In using assessment techniques, psychologists respect the right of clients to have full explanations of the nature and purpose of the techniques in language the clients can understand, unless an explicit exception to this right has been agreed upon in advance. When the explanations are to be provided by others, psychologists establish procedures for ensuring the adequacy of these explanations.

b. Psychologists responsible for the development and standardization of psychological tests and other assessment techniques utilize established scientific procedures and observe the relevant APA standards.

c. In reporting assessment results, psychologists indicate any reservations that exist regarding validity or reliability because of the circumstances of the assessment or the inappropriateness of the norms for the person tested. Psychologists strive to ensure that the results of assessments and their interpretations are not misused by others.

d. Psychologists recognize that assessment results may become obsolete. They make every effort to avoid and prevent the misuse of obsolete measures.

e. Psychologists offering scoring and interpretation services are able to produce appropriate evidence for the validity of the programs and procedures used in arriving at interpretations. The public offering of an automated interpretation service is considered a professional-to-professional consultation. Psychologists make every effort to avoid misuse of assessment reports.

f. Psychologists do not encourage or promote the use of psychological assessment techniques by inappropriately trained or otherwise unqualified persons through teaching, sponsorship, or supervision.

Principle 9: Research with Human Participants

The decision to undertake research rests upon a considered judgment by the individual psychologist about how best to contribute to psychological science and human welfare. Having made the decision to conduct research, the psychologist considers alternative directions in which research energies and resources might be invested. On the basis of this consideration, the psychologist carries out the investigation with respect and concern for the dignity and welfare of the people who participate and with cognizance of federal and state regulations and professional standards governing the conduct of research with human participants.

a. In planning a study, the investigator has the responsibility to make a careful evaluation of its ethical acceptability. To the extent that the weighing of scientific and human values suggests a compromise of any principle, the investigator incurs a correspondingly serious obligation to seek ethical advice and to observe stringent safeguards to protect the rights of human participants.

b. Considering whether a participant in a planned study will be a "subject at risk" or a "subject at minimal risk," according to recognized standards, is of primary ethical concern to the investigator.

c. The investigator always retains the responsibility for ensuring ethical practice in research. The investigator is also responsible for the ethical treatment of research participants by collaborators, assistants, students, and employees, all of whom, however, incur similar obligations.

d. Except in minimal-risk research, the investigator establishes a clear and fair agreement with research participants, prior to their participation, that clarifies the obligations and responsibilities of each. The investigator has the obligation to honor all promises and commitments included in that agreement. The investigator informs the participants of all aspects of the research that might reasonably be expected to influence willingness to participate and explains all other aspects of the research about which the participants inquire. Failure to make full disclosure prior to obtaining informed consent requires additional safeguards to protect the welfare and dignity of the research participants. Research with children or with participants who have impairments that would limit understanding and/or communication requires special safeguarding procedures.

e. Methodological requirements of a study may make the use of concealment or deception necessary. Before conducting such a study, the investigator has a special responsibility to (i) determine whether the use of such techniques is justified by the study's prospective scientific, educational, or applied value; (ii) determine whether alternative procedures are available that do not use concealment or deception; and (iii) ensure that the participants are provided with sufficient explanation as soon as possible.

f. The investigator respects the individual's freedom to decline to participate in or to withdraw from the research at any time. The obligation to protect this freedom requires careful thought and consideration when the investigator is in a position of authority or influence over the participant. Such positions of authority include, but are not limited to, situations in which research participation is required as part of employment or in which the participant is a student, client, or employee of the investigator.

g. The investigator protects the participant from physical and mental discomfort, harm, and danger that may arise from research procedures. If risks of such consequences exist, the investigator informs the participant of that fact. Research procedures likely to cause serious or lasting harm to a participant are not used unless the failure to use these procedures might expose the participant to risk of greater harm, or unless the research has great potential benefit and fully informed and voluntary consent is obtained from each participant. The participant should be informed of procedures for contacting the investigator within a reasonable time period following participation should stress, potential harm, or related questions or concerns arise.

h. After the data are collected, the investigator provides the participant with information about the nature of the study and attempts to remove any misconceptions that may have arisen. Where scientific or humane values justify delaying or withholding this information, the investigator incurs a special responsibility to monitor the research and to ensure that there are no damaging consequences for the participant.

i. Where research procedures result in undesirable consequences for the individual participant, the investigator has the responsibility to detect and remove or correct these consequences, including long-term effects.

j. Information obtained about a research participant during the course of an investigation is confidential unless otherwise agreed upon in advance. When the possibility exists that others may obtain access to such information, this possibility, together with the plans for protecting confidentiality, is explained to the participant as part of the procedure for obtaining informed consent.

Principle 10: Care and Use of Animals

An investigator of animal behavior strives to advance understanding of basic behavioral principles and/or to contribute to the improvement of human health and welfare. In seeking these ends, the investigator ensures the welfare of animals and treats them humanely. Laws and regulations notwithstanding, an animal's immediate protection depends upon the scientist's own conscience.

a. The acquisition, care, use, and disposal of all animals are in compliance with current federal, state or provincial, and local laws and regulations.

b. A psychologist trained in research methods and experienced in the care of laboratory animals closely supervises all procedures involving animals and is responsible for ensuring appropriate consideration of their comfort, health, and humane treatment.

c. Psychologists ensure that all individuals using animals under their supervision have received explicit instruction in experimental methods and in the care, maintenance, and handling of the species being used. Responsibilities and activities of individuals participating in a research project are consistent with their respective competencies.

d. Psychologists make every effort to minimize discomfort, illness, and pain of animals. A procedure subjecting animals to pain, stress, or privation is used only when an alternative procedure is unavailable and the goal is justified by its prospective scientific, educational, or applied value. Surgical procedures are performed under appropriate anesthesia; techniques to avoid infection and minimize pain are followed during and after surgery.

e. When it is appropriate that the animal's life be terminated, it is done rapidly and painlessly.

CODE OF ETHICS FOR THE AMERICAN ASSOCIATION FOR MARRIAGE AND FAMILY THERAPY

The Board of Directors of the American Association for Marriage and Family Therapy (AAMFT) hereby promulgates, pursuant to Article 2, Section 2.013 of the Association's By-laws, the Revised AAMFT Code of Ethics, effective August 1, 1991.

The AAMFT Code of Ethics is binding on Members of AAMFT in all membership categories, AAMFT Approved Supervisors, and applicants for membership and the Approved Supervisor designation (hereafter, AAMFT Member).

If an AAMFT Member resigns in anticipation of, or during the course of an ethics investigation, the Ethics Committee will complete its investigation. Any publication of action taken by the Association will include the fact that the Member attempted to resign during the investigation.

Marriage and family therapists are strongly encouraged to report alleged unethical behavior of colleagues to appropriate professional associations and state regulatory bodies.

1. Responsibility to Clients

Marriage and family therapists advance the welfare of families and individuals. They respect the rights of those persons seeking their assistance, and make reasonable efforts to ensure that their services are used appropriately.

1.1 Marriage and family therapists do not discriminate against or refuse professional service to anyone on the basis of race, gender, religion, national origin, or sexual orientation.

1.2 Marriage and family therapists are aware of their influential position with respect to clients, and they avoid exploiting the trust and dependency of such persons. Therapists, therefore, make every effort to avoid dual relationships with clients that could impair professional judgment or increase the risk of exploitation. When a dual relationship cannot be avoided, therapists take appropriate professional precautions to ensure judgment is not impaired and no exploitation occurs. Examples of such dual relationships include, but are not limited to, business or close personal relationships with clients. Sexual intimacy with clients is prohibited. Sexual intimacy with former clients for two years following the termination of therapy is prohibited.

1.3 Marriage and family therapists do not use their professional relationships with clients to further their own interests.

1.4 Marriage and family therapists respect the right of clients to make decisions and help them to understand the consequences of these decisions. Therapists clearly advise a client that a decision on marital status is the responsibility of the client.

1.5 Marriage and family therapists continue therapeutic relationships only so long as it is reasonably clear that clients are benefiting from the relationship.

1.6 Marriage and family therapists assist persons in obtaining other therapeutic services if the therapist is unable or unwilling, for appropriate reasons, to provide professional help.

1.7 Marriage and family therapists do not abandon or neglect clients in treatment without making reasonable arrangements for the continuation of such treatment.

1.8 Marriage and family therapists obtain written informed consent from clients before videotaping, audiorecording, or permitting third party observation.

2. Confidentiality

Marriage and family therapists have unique confidentiality concerns because the client in a therapeutic relationship may be more than one person. Therapists respect and guard confidences of each individual client.

2.1 Marriage and family therapists may not disclose client confidences except: (a) as mandated by law; (b) to prevent a clear and immediate danger to a person or persons; (c) where the therapist is a defendant in a civil, criminal, or disciplinary action arising from the therapy (in which case client confidences may be disclosed only in the course of that action); or (d) if there is a waiver previously obtained in writing, and then such information may be revealed only in accordance with the terms of the waiver. In circumstances where more than one person in a family receives therapy, each such family member who is legally competent to execute a waiver must agree to the waiver required by subparagraph (d). Without such a waiver from each family member legally competent to execute a waiver, a therapist cannot disclose information received from any family member.

2.2 Marriage and family therapists use client and/or clinical materials in teaching, writing, and public presentations only if a written waiver has been obtained in accordance with Subprincipal 2.1(d), or when appropriate steps have been taken to protect client identity and confidentiality.

2.3 Marriage and family therapists store or dispose of client records in ways that maintain confidentiality.

3. Professional Competence and Integrity

Marriage and family therapists maintain high standards of professional competence and integrity.

3.1 Marriage and family therapists are in violation of this Code and subject to termination of membership or other appropriate action if they: (a) are convicted of any felony; (b) are convicted of a misdemeanor related to their qualifications or functions; (c) engage in conduct which could lead to conviction of a felony, or a misdemeanor related to their qualifications of functions; (d) are expelled from or disciplined by other professional organizations; (e) have their licenses or certificates suspended or revoked or are otherwise disciplined by regulatory bodies; (f) are no longer competent to practice marriage and family therapy because they are impaired due to physical or mental causes or the abuse of alcohol or other substances; or (g) fail to cooperate with the Association at any point from the inception of an ethical complaint through the completion of all proceedings regarding that complaint.

3.2 Marriage and family therapists seek appropriate professional assistance for their personal problems or conflicts that may impair work performance or clinical judgment.

3.3 Marriage and family therapists, as teachers, supervisors, and researchers, are dedicated to high standards of scholarship and present accurate information.

3.4 Marriage and family therapists remain abreast of new developments in family therapy knowledge and practice through educational activities.

3.5 Marriage and family therapists do not engage in sexual or other harassment or exploitation of clients, students, trainees, supervisees, employees, colleagues, research subjects, or actual or potential witnesses or complainants in investigations and ethical proceedings.

3.6 Marriage and family therapists do not diagnose, treat, or advise on problems outside the recognized boundaries of their competence.

3.7 Marriage and family therapists make efforts to prevent the distortion or misuse of their clinical and research findings.

3.8 Marriage and family therapists, because of their ability to influence and alter the lives of others, exercise special care when making public their professional recommendations and opinions through testimony or other public statements.

4. Responsibility to Students, Employees, and Supervisees

Marriage and family therapists do not exploit the trust and dependency of students, employees, and supervisees.

4.1 Marriage and family therapists are aware of their influential position with respect to students, employees, and supervisees, and they avoid exploiting the trust and dependency of such persons. Therapists, therefore, make every effort to avoid dual relationships that could impair professional judgment or increase the risk of exploitation. When a dual relationship cannot be avoided, therapists take appropriate professional precautions to ensure judgment is not impaired and no exploitation occurs. Examples of such dual relationships include, but are not limited to, business or close personal relationships with students, employees, or supervisees. Provision of therapy to students, employees, or supervisees is prohibited. Sexual intimacy with students or supervisees is prohibited.

4.2 Marriage and family therapists do not permit students, employees, or supervisees to perform or to hold themselves out as competent to perform professional services beyond their training, level of experience, and competence.

4.3 Marriage and family therapists do not disclose supervisee confidences except: (a) as mandated by law; (b) to prevent a clear and immediate danger to a person or persons; (c) where the therapist is a defendant in a civil, criminal, or disciplinary action arising from the supervision (in which case supervisee confidences may be disclosed only in the course of that action); (d) in educational or training settings where there are multiple supervisors, and then only to other professional colleagues who share responsibility for the training of the supervisee; or (e) if there is a waiver previously obtained in writing, and then such information may be revealed only in accordance with the terms of the waiver.

5. Responsibility to Research Participants

Investigators respect the dignity and protect the welfare of participants in research and are aware of federal and state laws and regulations and professional standards governing the conduct of research.

5.1 Investigators are responsible for making careful examinations of ethical acceptability in planning studies. To the extent that services to research participants may be compromised by participation in research, investigators seek the ethical advice of qualified professionals not directly involved in the investigation and observe safeguards to protect the rights of research participants.

5.2 Investigators requesting participants' involvement in research inform them of all aspects of the research that might reasonably be expected to influence willingness to participate. Investigators are especially sensitive to the possibility of diminished consent when participants are also receiving clinical services, have impairments which limit understanding and/or communication, or when participants are children.

5.3 Investigators respect participants' freedom to decline participation in or to withdraw from a research study at any time. This obligation requires special thought and consideration when investigators or other members of the research team are in position of authority or influence over participants. Marriage and family therapists, therefore, make every effort to avoid dual relationships with research participants that could impair professional judgment or increase the risk of exploitation.

5.4 Information obtained about a research participant during the course of an investigation is confidential unless there is a waiver previously obtained in writing. When the possibility exists that others, including family members, may obtain access to such information, this possibility, together with the plan for protecting confidentiality, is explained as part of the procedure for obtaining informed consent.

6. Responsibility to the Profession

Marriage and family therapists respect the rights and responsibilities of professional colleagues and participate in activities which advance the goals of the profession.

6.1 Marriage and family therapists remain accountable to the standards of the profession when acting as members or employees of organizations.

6.2 Marriage and family therapists assign publication credit to those who have contributed to a publication in proportion to their contributions and in accordance with customary professional publication practices.

6.3 Marriage and family therapists who are the authors of books or other materials that are published or distributed cite persons to whom credit for original ideas is due.

6.4 Marriage and family therapists who are the authors of books or other materials published or distributed by an organization take reasonable precautions to ensure that the organization promotes and advertises the materials accurately and factually.

6.5 Marriage and family therapists participate in activities that contribute to a better community and society, including devoting a portion of their professional activity to services for which there is little or no financial return.

6.6 Marriage and family therapists are concerned with developing laws and regulations pertaining to marriage and family therapy that serve the public interest, and with altering such laws and regulations that are not in the public interest.

6.7 Marriage and family therapists encourage public participation in the design and delivery of professional services and in the regulation of practitioners.

7. Financial Arrangements

Marriage and family therapists make financial arrangements with clients, third party payors, and supervisees that are reasonably understandable and conform to accepted professional practices.

7.1 Marriage and family therapists do not offer or accept payment for referrals.

7.2 Marriage and family therapists do not charge excessive fees for services.

7.3 Marriage and family therapists disclose their fees to clients and supervisees at the beginning of services.

7.4 Marriage and family therapists represent facts truthfully to clients, third party payors, and supervisees regarding services rendered.

8. Advertising

Marriage and family therapists engage in appropriate informational activities, including those that enable laypersons to choose professional services on an informed basis.

General Advertising

8.1 Marriage and family therapists accurately represent their competence, education, training, and experience relevant to their practice of marriage and family therapy.

8.2 Marriage and family therapists assure that advertisements and publications in any media (such as directories, announcements, business cards, newspapers, radio, television, and facsimiles) convey information that is necessary for the public to make an appropriate selection of professional services. Information could include: (a) office information, such as name, address, telephone number, credit card acceptability, fees, languages spoken, and office hours; (b) appropriate degrees, state licensure and/or certification, and AAMFT Clinical Member status; and (c) description of practice. (For requirements for advertising under the AAMFT name, logo and/or the abbreviated initials AAMFT, see Subprinciple 8.15, below).

8.3 Marriage and family therapists do not use a name which could mislead the public concerning the identity, responsibility, source, and status of those practicing under that name and do not hold themselves out as being partners or associates of a firm if they are not.

8.4 Marriage and family therapists do not use any professional identification (such as business card, office sign, letterhead, or telephone or association directory listing) if it includes a statement or claim that is false, fraudulent, misleading, or deceptive. A statement is false, fraudulent, misleading, or deceptive if it (a) contains a material misrepresentation of fact; (b) fails to state any material fact necessary to make the statement, in light of all circumstances, not misleading; or (c) is intended to or is likely to create an unjustified expectation.

8.5 Marriage and family therapists correct, wherever possible, false, misleading, or inaccurate information and representations made by others concerning the therapist's qualifications, services, or products.

8.6 Marriage and family therapists make certain that the qualifications of persons in their employ are represented in a manner that is not false, misleading, or deceptive.

8.7 Marriage and family therapists may represent themselves as specializing within a limited area of marriage and family therapy, but only if they have the education and supervised experience in settings which meet recognized professional standards to practice in that specialty area.

Advertising Using AAMFT Designations

8.8 The AAMFT designations of Clinical Member, Approved Supervisor, and Fellow may be used in public information or advertising materials only by persons holding such designations. Persons holding such designations may, for example, advertise in the following manner:

- *Jane Doe, Ph.D., a Clinical Member of the American Association for Marriage and Family Therapy.*
Alternately, the advertisement could read:
Jane Doe, Ph.D., AAMFT Clinical Member.
- *John Doe, Ph.D., an Approved Supervisor of the American Association for Marriage and Family Therapy.*
Alternately, the advertisement could read:
John Doe, Ph.D., AAMFT Approved Supervisor.

- *Jane Doe, Ph.D., a Fellow of the American Association for Marriage and Family Therapy.*
Alternately, the advertisement could read:
Jane Doe, Ph.D., AAMFT Fellow.
More than one designation may be used if held by the AAMFT Member.

8.9 Marriage and family therapists who hold the AAMFT Approved Supervisor or the Fellow designation may not represent the designation as an advance clinical status.

8.10 Student, Associate, and Affiliate Members may not use their AAMFT membership status in public information or advertising materials. Such listings on professional resumes are not considered advertisements.

8.11 Persons applying for AAMFT membership may not list their application status on any resume or advertisement.

8.12 In conjunction with their AAMFT membership, marriage and family therapists claim as evidence of educational qualifications only those degrees (a) from regionally accredited institutions or (b) from institutions recognized by states which license or certify marriage and family therapists, but only if such state regulation is recognized by AAMFT.

8.13 Marriage and family therapists may not use the initials AAMFT following their name in the manner of an academic degree.

8.14 Marriage and family therapists may not use the AAMFT name, logo, and/or the abbreviated initials AAMFT or make any such representation which would imply that they speak for or represent the Association. The Association is the sole owner of its name, logo, and the abbreviated initials AAMFT. Its committees and divisions, operating as such, may use the name, logo, and/or the abbreviated initials AAMFT in accordance with AAMFT policies.

8.15 Authorized advertisements of Clinical Members under the AAMFT name, logo, and/or the abbreviated initials AAMFT may include the following: the Clinical Member's name, degree, license or certificate held when required by state law, name of business, address, and telephone number. If a business is listed, it must follow, not precede the Clinical Member's name. Such listings may not include AAMFT offices held by the Clinical Member, nor any specializations, since such listings under the AAMFT name, logo, and/or the abbreviated initials, AAMFT, would imply that this specialization has been credentialed by AAMFT.

8.16 Marriage and family therapists use their membership in AAMFT only in connection with their clinical and professional activities.

8.17 Only AAMFT divisions and programs accredited by the AAMFT Commission on Accreditation for Marriage and Family Therapy Education, not businesses nor organizations, may use any AAMFT-related designation or affiliation in public information or advertising materials, and then only in accor-

dance with AAMFT policies.

8.18 Programs accredited by the AAMFT Commission and Accreditation for Marriage and Family Education may not use the AAMFT name, logo, and/or the abbreviated initials AAMFT. Instead, they may have printed on their stationery and other appropriate materials a statement such as:

> *The (name of program) of the (name of institution) is accredited by the AAMFT Commission on Accreditation for Marriage and Family Therapy Education.*

8.19 Programs not accredited by the AAMFT Commission on Accreditation for Marriage and Family Therapy Education may not use the AAMFT name, logo, and/or the abbreviated initials AAMFT. They may not state in printed program materials, program advertisements, and student advertisement that their courses and training opportunities are accepted by AAMFT to meet AAMFT membership requirements.

Violations of the Code should be brought in writing to the attention of the AAMFT Ethics Committee, 1100 17th Street, NW, The Tenth Floor, Washington, DC 20036-4601, (telephone 202/452-0109).

Effective August 1, 1991.

INDEX

ABC Theory of Emotion, 124, 127
Ability
  career development and, 243
  tests of, 158–159
Abusive behavior
  drug use and, 259
  in group counseling, 197
Acceptance, 69, 73, 76
Achievement, tests of, 159
Action-oriented counseling, 90, 115–138
Action skills, 305
Addiction, 250–251
  depressants and, 254
  marijuana and, 254
  narcotics and, 256
Adler, A., 27, 31, 101, 111–113, 143
Adolescents, 296
  development in, 58
  drug abuse by, 257–259
  drug availability and, 252–253
Aged. See Elderly
AIDS, 282–284
Alcohol counseling, 249–265
Alexander, F., 101
Alibrandi, T., 258
Allers, C. T., 283
Amatea, E., 204
American Association for Counseling and
    Development (AACD), 32, 34, 280, 309,
    313, 329
American Association for Marriage and Family
    Therapy (AAMFT), 34, 204, 309, 313, 329
American Mental Health Counselors
    Association, 32–33
American Personnel and Guidance
    Association, 32
American Psychological Association, 309, 313, 329

Analysis. See Psychoanalytic counseling
Anastasi, A., 156–157
Anderson, B. S., 321
Anderson, P., 260, 261
Anderson, S. M., 184
Anderson, W. P., 306
Andrews, S., 231, 244
Anthony, W. A., 302
Anxiety, 104, 112, 113
  diagnostic criteria for, 169
  drug abuse and, 263
  in first session, 82
Aptitude, tests of, 159
Argyris, C., 89
Aristotle, 25, 31
Armor, D. J., 263
Arrendondo, P., 267
Art therapy, 136
Assessment
  in behavioral counseling, 117
  definition of, 153–154
  of elderly clients, 276–277
  individual, 39–40
  observational, 162
  process of, 152–175
  role of testing in, 154–155
  in sexual counseling, 222–223
  summary of principles, 164
  use of in counseling, 163–164
Association for Counselor Education and
    Supervision, 33
Atkinson, D. R., 298
Atkinson, G., Jr., 229
Attending skills, 30, 73–74, 302–303
Attractiveness, 76
  of counselor, 298
Authier, J., 302

Authority, 66, 77
Aversion therapy, 262
Avila, D. L., 17
Awareness, 106, 291
  layers of, 101
  personal, 18
Axelson, J. A., 267

Background, client, 79–80
Baird, J. E., Jr., 180
Baker, L., 272
Bandler, R., 128–130, 132
Bandura, A., 76, 117, 269, 294
Banikiotes, P. G., 298
Bank, B. J., 258
Barkley, W. M., 295
BASIC ID, 132–133
Bateson, G., 89–90, 128, 205, 293
Bauer, G. P., 101, 105
Beck, A. T., 122
Bednar, R. L., 321
Beers, Clifford, 29
Begley, P. J., 298
Behavioral counseling, 116–122
Behaviorism, 28
Behavior modification. See Behavioral
      counseling
Behaviors
  change theories, 269
  collective, 180
  disruptive, in children, 210–212
  ethical consequences of, 311
  facilitating, 69
  inhibiting, 69
  intentional, 93
  overconforming, 272
  self-defeating, 80
  self-destructive, 72, 251
Belkin, G., 23
Belle, D., 273
Bellet, W., 298
Bem, D. J., 269
Benedek, E. P., 271
Bennett, B. E., 321, 322
Bennett, M. J., 105
Bentel, D. J., 252
Berenson, B. G., 18, 30, 91
Berger, M., 315
Bergin, A. E., 15, 117, 184, 294, 301
Berg, J. H., 69
Berkeley, G., 28
Berne, E., 27, 101, 110, 143
Betz, B., 293
Beutler, L. E., 16, 165, 262
Bias, 317
  influence of, 267–269
  professional, 270
  in testing, 273
Biddle, B. J., 258

Biggs, D., 163
Binder, J. L., 101
Binet, A., 31
Biofeedback, 136
Birrin, J. E., 279
Blanchare, E. B., 269
Blau, D., 331
Blocher, D. H., 246
Block, J., 257–259
Bloom, J. W., 33
Blum, C. R., 244
Boorstein, D., 332
Borman, C.A., 242
Boy, A. V., 65, 92, 143, 172
Bradley, R. W., 163
Brammer, L. M., 16
Breuer, Joseph, 27
Brief therapy. See Strategic counseling
Brigman, S. L., 231
Brilhart, J., 189
Brown, M. T., 290
Bryant, B. K., 321
Buffone, C. W., 137, 263
Bugental, J. F. T., 98
Buhrke, R. A., 280
Burks, H. M., Jr., 89
Burnett, M., 251
Burn-out, 127, 189–190, 330
Buros, O., 154

Callanan, P., 267
Campbell, V. L., 142
Caplow, T., 233
Capuzzi, D., 264
Career choice, 238, 239–240
Career counseling, 28–29, 59, 226–248
  computer-based guidance systems, 230, 244
  gay issues in, 281–282
  standards for, 34
Career development, 42, 231–240
Career education, 240–243
Career guidance, computerized, 242–243,
      246–247
Carkhuff, R., 16, 18, 30, 32, 67, 73, 91–92, 290,
      294, 300–302
Carskadden, G., 298
Carter, J. A., 298
Casas, J. M., 275
Cash, T. F., 298
Castronovo, N. R., 283
Cattell, J., 154
Cautela, J. R., 118
Cayleff, S. E., 268
Certification, of counselors, 33–34
Change, 300–301
  discomfort and, 194
  expectation of, 13
  facilitation of, 303–305
  measurement of, 301

Chassin, L., 257
Chemical dependence, counseling principles for, 262–264
Cheung, F. K., 268, 275
Child abuse, 316
Child development, 58
Christensen, C. P., 273
Christensen, E. R., 301
Cianni-Surridge, M., 246
Claiborn, C. D., 67, 298, 302
Clarkin, J. F., 262
Classical-conditioning procedures, 121–122
Client
   history of, 21
   relationship with, 64
Client-centered counseling, 15, 29–30, 91–96
   assumptions of, 92
   criticisms of, 95
   personal applications of, 95–96
   techniques in, 93–95
Clientele
   of counselors v. psychotherapists, 22, 23
   preferred types, 270
Cocaine, 255
Cochran, S. D., 283
Cognitive behavior therapy. See Rational-emotive counseling
Cognitive development, 42
Cohen, R. J., 172
Coleman, E., 312
Combs, A. W., 17
Commitment, 7, 74–75, 78, 81, 144
Communication, 214
   in families, 204
   patterns of, 129
Competition
   in families, 208
   of mental health professionals, 24
Compliance, 218–219
Confidentiality, 68, 78, 81, 308, 315–316, 320–321
   in career counseling, 242
   in family counseling, 221
   in group counseling, 186, 193–194
   in group setting, 187–188
   in helping relationship, 76
Conflict, 13
   in group counseling, 196–197
   management of, 70
Confrontation, 11, 30, 40
Congruence, 71–72
Conoley, J. C., 161
Conroy, P., 11
Consciousness, 28
Consistency, 89
   of tests, 157
Contingency contracting, 120, 135
Contract, 64
   self, 120
Control, 4

of counselor, 65
   in families, 209–210, 212, 219–220
Controlled Substance Act (1970), 252
Cook, E. P., 271, 316
Corazzini, J. G., 184
Corey, G., 18, 33, 180, 183, 185, 199, 267, 313
Corey, M. S., 267
Cormier, L. S., 122
Cormier, W. H., 122
Cornacchia, H. J., 252
Corn, R., 298
Council for the Accreditation of Counseling and Related Educational Programs (CACREP), 34
Counseling
   chemically dependent, 262–264
   choosing career in, 4–7
   clinical v. mental health, 24
   definitions of, 12–15
   effectiveness of, 16
   family, 40
   flexibility in, 130
   generic skills of, 301–305
   group, 40, 179–202
   history of, 66–67, 143
   individual, 39
   outcome effects in, 300–301
   psychotherapy and, 21–24
   regulation in, 33–34
   role of in career choice, 228–229
   settings for, 36–62
   specialty areas in, 58–59
Counseling pragmatic. See Multimodal counseling
Counseling relationship, qualities of, 64–66
Counselor
   as client, 328
   perceptual base of, 17–18
   qualities of, 18
   role of in strategic counseling, 129–130
Covert, J. A., 316
Cox, W. M., 252, 263
Credentials, of counselors, 33–34
Crisis center, counseling in, 47–48
Cronback, L. J., 155
Cunningham, W. R., 279

Darwin, Charles, 39
Dasberg, H., 105
Davanloo, H., 101, 105
Death, 277–278
Deception, 314–315
Decision-making
   career and, 243–245
   ethical, 317–320
   skills in, 230–231
Defense mechanism, 103–104, 143
DeJulio, S. S., 301
Dependence
   of client, 66, 77

Dependence (*continued*)
  on drugs, 250
  liability for, 252
Depressants, 254–255
Depression, 8, 66, 209
  drug abuse and, 263
  elderly and, 260
  gay issues and, 282
  in women, 271
Derlega, V. J., 69
Descartes, R., 28, 31
Desensitization, 117, 121
Developmental orientation, 34–35, 42–44, 65
Diagnosis, 13, 313
  behavioral, 172–174
  cultural differences and, 275
  of elderly clients, 276
  ethical concerns in, 171–172
  in family counseling, 212–217
  formal and functional, 164–174
  psychiatric, 168–169
  treatment plan and, 165–166
DiClemente, C. C., 132
Dinkmeyer, D. C., 112
Dinkmeyer, D. C., Jr., 112
Directives, 215, 218–219, 395
Disabled
  counseling of, 59, 284–285
  drug abuse by, 260–261
Disadvantaged, counseling with, 52–54
Distraction, 9–10
Dixon, D. N., 298
Doherty, M. A., 272
Dollard, J., 16, 117, 293
Donigian, J., 201
Donovan, M. E., 272
Double bind, 205
Double chairing, 108
Douce, L. A., 280
Downing, H. D., 168
Dreams, 101, 106, 111
Dreikurs, R., 112
Driscoll, R. H., 16
Drug abuse, 250–252
  by adolescents, 257–259
  by disabled, 260–261
  effects of, 256–257
  by elderly, 259–260
Drug counseling, 59, 249–265
Dryden, W., 122
DSM-III-R, 168–172, 271, 280
Dworkin, S. H., 279
Dye, A., 199
Dyer, W. W., 80, 199

Eating disorders, 272
Eclectic counseling. *See* Multimodal counseling
Eclecticism, 16, 149
  technical v. prescriptive, 148
  theoretical, 142

Edgerton, R. B., 274
Edwards, R. B., 172
Egan, G., 65, 67, 75–76
Ego, 42, 103, 111
Eisdorfer, C., 276
Eisenberg, S., 18
Elderly, counseling of, 276–279
Eldridge, W. D., 290
Ellis, A., 27, 30, 101, 122–125, 143, 146, 269
Ellis, M. V., 208
Emotion, ABC Theory of, 124
Empathy, 12, 41, 71–73, 92–93
  in helping relationship, 75–76
Encounter group, 95, 182
Ericksonian therapy. *See* Strategic counseling
Erickson, M., 128, 130, 144, 214
Erikson, E., 42, 65, 101, 140, 147, 277
  stages of personality development, 43,
    102–103
Erlanger, M. A., 215
Ethical issues, 307–324
Ethics, 89
  in family counseling, 221
Ethnic minorities, counseling of, 273–275
Evans, R., 240
Exercise, 137
  drug abuse and, 263
Existential counseling, 96–100
Expectations, 4
  assessment of, 78–79
  of client, 81
  of group counseling, 187, 192–193
  positive, 16
  of treatment, 13
Experiential counseling. *See* Existential
    counseling
Expressive therapies, 135–136
Eysenck, H., 147, 293, 300–301

Fabrick, F., 204
Family counseling, 40, 129, 203–225
  case example of, 212–214
  ethical issues in, 221
  theoretical viewpoints in, 206–207
  theories of, 205–208
Family violence, 221
Farber, B. A., 331
Fassinger, R. E., 279
Feedback
  in counseling, 13
  in group counseling, 189–191, 196
Feelings
  catharsis of, 101
  experiencing of, 106
Fenell, D. L., 205, 208
Ferenczi, S., 26
Festinger, L., 269
Fiedler, F. E., 17, 293
First session, 76–82
Fisch, R., 129, 132, 218

Fish, J., 76
Fishman, H. C., 145, 204
Flaherty, J. A., 274
Flexibility, 142, 148
   in specialty, 329–330
Food and Drug Administration, 252
Forsyth, D. R., 295
Framo, J. L., 204
Frank, J. D., 16
Frankl, V., 32, 96–97, 99
Frazier, N., 242
Freedom, 96–98
French, T. M., 16
Fretz, B. R., 227, 298
Freud, Anna, 27, 101, 271
Freudian psychotherapy. *See* Psychoanalytic
      counseling
Freud, S., 31, 42, 105–106, 142
   accomplishments of, 27
   counseling relationship, 66
   insight theory of, 88
   methods of, 25
   photographs of, 26, 100
   psychoanalytic counseling and, 100
   stages of personality development, 44,
      102–103
   talking cure, 27
Friedlander, M. L., 208
Fromm, E., 101
Fromm-Reichmann, F., 18
Fuhrman, B. S., 263
Fukuyama, M. A., 243
Fuqua, D. R., 229, 244

Gallagher, K. M., 142
Galton, F., 154
Garfield, S. L., 15, 117, 184
Gay men, counseling of, 279–284
Geis, H. J., 88
Gelman, D., 231
Gendlin, E. T., 91
Gentner, D. S., 129
Genuineness, 41, 92, 142, 270
Gerson, R., 215
Gerstein, L. H., 33
Gestalt counseling, 30, 106–109
Gibbon, M., 170
Ginzberg, E., 240
Glantz, K., 66
Glasser, W., 135, 137
Glass, G. V., 294, 301
Goals
   of clients, 320
   of counseling, 13, 17, 23, 65, 81, 149
   group, 185
   of group counseling, 193
   identification of, 117
   professional, 41–42
   setting, 30, 40
Goldband, S., 136

Goldenberg, G. H., 204, 206–208
Goldenberg, G. I., 204, 206–208
Goldfried, M. R., 16
Goldman, L., 163
Goldstein, A. P., 69, 117
Gomberg, E. S. L., 259
Good, G. E., 271
Goodman, J., 276
Gordon, J., 282–283
Gordon, T. G., 73, 92
Gottlieb, M. C., 75, 312
Gottman, J. M., 80, 117
Gowing, M. K., 246
Gray, B. A., 268
Greenberg, L. S., 15
Green, S. L., 221
Greenspan, S. I., 65
Greenwood, A., 321
Greenwood, R., 284
Grieger, R., 122
Grinder, J., 128, 129, 132
Groden, G., 118
Gross, D. R., 221, 316
Groth-Marnat, G., 157, 158
Group counseling, 40, 179–202
   advantages of, 188–192
   chemical dependency and, 263
   limitations of, 187–188
   methods of, 180
   potential of, 186
   skills for, 200
   specialized skills for, 199–201
   use of modalities of, 184–187
Groups
   assumptions about, 192–197
   counseling, 183
   encounter, 182
   goals of, 185
   guidance, 182–183
   survey of, 180–184
   therapy, 184
   work styles of, 181
Guidance, 28–29
Guidance groups, 182–183
Gutierrez, F., 280
Gutierrez, J. M., 275

Haber, R. A., 257
Hadley, W. S., 301
Haley, J., 65, 80, 128–130, 205, 208, 211, 214, 293
Hall, E., 277
Hall, E. T., 274
Hall, G. C. N., 273, 274
Hall, G. Stanley, 26, 28, 31
Hallucinogens, 256
Handicapped
   counseling of, 284–285
   drug abuse by, 260–261
Haney, W., 155
Hansen, J. C., 221, 240, 321

Hare-Mustin, R., 271
Harper, R., 124
Harris, T. A., 110
Hartman, B. W., 229, 244
Harvill, R. L., 201
Hausman, C. P., 276
Hayman, P. M., 316
Hazler, R. J., 231
Healy, M., 316
Hegel, G. W. F., 27
Heitzman, D., 230
Held, B. S., 148
Helping relationship, characteristics of, 71–74
Hendrick, S. S., 69
Hepner, R., 261
Heppner, P. P., 298, 306
Herlihy, B., 313, 316, 323
Hermans, H. J., 163
Herr, E., 243
Herron, W. G., 4
Hester, R. K., 262
Hill, C. E., 185
Himmell, C. D., 142
Hippocrates, 27, 31
Hoffman, A., 262
Hoffman-Graff, M. A., 298
Hoffman, J., 23
Holland, J., 163, 235–236, 293
Ho, M. K., 270
Homosexuality, 279–284
Honesty, 4, 64, 75
  of counselor, 67
Hopkins, B. R., 321
Hoppock, R., 236–238
Horan, J., 244
Horne, A. M., 184
Horney, K., 101, 113
Hosford, R., 117
Hosie, T. W., 259
Hoyt, K., 240
Hoyt, K. B., 242, 245–246
Hudson, P., 316
Huey, W. C., 321
Humanistic counseling. See Client-centered
  counseling; Existential counseling
Hume, David, 28
Hurley, F. W., 230
Hussian, R. A., 277
Huxley, A., 278
Hypnosis, 27, 100, 106, 136

Iasenza, S., 280
Ibrahim, F. A., 267
Identification, 104
  in group counseling, 195
Identity, 135
  career and, 240
  of counselor, 39
  development of in gays, 280–281
  professional, 21, 24, 41, 330

  self, 17
Imagery, 128, 133–134
Individual assessment, 39–40
Industry, counseling in, 55–57, 59
Information, collecting background, 79–80
Initial interview, creating relationship in, 76–82
Insight, 105
Insight theories, 87–114
  v. action theories, 90
Insurance, 42, 323
  for counseling, 34
Integration, 16, 77
Intelligence tests, 158–159
Intentionality, 299
Interest inventories, 161
Interests, career development and, 243
Internship, 60, 147–148
Interpersonal relationships, as counseling
  specialty, 58
Intervention, 33
  assessment of impact, 117
  beginning, 80
  in client-centered therapy, 93
  cross-cultural skills in, 274
  in drug abuse, 251
  in family counseling, 208, 211
  in group counseling, 197–199
  rationale for choices, 149
  in sexual counseling, 222
  skills in, 40–41
Intimacy, 64, 68, 74, 81, 214, 311
  in group counseling, 191
  in therapeutic relationship, 79
  in transactional analysis, 110
Irrational thinking, 123
  intervention in, 126
Isaacson, L. E., 239
Isolation, 68, 97, 113
  gay issues and, 282
Ivey, A., 23, 34, 42, 294, 302

Jackson, D. D., 205, 293
Jacobs, E. E., 201
James, M., 110
James, W., 28, 142, 146, 149
Jochem, L., 189
Johnson, S. D., 275
Jones, B. E., 268
Jones, E., 26
Jones, G., 312
Jongeward, D., 110
Jung, C., 26, 27, 31, 101, 114, 143
Jurek, A. W., 204

Kagan, N., 299
Kaiser, H., 68
Kanfer, F. H., 117
Kapes, J. T., 242
Kaplan, H. S., 222
Kaplan, M., 271, 272

Karno, M., 274
Kass, F., 272
Katkin, E. S., 136
Katrin, S. E., 283
Kaul, T. J., 298
Keith-Spiegel, 312
Keller, K., 163
Kelly, K. R., 142
Kent, L., 272
Kershbaum, H., 261
Kierkegaard, S., 27, 31, 96
Kinnier, R. T., 231, 244
Klein, M., 271
Klinger, E., 252, 263
Knapp, S., 316
Kobos, J. C., 101, 105
Koffka, K., 106
Kohlberg, L., 42–44
Kohler, W., 28, 106
Kohut, Heinz, 101
Konner, J., 153
Koss, M. P., 273
Kottler, J. A., 16, 18, 33, 80, 89, 122, 132, 142,
    267, 317, 331
Kovacs, A. L., 80
Kramer, J. J., 161
Kroll, J., 171–172
Krumboltz, J. D., 30, 116–117, 239–240, 244
Kubie, L. S., 16
Kubler-Ross, E., 278

LaCrosse, M. B., 298
Lambert, M. J., 301, 321
Landes, D., 261
Lawe, C. F., 184
Lazarus, A. A., 16, 76, 132
Lecoq, L. L., 264
Legal issues, 307–324
Leiblum, S. R., 80, 117
Lesbian women, counseling, 279–284
Levinson, D. J., 279
Levitt, E. E., 301
Lewin, K., 147, 182
Lichtenberg, J. W., 297
Lieberman, M., 184, 187, 197
Linden, J., 157
Listening
    active, 40, 70, 74, 92, 93, 95
    effective, 302–304
Locke, J., 28, 31, 146
Loevinger, J., 42, 43
Lopez, F. G., 142, 231, 244
Lowenthal, A., 261
Lundin, R. W., 112

McBride, A. B., 271, 272
McCown, D. A., 298
McDowell, D. F., 246
McGoldrick, M., 215
Mackin, E., 240

McKusick, L., 284
Madanes, C., 128–129, 130, 209, 211, 218, 220
Magoon, T. M., 163
Maher, E. L., 330
Mahoney, M. J., 122
Mahrer, A. R., 16, 33
Malan, D., 101
Malnati, R., 201
Maloney, H. N., 273, 274
Malpractice, 322
Mangum, G., 240
Mann, L. M., 257
Marijuana, 253–254
Marital counseling, 203–225
Marlin, M. M., 258
Mar, M. E., 204
Marmor, J., 15
Marriage, 213, 271
Maslow, A., 18, 32, 97, 147
Masson, R. L., 201
Maultsby, M. C., 122
May, R., 5, 18, 68, 97, 98, 101
Mays, V. M., 283
Meadow, A., 189
Meagher, R., 274
Meichenbaum, D. H., 122, 294
Mental disorders, classification of, 26
Mental health clinic, counseling in, 46–47, 59
Mental health counseling, standards for, 34
Mental Measurements Yearbook, 154
Mentoring, 147–148, 279, 326–327
Merluzzi, T. V., 298
Mesmer, Anton, 31
Methodologies, analysis of, 294–296
Metzler, A. E., 243
Milby, J. B., 256
Miles, M., 184
Milford, D., 208
Miller, G. M., 163
Miller, N., 16, 117, 293
Miller, T. J., 301
Miller, W. R., 262
Mill, John Stuart, 28
Millon, T., 132
Minnesota Multiphasic Personality Inventory,
    154
Minorities. See Ethnic minorities
Minuchin, S., 65, 129, 145, 204, 209, 212, 272
Miranda, J., 280
Misjudgment, 313–314
Missbach, J. W., 298
Mitchell, L. K., 244
Modeling, 15, 41
    in group counseling, 195
Montague, P., 172
Moral development, 42
Moral issues, 309–310
Motivation
    career development and, 243
    of client, 18

Motivation (*continued*)
  drug abuse and, 264
  in minority clients, 274
Motives, 4, 6, 89
  of clients, 13
  of counselor, 18
Moustakas, C., 71
Mowbray, C. T., 271
Multimodal counseling, 132–135
Murphy, J. P., 259, 263
Murrell, P. H., 229
Myers, J. E., 278

Nace, E. P., 262
Narcotics, 256
Narcotics Manufacturing Act, 252
Nathanson, L. S., 172
National Association for Mental Health, 29
National Board for Certified Counselors
      (NBCC), 34
Neimeyer, G. J., 243
Nelson-Jones, R., 69
Neugarten, B., 42
Neurolinguistic programming. *See* Strategic
      counseling
Nevill, D. D., 243
Nevo, O., 245
Newman, B., 42
Nietzsche, Friedrich, 27
Nissenson, M., 278
Noble, F. C., 231
Nolan, E. J., 199, 201
Nondirective counseling. *See* Client-centered
      counseling
Norcross, J. C., 15, 33, 132, 142
North, R., 259

Oakley, R., 252, 258
Observation, in group counseling, 188, 195
Offermann, L. R., 246
O'Hanlon, W. H., 131
O'Hara, R. P., 240
O'Hare, M. M., 227
Ohlsen, M. M., 184
Oler, C. H., 275
Operant-conditioning procedures, 118
Orange, R., Jr., 259
Ordeal therapy. *See* Strategic counseling
Osberg, T. M., 163
Osipow, S. H., 301
Othmer, E., 168
Othmer, S. C., 168

Palmer, J. O., 16
Palo Alto Group, 128
Paradise, L. V., 168
Paritzky, R. S., 163
Parloff, M., 67
Parnes, S., 189

Parsons, F., 28–29, 31
Pascarelli, E. F., 260
Patterson, C. H., 23, 145, 186
Patterson, L. E., 18
Pavlov, I., 31, 117, 147
Pearce, J. K., 66
Pedersen, P., 267, 274, 275
Perception, 93
  of counselor, 17
Performance, tests of, 159
Perls, F., 27, 101, 107–108, 143, 144, 146
Perosa, L. M., 229, 231
Perosa, S. L., 229, 231
Personality
  career choice and, 235–236
  of counselor, 18
  types of, 235–236
Personality development
  in client-centered theory, 92
  stages of, 102–103
Personality inventories, 159–160
Personality theory, 42
Personal needs, subjugating, 9–10
Personal theory, 143–145, 148
Person-centered counseling. *See* Client-
      centered counseling
Phenomenological counseling. *See* Existential
      counseling
Phillips, J. S., 117
Piaget, J., 32, 42, 43, 147
Pietrofesa, J., 23, 262
Pine, G. J., 65, 92, 143
Plato, 25, 31
Play therapy, 136
Polick, M. J., 263
Ponterotto, J. G., 275
Pope, K. S., 312, 313, 315
Position hunger, 110–111
Positive regard, 71–72
Power, 4
  benevolent, 76
  in counseling relationship, 64–65
  of counselor, 77
  in families, 208–211, 212
  shared, 144
Practicum, 60, 147–148
Pragmatism, 16
  in personal theory, 149–150
Prediction, 89–90, 291–292
  from tests, 156, 158
Prejudice, 267–268
Pretending, 130, 220
Prevention, 42
  in counseling, 34
Privacy, 68, 267
  of clients, 320–321
  in group counseling, 187, 198
  test results and, 157
Private practice, 45–46
Probert, B. S., 243

Problem solving
  in multimodal counseling, 134
  in reality therapy, 135
Problem-solving therapy. *See* Strategic
  counseling
Process, nonconscious, 132–133
Prochaska, J. O., 16, 132, 142
Professional codes, 309–310
Professional development, 61, 140
Professional relevance, 61
Professional standards, 316
Prognosis, 26
Projection, 104, 109, 270
Psyche, structure of, 103
Psychoanalysis. *See* Psychoanalytic counseling
Psychoanalytic counseling, 15, 100–106
Psychodynamic therapy. *See* Psychoanalytic
  counseling
Psychology, history of, 28
Psychopathology, 29
Psychosexual development, 42
Psychosocial development, 42
Psychotherapy, 21–24, 33
Punishment strategies, 118–120
Purkey, W. W., 17

Questioning, 41

Rachman, S., 301
Rank, Otto, 101, 143
Rating scales, 162
Rational behavior therapy. *See* Rational-
  emotive counseling
Rational-emotive counseling, 122–128
Rational-emotive imagery, 126
Rationalization, 104
Raymond, L., 208
Rayner, R., 293
Reality testing, 60
Reality therapy, 30, 135
Reardon, R. C., 230
Reese, J., 189
Reflection, 30, 303
  of feelings, 93, 95
Reframing, 130, 131, 216–218
Regression, 104
Rehabilitation counseling, 34, 54–55
Reich, W., 27, 101
Reik, T., 101
Reinforcement, 15, 28, 41, 117, 305
  covert, 120
  negative, 118
  positive, 118
Rejection, 69
Relationship
  counselor/client, 13, 29–30, 64
  counselors as specialists in, 67–70
  healing, 68
  nurturing, 15
  quality of, 17

  therapeutic, 33
Relationship skills, rating scale, 69–70
Relaxation response, 121
Reliability
  in counseling, 298–300, 313
  in diagnosis, 172
  of tests, 157, 161
Remedial orientation, 42–44
Remer, R., 156, 294
Remley, T. P., 321
Repression, 104, 127
Research, 289–306, 327
  classic, in therapeutic counseling, 293
  in counseling, 40
Research methodologies, 294–296
Resentment expression, 108
Resistance, 117
  drug abuse and, 264
  in family counseling, 208
  in sexual counseling, 224
  to group strategies, 186
Resnikoff, A., 232
Respect, 41, 64, 69, 92
  of client, 73, 75
Responding skills, 70, 73–74
Responsibility
  of client, 13, 91, 92
  of counselor, 9, 65
  equality of, 144
  in existential counseling, 96–97
  in families, 209
  in Gestalt counseling, 106
  personal, 111
RET. *See* Rational-emotive counseling
Rice, L. N., 15
Risk taking, 17
  in group counseling, 189–190, 194–196
Ritter, R., 269
Rituals, 110
Robertiello, R. C., 4
Roberts, G., 231
Robinson, S. E., 221, 316
Roe, A., 238–239
Rogerian counseling. *See* Client-centered
  counseling
Rogers, C., 27, 30, 32, 65–66, 93, 143, 290, 293
  characteristics of helping relationship, 71–72
  client-centered counseling, 91–92
  encounter groups and, 95, 182
  insight theory of, 88
  therapeutic relationship, 67
Roles
  of counselor, 39–40
  flexibility of, 19
Rosen, E., 224
Rosenzweig, S., 16
Rosman, B., 272
Rossberg, R. H., 321
Rothman, S., 158
Rotter, J., 117

Rouslin, S., 4
Russo, N. F., 271, 273
Rutter, P., 312

Sachs, M. L., 137, 263
Sampson, J. P., Jr., 155, 163, 230
Sandgren, A. K., 204
Sanford, L. T., 272
Sartre, J.-P., 96, 98, 146
Satir, V., 129
Satisfaction, work, 234, 237
Schaefer, S., 312
Schafer, C., 312, 316
Scher, M., 271
Schlaadt, R. G., 257
Schlossberg, N. K., 42, 272
Schmidt, A. K., 230
Schmidt, L. D., 298
Schoenfeld, L., 75, 312
Schofield, W., 270
Schools
  counseling in, 48–52
  guidance groups in, 182
Searights, H. R., 204
Seduction, by client, 311–313
Segal, L., 129, 218
Self
  as instrument, 18
  significance of, 16–17
Self-actualization, 92
Self-assessment, 163, 302
  of counselor, 59, 60
Self-awareness, 69, 90, 229–230
  career choice and, 236–238
Self-disclosure, 40, 70, 79
  in gays, 280
Self-discovery, 11
Self-esteem, 33
  career and, 227
  drug abuse and, 264
Self-examination, 6, 93
  by client, 79
Self-judgment, 125
Self-knowledge, 11, 90
Self-monitoring, in multimodal counseling, 134
Self-talk, 127
Self Theory. See Client-centered counseling
Self-understanding, career choice and, 242
Seligman, L., 168
Seligman, M., 284
Sell, J. M., 75, 298, 312, 317
Sensate focus, 223
Settings, for counseling, 36–62
Sex counseling, 213, 221–225
  techniques in, 223–224
Sexton, T. L., 16
Sexual dysfunction, 222
Shahnasarian, M., 230
Shannon, J. W., 281
Shannon, P. T., 257

Shaping, 120
Shedler, J., 257–259
Sheeley, V. L., 316
Sher, K. J., 257
Shertzer, B., 157, 301
Shipley, A., 270
Shontz, F. C., 282–283
Shostrum, E. L., 16, 97
Siegal, R., 246
Siegel, J. C., 298
Siegel, S. M., 208
Sifneos, P., 101
Simek-Downing, L., 23
Simon, G. M., 142
Simulation, 246–247
Skills
  core, 33
  generic, for counselors, 40–41
  traditional, 10
Skinner, B. F., 28, 31, 116–118, 147, 277, 293
Skodol, A. E., 170
Slowing down (directive), 220–221
Smith, D. E., 252
Smith, D. S., 142
Smith, M. C., 294, 301
Snowden, L. R., 268, 275
Snyderman, M., 158
Socialization, 269
Social modeling, 117
Social reform, 28
Socrates, 25, 31, 96
Specialization, 57–61
  flexibility in, 57–58
  guidelines for selecting, 59–61
  of mental health professionals, 22, 24
Special populations, counseling of, 266–286
Sperry, L., 112
Spitzer, R. L., 170, 272
Splete, H., 23, 262
Stadler, H. A., 315
Stambul, H. B., 263
Standardization, of tests, 157–158
Standards for Educational and Psychological
    Testing, 157
Stanton, M. D., 208
Stefflre, B., 89
Stevic, R. R., 240
Stewart, B. J., 155
Stewart, M. R., 269
Stimulants (drugs), 255
Stimulation, in group counseling, 188–190
Stimulus hunger, 110
Stone, S., 301
Storms, M., 280
Strategic counseling, 128–131
Street ministry, 52–54
Stress, 56, 227
Strong, S. R., 67, 293, 298
Structural family therapy. See Strategic
    counseling

Structure, of families, 204, 210
Structured practice, 191–192
Structure hunger, 110
Strupp, H., 16, 101, 290
Strupp, H. H., 301
Stuart, R. B., 171
Style
  development of, 139–151
  personal, 17
Sublimation, 104
Sue, S., 267, 274, 275
Sullivan, H. S., 101
Summarizing, 30
Super, D., 42, 293
  developmental stage theory, 43
  theory of career development, 233–235
Superego, 103
Supervision, 40
Support groups, 191
  for AIDS victims, 284
  chemical dependency and, 262–263
  of counselors, 331
Sweeney, T. J., 112
Swensen, C. H., 279
Swerdlik, M., 172

Tabachnick, B. G., 312
Tactical therapy. *See* Strategic counseling
Talbutt, L. C., 309, 317
Talking cure, 25, 27, 100
Tall, K. M., 204
Taylor, B., 312
Teamwork, 44
Terkel, S., 228–229
Testing
  for ability, 158–159
  for achievement, 159
  for aptitude, 159
  bias in, 157
  construction of, 157
  criticisms of, 157
  intelligence, 154
  interpretation in, 164
  limitations of, 163
  nonstandardized measures in, 162
  for performance, 159
  personality, 154
  reliability and validity of, 157
  role of in assessment, 154–155
  selection of, 161–162
  standardized measures in, 156–162
  use of computers in, 155
  value of, 155–156
Theoretical orientation, 17
Theory construction, 88–90
Theory development, 15–16
Therapeutic attributes, 297–301
Therapeutic counseling
  era of, 32–33
  history of, 24–35

identity of, 21
Therapeutic environment, 11
Therapeutic relationship, 9, 63–83
  quality of, 143–144
Therapy groups, 184
Thoits, P. A., 271
Thomas, A. H., 269
Thomas, L., 17
Thoreson, C. E., 117
Thorne, F. C., 16, 132
Tiedeman, D. V., 240
Time structuring, 110–111
Tinsley, H. E., 163
Toffler, A., 57
Tolliver, L. M., 279
Tosi, D. J., 301
Training
  of counselors, 33
  of mental health professionals, 22
Training models, 15
Tramel, D., 12
Transactional analysis, 30, 110–111
Transference, 66, 77, 187
Treatment plan, 165–166
Troll, L., 42
Trotzer, J. P., 18
Truax, C. B., 16, 67, 73, 91, 290, 293, 301
Trust, 13, 64–65, 68, 71–72, 74, 81, 298, 308
  between client and counselor, 77–78
  in group counseling, 193–194
  in helping relationship, 75
Tuemmler, J. M., 298
Turkington, C., 272
Tyler, L., 150

University, counseling in, 54, 59

Validity
  in counseling, 298–300, 313
  of tests, 157, 161
Values
  career development and, 243
  of counselor, 142, 149, 311
  individual, 17
  work related, 229
Values clarification, 30
  of counselor, 60
Vandecreek, L., 316
VandenBos, G. R., 321
Van Hesteren, F., 34
Van Hoose, W. H., 122, 317
Vash, C., 261
Vasquez, M. J., 312, 313, 315
Violence
  against gays, 282
  against women, 273
Vocational guidance, 28–29
  See also Career counseling
Vriend, J., 80, 199
Vroman, C. S., 33

Wachtel, P., 16, 132
Wagner, E. E., 157
Wagner, M., 312
Waite, D. R., 321
Walsh, W. B., 301
Warnath, C. F., 284
Warner, R. W., Jr., 240
Washington, C. S., 263
Wass, H., 278
Waters, E. B., 276
Watkins, C. E., 142
Watson, J. B., 28, 31, 117, 147, 293
Watts, A., 243
Watzlawick, P., 129, 132
Weakland, J. H., 129, 132, 205, 218, 293
Wechsler Adult Intelligence Scale, 154
Weil, A., 250, 256
Weinberg, S. B., 180
Weiner-Davis, M., 131
Weinhold, B. K., 205
Weinstein, E., 224
Weise, B. C., 298
Weissman, M., 271
Weltner, J., 165
Wertheimer, Max, 28
Westerman, M. A., 91
West, J. D., 259
Weyer, Johann, 66
Whiston, S. C., 16

Whitehorn, J., 293
Whiteley, J. M., 122, 227, 232
Wieder, S., 65
Wiener, E. A., 155
Williams, J. B. W., 170, 272
Winoker, M., 105
Winstead, B. A., 69
Wise, R. A., 250
Withdrawal, 110
Wolberg, L. R., 68
Wolpe, J., 117, 121, 132, 293, 301
Women
   counseling, 271–273
   stereotypes of, 271
Woods, S. M., 15
Woods, W. J., 281
Woody, J. D., 317
Woody, R. H., 321
Work, functions of, 227–228
Wundt, W., 28, 31, 142

Yalom, I., 68, 97, 99, 143, 184
Yamamoto, K., 279

Zane, N., 275
Zarski, J. J., 259
Zeig, J. K., 16, 33
Zucker, R. A., 259

To the owner of this book:

We hope that you have enjoyed *Introduction to Therapeutic Counseling*, 2nd Edition, as much as we enjoyed writing it. We'd like to know as much about your experiences with the book as you care to offer. Only through your comments and the comments of others can we learn how to make this a better book for future readers.

School: _____

Address of school (city, state, and ZIP code): _____

_____

Your instructor's name: _____

1. What did you like most about *Introduction to Therapeutic Counseling?* _____

_____

2. What did you like *least* about the book? _____

_____

3. Were all the chapters of the book assigned for you to read? _____

(If not, which ones weren't?) _____

4. How interesting and informative was the last chapter (Chapter 16)? _____

_____

5. What material do you think could be omitted in future editions? _____

_____

_____

6. If you used the student workbooks, how helpful was it as an aid in understanding concepts and theoretical approaches? _____

_____

_____

7. In the space below or in a separate letter, please let us know what other comments about the book you'd like to make. (For example, were any chapters or concepts particularly difficult?) Please recommend specific changes you'd like to see in future editions. We'd be delighted to hear from you!

Optional:

Your name: _____ Date: _____

May Brooks/Cole quote you, either in promotion for *Introduction to Therapeutic Counseling* , 2nd Edition, or in future publishing ventures?

    Yes: _____ No: _____

    Sincerely,

    Jeffrey A. Kottler
    Robert W. Brown

- -
FOLD HERE

NO POSTAGE
NECESSARY
IF MAILED
IN THE
UNITED STATES

BUSINESS REPLY MAIL
FIRST CLASS   PERMIT NO. 358   PACIFIC GROVE, CA

POSTAGE WILL BE PAID BY ADDRESSEE

ATT: *Drs. Jeffrey A. Kottler and Robert Brown*

**Brooks/Cole Publishing Company
511 Forest Lodge Road
Pacific Grove, California 93950-9968**

- -
FOLD HERE